M. Göbel
J. Landauer
U. Lang
M. Wapler (eds.)

Virtual Environments '98

Proceedings of the Eurographics Workshop
in Stuttgart, Germany,
June 16–18, 1998

Eurographics

SpringerWienNewYork

Dr. Martin Göbel
GMD-Forschungszentrum Informationstechnik, IMK-VMSD
Schloß Birlinghoven, St. Augustin, Federal Republic of Germany

Dr. Jürgen Landauer
DI Matthias Wapler
VIS-LAB, Fraunhofer Institute for Industrial Engineering (FhG IAO)
Stuttgart, Federal Republic of Germany

Dr. Ulrich Lang
HLRS Visualisation Department, University of Stuttgart
Stuttgart, Federal Republic of Germany

© 1998 Springer-Verlag/Wien

Typesetting: Camera ready by authors

Graphic design: Ecke Bonk

SPIN: 10684759

With 206 partly coloured Figures

ISSN 0946-2767
ISBN-13: 978-3-211-83233-2   e-ISBN-13: 978-3-7091-7519-4
DOI: 10.1007/978-3-7091-7519-4

Preface

Virtual Environments '98 – the Conference and 4th Eurographics Workshop on Virtual Environments – was organized in a different frame than the previous Eurographics Workshops in 1993, 1995 and 1996.

This fourth EG workshop was held together with the VE 98 conference and the VE Yuforic taking place in Stuttgart from June 16–18, 1998. The event was cosupported by the IEEE Computer Society and well organized by the Fraunhofer IAO and IPA institutes, RUS at the University of Stuttgart and GMD in Bonn.

Following a call for participation, about 65 technical contributions were received electronically. All extended abstracts were carefully reviewed by at least 3 members of the international programme committee, and 35 authors were invited to present their papers during the workshop. Following the concept, to be attractive for people from academia as well as for people from industry, the workshop took up four different streams which are included in this book:

– the keynote presentations of leading experts from the US, Japan and Germany;
– the technical papers, reviewed by the international programme committee;
– the panel discussions;
– and the industrial case studies.

The invited keynote papers discuss the strategic importance of Virtual Environments for information technology, also covering different application fields such as visualization of massive amounts of data, the medical field, but also entertainment and arts.

21 technical papers were chosen by the programme committee for publication. These papers cover aspects of human computer interaction, novel navigation metaphers, interaction and feedback devices; telepresence, distributed, collaborative and inhabited Virtual Environments; as well as a number of novel applications in which VE techniques are explored.

The panels were organized including representatives from companies experienced in Virtual Reality applications, such as the automotive and the telecommunication industries, the medical and geoscience field and others. In this book, reports from two panels are included.

Finally, more than 20 industrial case studies were presented during the conference. We have selected 5 of them to report in these proceedings about the state of the art on using VR in industries.

At this point we would like to acknowledge the support of Heinrich Müller and Dieter Fellner for their assistance on behalf of EUROGRAPHICS. We owe gratitude to the international programme committee, most of them IPC members who have been working for the EG Virtual Environments workshops already for years. In particular, we would like to thank the local organization teams from Stuttgart and Petra Unnützer and Simone Paponja for the editorial support to complete this volume.

Bonn, Stuttgart, September 1998

Martin Göbel
Jürgen Landauer
Ulrich Lang
Matthias Wapler

Contents

VIII   Contents

Panel Reports

Industrial Case Studies

Advances in Bridging the Gap: Using Virtual Reality to Enhance Productivity

Hans-Joerg Bullinger
Andreas Roessler

Fraunhofer-Institute for Industrial Engineering IAO
Nobelstrasse 12, 70569 Stuttgart, Germany
E-mail: andreas.roessler@iao.fhg.de

Abstract

This paper presents an overview on actual trends in Virtual Reality. The paper discusses trends in presentation and interaction technology, applications, particularly in automotive industries and in research.

Keywords: Virtual Reality, Virtual Prototyping, Usability

1.   Introduction

In the end of the eighties and the beginning of the nineties there was a lot of hype in Europe and USA about the new medium and tool Virtual Reality. Datahelmets and datagloves always attracted many people on trade shows and exhibitions. The promoters of VR promised huge benefits in a broad range of applications. But meanwhile the fascination of the media for this technology has clearly dropped. On the other hand, there still is a growing community of research institutions and companies, who are hoping to benefit from the use of VR.

For a better understanding of potential user and investors, this papers tries to show the most recent trends in the development of VR. The presented trends are mainly derived from observations in Germany and USA.

2.   Trends in VR

Obvious Trends

Trend 1: Price of computer hardware drops, performance rises

The fact, that the performance of processors and graphics engines drop rapidly, is well known. And it is essential for the VR community, as VR is one of the most performance demanding computer application – the hardware for an excellently equipped VR lab easily adds up to more than three million US dollars. Moore's Law (e.g. Schaller, 1996) predicts a doubling of processor power every 18 months. Graphics performance, which is even more important for VR, seems to evolve faster.

Trend 2: Community Grows

Despite decreasing media coverage, there is a growing VR community in Germany. Meanwhile it includes the major German car manufacturers (Mercedes-Benz, Volkswagen, BMW), other large industrial groups like Siemens, some smaller companies and more and more universities and research organisations. Interestingly, no one stopped using VR yet. Figure 1 shows our prediction for the availability and use of high-end 3D graphics for VR. According to our assumptions, home users will have graphics adapters with a performance of one million polygons per second in the end of 1998.

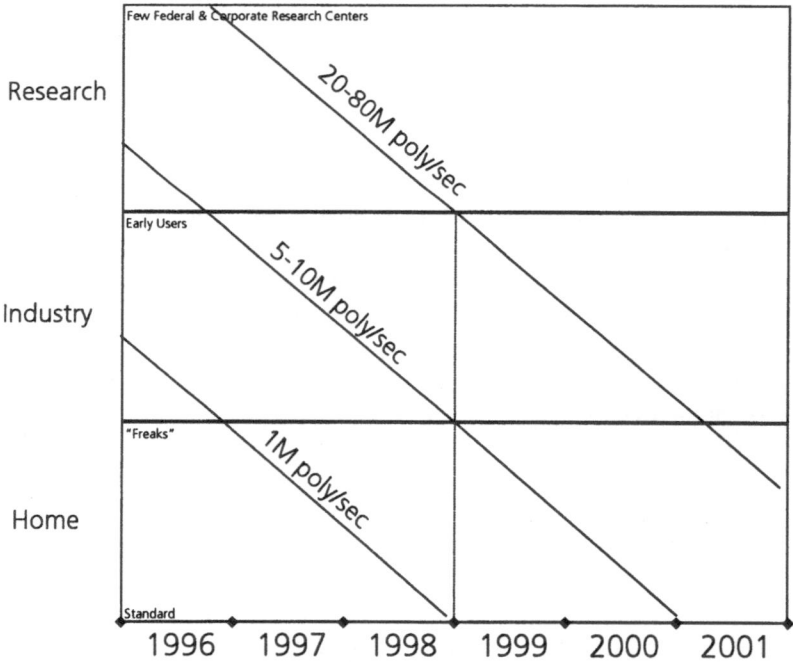

Figure 1: The use of 3D-graphics in three sectors: home, industry & research

(Roessler and Ziegler, 1997)

Technology Trends

Trend 3: Less head-mounted displays, more projection systems

In the beginning of VR, head-mounted displays (HMD), also known as datahelmets, were standard device for VR. Meanwhile, nearly all major VR groups in Germany switched to stereoscopic projection systems. These systems have several advantages: they provide a higher screen resolution, offer a better comfort and they can be used by several people. Figure 2 shows the four-wall projection systems used by Fraunhofer IAO.

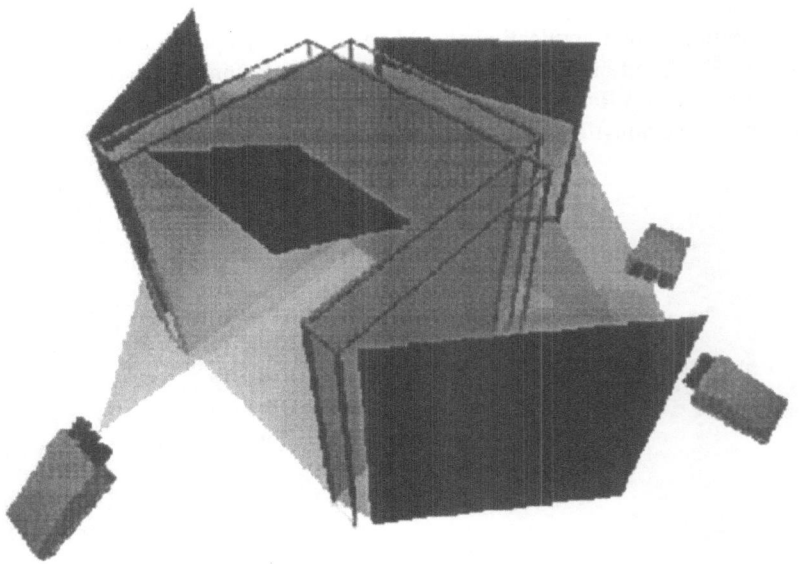

Figure 2: Fraunhofer IAO multi-wall projection system CAVEEE

Trend 4: Less datagloves, more button devices

The datagloves (and HMD) are the symbols of VR. Likewise the HMD, the use of datagloves decreases. The main reason is, that there are simple devices with push buttons, which give a very easy access to user's actions. The initial promise of a very intuitive gestural device could not be fulfilled.

4

Trend 5: More VRML, more PC

A few years ago, it was very difficult to exchange geometrical 3D data between CAD-packages, modelling packages and VR. With VRML (Virtual Reality Modelling Language), this obstacle is gone. Additionally VRML is used to present interactive 3D content via internet on standard PCs. And the PC will be the platform for VR in five years. Even SGI, the de-facto monopolist for high-end VR workstations, will possibly present a (W)Intel-based workstation soon.

Application Trends

Trend 6: Less presentations & shows, more r e a l applications

In the past, most of the published VR applications were show cases and prototypes. In our definition, a real application should be used daily and should help to solve a real problem. This kind of application is emerging: e.g. Fraunhofer IAO installed a stereo-projection and a VR software for BMW engineers, who evaluate large press tools. Their average evaluation time decreased by 80 percent using VR.

Figure 3: VR simulation of Assembly of A-Class Mercedes-Benz

Trend 7: More Digital Mock-Ups, more Virtual Prototyping

The most important application trend is the use of VR technology to replace physical by virtual prototypes. The virtual prototypes help to save substantial amounts of time and money. VR adds 3D visualisation and interaction in a natural scale.

Trend 8: More dynamic simulation in VR

Dynamic simulation of robots (figure 3) or virtual man models (figure 4 + 5) is getting more important. There is an increasing interest to simulate not only static virtual prototypes, but also dynamic processes, e.g. in manufacturing. The man models are used for ergonomic evaluation of prototypes.

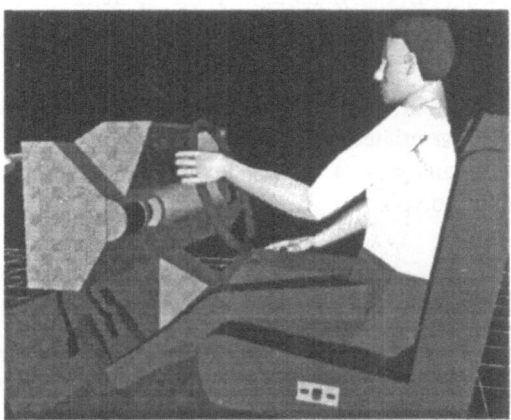

Figure 4 (above): VirtualANTHROPOS by IAO and IST,

Figure 5 (below): Jack by University of Pennsylvania

Trend 9: More usability – better concepts, devices, software

The technological problems of the beginning, i.e. data exchange, price and poor quality (Bullinger, 1994), are almost solved. At least there are fields of applications where the benefit of VR exceeds the cost. The fact, that there are real users and not only scientists and experts, raises the need for a better usability. The first "victims" of this trend were datahelmet and datagloves (see above). New concepts like the multi-wall projection systems (CAVE) improve the human perception, new interaction devices enable two-handed spatial interaction. But still, a consistent software usability concept is mostly missing. Most of the so-called applications developed in the last years are as mentioned above single purpose prototypes and show cases. To improve usability, a lot of experiments are needed with real users. These experiments should have the following objectives:

A better understanding of the nature of VR:

What is similar to reality? How can we use the similarity?
E.g. if users react similar to virtual heights, we can use VR for therapy of phobia.

What is different from reality? How can we use these differences?
E.g. if it is useful to change the environment to stimulate human creativity, it can be easily done in VR.

The improvement of the usability of VR:

Improving the usability includes better stability of hardware and software as well as reduction of complexity of the handling of the systems. Additionally, the basic interactions, i.e. navigation and object manipulation, have to be adapted to user's needs.

Given these improvements of quality and understanding and the reduction of cost, VR promises to be an appropriate tool for perception and manipulation of spatial information, either for analysis of human behaviour, learning and training or for industrial design and prototyping.

3.   The Future: Evaporation of VR

The last years there were VR-applications and today we have real applications powered by VR. In the future the use of technologies which belong today to VR will be very natural: you will not see VR, but it will be there.

4. References

Blach, R.; Simon, A. and Riedel, O. (1997): Experiences with user interactions in a CAVE-like projection environment. In: Smitz, M.J.; Salvendy, G.; Koubek, R.J. (Eds.) Advances in Human Factors/Ergnonomics. Amsterdam: Elsevier Science

Bullinger, H.-J. and Bauer, W. (1994): Strategische Dimensionen der Virtual Reality. In: Proceedings of Virtual Reality '94. Springer Verlag, Heidelberg, pp. 13-26

Fraunhofer IAO (1997): Home-Page of VirtualANTHROPOS. http://vr.iao.fhg.de

HIT Lab (1998): On the Net: Research Centers. http://www.hitl.washington.edu/projects/knowledge_base/research.html

Mine,M. (1995) Virtual Environment Interaction Techniques, UNC Chapel Hill Computer Science Technical Report TR95-018

Poupyrev, I., Weghorst, S., Billinghurst, M., and Ichikawa, T. (1997): A study of techniques for selecting and positioning objects in immersive Ves: effects of distance, size and visual feedback, Human Interface Technology Laboratory Report R-97-45

Roessler, A., and Ziegler, J. (1997): Mulitmediale and virtuelle Netzanwendungen. Report für die Swiss Telekom. Stuttgart

Schaller, B. (1996) : The Benchmark of Progress in Semiconductor Electronics. http://www.advtech.microsoft.com/research/BARC/Gray/Moore_Law.html.

University of Pennsylvania (1997): Jack Home-page. http://www.cis.upenn.edu/~hms/jack.html

New Trends in Virtual Environment User Interface Research:
Case Studies at the Human Interface Technology Laboratory

Toni Emerson

Human Interface Technology Laboratory, University of Washington, Box 352142, Seattle, WA 98195-2142, USA. Email: temerson@hitl.washington.edu

1   Introduction

The user interface of the future characterizes itself as ubiquitous, transparent, collaborative, and networked. This outlook reflects a culture rapidly assimilating to the information infrastructure and connectivity provided by the World Wide Web. Virtual environment (VE) research has served as a foundation for this current view and is also challenged by the goals that such a vision presents. The demand for ubiquitous, transparent computing is a double edged sword to VE research. On one hand, mobile computing drives the development of wearable VE interfaces. However, ubiquitous computing stipulates that the computer be accessible everywhere in the user's world. Since VE interfaces develop computer generated worlds to immerse the user in an artificial reality or augment the user's world, such a requirement is counterpoint to the definition of a virtual interface display (Weiser, 1996). Transparent interfaces, on the other hand, are supported by VE research working toward the goal of producing natural interfaces that enhance the use of human modalities for human computer interaction.

Collaborative, networked multi-users have been an active component in virtual environment research since VPL developed "Reality Built for Two" (Blanchard, et al., 1990). Distributed virtual environment research has been underway for over a decade; beginning with military networks of SIMNET and DIS, networked games such as Doom, and academic research represented by DIVE, NPSNET, and MR Toolkit (Singhal and Zyda, forthcoming). In fact, distributed virtual environment (DVE) research has been around so long that another category has evolved: collaborative virtual environments (CVE). Collaborative systems account for the individual needs of users while empowering them to communicate with other members in the virtual community (Churchill and Snowdon, 1998).

2   Trends

A change in the user's relationship to the computer has created a shift in consciousness. People no longer want to sit in front of a screen. Intent on discarding the "user" role and becoming active participants, they are communicating with each other in real-time and creating significant effects collaboratively. As this transformation occurs, trends in the general computing prototype point directly to the multidisciplinary research in virtual reality. The trend in virtual environments is no longer to put the human inside the machine, forcing the computer into some anthropomorphic exo-skeleton. Virtual interfaces are now centering on the user side as a dynamic intermediary pushing the technology forward, rather than the technology pushing the human element to adapt. The progression diverges away from the technology towards the human problem-solving experience.

The focus is on a natural user interface that fits the human's tasks, personality, and lifestyle. The goal is modality and medium independence-- translating information representation from machine to haptic, audio and visual displays (National Research Council, 1997). From the beginning, VE interfaces have been touted as a step forward in displaying information in three-dimensions allowing the human to process information the "natural way". Multimodal research incorporates and presents information via natural human modalities: gesture, voice, and facial expression. This increased complexity in the interface promotes the development of new interaction metaphors that amplify the user capabilities in the virtual space (Poupyrev, 1997). Multidisciplinary research also includes human factors and presence measures and neuro-psychophysiological study into adapting the environment to meet the cognitive, sometimes physical needs, of the human. Investigators are examining how to design virtual environments to avoid negative human reactions, such as simulator sickness (Draper, 1996).

This same trend of designing for the human, exists in the development of virtual communities and virtual space design. The World Wide Web has penetrated our work and our play. It's natural for the community to move itself online. The exodus to cyberspace has generated many areas of study. Sociologists (Smith and Kollack, 1998), anthropologists (URL= http://www.ccon.org/socioanthro/index.html) and other cultural theorists now study virtual community interactions. Scene graph manipulation languages such as Virtual Reality Modeling Language (VRML) and Java3D give the community tools to develop virtual spaces. In the popular mode, we build them together in online chat rooms. However, many virtual architects (Campbell, 1996) create spatial architectures that fit the user group objectives and task.

The popularization of avatars and virtual humans in VE interfaces exemplify the user wanting to influence and personify the virtual interface. It's difficult to get a sense of presence when your representation is a disembodied icon that doesn't even look like you—much less resemble your personality. Virtual humans are graphical representations of people that can be used as avatars, real time embodiments of the users in the virtual environment or as agents, human surrogates (Badler, 1997). Virtual humans have been successfully represented in a number of networked virtual environments. MIRALab's Virtual Life Network (VLNET) (Capin, et al., 1997) and the MedSIM project (Chi, et al., 1997) are examples of successful implementations of this research.

Animated Interface Agents indicate a shift towards highly personalized interfaces in which communication between the user and the computer will be mediated by life-like agents. Research in this area combines an interesting mix of advances in computer graphics and applied artificial intelligence. The realization of visually appealing agents is coupled with the need for agents to behave in a natural manner.

Strong opinion exists that humans don't want electronic "buddies" to assist them, even in the digital environment (Shneiderman, 1997). Yet, there is a trend toward autonomous agents working with us online.

3   Drawing the VE Interface

A dilemma in VE interfaces lies in the perception of what constitutes a virtual environment interface. It's a variation of Bill Buxton's test of having the audience draw what they think a computer looks like. In 15-20 seconds, take a piece of paper and draw what your VE interface looks like (Buxton, 1993). Did you draw a head mounted display? What was your input device? Was your avatar wearing a body suit? What did your software look like? The flat 2D screen is a far cry from an occluded head mounted display. Visualization has given us such creative new displays as the CAVE ™ (Cruz-Neira, et al., 1992), the Responsive Workbench (Wesche, et al, 1997). There are many types of 3D displays: high resolution and other spatially immersive displays (Emerson, 1997). The critical determinant is that the interaction and presence serve the goals of the application.

Input/Output devices are also diversifying. Manipulation devices include: flat surface tablets, joystick, glove, thimble, stick or pen, exo-skeletal structures, treadmills (OTT, 1997). The entertainment industry is driving the trend towards desktop users producing force-feedback joysticks, mice, flight yokes and steering wheels (URL=http://www.force-1.com/). Current displays such as SensAble's PHANToM (URL=http://www.sensable.com/) and Immersion Technologies' force-feedback devices (URL=http://www.force-feedback.com) have led the way to new rendering tools and techniques as well as development environments. New research tracks the use of graspable objects (Fitzmaurice and Buxton, 1997) or "tangible bits" (Ishii and Ullmer, 1997) to manipulate the interactive surface. It's an interesting variation on augmented reality. Instead of having the virtual objects overlaid on the real world, you use actual objects to interact with the virtual world.

4   Where does HITL fit in?

Research at Human Interface Technology Laboratory (HITL) supports the following project thrusts:

- Understanding Humans
- Interfaces that Amplify
- Collaboration
- Learning
- Vanquishing Human Limitations

These project thrusts support a mission "to empower people by building better interfaces with advanced machines that will unlock the power of human intelligence" (excerpt from HITL mission statement). HITL's multidisplinary research encompasses the development of wearable hardware, advanced interface metaphors, cognitive psychology and human factors.

4.1   Understanding Humans: The Virtual Effects Laboratory

Investigations of simulator sickness have come to the forefront and there are increasing demands for understanding the processes underlying a positive or aversive immersive experience. Continuous access and group interactions necessitate progress be made in developing presence measures and solving such problems as simulator sickness. The VR Effects Laboratory at HITL (URL=http://www.hitl.washington.edu/projects/vrefx) explores the physiological and psychological effects of virtual interfaces on the users of this technology. VR effects research focuses on simulator sickness, adaptation, and presence.

Research conducted at the VR Effects lab showed that changes in the geometric field of view cause simulator or motion sickness. The most provocative stimulus is the minimized view. Time delay experiments showed no significant provocative affect. The experiments also proved that the human brain adopts to the virtual environment (VOR adaptation) (Draper, 1998). Dr. Erik Viirre is currently developing a technique which can be beneficial for patients with vestibular disorders (Viirre, forthcoming).

Recent presence research produced results indicating that a meaningful virtual scene, as opposed to a random one, increased both reported presence and the level of inertial motion required to overcome perceived self-motion elicited by scene motion. A procedure was introduced involving rest frames (Rest Frame Construct - RFC), possibly based on brain-stem level neural processing, to measure the salience of virtual environments (Prothero, 1998).

4.2   Interfaces that Amplify: Wearables Project, Multimodal Project, FLIGHT, Sound Lab, and the Virtual Retinal Display (VRD)

4.2.1   Wearables Project

(URL=http://www.hitl.washington.edu/projects/wearables/)

Wearable computer research at the HIT Lab is focused in two directions: intuitive interfaces for wearable computers and using wearable computers to enhance collaborative work. The HIT Lab has been experimenting with body-stabilized spatial information displays on a wearable platform. HITL researchers have found that users perform faster with a spatial display and are able to remember more displayed information. In collaboration with the Advanced Perception Unit at BT Laboratories, HITL combined research in wearables and augmented reality. The study examined display performance effects and the benefits of spatial cues. (Billinghurst, et al., 1997)

4.2.2   Multimodal Project

(URL= http://www.hitl.washington.edu/projects/advanced/multimodal/)

The Multimodal Project at HITL involves the development of software libraries for incorporating multimodal input into virtual interfaces. GloveGRASP is a set of C++ class libraries that allow developers to add gesture recognition to their SGI applications. The Hand Motion Gesture Recognition System (HMRS) is a generic software package for hand motion recognition system using hidden markov models.

In collaboration with the HITL, El Laboratorio de Interfaces Inteligentes at the University of Mexico (UNAM) is developing an expert system architecture for building intelligent agents that respond to voice and gesture commands in the virtual environment (Savage-Carmona, et al., forthcoming).

4.2.3 FLIGHT

Feedback-based muLti-Dimensional Interface as a General Human-Computer Technology (FLIGHT) is a three dimensional human-computer interface software and Application Programming Interface (API) developed at Sandia National Labs. FLIGHT incorporates force-feedback and spatialized sound into its interface and interaction. FLIGHT is now being used at HITL for graduate research to design a computer animation system that includes a variety of modeling and animation techniques (Anderson, 1997).

4.2.4   Sound Lab

HITL research in virtual audio has produced new methods for representing three dimensional data through audio mastering and for measuring the cognitive and perceptual effects of simulated auditory environments (Hollander, 1994) (Hollander and Furness, 1994) (King and Weghorst, 1995).

Funded through a Defense University Research Instrumentation Program (DURIP) proposal, the new Audio Lab at HITL contains two double-walled acoustic sound chambers allowing work within a low reverberation environment. The chambers are connected by a patch panel allowing audio, video, serial, etc. throughput between booths, providing synchronization, editing, mixing and audio processing.

The HITL Audio Group's areas of interest include room acoustics modeling and simulation, spatialized hearing, and auditory navigation. A recent graduate study of desktop conferencing has found that spatialized sound significantly enhances the listener's perceived comprehension and memory of the communication that took place during the conference.

4.2.5   Virtual Retinal Display (VRD)

(URL=http://www.hitl.washington.edu/projects/vrd/)

The VRD, based on the concept of scanning an image directly on the retina of the viewer's eye, was developed under a four-year program funded by Microvision, Inc. (URL= http://www.mvis.com).   Currently, the HITL hardware team is developing a custom high speed, high Sensitivity Optical Beam Profiler (SPOT). SPOT will allow the determination of the beam shape, power density, field distortion, optical resolution, and temporal stability characteristics of the system. In addition to hardware development for SPOT, the VRD team has been developing and extensive software package of control, acquisition and test programs to automate much of the characterization process. Other design improvements have been made to the VRD benchtop system. The new layout has provided a reduction both in the amount of time needed for system alignment and in the amount of space needed for the system.

The VRD team is also working on a VRD emulator system which will allow various aspects of the VRD to be simulated independently. This will permit the study of why the VRD appears to have different perceptual properties than a conventional display, especially for patients with different vision disorders.

4.3   Collaboration: Virtual Playground Project

(URL=http://www.hitl.washington.edu/projects/greenspace/)

The Virtual Playground project at HITL continues the collaborative virtual world research of the GreenSpace Project. The purpose of the GreenSpace Project was to develop a testbed to demonstrate the power of an ideal communications environment in which geographically separated participants can interact in a common space. Virtual Playground goals include developing a hospitable environment for users and affordances for social interaction, giving users "a reason and a place to go". The Virtual Playground Netgate Mall application uses hybrid patterns of virtual architecture, patterns encouraging a creative use of space and prior knowledge of spatial relations. The shared virtual environment was built for the users and their tasks (Schwartz, et al., submitted).

4.4   Learning: Virtual Classroom

(URL=http://www.hitl.washington.edu/projects/learning_center/)

The Virtual Classroom project empowers children hospitalized for long periods to use virtual reality technology and share learning experiences with children in public school classrooms. Through the use of helmets that present stereo graphics and sounds, virtual reality (VR) technology will allow students to enter and interact with other students in virtual environments. The immersive environment which will be used for this study is called Global Change World, an environment prototyped and tested last year. It is the goal of the project to have pairs of children at each site collaboratively study and work towards reducing the "greenhouse effect" on the world.

4.5   Vanquishing Human Limitations: Virtual Retinal Display - Low Vision Group and Therapeutic VR Group

Visual displays are also advancing into the field of rehabilitative interfaces. HITL pioneered the use of Virtual Vision™ multi-plexed display (URL= http://www.virtualvision.com) to therapeutic aid to Parkinson's disease patients suffering from akinesa (Reiss and Weghorst, 1995). In this vein, HITL is moving from the engineering development of the Virtual Retinal Display (VRD) as a product to research and development of biomedical applications of the VRD. For example, designing visual aids for people that are partially sighted (people who may be legally blind, but their eyes/retina are still responsive to light). The aids use the VRD to more easily read books, work at a computer, watch television and navigate inside and outside using the portable (and soon, wearable) head-mounted VRD. Other therapeutic uses of virtual interfaces at HITL (URL=http://www.hitl.washington.edu/projects/therapeutic/) include pain distraction for burn patients (Hoffman, 1998) and phobia desensitization (Carlin et al., 1997).

5 Conclusion: Transformation - Human Centered Systems

VE interfaces show great progress, evolving into human centered systems, not just peripherals to computers. This system will not only consist of a delivery device, but context and content as well. Message and medium will be optimally combined in the form of a system that matches the perceptual and cognitive perception of the human. What are the challenges?

Virtual interfaces should be adaptive, conforming to the needs and tasks of the individual, allowing interactive modification of form and content.

Determining where we benefit most by upgrading from a 2D to a 3D interface in our daily activities. VE users should be empowered, able to accomplish more with the interface than without it.

Technological advances need to go hand in hand with content theory and development.

6   References

Anderson, T. (1997). FLIGHT: A 3D Human-Computer Interface and Application Development Environment. In Proceedings *of Second PHANToM User's Group Workshop*, October 19-22, 1997, Cambridge, MA (preprint).

Badler, N. (1997). Real-Time Humans. Paper presented at *Pacific Graphics 1997*. [Online: WWW] URL=http://www.cis.upenn.edu/~badler/paperlist.html

Billinghurst, M., Bowskill, J., Dyer, N., and Morphett, J. (1998). An Evaluation of Wearable Information Spaces. In Proceedings of *IEEE Virtual Reality Annual International Symposium* (pp. 20-27). Los Alamitos, CA: IEEE Computer Society Press. [Online:WWW] URL=http://www.hitl.washington.edu/publications/r-97-35/

Blanchard, C., Burgess, S., Harvill, Y., Lanier, J., Lasko, A, Oberman,M. and Teitel, M. (1990). Reality Built for Two: A Virtual Reality Tool. *Computer Graphics, 24*(2), pp. 35-36.

Buxton, B. (1993). Absorbing and Squeezing Out: On Sponges and Ubiquitous Computing. Paper presented at *Xerox Ubiquitous Computing Workshop*, Los Altos, CA , April 5 & 6, 1993. [Online: WWW] URL= http://www.dgp.toronto.edu/OTP/papers/bill.buxton/ubicompIO.html

Campbell, D. (1996). *Design In Virtual Environments Using Architectural Metaphor: A HIT Lab Gallery.* Unpublished Masters thesis. Seattle, WA: University of Washington, Human Interface Technology Lab. [Online: WWW] URL= http://www.hitl.washington.edu/publications/campbell/

Capin, T.K., Pandzic, I.S., Noser, H., Magnenat Thalmann, N., Thalmann, D. (1997). Virtual Human Representation and Communication in VLNET. *IEEE Computer Graphics and Applications, 17*(2), pp. 42-53.

Chi, D., Kokkevis, E., Ogunyemi, O., Bindiganavale, R., Hollic, M., Clarke, J., Webber, B., and Badler, N. (1997). Simulated Causalities and Medics for Emergency Training. In K.S. Morgan, H.M.Hoffman, D. Stredney, and S.J. Weghorst (Eds.), *Medicine Meets Virtual Reality 5* (pp. 486-494). Amsterdam: IOS Press.

Churchill, E.F. and Snowdon, D. (1998). Collaborative Virtual Environments: An Introductory Review of Issues and Systems. *Virtual Reality: Research, Development and Applications, 3*(1), pp. 3-15.

Cruz-Neira, C.; Sandin, D. J.; Defanti, T. A.; Kentyon, R. V.; Hart, J. C. (1992). The CAVE: Audio Visual Experience Automatic Virtual Environment. *Communications of the ACM, 35*(6), 64-72.

Cruz-Neira, C.; Leigh, J.; Papka, M.; Barnes, C.; Cohen, S. M.; Das, S.; Engelmann, R.; Hudson, R.; Roy, T.; Siegel, L.; Vasilakis, C.; DeFanti, T. A.; Sandin, D. J. (1993). Scientists in Wonderland: A Report on Visualization Applications in the CAVE Virtual Reality Environment. In Proceedings of *1993 IEEE Symposium on*

Research Frontiers in Virtual Reality (pp. 59-66). Los Alamitos, CA: IEEE Society Press.

Draper, M. (1996). *Can Your Eyes Make You Sick? Investigating the Relationship Between the Vestibulo-Ocular Reflex and Virtual Reality.* HITL Technical Report R-96-3. Seattle, WA: Human Interface Technology Laboratory. [Online:WWW] URL=http://www.hitl.washington.edu/publications/r-96-3/

Draper, M. (1998). *The Adaptive Effects of Virtual Interfaces: Vestibulo-Ocular Reflex and Simulator Sickness.* Ph.D. dissertation. Seattle, WA: University of Washington, Human Interface Technology Laboratory.

Emerson, T. (1997). *Visual Display FAQ*, sci.virtual-worlds. [Online:WWW] URL=http://www.hitl.washington.edu/scivw/visual-faq.html

Fitzmaurice, G. and Buxton, W. (1997). An Empirical Evaluation of Graspable User Interfaces: Towards Specialized Space-Multiplexed Input. In *Proceedings of the 1997 ACM Conference on Human Factors in Computing Systems, CHI '97*, (pp. 43-50). New York, NY: ACM. URL=http://reality.sgi.com/gordo_tor/papers/gf/CHI97.GraspUI/GraspExpt.html

Hoffman, H.G., Doctor, J.N., Patterson, D.R., Carrougher, G.C., Taylor, W., Weghorst, S., and Furness, T. III. (1998). VR for Burn Pain Control During Wound Care. Paper presented at *Medicine Meets VR 6*, San Diego, CA, January 28-31, 1998.

Hollander, A. (1994). *An Exploration of Virtual Auditory Shape Perception.* Unpublished masters thesis. Seattle, WA: University of Washington, College of Engineering. [Online:WWW] URL=http://www.hitl.washington.edu/publications/hollander

Hollander, A. J. and Furness, Thomas A. (1994). *Perception of Virtual Auditory Shapes.* Paper presented at Proceedings of the International Conference on Auditory Displays, Santa Fe, NM, November, 1994. [Online: WWW] URL=http://www.hitl.washington.edu/publications/p-94-3/index.html

Ishii, H. and Ullmer, B. (1997). Tangible Bits: Towards Seamless Interfaces between People, Bits, and Atoms. In *Proceedings of CHI'97*(pp. 234-241). New York, NY: ACM. [Online: WWW] URL=http://tangible.www.media.mit.edu/groups/tangible/papers/Tangible_Bits_html/index.html

King, J. and Weghorst, S. (1995). Ear Tracking: Visualizing Auditory Location Strategies. In Proceedings of *CHI '95*, (pp. 214-215), Denver, Colorado, USA: ACM.

National Research Council (1997). *More Than Screen Deep : Toward Every-Citizen Interfaces to the Nation's Information Infrastructure.* Washington, DC: National Academy Press.

17

Office of Training Technology (OTT), Chief of Naval Operations' (1997). Haptic (Sensory/Touch) Interfaces. In *Modeling and Simulation*. [Online:WWW] URL= http://www.ott.navy.mil/1_3/1_3_5/

Poupyrev, I., Weghorst, S., Billinghurst, M., Ichikawa, T. (1997). A Framework and Testbed for Studying Manipulation Techniques for Immersive VR. In *Proceedings of ACM Symposium on Virtual Reality Software and Technology, VRST '97* (pp. 21-28). New York, NY: ACM.

Prothero, J. (1993). *The Treatment of Akinesia Using Virtual Images*. Unpublished Masters thesis. Seattle, WA: University of Washington, College of Engineering. [Online:WWW] URL=http://www.hitl.washington.edu/publications/prothero/

Prothero, J. (1998). *The Role of Rest Frames in Vection, Presence and Motion Sickness*. Ph.D. dissertation. Seattle, WA: University of Washington, Human Interface Technology Laboratory. [Online: WWW] URL=http://www.hitl.washington.edu/publications/r-98-11/

Savage-Carmona, J., Billinghurst, M., and Holden, A. (1998, forthcoming). VirBot: A Virtual Reality Robot Driven with Multimodal Commands. Paper to be presented at the *Intelligent Virtual Environments Workshop* to be held at the European Conference on AI on Brighton, UK, August 25,1998.

Schwartz, P., Campbell, B., Tanney, S., Yen, S., Shen, L-S., and Furness, T. (submitted). Virtual Playground: Architectures for a Shared Virtual Worlds. Submitted to *ACM Symposium on Virtual Reality Software and Technology*, November 2-5, 1998, Taipei, Taiwan.

Singhal, S. and Zyda, M. (forthcoming). The Origins of Networked Virtual Environments. In *Networked Virtual Environments*. New York, NY: ACM Press. [Online:WWW] URL=http://www.npsnet.nps.navy.mil/zyda/NVEBook/Book.html

Smith, M. and Kollack, P. (1998). *Communities in Cyberspace*. New York, NY: Routledge. [Online: WWW] URL= http://netscan.sscnet.ucla.edu/csoc/cinc/

Shneiderman, B. (1997, Nov/Dec). A Grander Goal: A Thousand-Fold Increase in Human Capabilities. *Educom Review, 32* (6), pp. 4-10.

Reiss, T. and Weghorst, S (1994). Augmented Reality in the Treatment of Parkinson's Disease. *Medicine Meets Virtual Reality 3 (pp. 282-302)*. Amsterdam: IOS Press.

Viirre, E. (forthcoming). Adaptation of the VOR in Patients with Low VOR Gains. [short communication]. *Journal of Vestibular Research*.

Weiser, M. (1996). Ubiquitous Computing (home page). [Online: WWW] URL= http://www.ubiq.com/hypertext/weiser/UbiHome.html

Wesche, G., Wind, J., Gobel, M., Rosenblum, L., Durbin, J., Doyle, R., Tate, D., King, R., Fohlich, B., Fischer, M., Agrawala, M., Beers, A., Hanrahan, P., and Bryson, S. (1997, July/August). Applications of the Responsive Workbench. *IEEE Computer Graphics and Applications, 17*(4), pp. 10-15.

Teraflop Visualization

Arthurine R. Breckenridge
Computer Architectures Department
Sandia National Laboratories, New Mexico, US
arbreck@sandia.gov

Abstract

The key to insight is coupling the power of the computer with unique skills of the human. At Sandia National Laboratories' Interaction Laboratory, we call this teraflop visualization. We are concentrating research in three main areas: 1) using the computer as a facility for authoring content, 2) adding the physics to model real behaviors, and 3) allowing the human to utilize the improved precision and resolution provided by this new class of compute power.

Keywords

Scientific Visualization, Virtual Environments, Parallel Algorithms, Haptics, Teraflop, 3D widgets, human computer interface

Introduction

> *"The primary research instrument of the sciences of complexity is the computer. Ever since the rise of modern science three centuries ago, the instruments of investigation such as telescopes and microscopes were analytic and promoted the reductionalist views of science. Physics, because it dealt with the smallest and most reduced entities, was the most fundamental science. From the laws of physics, one can deduce the laws of chemistry, then of life, and so on up the ladder. The computer, with its ability to manage enormous amounts of data and simulate reality, provides a new window on that view of physics. We may begin to see reality differently simply because the computer produces knowledge and insight differently from the traditional analytic instruments. It provides a different angle on reality."*
>
> *Heinz Pagels, The Dreams of Reason, 1988.*

Ten years later, Sandia National Laboratories researchers are providing this different angle on reality by addressing two important concepts: a) how do we get knowledge from the computer into the human, and b) how do we get insight from the human into the computer? The answers inevitably leads one to computer graphics, because the eye is the human's broad-bandwidth information channel. This is now called "scientific visualization." It has only been recently, after video games and educational software were established industries, that the scientific world has accepted the idea of computer graphics can help them understand their piles of numbers. At Sandia's Interaction Laboratory, we do not want another decade to pass before our scientists see what was obvious to every kid the first time he/she touched a video game-- the power of interactive graphics. To go one step further, we want to use all the channels of communicating with the human being that the mind already knows how to interpret. Ivan Sutherland (often called the father of computer graphics) stated you create the mathematical model of a virtual world in the computer then you want this model to look, feel, and sound as much as possible like a real world to the human mind coupled with the it. [Sutherland, 1965] This is the definition we use for "virtual environments." (VE s) Taking this definition one step further is teraflop visualization where the computing model and the virtual environment are an integral whole needed to provide computing for insight.

In order to implement teraflop visualization we are concentrating research in three main areas: 1) authoring content (the computer) , 2) adding behaviors (the physics) , and 3) enhancing precision and resolution (the human).

1. Authoring Content.

The first area of research focus is using the computer as a facility for authoring content. Having participated in decades of research, Sandia researchers are convinced that today's computers empower us to build sophisticated models of complex natural phenomena and to explore them from new perspectives. Noting that the greatest scientific revolutions of Newton's times were empowered by the new mathematical capabilities of the calculus and other analytic equations. We believe that the power of modern computers to represent complex mathematical models can leverage yet further exponential progress in science.

In Sandia's Interaction Laboratory, the success stories of insight gained by using VEs are numerous. Our simulation codes are working on problems that are too hard to do by machine algorithms alone and require human insight, and are too hard to do by human insight alone and require a lot of calculations. In other words, a terabyte of information has become easy to generate; indeed, datasheets of this size regularly being produced on the massively parallel Intel teraflop supercomputer located at Sandia. More recently, clusters of personal computers have begun to reach gigaflop scale of computation. How can a scientist hope to comprehend this volume of data effectively?

Effective ways to answer this question are:

• Building parallel virtual environment hardware

    The Intel Teraflop machine provides an unique opportunity to author content. The visualization shown in Figure 1 is one of the result files calculated during the initial benchmark of the machine. Since the Teraflop is simplistically a hybrid of personnel computer processors, one could, if able to overcome memory, disk and other bottlenecks, estimate that it would have take almost 10 years to complete this same problem on a single PC. [i.e., (4096 processors

X 18 hours) / (24 hours in a day X 365 days in a year)] The fact that the cost of computer chips keep dropping as their power increases, is making it possible to link hundreds, even thousands, of computer chips in special systems. Today, computing speeds are measured in MIPS (millions of instructions per second) and strange new rates such as "teraflops". However, virtual environments consume CPU cycles. Or, VE eat MIPS for breakfast. All who have ventured into the realm of real-time multi-dimensional simulations have discovered that VE requires a hybrid of general purpose and special processors to create even a crude approximation of reality.

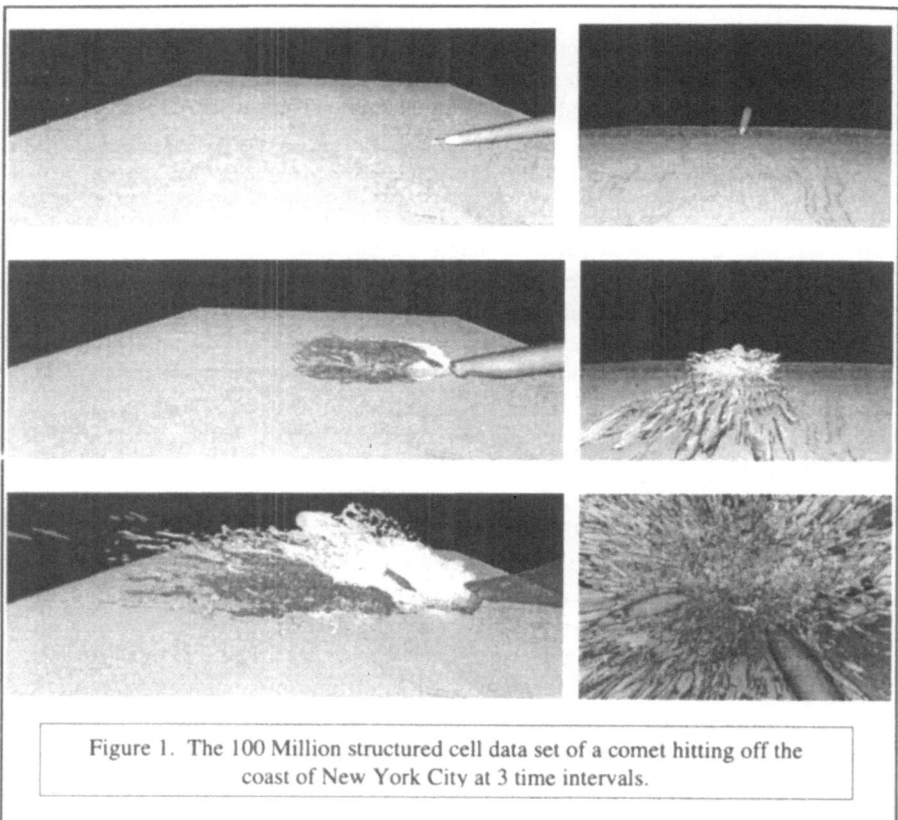

Figure 1. The 100 Million structured cell data set of a comet hitting off the coast of New York City at 3 time intervals.

The solution is to develop a general pathway for VE that can utilize the extremely high rates of processing speed in the computer architecture known as "massive parallelism," in which many instead of one is devoted to the same task, which is logically parceled out in some manner. All machines will be based on commodity off the shelf products. (The EIGEN/VR project focus addressing this limitation is named CPLANT.[1])

- Building integrated simulation and virtual environment software

The Intel Teraflop machine provides an unique opportunity to implement the VE foresight provided by Fredrick Brooks (often called the father of virtual reality) even before computing hardware was powerful enough. Brooks believes the use of computer systems for intelligent amplification (IA) is much more powerful today and will be at any given point, than the use of the computers for artificial intelligence (AI) where the objective is to replace the human mind by the machine and its simulation codes. The virtual environment IA objective is to build systems that amplify the human mind by providing it with computer-based auxiliaries that do the things that the mind has trouble doing. Brooks offers several areas of in which human minds are more powerful than any computer algorithm designed. The computer's strength is in storing massive amounts of data and recalling the data without forgetting it upon well-defined commands. The human strength is to recall data at the appropriate time, in a reference to a completely different subject, that we suddenly see to be meaningful. Human evaluation and recall are very hard processes to translate into a well-defined computer data retrieval command. Humans are more skilled than computers at pattern recognition, whether visual or aural. [Brooks, 1977]

The solution is to develop a general pathway for VE that utilizes the strengths of both the human and the computer. Qualitative algorithms are needed to get a high level view of what the large data sets looks like. Quantitative algorithms are needed for the human to probe beyond sight into the raw data. And, amplifying algorithms are being developed so the computer can focus on preset reduction criteria and the human has a mechanism to steer the computation based on his/her evaluation and pattern recognition strengths. (The EIGEN/VR project focus addressing this limitation is named Parallel Algorithms.[1])

2. Adding Behaviors

The second area of research focus at Sandia is adding the physics to model real behaviors. Simply specifying an object "static" 3D-geometry is not sufficient for analysis. The object's behavior in the VE involves changes in position, collisions, grasping, scaling, surface deformations, etc. Virtual objects also need to be modeled physically by specifying their mass, weight, surface texture (smooth or rough), deformation mode, etc. These features are merged with geometrical modeling and behavior laws to form a more realistic VE. Figure 2 shows the crating results from the high velocity impact physics of the comet.

In the Interaction Laboratory, we not only concentrate on the behaviors coded into the simulation, we also focus on the behaviors needed to interact with the data and the computer. There is more to the modeling the real world than drawing a nice image. We make all of our scientists handicapped when interacting with a computer if we only give them their sense of sight and no tools to manipulate the images. How can a scientist examine the volume of data and its behaviors?

Figure 2. Illustrates the impact of the comet on the ocean floor.

Effective ways to answer this question are:

- Mapping force and tactile (haptics) feedback

    Our eyes may be the main broad-bandwidth information channel but we quickly realize the importance of our other senses when we operate without them in the VE. Much progress has been made in adding visual and auditory feedback possibly since the human receptors are localized. This is not true for haptic feedback. Not only are the receptors not localized, they are not consistent over the body surface. A great impact can be made by starting with the fingers. The maximum density is at the fingertips, where the density is up to 135 sensor/cm^2 [Kokjer, 1987].

    The sensation associated with haptic sensors also involves the melange of senses we lump together under the category of "touch." Haptic is not strictly tactile in the same way one's fingertips convey tactile information about the outside world. Haptic tasks also include tasks that use the body's sense of proprioception that informs us about the position of our own limbs in relation to one another and to the space around us. [Boff, 1986] We hardly notice the mind's fast, silent information-processing and fine muscular coordination skill that enables you to move your hand in exactly the right direction when you decide to reach for a glass of water. A ballet dancer is a virtuoso of proprioception. Haptics involves both proprioceptive and tactile senses, in concert with other senses.

    The solution is to add as many natural behaviors as possible to the VE. The VE is enhanced by adding auditory cues and haptic feedback. Sound but especially touch are critical elements in developing effective human/computer interaction. (The EIGEN/VR project focus addressing this limitation is named FLIGHT.[1])

- Mapping human imperceptible phenomena.

    We have certain built-in senses such as vision, hearing, and touch, but there are many phenomena which are completely imperceptible to us. Some examples are x-rays, radioactivity, and electricity. One could say we lack the senses to perceive these things. But, by using electronic sensors and computer interfaces, we can make these imperceptible phenomena visible, or audible or touchable. One example would be magnetic field which are traditionally visualized with vector arrows in a 2D visualization (called the hedgehog). In 3D, the arrows get very confusing due to occlusion problems. A human can see iron filings moving or the effect of a magnetic field but can not see the magnetic force itself. We must look beyond vision to convey these imperceptible phenomena.

    The solution is to use develop innovative interfaces that map very hard physics into the appropriate sense which will enhance comprehension. (The EIGEN/VR project focus addressing this limitation is named HEDGEHOG.[1])

3. Utilizing Precision and Resolution

The third area of research focus at Sandia is allowing the human to utilize the improved precision and resolution. The Teraflop machine provides an unique opportunity to increase the resolution and precision of the simulation. Figures 3a and 3b illustrate the difference in detail of a 54 Million cell volume representation of the comet computed in 1996 and a 100 M cell surface representation from 1997. Besides the well known limitations such as system latency and display resolution, the precise manipulation of virtual objects is very difficult. Why add resolution and precision if it must be removed in order to visualize the data?

Effective ways to answer this question are:

- Upgrading the settings

    Thirty thousand years ago, many of the ochre paintings on limestone cave walls at Lascaux were painted in precisely distorted manner in order to give the rendering of 3D appearance. The art itself is only part of the experience, often rather a small part at that. The ochre figures viewed out of context and in two dimensions, reproduced in books are far less interesting and informative. The setting was a major factor in the effect of the figures. Considering the technologies at the time, the people seemed to have made use of every trick, using special effect upon special effect in an effort to create a specific state of consciousness to focus the human mind's attention on the information. [Pfeiffer, 1982]

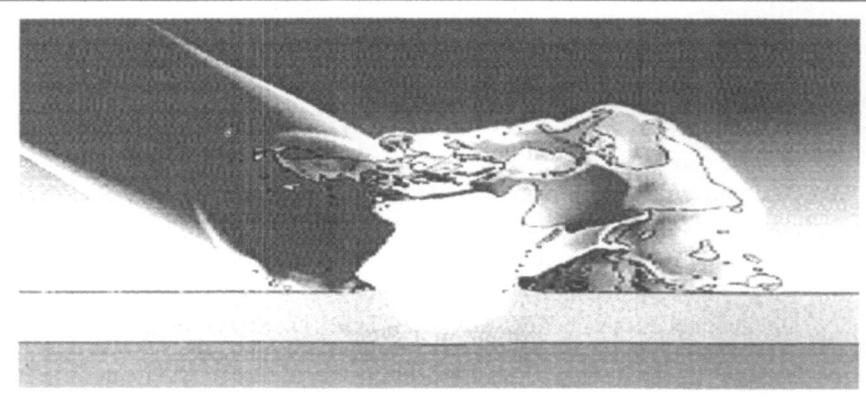

Figure 3a: 54 Million cell representation of two variables (water and comet)

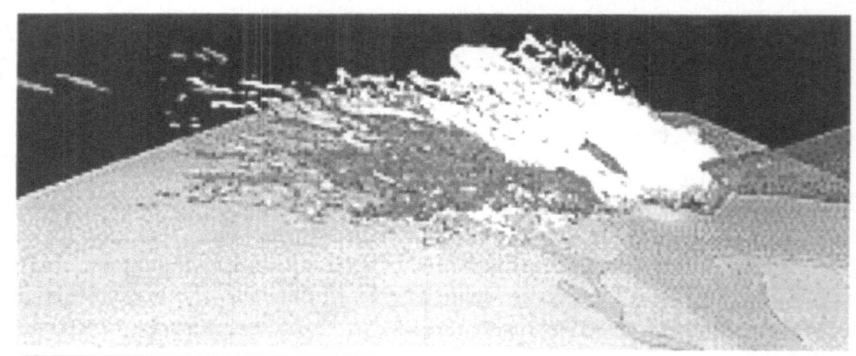

Figure 3b: 100 Million cell representation with five variables (air, water, land, temperature and comet)

Like the caves at Lascaux, recent years have invented alternative output devices such as CAVE (TM)-like environments or stereoscopic wall projections and more precise input devices for enhancing the experience. [Cruz-Neira, 1992] These environments have gone far in providing the settings for making the computer become transparent and focus on the information. The next step is to reduce the cost of these tools, extend the domain space to more collaboration than a few individuals, and improve the resolution and precision of interaction. In these CAVEs, as in the caves at Lascaux, people in altered state of consciousness were educated in the use of tools for creating and maintaining knowledge.

The solution is to provide the "setting" for focused attention whether in a CAVE, VE on the desktop, or the next generation setting. Real environments require people to be in the same space at the same time. VEs will hopefully get rid of the real space requirement allowing distance settings to collaborate. We are going to use this new communication medium to take us beyond the boundaries of our minds and push our society to create and transmit information from generation to generation. (The EIGEN/VR project focus addressing this limitation is named KIVA [1].)

- Upgrading from a 2D to 3D interface

Thirty thousand year ago, well not really, but about three decades have passed since devoting a single computer to the use of one person was a revolutionary idea that converged with another revolutionary idea-- the notion that the human interfaces for computers should accommodate human needs and abilities, rather than shaping human behavior to fit the demands of the computer technology. Today, the word computer brings to mind monitor, keyboard, and mouse attached to a desktop machine. VE s are supporting technologies that will explode that image.

Let's begin with the human/computer interface or the lack thereof. To solve problems with the aid of a computer, a user must be able to easily and accurately communicate to the machine and control what need to be done. Designing the means to do so (i.e., the human/computer interface) is by no means trivial. The way in which a person enters commands or data into a computer is the input part of the interface, and the way the computer shows the user the results of the computations is the output part of the interface. In the 1950s, the first input and output devices were designed with the limitations of computers rather than the capabilities of humans in mind. A computer that accepts input only in the form of punched cards and spits out answers on a roll of paper, is an example of a user interface designed to meet the needs of computing machines.

The mouse pointing device, now ubiquitous with human/computer interfaces of all kinds, was invented in the 1960's, although it was not commercially available until the 1980s. The use of a mouse as a pointing device signaled a concrete break-through in the human-computer interface, one that moved directly to the core of VE: gestural input as a command language. However, the mouse implementation (WIMP: Windows, Icons, Menus, and Pointers) was in a 2D environment that reduced the look and feel so any object/widget could never be more than flat object and not intuitive. Although standardization of user interfaces (Motif) have been an important development in this decade, Sandia researchers feel this is still one of the largest areas of improvements. The invention of the keyboard and mouse is better; however we can still improve on this.

The solution is stop mapping 3D functions into 2D space when at all possible. Our simulations are moving to 3D as quickly as possible; we should move to 3D interface as quickly as possible. We need a next-generation mouse but more importantly we need "de-facto standard" 3D widget software that operates with the peripherals of the future based on 6 DOF (x, y, z, row, pitch, and yaw) plus force, plus sound, etc. Today, our scientists are not enamored with the encumbering devices like "goggles and gloves" as some people call VE peripheral equipment. But as the devices become more natural and the interfaces comfortable, familiar, and effortless (like the telephone), we can unconsciously subtract the VE peripherals out and focus on the function -- the information. (The Sandia project team addressing this limitation is named VRML widgets[1])

Changing the angle of reality

In summary, virtual environments offer the potential for another technological revolution like the telephone and television. Sandia researchers think VE will be the technological medium for advancing computing for insight. Alexander Graham Bell thought the telephone would be useful as a way to pipe music to people. The developer's of radio and television thought that their devices would launch a world of 2-way communications to replace the telephone. Ideas abounded about possible implications of VE s.

In retrospect, we now understand something about the way telephones and television expand far beyond the expectations of their inventors. In fact, it is interesting to compare the introduction of television with the introduction of virtual environments. Here was a technology fascinating to view, though limited in content and image quality. Crowds formed wherever it was initially demonstrated. In wide spread use, the main application of television turned out to be the introduction of the concept of telepresence, the sense of being there through the eyes of a camera in real-time. In wide spread use, the prime application for coupling computers with VE s is still to be determined.

It is hoped that reading the focus areas of Sandia's Interaction Laboratory staff was useful and informative. The VE peripherals will change (i.e., holovideos and autostereosopic displays) and our environment will become more natural. The author has no doubt that teraflop visualization (coupling computers and VE s) will influence our society greatly in the not too distant future. As John Thomas (often called the father of innovative interfaces), puts it:

> "VE, at best, will not only affect the world we live in, it may
> help ensure we have a world to live in." [Thomas, 1993]

Boff, K. R., L. Kaufman and J.P. Thomas, Eds. Handbook of Perception and Human Performance, New York: John Wiley and Sons, 1986.

Brooks, F.P, Jr., "The Computer Scientist as Toolsmith: Studies in Interactive Computer Graphics," Information Processing 77, B. Gilchrist, ed., Amsterdam: North-Holland, 1977, pp. 625-634.

Cruz-Neira, C., Sandin, D.J., DeFanti, T.A., Kenyon, R., and Hart, J.C. The CAVE, Audio Visual Experience Automatic Virtual Environment. Communications of the ACM, June 1992.

Kokjer, K., "The Information Capacity of the Human Fingertip," IEEE Transactions on Systems, Man and Cybernetics, 1987, Vol. SMC-17, No. 1, pp. 100-102.

Pagels, H., The Dreams of Reason, New York: Simon & Schuster, 1988.

Pfeiffer, J. E., The Creative Explosion: An Inquiry into the Origins of Art and Religion, Ithaca, NY: Cornell University Press, 1982.

Sutherland, I., "The Ultimate Display," Proceedings of the IFIP Congress, 1965, pp. 506-508.

Thomas, J., "The Shape of Things to Come," Proceedings of VR Systems '93 Conference, New York, NY, pp. 342-346, March, 1993.

[1]This keynote address at Visualization Environment '98 was meant to identify trends in VE. For more specific information about Sandia's work in removing these limitations please see details on our web pages at http://www.cs.sandia.gov/ILAB. All sub-projects mentioned are part of the EIGEN/VR teraflop visualization project.

This work was supported by Sandia National Laboratories, a multi-program laboratory operated by Sandia Corporation (a Lockheed Martin company) for the United States Department of Energy under contract DE-AC04-94AL85000.

Virtual Reality in Medicine: Developing the Visualization and Interaction Technology for the 21st Century

Prof. Dr.-Ing. Dr. h.c. Rolf Dieter Schraft, Dipl.-Ing. Matthias Wapler
Fraunhofer-Institut für Produktionstechnik und Automatisierung (IPA)
Nobelstraße 12, D-70569 Stuttgart, Germany
Tel: +49 (0)711 970-1307 Fax: +49 (0)711 970-1005, wapler@ipa.fhg,de
http://www.ipa.fhg.de/medizin

Abstract - New high-performance graphic PCs and a young generation of computer literate surgeons have paved the way for new high technology solutions in medicine. Virtual Reality technology is the basis for many of the innovative visualization and interaction techniques being implemented. In this paper we present an overview of current developments worldwide and describe our vision of how several developments may be integrated in the virtual hospital and operating room of the future. We conclude with a discussion of the major research issues in medical applications of Virtual Reality.

1   Introduction

The ultimate goal of all medicine is to achieve the perfect therapeutic result with no side-effects or pain for the patient. Some of the elements needed to realize this vision are non-invasive diagnosis techniques, preferably without any ionizing radiation, effective communication of appropriate prophylactic measures and minimal micro-surgical procedures which only manipulate those structures directly responsible for the illness. This paper looks at these developments in the context of the virtual hospital of the future and examines the role of Virtual Reality in this scenario. Based on an overview of several available or experimental systems, this paper intends to show that Virtual Reality provides many of the key technologies needed to achieve this goal, but that there are still many research challenges left to be overcome.

2   The Virtual Hospital of the Future

Foreseeable changes and developments in the way hospitals operate are laying down the framework within which Virtual Reality will find its place. Therefore, any discussion on Virtual Reality must start with a look at these developments. Already today, cost pressure on the healthcare providers is changing many processes within hospitals. The future will see many more non-stationary treatments and even electronic house calls. The result will be the creation of virtual hospitals, relying on sophisticated networks to maintain the integrity of patient data. Information must be securely retrievable everywhere and at any time. Standardized low cost interfaces to different measurement devices such as blood pressure gauges, glucose analysis or thermometers will ensure quick and correct data input [1].

The operating room of the future is one of the central nodes in the future virtual hospital. Together with the Dr. Horst-Schmidt-Kliniken in Wiesbaden, the Fraunhofer IPA is developing a scenario for the operating room of the future, the OR 2015 [2]. Figure 1 shows an early simulation of the OR 2015. The OR 2015 stands for a workplace where the patient is once again the focus of activities. The surgeon is next to the patient, thus establishing the patient-surgeon relationship as the major axis. At the same time appropriate surgeon-computer-patient-interfaces serve as a means to transfer the manual dexterity of the surgeon to the tip of the endoscope as well as keeping the surgeon informed about the patient status, anatomical and navigational information. Quality assurance will mean on-line documentation of all equipment settings and procedures carried out.

Fig. 1. Simulation of the OR 2015 (Dr. Urban, Art+Com)

Similar scenarios for the operating room of the future are currently being developed by the Human Interfaces Technology Laboratory [3] and others.

In summary it can be stated that within the virtual hospital Virtual Reality will play an important role as a visualization and interaction medium, as discussed in more detail in the next session.

3   The Role of Virtual Reality in Medicine

The term Virtual Reality has been applied to so many different applications that an exact definition of the scope is almost impossible. Virtual Reality in the sense of its original developers refers to a feeling of immersion in an artificially created environment in which the user can perceive and manipulate virtual objects. Applied to medicine, an example would be the ability to go inside a virtual patient in a minimally invasive procedure and control an instrument. To give the user the feeling of immersion the stimuli to the body senses are artificially generated with appropriate hardware and software. This includes not only the visual and auditory senses, but also haptic and tactile senses as well as the sense of balance. Finally, since most real-life situations are changing with time, real-time behavior is also an important feature of most Virtual Reality systems. Based on this quite restrictive definition, Virtual Reality offers three basic technologies of use in medical applications:

- A visualization technology to present efficiently and intuitively patient data from different imaging techniques as well as from remote diagnoses.
- A interaction technology using the sense of immersion to tele-operate robot-assisted systems, thus opening up inaccessible dimensions to the surgeon
- An interaction paradigm by using intuitive spatial metaphors to manipulate large amounts of data

This paper will look at the application of these technologies in three areas of medicine (see Figure 2):

- Virtual Reality-assisted diagnosis
- Virtual Reality-assisted therapy planning and execution
- Education and training systems

Other applications, which are not discussed here are, for example, Virtual Prototyping to assist medical product development.

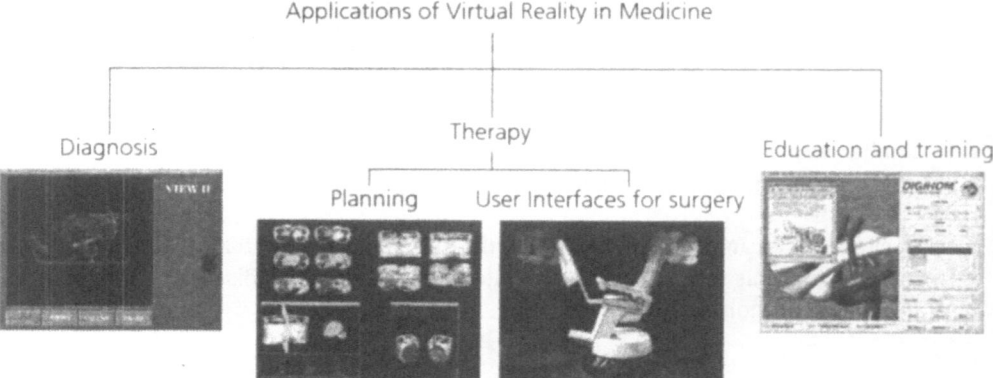

Fig. 2. Applications of Virtual Reality in Medicine

4 Virtual Reality-assisted Diagnosis

Modern imaging techniques such as magnetic resonance imaging (MRI), computer tomography (CT) and medical ultrasound allow us to look into the patient non-invasively. Virtual Reality provides the tools to understand the resulting images. Therefore, a large number of teams are developing systems for virtual endoscopy. An example is the VEMA System developed by General Electric Research for use in colonoscopy and bronchoscopy [4] shown in Figure 3. Other similar systems are being developed by HT Medical [5], Fraunhofer IGD [6] and others.

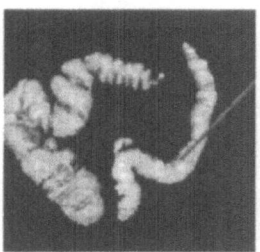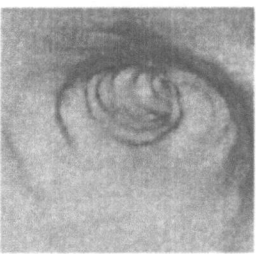

Fig. 3. Virtual Endoscopy (GE Research)

Another key aspect of Virtual Reality-assisted diagnosis is the ability to perform diagnoses by remote experts. Cost and quality constraints will certainly favor this kind of procedure for non-standard conditions in future. An example of a Virtual Reality based assistance system for remote diagnosis are some of the features of the UltraTrainer System [7] developed at Fraunhofer IPA, shown in Figure 4. The system allows a specialist to perform a remote ultrasound examination off-line, in the same way as he or she would if the patient were present. Basis for the examination is a 3D-ultrasound dataset which can be locally acquired from the patient by a less experienced physician.

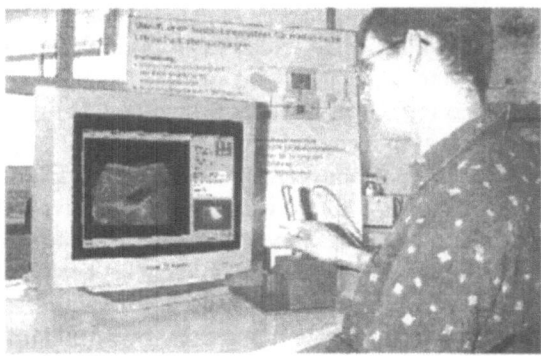

Fig. 4. UltraTrainer System for off-line medical ultrasound diagnosis (Fraunhofer IPA)

5 Virtual Reality-assisted Therapy

Virtual Reality plays a role in therapy in both surgical planning and actual surgery itself. Therapy planning is a rapidly growing market in the area of neurosurgery, orthopedics, otology, maxillo- and craniofacial surgery. Therapy planning utilizes the same imaging techniques as Virtual Reality-assisted diagnosis and can improve the final outcome as well as minimizing the surgical risks. Several commercial systems are already available, for example the Stealth System by Sofamor Danek or the VectorVision system [8] from BrainLAB, to name just two examples. Figure 5 shows an example of a system used at the Mayo Clinic for surgery planning for the separation of conjoined infant twins.

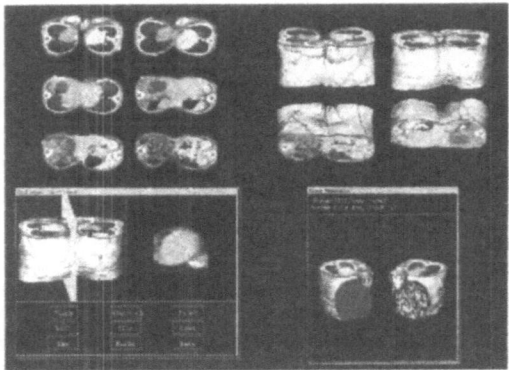

Fig. 5. Surgery planning for the separation of conjoined infant twins (Mayo Clinic)

The aim of most Virtual Reality-assisted surgery systems is to help surgeons in navigation and spatial co-ordination as well as improving the ergonomics of minimally invasive surgery. Virtual Reality provides the enabling technology to give the surgeon virtual access to the operating situs. Most systems use additional visual clues to augment the endoscope or microscope images. A new approach is currently being implemented at the Fraunhofer IPA using additional motion clues for navigation [9]. Our motivation for selecting orientation and motion feedback is that it is directly related to the task being performed in several ways:

- By transferring the scaled movements of the vision system, e.g. endoscope to the surgeon, his sense of balance and movement provides additional cues about the current orientation and position of the vision system relative to the anatomy. This sensation is the same as the surgeon would notice if he would observe the anatomy directly from different perspectives by moving his head, as in open surgery.
- The acceleration and velocity experienced by the surgeon gives him an intuitive feeling for the magnitude of motion of the vision system and instruments.
- Forces sensed by instruments can be felt by the surgeon in the form of "shudders" or opposing movements.

The key components of the system are a robot for handling the endoscope and an operating cockpit from which the surgeon controls the endoscope. The robot and operating cockpit are shown in Figure 6. Since the system is intended to be used in sub-millimetre surgery, e.g. neurosurgery, a hexapod robot is used for the precise handling of the endoscope. The operating cockpit is mounted on a second hydraulic hexapod to realise the motion feedback. Using a joystick the surgeon can control the endoscope. The magnified movements of the endoscope tip are then transferred to the operating cockpit.

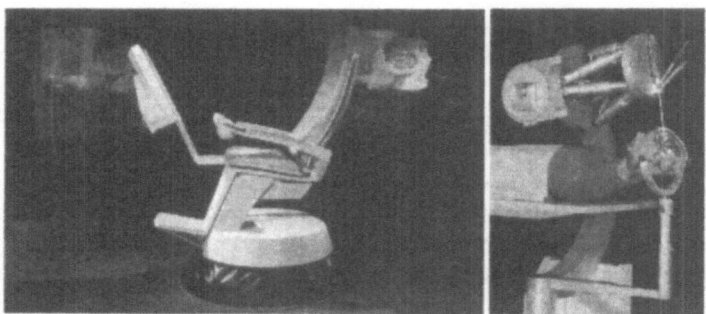

Fig. 6. Virtual Reality-assisted surgery system (Fraunhofer IPA)

Another approach using Virtual Reality concepts for robot-assisted surgery is the EndoSista System developed by Armstrong Healthcare [10]. The surgeon dictates the movement of the endoscope tip in laparoscopic surgery with his head motions as shown in Figure 7.

Fig.7. EndoSista system for laparoscopic surgery (Armstrong Healthcare)

6   Education and Training Systems

Certifiable quality criteria combined with lower cost education of medical personnel can only be achieved with new technology in education and training. While nobody disputes that experience with patients, in the OR and in the dissection laboratory will always be an essential part of student and resident training, the next four sections will look at areas where there is considerable justification for the use of Virtual Reality.

6.1   Practicing principal dexterous skills

Surgery will always not only require analytical skills but also manual and hand-eye coordination skills. Learning minimally invasive techniques poses a special challenge. Several teams are working on computer simulators to train such procedures, as shown in Figure 8. One of the most advanced is the system developed by Kühnapfel [11], which can be used to train certain steps in a laparoscopic cholecystectomy. The system uses high performance computer graphics, including soft tissue simulation, to allow some of the steps in the operation, such as the applications of clips or cutting of the cystic duct to be simulated. The interaction is very similar to true surgery, with realistic models of the endoscopes and surgical instrument handles. Force feedback is also foreseen. The training system is very useful to practice the manipulation of endoscopes and surgical instruments in minimally invasive surgery. However, all current surgery simulators show the limitations of current behavioral models and computer power. The behavior of the anatomy is usually limited to a very simplified elastic model and no account is taken of biochemical functions, bleeding or adhesions. Therefore, a more simplified approach is that presented by the Virtual Presence MIST system [12]. This concentrates on measurable teaching of hand-eye coordination skills. This may well be the most feasible form of Virtual Reality trainer in the near future.

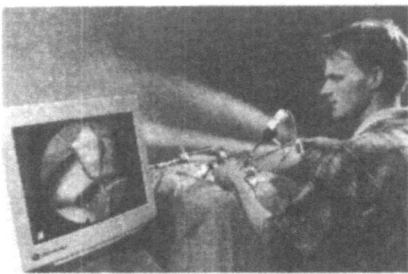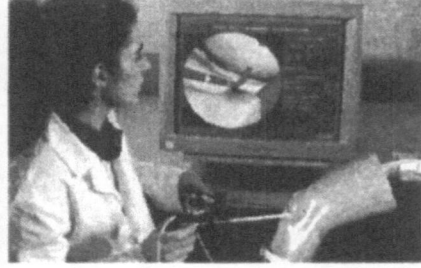

Fig. 8. KISMET simulator for laparoscopic cholecystectomy (FZK) and virtual
arthroscopy trainer (Fraunhofer IGD)

6.2   Systems Training

For standard operations with large case numbers the goal of the one button does-it-all system may well be a realistic vision. However, any specialized therapy will be patient specific and as such the system will require to be configured by the surgeon.

Here it has to be accepted that a system with many configurable parameters will be more useful than one with just one or two principal parameters. Undeniably, intelligent and more intuitive user interfaces are not only possible but also a definite requirement and a major research topic at Fraunhofer IPA. However, these systems will always require some form of training and here computer based learning systems prove to be most cost effective.

6.3 Learning about special cases

A certifiable training must ensure that the student has experience with rare but significant cases, which presence in the OR often cannot. An example of such a system is the UltraTrainer system for the training of medical ultrasound, developed at Fraunhofer IPA [7]. The student can perform simulated ultrasound examinations under realistic conditions and using real patient data. Recordings of data from patients suffering from rare diseases or malformations can be made available to all students using the UltraTrainer system.

6.4 Teaching basic anatomy

While dissection courses can teach dexterous skills, it cannot show all aspects of anatomy and is also too expensive for basic anatomy teaching. Hence the interest in setting up virtual representations of the human. The visible human project [13] has generated much of the data necessary for such a task. The Voxel-Man system developed by Höhne [14] shows how high quality images can be generated from these data. An example of a future education application is the digital anatomical atlas DIGIHOM® [15], a prototype of which is shown in Figure 9.

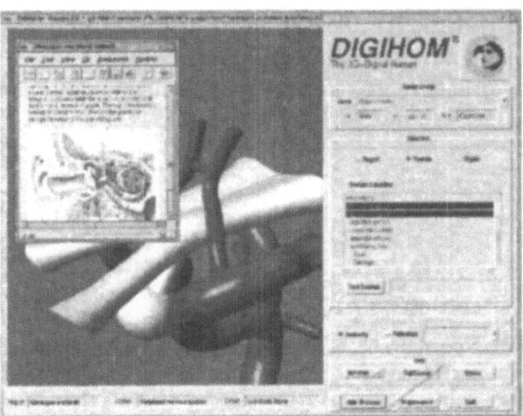

Fig. 9. DIGIHOM 3D interactive anatomical atlas (Fraunhofer IPA)

This software uses real-time interactive 3D computer graphics to show the human skeletal systems and its movements. To achieve the real-time interaction, the presentation of the anatomy has been simplified. The principal benefit of this approach is that spatial relationships and movements can be perceived very intuitively. Optionally, the user can use shutter glasses for stereoscopic viewing. DIGIHOM also uses other features of information systems such as a hypertext browser which permits other multimedia information to be associated with the 3D anatomy.

7 Discussion

Increasing computer performance and intensive research into Virtual Reality applications has already brought the benefits of real-time 3D interactive computer graphics to many medical users. However, many topics still require more research effort before they can become marketable products.

- Realistic modeling of anatomical behavior: It is fair to say that the accurate modelling and simulation of the complex physical and biochemical behaviour of living organisms is still largely unsolved. The complexity and number of interrelationships are too great to be solvable deterministically or by simple empirically derived look-up tables. Therefore, much research is still needed to find better iterative models of the behavior. Even then, the real-time solving will require computer performance many orders of magnitude greater than that available today.
- Many diagnoses as well as therapy planning procedures require image segmentation. Although automatic segmentation has been a major research topic for well over a decade now, we are still far away from satisfactory solution. It should, therefore, be accepted that the one solution does-it-all will not happen. However, new knowledge-based approaches for specific organs may be the right direction to go.
- Standardization will always be a subject, especially in a fast evolving technology. However, only standards, be they de facto industry standards or other standards can make a modular development possible. Areas where standards are needed are 2D and 3D-data formats, software applications and certain libraries and also very importantly, processes.

References

[1] J. Pfeifer, A. Hopper, B. Sudduth, A Patient-Centric Approach to Telemedicine Database Development, Medicine Meets Virtual Reality 6, pp. 67-73, IOS Press and Ohmsha 1998.

[2] V. Urban, Operieren im Submillimeterbereich - Der interdisziplinäre Operationssaal der Zukunft, Bericht über die Unfallmedizinische Tagung des Landesverbandes Hessen-Mittelrhein und Thüringen der gewerblichen Berufsgenossenschaften in Mainz, pp. 81-86, No. 96, Hauptverband der gewerblichen Berufsgenossenschaften, Sankt Augustin, 1996.

[3] LIMIT: Laboratory for Integrated Medical Interface, http://www.hitl.washington.edu/projects/medicine/limit.html, June 1998.

[4] A. M. Alyassin, W. E. Lorensen, Virtual Endoscopy Software Applications on a PC, Medicine Meets Virtual Reality 6, pp. 84-89, IOS Press and Ohmsha 1998.

[5] HT Medical Systems Inc., http://www.ht.com/, June 1998.

[6]   VR Medicine, http://www.igd.fhg.de/www/igd-a4/flyers/medicine, February 1998.
[7]   J. Stallkamp, M. Wapler, UltraTrainer-A Training System for Medical Ultrasound Examination, Medicine Meets Virtual Reality 6, pp. 298-301, IOS Press and Ohmsha 1998.
[8]   BrainLAB GmbH, http://www.brainlab.com/Vvision.htm, 1997.
[9]   M. Wapler, J. Neugebauer, T. Weisener, V. Urban, Robot-assisted Surgery System with Kinesthetic Feedback, Proceedings of the 29th International Symposium on Robotics, Birmingham, April 1998.
[10] P. Finlay, Endosista: A Telemanipulator for Endoscopic Control in Minimally Invasive Therapy, Proceedings of the 29th International Symposium on Robotics, New Sector Session: Medical and Healthcare, Birmingham, April 1998.
[11] U. Kühnapfel, Ch. Kuhn, M. Hübner, H. G. Krumm, H. Maaß, B. Neisius, The Karlsruhe Endoscopic Surgery Trainer as an example for Virtual Reality in Medical Education, Minimally Invasive Therapy and Allied Technologies (MITAT), pp. 122-125, No. 6, Blackwell Science Ltd. 1997.
[12] Virtual Presence, http://www.vrweb.com/WEB/DEV/MEDICAL.HTM May 1998
[13] The visible human project, http://www.nlm.nih.gov/research/visible/, June 1998
[14] Voxel-Man, http://www.springer.de/newmedia/medicine/voxel/voxel.htm, June 1998
[15] DIGIHOM 3D, http://www.ipa.fhg.de/300/340/vr/digihom/digihom_englisch.html, April 1998.

MAKING VIRTUAL WORLDS WORK IN A REAL WORLD

Mark R. Mine

Walt Disney Imagineering Research & Development, Inc.

1 The Promise

The promise of immersive virtual environments is one of a three-dimensional environment in which a user can directly perceive and interact with three-dimensional virtual objects. The underlying belief motivating most virtual reality (VR) research is that this will lead to more natural and effective human-computer interfaces. Promising results have been demonstrated in several key application domains such as architecture [Brooks, 1986], scientific visualization [Taylor, et al., 1993], phobia therapy [Rothbaum, et al., 1995], and entertainment [Pausch, et al., 1996].

The number of successful virtual-environment applications, however, still remains small, with even fewer applications having gone beyond the research laboratory. Why?

Many of the successful applications fall within the realm of spatial visualization. The applications exploit the intuitive view specification (via head tracking) offered by VR systems but make little use of direct virtual-object manipulation. Why is it difficult to do much more than look around in a virtual world?

In this talk I present some of the lessons I have learned about building virtual world applications that work in a real world. I describe characteristics of virtual environments which hamper the development of successful virtual environment applications. I discuss effective techniques which compensate for some of the limitations of working immersed. Finally I talk about ways to enhance virtual-environment interaction by providing real-world haptic surfaces such as tablets and projection desktops.

2 The Problems

Besides the well known technological limitations such as system latency and display resolution, several less obvious factors have hampered development of "real-world" virtual-environment applications.

1) *The precise manipulation of virtual objects is hard.* Although immersion, head-tracked view specification, and six degree-of-freedom (DoF) hand tracking facilitate the coarse manipulation of virtual objects, the precise manipulation of virtual objects is complicated by:

- *Lack of haptic feedback*: Humans depend on haptic feedback and physical constraints for precise interaction in the real world; the lack of physical work-surfaces to align against and rest on limits precision and exacerbates fatigue. Though there is considerable ongoing research in the area of active haptic feedback [Durlach and Mavor, 1995], general-purpose haptic feedback devices that do not restrict the mobility of the user are not yet practical or available.

- *Limited input information*: Most virtual-environment systems accept position and orientation (pose) data on the user's head and (if lucky) two hands. One also typically has a button or glove to provide signal/event information. This suffices for specifying simple 6 DoF motion and placement but falls short for many more complex forms of interaction.

- *Limited precision*: The lack of haptic and acoustic feedback, inaccurate tracking systems, and whole-hand input typical of current VR systems restricts users to the coarse manipulation of virtual objects. Fine-grained manipulations are extremely difficult using this "boxing glove" style interface.

2) *Virtual environments lack a unifying framework for interaction,* such as the desktop metaphor used in conventional through-the-window computer applications. Without haptics, neither real-world nor desktop computer interaction metaphors are adequate in a virtual environment.

The desktop metaphor further breaks down when the user is inside the user interface. Interface controls and displays must move with the user as he moves through the environment and be made easy to locate. The differences between working in a conventional computer environment and working immersed are analogous to the differences between a craftsman at a workbench and one moving about a worksite wearing a toolbelt. His toolbelt had better be large and filled with powerful tools.

3 Proprioception and Body-Relative Interaction

Without touch, a user can no longer feel his surroundings to tell where he is nor use the felt collision of a manipulandum (an object being manipulated) with stationary objects to refine spatial perception. It is imperative, therefore, to take advantage of one thing every user can still feel in the virtual world, his body.

A person's sense of the position and orientation of his body and its several parts is called *proprioception* [Boff, et al., 1986]. I have found that one can use proprioception to develop a unified set of interaction techniques that allow a user to interact with a virtual world intuitively, efficiently, precisely, and lazily. I have also found that these body-relative ineraction techniques are more effective than techniques relying solely on visual information. Body-relative interaction techniques provide:

- a physical real-world frame of reference in which to operate
- a more direct and precise sense of control
- "eyes off" interaction (the user doesn't have to constantly watch what he's doing)

A user can take advantage of proprioception during body-relative interaction in at least three ways:

Direct manipulation:

If a virtual object is located directly at the user's hand position, the user has a good sense of the position of the object (even with eyes closed) due to proprioception, and thus a greater sense of control. It is easier to place an object precisely by hand than when it is attached to the end of a fishing rod.

Often, however, the target of manipulation lies outside of the user's reach. Though he can move to reach it, constantly switching between object interaction and movement control breaks the natural rhythm of the operation and adds significant cognitive overhead. As an alternative, users can manipulate objects using *scaled-world grab*. When using scaled-world grab, selected objects that fall outside of the reach of the user are brought instantly into reach by automatically scaling down the world about the user's head every time he grabs an object and scaled back up when he releases it (Figure 1).

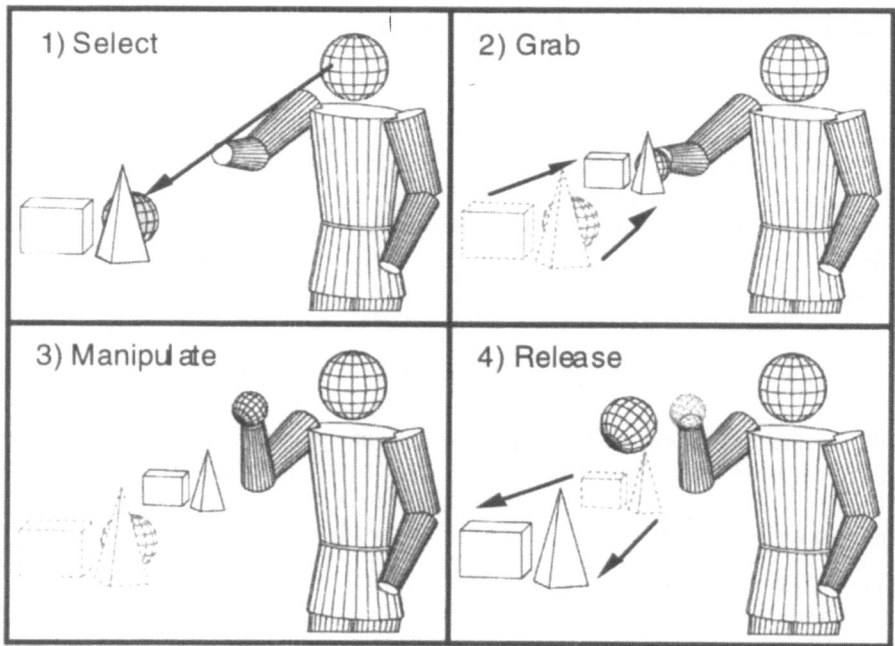

Fig. 1: Automatic scaling of the world when the user grabs and releases an object.

For example, if the user's arm is extended 0.5 meters, the application brings a selected object that is 5 meters away to the user's hand by scaling down the world by a factor of ten. Scaling takes place at the start of each manipulation and is reset when the user is done (when the user grabs and then releases an object, for example).

With the object at the user's hand he can exploit proprioception, stereopsis, and head-motion parallax as he grabs an object and moves it.

If the center of the scaling operation is chosen to be the point midway between the user's eyes, he will be unaware, usually, that scaling has taken place, due to the ambiguity of perspective projections. This is particularly true if the inter-pupilary distance used to compute stereo images is also adjusted by the same scaling factor. This saves the user's having to reconverge the eyes.

Automatic world-scaling also yields a useful locomotion mode, in which the user transports himself by grabbing an object in the desired travel direction and pulling himself towards it. With scaled-world grab the user can reach any visible destination in a single grab operation.

Since the point of interest is attached to the user's hand he can quickly view it from all sides by simply torquing his wrist. Alternately, if the virtual world stays oriented with the laboratory (which aids wayfinding), the user can swing himself about the point of interest, in a fashion similar to orbital mode (discussed later), by holding it in front of his face while he turns around (the world pivoting about his hand).

Scaled-world grab is a powerful technique with an important property: it minimizes user work for a given result. With scaled-world grab the user can bring the most remote object in the scene to his side in a single operation; he doesn't have to fly (or worse, walk) to reach it or repeatedly grab, drop, and regrab the object to reel it in.

Fig. 2: Pull-down menus

Physical mnemonics:

Since a user can no longer feel the world around him, it can be difficult to find, select, and use virtual controls in world space, especially if the user is free to walk about the environment. Users can store virtual objects, in particular menus and widgets, relative to his body. If controls are fixed relative to the user's body, he can use proprioception to find the controls, as one finds his pen in his pocket, or his pliers in his tool belt. If controls are attached to the user's body, they move with him as he moves through the environment and are always within reach. Finally, controls can be stored out of view (behind the user's back for example), reducing visual clutter, yet remaining easily accessible (like an arrow from a quiver).

For example, one can hide virtual menus just above the user's current field of view (Figure 2). To access a menu the user simply reaches up, grabs it, and pulls it into view. The user can then interact with the menu using his other hand (if two hands are available) or through some form of gaze-directed interaction. Once the user is done with the menu he lets go, and it returns to its hiding place. This obviates a dedicated menu button, avoids occlusion by the menu, uses an existing operation for menu invocation, and keeps menus easy to find and access.

Gestural actions

Just as a user's body sense can be used to facilitate the recall of objects, it can be used to facilitate the recall of actions, such as gestures used to invoke commands or to communicate information.

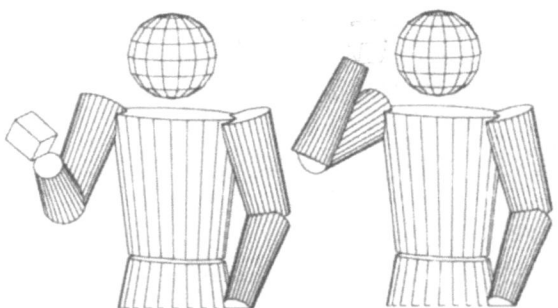

Fig. 3: Over-the-shoulder deletion.

A common operation, for example, is deletion; users need an easy way to get rid of virtual objects. Over-the-shoulder deletion is an intuitive gesture that exploits body sense. To delete an object the user simply throws it over his shoulder (Figure 3). It is easy to do, easy to remember, and it does not use up any buttons or menu space. It is unlikely to be accidentally invoked, since users do not typically manipulate objects in that region.

The space behind a user's head can be treated as a virtual clipboard. A user can later retrieve the last object deleted by simply reaching over his shoulder and grabbing it.

4 Providing Haptic Work Surfaces

Though proprioception greatly enhances virtual-environment interaction, precise manipulation is still harder in virtual spaces than in real space. Several factors complicate fine-grained manipulation.

First, the lack of physical work surfaces and haptic feedback makes the controlled manipulation of virtual objects much more difficult. Users typically manipulate virtual objects by holding their arms out without support. In the real world, a person generally grounds the arm at the forearm, or elbow, or heel of hand to steady hand motions and to reduce fatigue when performing precise manipulation.

Second, humans depend upon naturally occurring physical constraints to help determine the motion of objects they are manipulating (sliding a chair along a floor, for example). Whereas it is possible to implement virtual equivalents of physical constraints [Bukowski and Sequin, 1995], it is more difficult for the user to take advantage of these constraints without haptic feedback. He can only see that the chair is on the floor, he can't feel the contact, hear it, or sense the vibration as the chair slides.

Third, users in a virtual world must typically do without the fingertip control they rely on for the fine-grained manipulation of objects in the real world. Instrumented gloves have shown some promise for the fine-grained manipulation of objects, but they have proven difficult to use in practice [Kijima and Hirose, 1996].

To overcome these limitations, several researchers are exploring the benefits of giving users a real surface on which they can work using haptic constraints. This can be in the form of a hand-held tablet (following the lead of [Sachs, et al., 1991] and [Stoakley, et al., 1995]), or a drafting table [Mapes and Moshell, 1995]. The tablet can be used as a two-dimensional drawing surface (to define detailed two-dimensional shapes) or it can be used as the input space for a two-dimensional menu (allowing users to interact precisely with widgets and controls). If the user interacts with the tablet using a hand-held stylus, he can take advantage of the user's fingertip control precision. In addition the friction between tablet and stylus and the grounding of the stylus against the tablet give the user better control. Interesting results can be found in papers such as: [Szalavari and Gervautz, 1997; Bowman, et al., 1998; Poupyrev, et al., 1998]

5 References

Boff, Kenneth R., Lloyd Kaufman and James P. Thomas, Eds. (1986). *Handbook of Perception and Human Performance*. New York, John Wiley and Sons.

Bowman, Doug A., Jean Wineman and Larry F. Hodges (1998). "Exploratory Design of Animal Habitats Within an Immersive Virtual Environment." *Georgia Institute of Technology GVU Center*, Technical Report GIT-GVU-98-06.

Brooks, Frederick P., Jr. (1986). "Walkthrough-a dynamic graphics system for simulating virtual buildings." *Proceedings of the 1986 Workshop on Interactive 3D Graphics* (Chapel Hill, NC), ACM, pp. 9-22.

Bukowski, Richard W. and Carlo H. Sequin (1995). "Object associations: a simple and practical approach to virtual 3D manipulation." *Proceedings of the 1995 Symposium on Interactive 3D Graphics* (Monterey, CA), ACM, pp. 131-138.

Durlach, Nathaniel I. and Anne S. Mavor, Eds. (1995). *Virtual Reality: Scientific and Technological Challenges*. Washington, D.C., National Academy Press.

Kijima, Ryugo and Michitaka Hirose (1996). "Representative spherical plane method and composition of object manipulation methods." *Proceedings of the 1996 Virtual Reality Annual International Symposium* (Santa Clara, CA), IEEE, pp. 196-202.

Mapes, Daniel P. and J. Michael Moshell (1995). "A two-handed interface for object manipulation in virtual environments." *Presence* 4(4), pp. 403-416.

Pausch, Randy, Jon Snoddy, Robert Taylor, Scott Watson and Eric Haseltine (1996). "Disney's Aladdin: first steps toward storytelling in virtual reality." Proceedings of SIGGRAPH '96 (New Orleans, LA). In *Computer Graphics* Proceedings, Annual Conference Series, ACM, pp. 193-202.

Poupyrev, Ivan, Numada Tomokazu and Suzanne Weghorst (1998). "Virtual Notepad: Handwriting in Immersive VR." *Proceedings of VRAIS '98* (Atlanta, GA), IEEE, pp. 126-132.

Rothbaum, B., L. Hodges, R. Kooper, D. Opdyke, J. Williford and M. North (1995). "Effectiveness of computer-generated (virtual reality) graded exposure in the treatment of acrophobia." *American Journal of Psychiatry* 152(4), pp. 626-628.

Sachs, Emanuel, Andrew Roberts and David Stoops (1991). "3-Draw: a tool for designing 3D shapes." *IEEE Computer Graphics and Applications* 11(6), pp. 18- 26.

Stoakley, Richard, Matthew J. Conway and Randy Pausch (1995). "Virtual reality on a WIM: interactive worlds in miniature." *Proceedings of CHI '95* (Denver, CO), ACM, pp. 265-272.

Szalavari, Zsolt and Michael Gervautz (1997). "The personal interaction panel - a two-handed interface for augmented reality." *Proceedings of Eurographics '97* , pp. 335-346.

Taylor, Russell M, Warren Robinett, Vernon L. Chi, Frederick P. Jr. Brooks, William V. Wright, Stanley Williams and Erik J. Snyder (1993). "The Nanomanipulator: a virtual-reality interface for a scanning tunnel microscope." Proceedings of SIGGRAPH '93 (Anaheim, CA). In *Computer Graphics* Proceedings, Annual Conference Series, ACM, pp. 127-134.

Experiences from an Inhabited Television experiment

Paul Rea

{paul.rea@bt-sys.bt.co.uk}

BT Advanced Research & Technology, UK

Abstract

In this paper we present a vision for a new class of network service aimed principally at the emerging digital television platform. Inhabited Television embraces the proven pulling power of professionally produced broadcast content, with the enduring appeal of online chat and interactive virtual environments.

Commissioned by the Channel 4, a public service broadcaster based in the UK, 'Heaven & Hell – live' was conceived as an experimental Inhabited Television service. In this paper we describe the technical and design background to the project, and present the main findings arising from delivering it as an experimental service.

1. What is Inhabited Television?

In 1996, there were an estimated 909-million television sets [1] in households around the world making it the most pervasive communication medium of the late-twentieth century. Television, which has remained largely unchanged for fifty years or more, is about to undergo a revolution. Old-style analogue delivery systems are poised to be replaced by digital systems, which promise greater choice and unprecedented levels of interaction with the broadcast content. One likely side effect of this revolution in digital broadcasting will be the convergence of television and the Internet. Indeed, one can envisage a point in the near future when the distinction between viewing and browsing will disappear for any practical purpose.

The emergence of digital broadcasting coupled with the convergence of television and the Internet leads inevitably to the question what services will be supported in this new domain and how consumers interact with them? Detailed answers to these questions are beyond the scope of this paper, however, we do offer a radical vision of where these new technologies might be leading which we illustrate through our experiences gained while delivering an experimental *Inhabited Television* service.

The term Inhabited Television was coined to describe a new class of service that could be deployed on the emerging digital infrastructure. The vision embraces the proven pulling power of professionally produced broadcast content with the enduring appeal of online chat and interactive virtual environments. Combining content and user participation as basic service components will result, in our opinion, in a proliferation of commercial Inhabited Television services.

Previous work on using shared spaces, more commonly referred to as multi-user virtual environments, to support computer supported collaborative working suggested that it would make a suitable candidate technology to underpin an experimental Inhabited Television service. Users in a shared space are embodied through a graphical object, often referred to as an avatar, and share a common model of a computer-generated world. Users are free to navigate around the world, they are able to manipulate applications and artefacts, and can communicate with other users. In terms of Inhabited Television, the world is the studio from where the broadcast originates.

This paper is organised as follows: Section 2 discusses previous experiments related to the Inhabited Television vision. In Section 3, we outline the experimental aims of 'Heaven & Hell – live'. Section 4 reflects on the conceptualisation process and content creation. In Section 5, we discuss participant involvement and engaging user's interest during the broadcast. In Section 6, we provide a brief overview of the delivery platform. In Section 7, we outline the methods employed to govern participation in the broadcast. Section 8 presents the main results from the experiment and, in Section 9, we discuss the experiment and outline future directions for our work.

2. Background

The seeds for Inhabited Television were sown in number of early experimental services. Prominent amongst these was The YORB [2], a service developed through New York University's Interactive Telecommunications Program. Broadcast once a week on Manhattan cable, a public access channel, The YORB was created specifically to support the needs and aspirations of a community derived from the viewing audience. Central to the broadcast stream was a three-dimensional environment, shown in Fig. 1. During the weekly broadcast viewers were invited to phone-in and contribute to the broadcast by chatting to the host. Additionally, while chatting to the host, it was possible for the contributor to use telephone generated DTFM tones to control the broadcast viewpoint. Community members were also able to make contribution via a bulletin board and an IRC channel, which appeared on the screen during the broadcast. The YORB's treatment of viewers as first-class members of an extended community makes it a truly significant precursor for Inhabited Television.

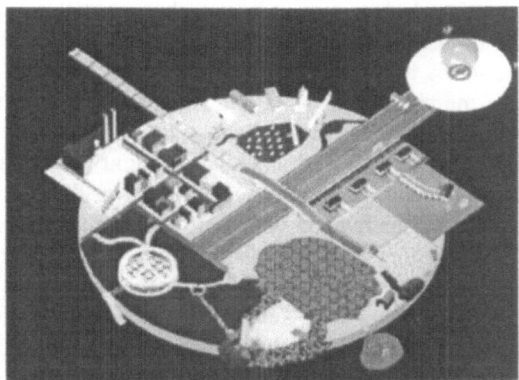

Fig. 1. View of the YORB

The World Wide Web was the catalyst for the development of a number of key technologies that enabled the creation of three-dimensional environments to support distributed communities. In particular, the emergence of VRML and Java provided platform- and vendor- independent mechanisms for creating and distributing virtual environments layered over existing network protocols. It was now possible to explore levels of interaction beyond the relatively crude forms supported by The YORB.

On July 10th, 1996, MTV and OnLive! Technologies announced the launch of a three-dimensional virtual environment based around a mythical tropical island called TikkiLand [3]. In a press release that accompanied the launch, MTV justified the project by restating its ongoing commitment to developing new and innovative approaches to delivering programming. To connect to the service users first had to download the browser software. They were then able connect to the world and speak to other people through OnLive!'s group chat server. Segments from the world showing avatars introducing videos and chatting to other avatars were incorporated into the normal broadcast stream. The true significance of Tikkiland for Inhabited Television came from the tight coupling between the virtual world and television broadcast.

The Mirror [4], created by a collaboration of BT, the BBC, Sony and Illuminations, was an experimental social environment run in association with the BBC's information technology television programme 'The Net'. The Mirror focused on how a virtual environment might be used to support communication and interaction within an online community formed around a television series. The worlds comprising The Mirror were opened to the public on January 13th, 1997, and were closed after seven weeks to coincide with the end of the television series. During the experiment a number of special events were staged, including a debate between Peter Cochrane and Douglas Adams on the future of the book; a virtual art exhibition; a game show; and a virtual marriage. The importance of the special events should not be underestimated as they provided a focus for the community to gather and interact in the world.

Evidence, both reported and observed, indicated that a small community had formed in The Mirror during its relatively brief existence. However, it was less clear to what extent the television series had contributed to this other than by delivering a ready source of community members and providing a channel to report significant events and activities back to the wider viewing audience. It was with this in mind that 'Heaven & Hell – live' was conceived as an experiment that attempted to develop a much tighter coupling between the community in the world and television broadcast. Indeed, the shared space and the events within it were to form the major part of a live one-hour broadcast shown on national television in the UK. The broadcast component of 'Heaven & Hell – live' was commissioned by Channel 4 as part of late-night series of programming entitled Renegade Television. Celebrating the subversive, the marginal and the underground, Renegade TV consisted of three blocks of programming shown over a three-week period in the late summer of 1997. Scheduled for broadcast in the third week, 'Heaven & Hell – live' was expected to benefit from the coverage given to it in the previous weeks programming.

3. Experimental aims of 'Heaven & Hell - live'

We are now starting to see the results from experiments assessing the applicability of shared spaces for supporting communication within distributed communities [5]. However, these experiments often require high-end workstations, sophisticated network configurations and use proprietary academic platforms. In addition, participants in these experiments are often derived from developers and advocates of the technology. For 'Heaven & Hell – live', as with The Mirror, we wanted to look beyond these relatively exclusive confines by involving members of the general public. Consequently, we had to support hardware configurations and network connectivity available to a typical Internet user, namely a PC configuration running over a narrowband dialup connection. The broad reach of 'Heaven & Hell – live' meant it was difficult to conduct it under rigorous experimental conditions. Nevertheless, certain experimental aims for the project were established covering the content delivery through to the post-event analysis.

These aims are summarised as follows:

- Deliver a compelling shared space capable of supporting the aspirations of the community and the needs of the broadcaster.
- Create a technically excellent service infrastructure to support all parties involved in the project.
- Learn through a process of formal data collection and observation how *real* people use shared spaces.

4. Conceptualisation and content creation

'Heaven & Hell – live' was conceived as a dramatic stage upon which the television event would be situated. Much of the early discussion centred on the themes to be incorporated in the world and how might translate into a familiar television format. After a period spent brainstorming and storyboarding ideas, Fig. 2, the strongest format to emerge was a post-modern game show based around themes from Heaven and Hell. This would provide, it was felt, wide ranging opportunities for the creation of a credible television programme that would demand participation from the world's inhabitants to make it a success.

Fig. 2. Storyboard showing purgatory

One of the goals of the project was to develop the concept in such a way that it might be possible to sustain a series at some point in the future. Inevitably, this lead to the conclusion that a programme based solely around technological novelty would not provide a theme strong enough to be carried forward. The structure developed for the show followed a series of structured activities including a treasure hunt, soul stacking, a quiz game and a gambling game. Intermingled between these activities were a series of contributions from the host, contestants, virtual camera-people or correspondents, and inhabitants.

The world was divided into three locations; Purgatory, Heaven and Hell. Each location was intended to have its own very distinctive and contrasting visual and audio qualities, which was emphasised by organising the world into a series of connected planes, Fig. 3. Purgatory, positioned as it was between Heaven and Hell, was the entry point to the world. In terms of the television broadcast, this area was also intended to double as the home location for the show's presenter, Dante. Heaven was connected to Purgatory by a shaft of light that, if stepped into, would draw the user up. As well as providing a link between locations, the light assisted user navigation. Hell was designed as a set of connected caverns with the intention of confusing and unnerving users. Hell was linked to Purgatory by a tube down which unsuspecting users would fall. Inspiration for the world's overall look and feel were drawn from classical and contemporary influences including works by Georgia O'Keeffe, Maxwell Parrish, William Blake and H. R. Giger. The themes embraced in the world were carried forward into the supporting web site and the CD containing the content and browser software. Brand identity was believed to be very important to the overall success of the project.

Fig. 3. Structure of the world

The creation of the characters that would inhabit the world of 'Heaven & Hell – live' was considered to be as important as the world construction. Fig. 4 shows a storyboard reflecting some initial ideas for avatars. Previous work on the Mirror had taught us the importance of providing a range of avatar forms with appropriate forms of customisation. Taking inspirations from Sony's Sapari world [6], it was decided to implement a facility whereby users, having chosen an avatar, could customise its appearance by applying colours and changing the relative proportions of the various body elements. In total six avatars were created each with its own very distinctive personality and set of emotions expressed through animations.

Fig. 4. Avatar storyboard

In addition to the normal avatars, a new class of avatar was created called Super Avatars. The main role for this type of avatar was to embody the contestants in the show. From a users perspective a Super Avatar is like any normal avatar in all respects except one. Most shared space systems, including the system used for 'Heaven & Hell – live', use some form of grouping mechanism to achieve scalability both at the server and client. However, this does have the side effect that at any point in time each user is only aware of a small subset of the total population. While this may be tolerable for conventional chat-based applications, for 'Heaven & Hell – live', this presents a major barrier to user participation. Our technical solution to this problem will be discussed later in this paper.

VRML and Java were used as the principal languages for coding the world, the avatars and all associated behaviours. This combination proved to be extremely powerful, and lead to a working style that encouraged content prototyping and experimentation. In a relatively short time and with limited resources (approximately three people worked full-time over four months from the initial prototypes to the final CD pressing) the content was completed, tested and delivered. The choice of VRML and Java did have an adverse effect on the final achievable frame-rate when compared to an implementation based, for example, on C++ and DirectX. However, it is questionable whether it would have been possible to deliver the project using these lower-level mechanisms particularly given the limited resources and time constraints.

5. Involving participants and engaging viewers

One of the main roles of the Television Production Company is to create programming content that matches the broadcaster's requirements with viewers' expectations. Inhabited Television challenges this relationship by empowering audience members to make significant contributions, if they so choose, to a programme's narrative structure. In 'Heaven & Hell – live' we wanted to explore the extent to which an audience might actively pursue and contribute to the events as they unfolded. The main contributors to the television programme were the contestants in the studio taking part in the activities and the pre-registered community members. Beyond this, we wanted to provide a channel for spontaneous contributions from anyone who had access to an e-mail account or the Internet. An IRC forum was created for online discussions and e-mail address was advertised for viewers to send reactions to what they were seeing.

Fig. 5 illustrates the various participation zones open during the live broadcast. At the periphery we have the traditional television viewer, for the most part their role is as passive observers. Moving to the next zone we have forum and e-mail contributors. Likely to be watching the broadcast at the same time, viewers in this zone were encouraged to engage in open discussions about what they were seeing and hearing in the broadcast stream. Access to the forum was open to anyone who had a PC with a suitable network connection. Admittance to the participant zone relied on pre-registering for a CD containing the content. Contestants competing in the game show and the correspondents, who were observing and reporting back events in the world populated the innermost zone. Located in a television studio, admittance to this zone was necessarily restricted.

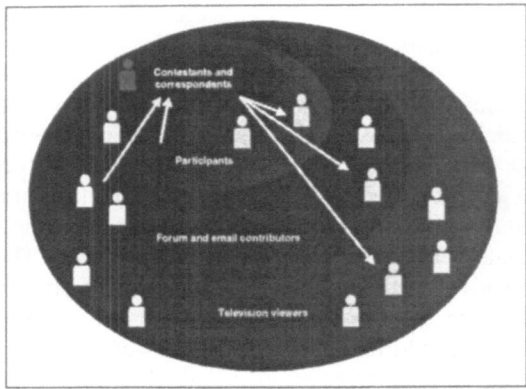

Fig. 5. Participation zones

Interfaces between certain zones where open, albeit subject to certain technical and organisational restrictions. It was possible, therefore, for a 'viewer' to contribute to the broadcast through the forum and then move back to the viewer zone. Evidence also suggested that people were co-present in multiple zones at the same time. For example, to view the television stream, contribute to the forum and control a client in the world – the reader is left to consider the impact this might have on an individual's cognitive loading over the one hour broadcast!

6. Delivery platform

Experiences from The Mirror highlighted the need to deploy a delivery platform that was reliable and scalable. Although not intended to be a commercial service in the first instance, it was important to use the project to learn what would be required in terms of a service-surround to support such a venture in the future. The delivery platform consisted of two elements; the registration platform and the shared space server, distributed over three physical sites; the Channel 4 web site, a server farm maintained at BT Laboratories, and, for the actual broadcast, the television studio.

6.1 Registration platform

Calls for participation were made variously through television publicity, newspaper articles and postings made to related mail lists. User registration was fronted by the Channel 4 web site [7], which contained the top-level pages describing the experiment and how people might participate in the experiment. The web material was distributed across two servers; the main Channel 4 web server primarily containing static information, and a server at BT Laboratories containing the registration code, database and any information designated as dynamic, for example FAQ lists. This separation was important as it simplified the on-going maintenance in the weeks leading up to the broadcast. From a user's point of view this separation was transparent.

Once an individual had decided they wished to take part in the experiment, they were required to follow a simple online registration procedure involving agreeing to the terms of a legal agreement and completing a simple form. Having correctly filled in the form, an identifier and password was generated and e-mailed to the user and the details supplied were logged in an Object Store database [8]. The database proved to be a core resource for the project and provided input to the administration, authentication and governance processes. Fig. 6 shows the components in the registration platform deployed for the experiment.

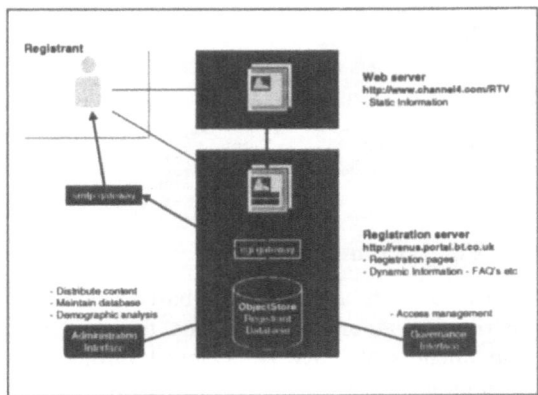

Fig. 6. Registration platform

The registration process was configured to accept 450 applications, a figure achieved two weeks after the experiment had been publicly announced. This figure of 450 was based upon the fact that the shared space server was configured to support 200 sessions and, from our experiences during The Mirror, it was expected that approximately 50% of pre-registered users would connect during the broadcast.

6.2 Shared space server

Sony's Community Place system [9] was used as the shared space server during the experiment. Community Place had been used successfully before to support The Mirror where it proved to be robust scalable solution. Fig. 7 shows a schematic representation of Sony's system. The system consists of three main functional components; the server or Bureau, the Application Object and a VRML client supporting the Virtual Society protocol. The Administration and Authentication Objects provide management and access control interfaces.

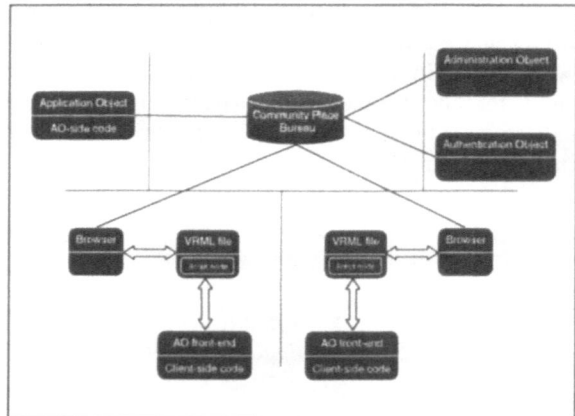

Fig. 7. Community Place architecture

In simple terms, the Bureau acts as a software-based router. Its main roles are to manage message distribution amongst clients and to maintain a lightweight state database. Bureau and client scalability is achieved through the use of a simple awareness model based upon aura groups [10]. Each client connected to the world has an associated spatial volume known as an aura, which is used to define a client's volume of interest or event horizon. The size of the aura for a particular world is specified through a Bureau configuration option. When a client connects to a Bureau, it has no initial knowledge of any other clients connected to the Bureau. Awareness of other clients is gained by the Bureau detecting aura collisions and using this information to route messages between clients. The Bureau guarantees all relationships are reflexive, i.e. if user A is aware of user B, then user B will be aware of user A. Allowing each client to maintain a fixed number of awareness relationships reduces the network traffic and reduces the rendering overhead on the client.

Community Place system supports a construct called an Application Object (AO). These are non-graphical clients that connect to a Bureau and dynamically inject shared VRML objects into a scene at runtime. AO's have an advantage over normal graphical clients in that they are able to declare a message distribution policy that regulates the message traffic to the Bureau. During 'Heaven & Hell – live' AO's were used to regulate the appearance of content related to the activities in the programme. Although the content resided on a CD local to the user, it was possible to manage its appearance and location in the world through the AO.

One of the problems identified early in the development process was the apparently stochastic behaviour of the simple aura model. In order to achieve any sense of structure in the broadcast stream it was essential to be able to consistently locate certain users namely the host and the two contestants. Without the Super Avatar there was the distinct possibility that the contestants would be aware of each other only at the start of the programme and the inhabitants would not be able to follow or participate in the activities. The Super Avatar exploited the fact that AO's, unlike normal graphical clients, are free from the restriction in the number of awareness relationships they are allowed to maintain. The implementation, as illustrated in Fig. 8, involved linking a normal graphical user to an AO by a separate TCP connection. As the user controlling a Super Avatar moves through the space, position updates are relayed to the Bureau via an AO. Because the number of clients using this mechanism was relatively small, the increase in the network traffic was also relatively small. Sending position and orientation update messages once every second further reduced traffic between AO and the Bureau.

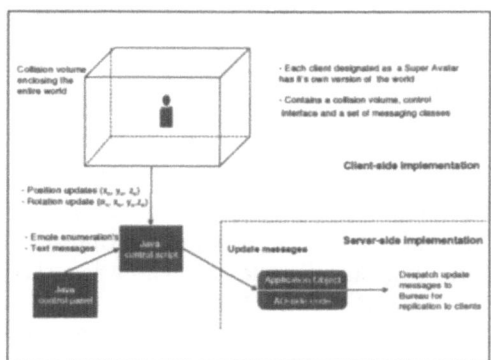

Fig. 8. Super avatar implementation

The servers used during the broadcast were distributed across the studio and the BT labs server farm. The AO's were the located in the studio, which made it much easier to start and stop them according to the programme schedule, and restart them after potential crashes.

7. Governing the broadcast

Like most broadcasters, Channel 4 is legally obliged to ensure that the programmes they broadcast satisfy the terms and conditions of the license under which they are regulated. Mindful of the regulatory framework, the programme's Commissioning Editor identified governance as a major cause for concern. This was expressed through a worst case scenario involving a group infiltrating the broadcast intent on inciting racial hatred. However extreme and unlikely this scenario sounded the possibility had to be treated seriously and a viable counter-strategy was demanded. Often virtual communities are seen as an opportunity for exploring alternative and emergent models of governance. The link between the television domain and virtual world in the 'Heaven & Hell – live' meant this luxury was not available.

The strategy developed for governing the world was based around determining whether the attack was by an individual or group. If the attack was by a single user then we would attempt to remove that person from the space and revoke their access rights while trying to maintain continuity for the rest of the community. If the attack appeared to be from a group, the approach was to withdraw the stream from Channel 4 and withdraw the service. This would have a catastrophic effect on the community and, therefore, would only be invoked as a last resort.

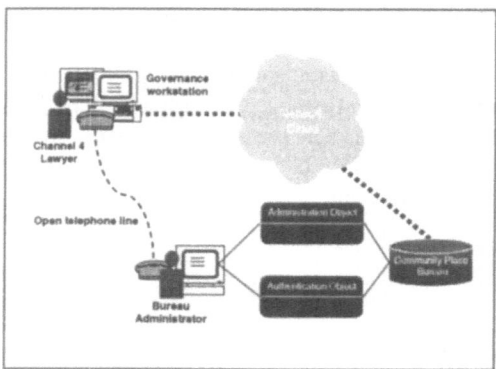

Fig. 9. Governance interface

The system devised for governing the space, Fig. 9, was based upon combining human judgement with a management interface to the Bureau. The human judgement was supplied in the form of a Channel 4 lawyer who was tasked with monitoring the broadcast stream and the chat log. Ultimately, the lawyer was responsible for taking the programme off-air or removing an individual from the world. Once an offender was identified the decision was relayed to the Bureau administrator whose responsibility was to remove the user and revoke their access rights. The technical solution relied upon regulating access to the world through user authentication scheme. In addition to governance, the authentication interface made it possible to construct a rich picture of user behaviour within the world.

8. Key results from 'Heaven & Hell – live'

'Heaven & Hell – live' produced a large body of objective and subjective data. Collected mainly from the delivery platform, the objective data was used for two purposes; to build a profile of the participants taking part in the experiment, and to observe patterns of behaviour in the world before and during the broadcast. The subjective data, supplied by a cross-section of participants and viewers, was used to assess reactions to the broadcast and gather opinions on the concept of Inhabited Television.

There now follows a summary of the main results from the data analysis.

8.1 Participant demographics

In total 456 people pre-registered to take part in the experiment. Of these 425 were male and only 36 were female, a staggering ratio of 11:1. This might be explained partly by the type of viewer attracted by late night programming on Channel 4 and partly by the perception that males dominate the Internet domain. Of the registered users, 219 connected to the world during the five days when the server was available to the public.

Fig. 10 shows the age distribution of registered participants. Nearly 50% of the participants were aged between 25 and 34 with the next largest age group being between 18 and 24. Renegade Television was considered, by Channel 4, to contain material inappropriate for viewers less than 18 years. Consequently, an age limited was imposed on participation in 'Heaven & Hell – live'.

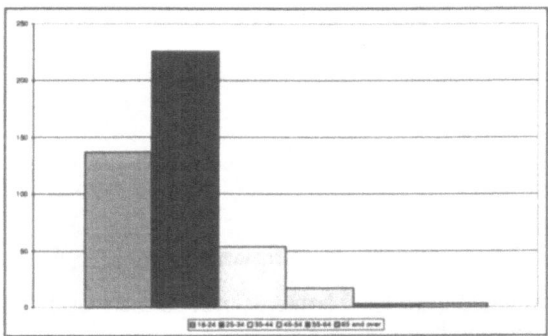

Fig. 10: Age distribution

The occupational information supplied indicated that the majority of participants were employed in an information technology related occupation. The profile of a typical 'Heaven & Hell - live' participant, therefore, was male, aged between 25 and 34 years and worked in an information technology related occupation.

8.2 World usage patterns

Heaven & Hell was opened to the public five days before the live broadcast. With hindsight, this period could have been extended as five days proved too short to form any recognisable communal structure or for users to develop a sense of personal identity. In comparison, during the seven weeks The Mirror was online there were definite signs that a community had formed, and users had established identities and formed meaningful interpersonal relationships with other users.

Fig. 11: Population variance

Participants' accumulated over 1100 hours of time in the world. Not surprisingly, the highest number of session hours, over 430, was recorded on the day of the broadcast. The average session length on the day of the broadcast was 20 minutes, which was of similar duration to that observed during The Mirror.

On 18 August, the day of the broadcast, 175 users connected to the world. The population in the world peaked during the broadcast at 142, a high number by virtual world standards. Fig. 11 shows the population density before the broadcast, during and just after the broadcast. In the hour before the broadcast the population is observed to rise almost linearly from 20 users to a peak of 142 people ten minutes into the broadcast. The population then remained relatively stable until the last twenty minutes of the broadcast when it starts to drop. Once the broadcast ends, the population in the space rapidly falls until it reaches a level below that seen before the broadcast. This profile reinforces the assertion that people were attracted by the relationship the shared space had to the television broadcast.

8.3 User movement during the broadcast

Analysing user movement during the programme makes it possible to establish the extent to which users in the world followed the programme's narrative structure. The programme was purposely structured to exploit the scale and diversity of the world. The activities were defined so as to encourage integration between the contestants and the participants within the world.

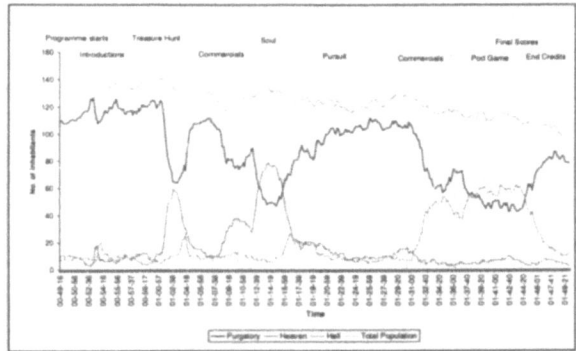

Fig. 12: Population movement during the broadcast

Fig. 12 shows the number of participants in the three main areas of the world during the broadcast. For the majority of the time, participants were mainly located in Purgatory and only small residual populations were observed in Heaven and in Hell. However, the graph does show a clear correlation between the location of participants and the televised activities. The treasure hunt, as one example, involved searching for clues in Purgatory and Heaven. Approximately halfway through the treasure hunt, a significant population shift is seen that would appear to correlate with the search for an object in Heaven.

8.4 Participant feedback

After the broadcast, participants were invited to fill in a short questionnaire to illicit their reactions, negative as well as positive, to the programme. In the event 56 questionnaires were completed and returned. Generally, participants seemed to like the overall concept, although they cited certain technical issues, including problems with aura, browser stability and network latency, that need to be resolved before they felt they could more fully participate.

A number of users felt that the broadcast stream was being censored as they observed significant delays between the events being triggered within the world and observing the effect on television. In actuality, any observed delays can be explained by the variability in round-trip times seen over the Internet and by the server and client performance. There is little evidence to suggest that the management interfaces such as that used for governing the broadcast had any significant impact on the overall performance of the system.

When asked how they would improve the experience, participants expressed a wish to be more involved with the activities in the world. Some noted that interaction between contestants and participants appeared almost incidental at times. Some thought that reducing the numbers of people in the world would have made it easier to involve participants. Others felt that the programme lacked an overall objective – bluntly expressed by one individual as 'the show lacked a script'. One of the challenges facing Inhabited Television is achieve a balance between spontaneous and constructive contribution against the need for a rigidly scripted programme.

8.5 Viewer feedback

An estimated 200,000 people watched 'Heaven & Hell – live' and, in many ways, the viewers provided the least encumbered source of comments about the experiment. In general, viewers felt confused by what was going on within the programme. Although the show was produced without any presumed knowledge, access to the web pages would have offered a clearer idea of the show's aims. Viewers thought the idea worked as a shared space but did not quite make the transition to a television programme.

There was little doubt that 'Heaven & Hell – live' was a success as an exercise in design and delivery of Inhabited Television. It was less obvious, however, how successful it had been for participants and viewers as an engaging and coherent experience. Given Inhabited Television's immaturity, this was hardly an unexpected conclusion!

9. Discussion

Clearly, 'Heaven & Hell – live' served an important role in refining what is actually meant by the term Inhabited Television and building an understanding of the issues to be addressed before migration from a proof-of-concept experiment to an enduring service capable of generating a sustainable revenue stream. The issues arising from the experiment can be broadly classified as relating to either the delivery platform, programme format, or surrounding commercial environment.

9.1 Delivery platform

The vision for Inhabited Television was forged on the back of the impending revolution in digital broadcasting. However, 'Heaven & Hell – live' was actually delivered using existing Internet access technology. Quite clearly, and for obvious reasons, there is a mismatch between the platform as envisioned and that deployed for the experiment.

9.1.1 Client hardware

To take part in the experiment users were required to have access to a relatively low-end PC with a connection to the Internet. Very little emphasis was placed on the availability of high performance hardware or high-speed, low latency network access for fear of excluding too many potential users from the experiment. Consequently, it was impossible to offer any guarantees on either client frame rates or overall network performance. Clearly, the transition from experiment to service will have to be marked by the imposition of certain, as yet undefined, quality of service targets.

When considering performance, one aspect that needs to be addressed is reliability. From the e-mail responses sent to the support-desk, it was evident that users were experiencing problems with resources when they tried to use the client software. Running fewer applications at the same time solved some problems, but the biggest source of problems was the variability of hardware and software configurations. Indeed, in the studio area, six apparently identical machines failed at different times for unknown and untraceable problems. To provide an Inhabited Television service or any other consumer oriented service for that matter, a delivery platform with the reliability and performance profile usually associated more with a gaming console than a PC will be necessary.

9.1.2 Access network

Like so called *twitch-games*, Inhabited Television is more sensitive to variance in network latency on a connection than it is to the availability of high bandwidth data connections. The control signals, generated as a client moves, sends a message or interacts with a shared object, are relatively compact. Bandwidth will become a greater concern as video, voice and other media types are integrated into the world and when the content for a world is delivered to the user across the network.

Optimising the content for network delivery represents an important departure from the approach adopted for 'Heaven & Hell – live' involved delivering content on a CD. Push-technology represents an obvious choice for delivering the browser software and world to the consumer. Assuming the set-top device contains secondary storage to cache software, updates could be delivered periodically to the consumer in the background.

9.1.3 Software platform

Requirements for a software platform to support an Inhabited Television service are, at this stage, somewhat dependent upon on the characteristics of the event being staged. From 'Heaven & Hell – live', certain fundamental requirements emerged, which included:

- Distributed object state and behaviour
- Flexible aura management
- Admission control
- Dynamic content management

More specific requirements, such as to whether to deploy a peer-to-peer, server-based, or a hybrid communication architecture, will depend upon the capabilities of the network and client. A server-based solution, similar to that employed by Community Place, is likely to be the architectural solution utilised in any early Inhabited Television incarnations.

9.2 Programme format

From a Producer's perspective, the development of a programme format that worked both as television for the viewing audience and as shared space for the online participants was a key aspect of 'Heaven & Hell – live'. Indeed, the search for a workable format appears to form an important stage in the evolution of any new form of communications media. As stated previously, the format chosen for 'Heaven & Hell – live' was based upon a television game show, a format familiar to most people. Care was taken not to create a programme based solely upon technical novelty derived from shared spaces. However, it was important to recognise that the majority of viewers would be unfamiliar with the shared space concept and that a certain amount of education was required. A post-programme review revealed that certain elements introduced to the world to create interest, like swapping the gender of the contestants and their avatars, merely served to increase confusion in the minds of participants and viewers.

The greatest challenge, in many ways, faced by advocates of Inhabited Television vision does not result from the technology but from the form the performance takes and how participants interact with the performers. These and many other issues will be addressed by eRENA [11], a collaborative project embracing technology, television production, and performance art. A panel session entitled *Narrative Environments: Virtual Reality as a Storytelling Medium* [12] was held at SIGGRAPH '97. During this session, the chair introduced the term *omni-directional storytelling* to describe a form of storytelling pertinent to multi-user virtual worlds. The challenge, as stated by the panellists, is to 'harmonise the seeming contradiction between narrative and interaction'. This succinctly describes the challenge facing those wishing to make sense of the intersection of television and shared spaces.

9.3 Commercial environment

Ultimately the success of Inhabited Television will be measured in terms of whether there is a viable market capable of sustaining it as a commercial enterprise. The funding model for digital television is, to say the least, uncertain. Revenue streams are predicted to originate from sources including subscriptions, advertising, and transactions. In this climate of uncertainty, we cannot give detailed answers to questions about generating revenue from Inhabited Television services. Nevertheless, the three methods of funding mentioned are all compatible with the Inhabited Television concept, though advertising is likely to generate any initial revenues.

10. Summary

History teaches us not to overestimate the short-term impact new technologies have on society. Laboratories around the world are littered with ideas that were going to fundamentally change society. History also teaches us not to underestimate the impact technologies have as they become ubiquitous and essential to the way we live our lives. The question is, will Inhabited Television be one of the ideas that languishes in the laboratory? In our opinion the answer to this question will be no. 'Heaven & Hell – live' demonstrated what was possible with a service based upon analogue television and the Internet. The impending revolution in digital television will result in Inhabited Television moving beyond a proof-of-concept demonstration to a viable and engaging commercial service.

Acknowledgements

'Heaven & Hell – live' was only made possible through the efforts of a dedicated and extremely talented technical team. Special thanks go to Amada Oldroyd, John Dent, and Richard Munn, who worked many late nights and long weekends to complete the project. I would also like to thank Saturo Matsuda, from Sony's Community Place team, who supported the project so admirably but, alas, missed all the fun.

References

[1]   George A.: Residential Broadband, *Cisco Press*, 1997.

[2]   Galanter P.: Just an Ordinary New York Cyberneighborhood, 1995.
http://www.nyu.edu/acf/pubs/connect/summer95/DigArtsYORBSum95.html

[3]   MacLean S., et al: MTV and Onlive! Technologies take the Internet to exotic new destinations, 1996.
http://www.onlive.com/corp/press/jul1096.html

[4]   Walker G. R: The Mirror - reflections on Inhabited TV, *British Telecommunications Engineering Journal*, vol. 16, part 1, pp. 29-38, 1997.
http://virtualbusiness.labs.bt.com/msss/IBTE_Mirror

[5]   Greenhalgh C., Bullock A., Tromp J., Benford S.: Evaluating the network and usability characteristics of virtual reality conferencing, BT Technology Journal, vol 15, No 4, pp 101-119. October 1993.

[6]   http://vs.sony.co.jp/

[7]   http://www.channel4.com/

[8]   http://www.odi.com

[9]   Lea R., Honda Y., Matsuda S., Matsuda M.: Community Place: Architecture and Performance, Proc Second Symposium on the Virtual Reality Modeling Language (VRML '97), February 1997.

[10]   Benford S., Fahlen L. E.: A spatial model of interaction in virtual environments'. Proc third European Conference on Computer Supported Co-operative Working (ECSCW '93), September 1993.

[11]   http://www.nada.kth.se/erena

[12]   Pearce C., deGraf B., Scott Young C., Ludtke J., Goldberg A.: Narrative Environments: Virtual Reality as a Storytelling Medium, *Panel Session at SIGGRAPH '97*.

Grounding & Awareness Management: Two Architectural Principles for Collaborative Virtual Worlds

Dr. Avon Huxor

Centre for Electronic Arts
School of Art, Design and Performing Arts
Middlesex University
Cat Hill, Barnet
London EN4 8HT
UNITED KINGDOM

a.huxor@mdx.ac.uk

Abstract

This paper considers how certain abstract aspects of design might effectively be brought over from the domain of architecture and planning into virtual world design. Two issues are specifically investigated, the management of 'awareness' and encounter in shared spaces, and the 'grounding' of the virtual space onto a real geographical site to assist in the legibility of the space. Both considerations inform the sketch design of a shared space to support distributed working in an organisation, in which the user is aided in 'chance encounter' with others, and in which the culture of the space is made more visible. Finally, these two issues are integrated in a manner which acknowledges the increasingly local use of the Internet, and the possibilities for virtual worlds to help support physical communities. The main concern that arises is the importance of encounters with others that are unplanned, but also appropriate, be they for work or for social reasons, resulting in face-to-face meeting.

1. Introduction

In the development of 3D shared spaces, the role of architecture and urban planning has, conventionally, been one of providing a very direct metaphor. Thus the model of the standard office, with tables, chairs, filing cabinets, etc., is one that is frequently used in shared collaborative spaces, such as DIVE (Carlsson & Hagsand 1993). Similarly, a VRML model is being constructed of the city of Helsinki to act as a 3D interface to telematic services within the city. However these designs do not really address the issue that the form and nature of physical buildings and urban spaces are, to a great extent, a product of physical constraints and requirements of both building materials and human activity. Virtual spaces need not be so constrained but have the opportunity to exploit their own characteristics. They do not, for example, need not be concerned with fire escapes, the structural safety of the building envelope, or its ability to keep out inclement weather.

Other recent work, however, has explored the characteristics of the built environment to identify those features that can be applied to 3D spaces. For example, Ingram, Bowers & Benford (1996) look at how features such as landmarks, paths and districts can aid the legibility of data spaces. This paper equally concerns itself with abstract elements, but concentrates on the more social aspects of the building and the city: the manner in which its spatial layout can facilitate informal social interaction in shared spaces, as well as facilitating access to content.

The specific work described below arose from a requirement of a large telecommunications research laboratory: the BT Labs at Martlesham Heath near Ipswich. Increasingly, many of the researchers at the Labs (and the Shared Spaces Group in particular) are working in new, distributed and collaborative arrangements. These include teleworking from home, intergroup collaborations across the whole laboratory site, and close collaborations with other, often international, organisations. These concerns parallel those that are also arising at the Centre for Electronic Arts (CEA), in which an increasing number of students are part-timers, often working from outside the CEA, and in which many research projects undertaken at the Centre involve collaborations with far-flung institutions.

Such working arrangements are slowly beginning to emerge in the wider economy. For example, Line and Syvertsen (1996) report on a medium-sized Norwegian company which is using the technology to create 'virtual engineering teams' spread across 16 regional offices. This will support a more project-based style of management, one in which specific skills are required to be brought together to undertake a particular project for a limited period. It has been suggested that in the U.S., teleworkers presently make up more than 11% of the workforce (Bélanger & Webb Collins 1998), and looks likely to increase. For this reason it appears worthwhile to address the problems that arise with this form of working, and seeking new solutions.

The design sketch outlined in Section 4 below began with the intention of exploring the potential of the technology being developed at BT Labs, in the field of multi-user 3D worlds - could it help create virtual places where distributed co-workers could meet and work? However, the experience of the author as a visitor to many of the widely available Internet-based 3D worlds, and especially in using them to support online meetings (Huxor 1997), pointed to a number of problems. I found that, once the novelty had worn off, these spaces seemed to offer little to support distributed working. Amongst the main issues that arose were:

a) The lack of use of the space by participants who tended to just use the text-chat facilities. Indeed one shared world technology provider employed, Blaxxun[1], released a chat only version of the world browser soon after.

b) The often inappropriate behaviour of others in the space, which made them less than inviting for many users.

From these concerns two design directions were investigated: awareness management and grounding, described below. Section 2 will address the manner in which spatiality might be used to support awareness in collaboration. Section 4 considers how the nature of a space, its host organisation and culture, may be made more visible by locating the virtual in the physical space, hopefully reducing the potential for conflicts between users of the space.

2. Spatial Management of Encounters

The majority of work in collaborative spaces has concentrated on creating a 'virtual meeting room', in which users gather at set times for pre-arranged meetings (Greenhalgh & Benford 1995). But one of the major problems for distance working is the maintenance of informal communications, those that typically occur by the coffee machine or copying machine. Empirical work has shown the value of these for effective working (for a review see Isaacs, Tang & Morris 1996): such unscheduled meetings are not just time-wasting, but crucial to the flow of information and maintenance of commitments within the workplace. Isolation from colleagues has been reported as a major problem for teleworking (Lewis 1996), one that must be overcome if it is to succeed. The need to chat seems strong: Tom Erickson (writing in Scholtz et al. 1998), who works in a distributed manner, reports that when he does visit the office, he will catch up on the informal aspects of the work place and "wander the hallways on purpose so I can bump into people" (1998: 52).

To support these unplanned meetings, usually known as *chance encounters*, a number of new Internet-based tools, such as ICQ[2] and, Virtual Places[3] have become available. These partly address the problem, by allowing for users to encounter other users who are online at the same time. However, the criteria for the encounters to occur are problematic. For real world encounters are not really chance alone. With ICQ a user must create a list of nominated users, all of whom are made aware of his or her presence. This can lead to distraction as all one's friends, colleagues and family see that one is available online. Furthermore, ICQ does not support the 'weak ties', those persons that one would not add to a list of contacts, but which have also been shown to be important to the working of an organisation (Hillier 1996). On the other hand, systems such as Virtual Places allow for contact between users who happen to be 'on'

---

[1] http://www.blaxxun.com

[2] http://www.mirabilis.com

[3] http://www.vplaces.com

a particular web-page at the same time. Clearly the chances of colleagues viewing the same web-page at the same time are very low, reducing the chances of encounter to almost nothing.

However, these problemsof encounter management are well addressed by physical architecture. The arrangement of spaces, grounded in the reality of the workplace, allow for users to be aware of colleagues (and content) appropriate to the task at hand. Unlike ICQ, it also encourages the 'weak ties', as a variety of people pass through the building and meet in corridors, foyers and other such semi-public areas. But the building form also ensures that those persons related to the task at hand are likely to be co-present, even if they are working on another task at the time, as colleagues usually have offices or studios in close proximity, and greater visibility. Spaces thus become sites which act as locales for task-specific content, and also manage the 'chance encounters' with others either working on a similar task, or coming from within the same organisation. It is this subtlety of awareness management that teleworking disrupts, and which current collaboration tools do not fully address. It also leads us to reconsider what the role of 3D worlds might be. It seems possible, if not likely, that there is something about the spatial nature of architecture, both the building and the urban setting, that can be abstracted out to assist in managing awareness in distributed working.

A simple exploration of the idea is under construction by the author within AlphaWorld, a shared 3D world accessible through the Active Worlds[4] browser, which supports text chat between users in a region. This is an easily available and 'light' browser to a number of multi-user worlds, of which the oldest and most popular is AlphaWorld. This particular technology has a number of advantages for such experimentation: It is very simple to built within the world using copy/move/edit of existing components, each of which can be linked to other web content that is then displayed in an associated web browser.

A virtual CEA (Centre for Electronic Arts) within AlphaWorld aims to facilitate collaboration between myself, the students, and with external parties. The various 'walls' within the space have two roles:

a) The surfaces have 'hot' links to content contained within the BSCW system[5]. This is a web-based collaboration tool, in which documents, URLs and messages are placed in workspaces that are only accessible by project members. It has various features, such as document version control and access logging, that facilitate group working. BSCW is crucial to the working of the space, as encounter can only occur if users are present, and work-related content provides the reason for being there.

---

[4] http://www.activeworlds.com

[5] http://bscw.gmd.de

68

b) By means of having various degrees of opacity, the walls allow the avatars of other users to be more or less visible. Although the avatars are always visible in Active Worlds (they are not fully hidden behind surfaces), the textures of intermediate surfaces creates the required effect. It is very easy to spin around and see which other users are present. Their visibility is dependent upon the size of the avatar, itself a measure of the conceptual and organisational closeness of the tasks they are currently undertaking. The avatars are further made more or less visible (present) by the nature of the walls in the space, giving further control.

Being an open system, AlphaWorld also allows for other users to visit[6] - control of access to BSCW content is handles by its own password-based user authentication mechanisms, rather than restricting access to the space. This openness of space access allows for weak ties to be better supported, and for interested visitors to come by.

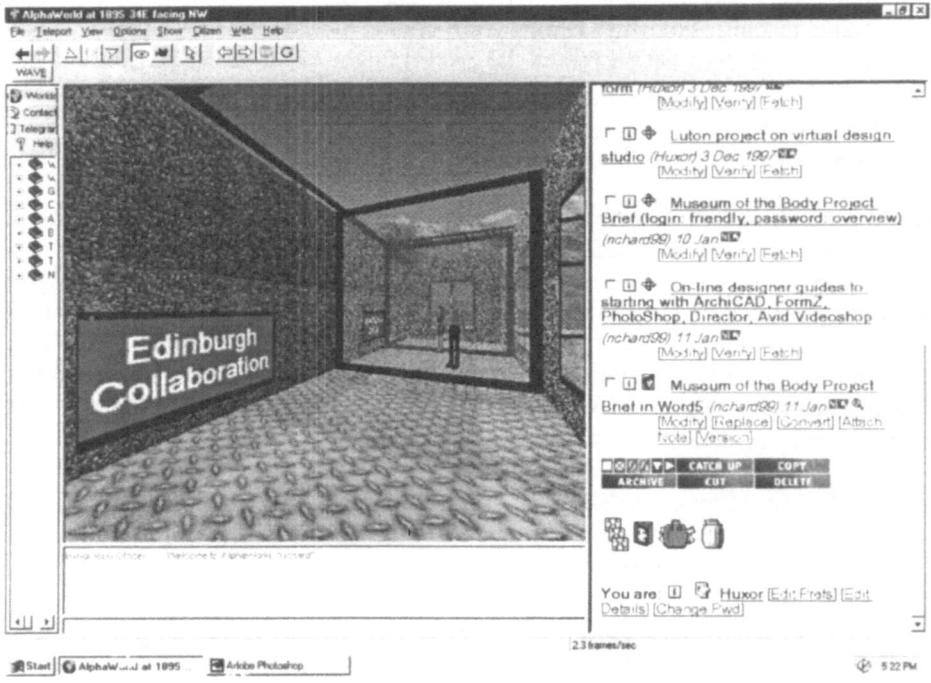

Fig. 1. Virtual CEA building in AlphaWorld with related BSCW content

---

[6] Visitors are welcome, and I am often within the space. Users must download and install the ActiveWorlds browser (see footnote above). The virtual CEA is in the world titled 'AW', at co-ordinates 192S 35E.

Figure 1 above shows a screen shot of the virtual CEA in AlphaWorld. The 3D space in the left hand pane, illustrates the management of awareness, through the use of glassy walls, and of the differing avatar sizes. Below the space are the two panes for text chat: the small lower pane for the user to type input, and above the display pane for the chat that is occurring. The right hand pane is a standard web browser, built into Active Worlds, in which the BSCW workspace associated with the 3D space is shown. The content, such as Word documents or URLs can be brought up as required.

I can access the space from any PC, be it at home, at the CEA, BT Labs or elsewhere. Although early days, it has already proven useful, and a number of chance encounters have occurred. For example, it is being used by a collaborator, Dr. Paul Rodgers, at Cambridge University, for whom I have created a guest room next to my office. He often passes by, and if I am online we can chat about matters arising. The link with the BSCW content means that a single click on the glass wall between the two rooms brings up the shared documents from the collaboration. I usually keep the 3D world open in the background of the PC, moving from space to space to access the BSCW content (in other words, the space acts a kind of spatial bookmarking system) and work on the documents therein. Experience thus far seems to indicate the potential of the approach, in that encounters with the students in particular have many of the characteristics of the 'meeting by the coffee machine'. They were not looking for me for anything specific, just at content in the space nearby, but saw me in the distance through the glass walls. But, as it happened there was an question that needed to be answered so they initiated a chat session.

The approach employed by the AlphaWorld CEA tries to capture elements from physical spaces. Unlike ICQ it is open to weak ties and interedted visitors, not only a closed set of nominated users. But chaos is limited by using the closeness of avatars to keep the most pertinent users as likely encounters. And unlike Virtual Places, it does not rely on users being engaged on the same task to allow encounter, as the spaces can contain a range of content.

3. Towards a Virtual BT Labs

The ideas of spatial co-ordination of awareness in CSCW are currently being applied to a 'sketch design' of a shared space for BT Labs. It is currently being constructed in 3D Studio MAX, although only a limited set of the features found in MAX are being used, as the eventual aim is for a functioning shared space to be exported as VRML 2, and to be placed into a shared space technology.

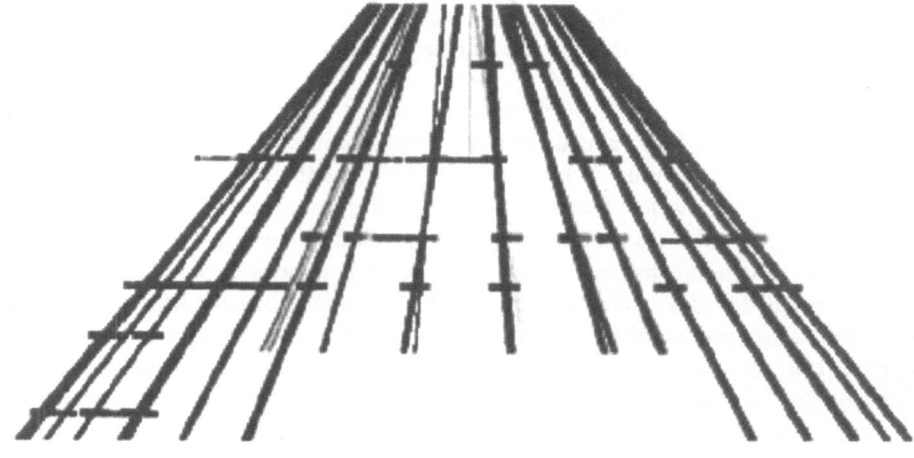

Fig. 2. Elevation View of Virtual BT Labs

The overall structure is based upon an understanding of the working practice of the Labs, which consists of a number of research groups. These are inter-related in two ways: as part of a hierarchy in the traditional manner for general administration purposes, but also into project specific clusters, which are formed and broken up as appropriate to undertake specific projects. The (near) vertical elements are circulation routes - elevators - each one of which is 'owned by' a research group. The horizontal elements relate to the interactions between the groups, both the higher level management clusters, and the project clusters. Content for each 'cluster' is contained within 'rooms' that connect the vertical elements: those closer to the vertical being more relevant to the nearest group.

The horizontal levels are composed of a series of interconnecting high-level 'walkways' that link the various group home spaces to both each other and to a number of 'public squares'. Along these walkways and around the squares many 'rooms' will be located. At the more detailed level, the rooms are similar to those found in the virtual CEA in AlphaWorld described above. They are not just chat areas, but link to content: to documents, spreadsheet, CAD models etc., that make up the tasks being undertaken by the various research groups.

Thus, in the Figure 3 below, consider two of the research groups (Shared Spaces and Human Factors) involved in a collaboration. Once a new collaborative project is set up, walkways and squares are set up on a free horizontal level. These lead from a Home Space that each group has attached to the vertical circulation element. Rooms are generated automatically upon demand, as content arises, along the walkways and around the public squares. The spatial layout indicates the degree of ownership, thus those rooms along the walkway linking the Shared Spaces home space to the square is primarily for content created by this group. Likewise those along the other walkway are primarily those belonging to the Human Factors Group. The rooms around the public square are the most 'public'. Users will move to rooms (and hence content) in two ways: either manually in the conventional manner, or automatically. In the latter case, the user does not have to control the avatar - after selecting a room from a menu, the avatar moves automatically along walkways to it. If the user sees another person, or new content that interests them, they can stop the avatar, and return to manual control.

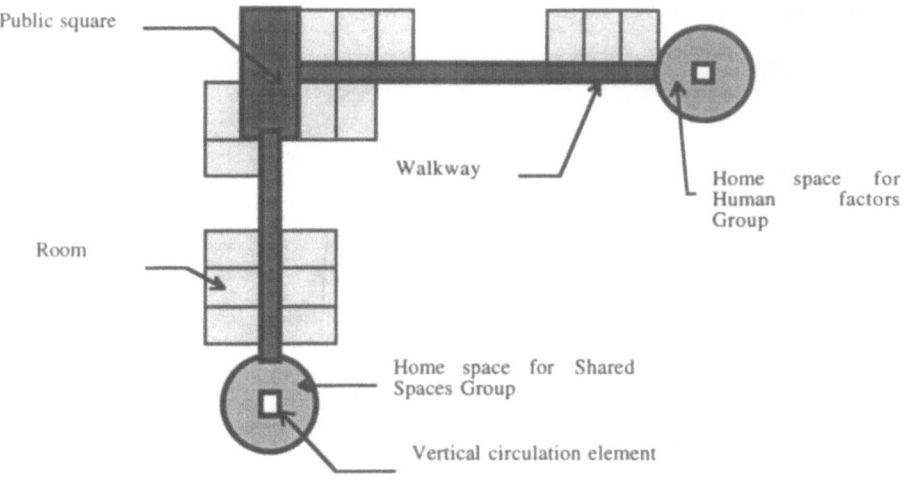

Fig. 3. Schematic Plan of Typical Horizontal Layer

Users will from room to room to access content, passing others, seeing them through the glassy walls in their own room spaces, and can stop to engage in chat, as in AlphaWorld. The actual routes will be determined by a combination of taking the shortest route, the need to respect certain areas belonging to other user groups, and a random element, to ensure that new users and content may occasionally be passed. It is envisaged that, if they desire, the user can override the automated movement mechanism, and jump to the target room. However, just as I often make none too urgent trips to the coffee shop or the laser printer at Middlesex University to allow for possible encounters, so I imagine that many users would make occasional wanders around the walkways to see who is around. Backhouse and Drew (1992) observed that in the physical workplace much recruitment into conversation occurs when people are moving between one work area and another. Possibly the same effect will translate into the virtual world, as movement will represent that the user is moving from one task to another, and hence less likely to have a train of thought disturbed by a causal conversation. (For a fuller account of these issues, see Huxor 1998).

The virtual space thus becomes a set of circulation routes, vertical and horizontal, that link task-specific *locales* (Fitzpatrick, Mansfield & Kaplan 1996), containing digital content. The applications and files would sit in a distributed network than manages access in manner similar to BSCW, to ensure security. From a perspective view (below) the space evokes images of a visual representation of the abstract data space of the organisation. Unlike many such representations, however, it makes a social world of the 3D space, adding new considerations of ownership, access and interpersonal encounter. Equally, although it does not look like a conventional physical building, its structure is informed by architectural principles, and can be considered as an architectural response to an increasingly online world.

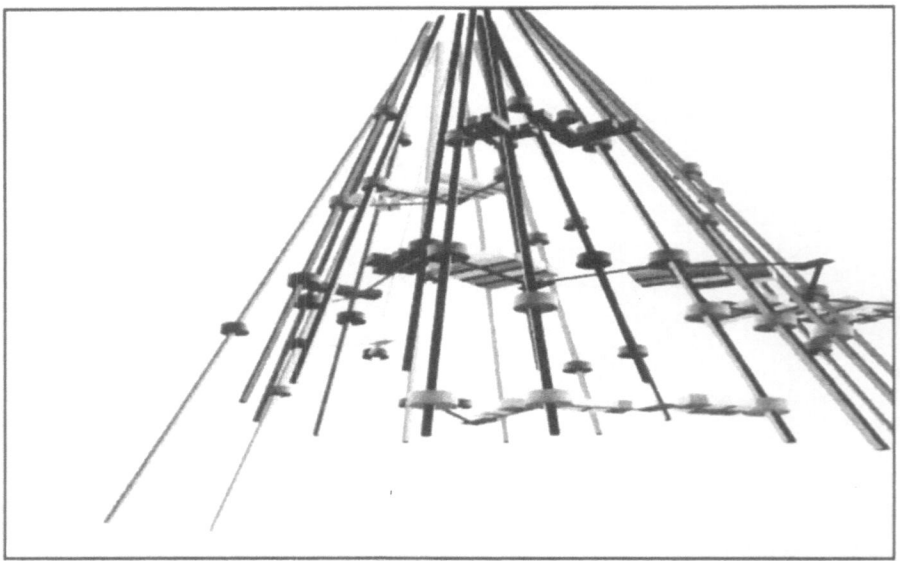

Fig. 4. Perspective View of Virtual BT Space

The value of moving from an imitative approach to a more abstract view of architecture is that the affordances of the digital medium can be exploited. So, one could use the generative techniques of Broughton, Coates & Jackson (1998), in which space syntax (Hillier 1996) guides the process, to create the rooms for the BT space.

4. Grounded Virtual Spaces

In addition to awareness, a second problem, identified in the introduction, is that of user behaviour in many of these shared spaces. All too often one experiences verbal abuse, racial and sexual harassment, from those who are visiting the space. Clearly this could be managed in a very simple way by creating a specific world for an organisation and restricting access to authenticated participants. However this would also reduce the possibility for chance encounters between weak ties, who would be excluded from the space. It also seems a rather negative solution. The approach being pursued here is based on the assumption that many of the social problems of shared spaces are due to the nature of the space - its 'citizens' and its purpose - being unclear. Clearly restrictions to sensitive content will have to be made to keep out determined people, but I am hopeful that many of these situations can be managed better by making the *culture* of the space more legible.

One solution would be to build a space that conveys the culture of the organisation by building a model that includes many clues, such as the DIVE office space that looks like a serious work area, as opposed to a gaming area. This however involves extensive modelling as the designer tries to capture the subtle elements, the furniture of the world, that makes up the visual 'look and feel' of a place.

Another solution (Huxor 1996) is to 'ground' the shared virtual work-space to the physical organisation that is responsible for the content. This is achieved through an extension of augmented reality techniques, applied to an architectural and urban scale. The virtual space is perceived to sit above the physical site of its host, and thus inherits the organisational and cultural characteristics of the site, making the nature of the world, and forms of activity appropriate to it, clearer to users. In other words, a virtual 'urban landscape', co-located with real space, is set upon the real landscape, a virtual space associated with each physical building below it. This virtual space is 'grounded' to the real space through the traditional media of video. Thus, real buildings have a multi-user virtual extension to their physical structure, rising above it. People would come to identify the connection between the two through the use of video techniques: the virtual component to the building being superimposed on a live video image of the physical building.

It is imagined that this superimposed image would be provided online using existing webcam technology, and video images provided by security cameras. Through these means, the virtual will gain a presence in the public imagination, and can become part of the physical space through constant presentation in the video media. Remote users, accessing a virtual space from the Internet, would enter it through selecting a part of the virtual space as presented on this superimposition. Visitors to the actual building, on the other hand, would become aware of the virtual component through the usual security monitors placed in the building.

74

This approach is being applied to the 'sketch' design for the shared BT virtual space above. Cameras would be distributed about the site at Martlesham Heath, and the virtual model would be mixed in real-time from the appropriate viewpoint. Thus below is an example of how the virtual world, 'grounded' on the geographical location, might appear. Remote users get a sense of place: They can see the geography, the time-of-day, and the architecture of the site, and get a measure of the activity as people move from building to building.

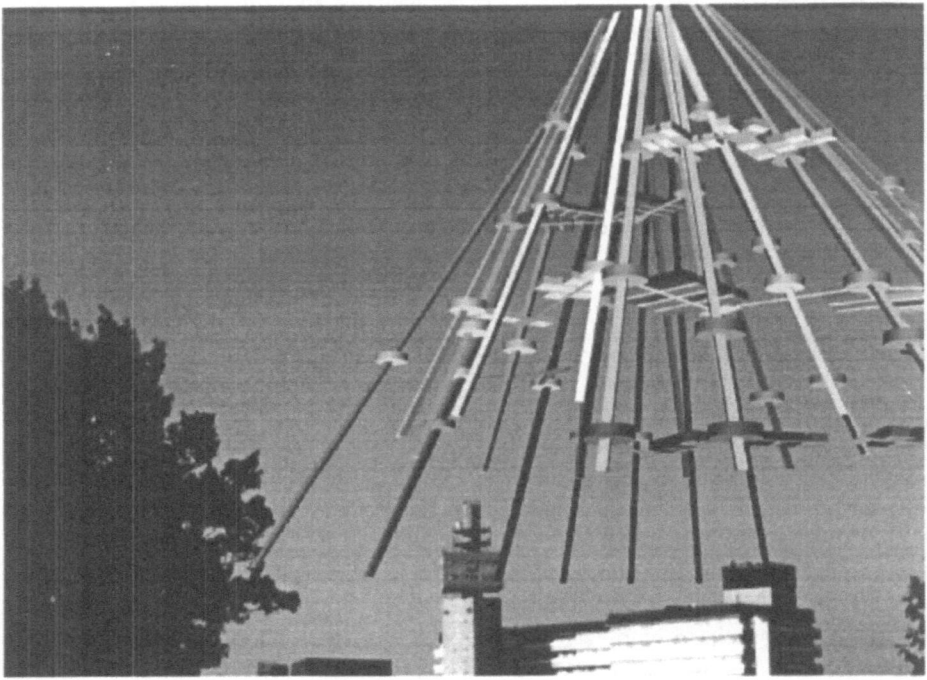

Fig. 5. A Putative Virtual Space above BT Labs

It is not difficult to imagine a future when architects, whose clients will increasingly will be organisation with a substantial virtual component, will design the physical and virtual spaces as an integrated whole. Certain architects are already pointing this way. The integration of video and built form is found in the work of Jean Nouvel. His design for the Cologne Mediapark, for example, which has grey glass facades, upon which he will "display messages in dense colours similar to those on computer screens or videos...The occupants will also become part of the display" (De Bure 1992: 44). Nouvel also illustrates theme implicit in the BT design above, the continuing motif in architecture in which the move from the ground to the heavens is reflected in the forms that become more immaterial. In his design "Tour Sans Fins", the building exterior goes from rough granite on the lower floors up through various materials to glass at the top, and lights continue the theme upwards at night. The proposal in this paper goes further, arguing for virtual spaces to extend outside the physical building, upwards and onwards, the lights becoming dancing spaces on a monitor screen, in which occupants can work, meet and play.

5. Community & Encounter

The original and intention of introducing 'grounded spaces' was to make the nature of a 'space' legible to users, from wherever they come. But it has since become clear that there is an additional benefit to tying a virtual space for an organisation to its physical site in some way, one that may integrate the ideas of awareness management and grounding in geography. The issue arose from a consideration as to why AlphaWorld has proven so successful, socially, of all the shared technologies that have been released for the Internet. AlphaWorld is unlike other shared spaces, such as Cybergate in which the meetings described in Section 1 occurred, in two features - its size, and the ability for users to easily construct buildings, to own a site in the space. With the alternative technologies, a designer builds a self-contained world in which others can meet. They are small and separate, individual worlds floating in the darkness. Users to the world are either 'in or out', but only a few own the space. AlphaWorld, however, is a large continuous area of space (currently equivalent to 400 square kilometers), within which users can stake-out a site of their own and build. This has a number of advantages.

1) One can be in the world, yet move far enough away from the busy central area to have a private discussion. But other users can pass by - it is not closed.
2) Sites are owned within the world, but these are within a network of visibly public areas, such as roads. Users can enter sites, to meet others, but the visual cues makes the private status of these clear.

That is, AlphaWorld combines both ownership and community through having personal sites set within a singular, coherent and *semi-permeable* framework.

If we need to create a singular, coherent framework for virtual spaces, one obvious option is to adopt that provided by the physical world. This is not an arbitrary choice, however. There are reasons for having neighbours in a virtual world that correlate with those found in the physical, arising from the increasingly interpersonal and local nature of the Internet. For a recent survey study showed the significance of interpersonal communication as "a stronger driver of Internet use than information and entertainment applications" (Kraut et al. 1998: 368). Increasingly as the Internet expands and moves into more everyday activities it takes on more of the character of the telephone, and Mayer (1977) notes that all studies show that about 50% of household calls are made within a two mile radius. That is, people make most calls to the neighbourhood in which they live. Although the new communications technologies allow for the maintenance of distant relationships, the importance of the local is often under-represented, relationships usually maintained through physical meetings.

The importance of such face-to-face meetings as a supplement to online interaction has recently arisen as an important issue. For instance, the title of a paper by Elena Rocco (1998) "Trust Breaks Down in Electronic Contexts but Can be Repaired by Some Initial Face-to-Face Contact" summarises her results very succinctly. Weinreich (1997) reports further evidence from the world of bulletin boards. In the German-speaking world, one study of the use of BBS's showed that 62% had met each other. This was facilitated of course by the geographical nearness of most of the bulletin board users due to the language being used. Another, wider study of the Usenet by Volker Kneer, also reported by Weinreich, found that 80% of respondents personally met people that they had first contacted on the Net. Similar results were also found by Katz & Aspden, whose survey suggests that the Internet is indeed "emerging as a medium for cultivating friendships which, in a majority of cases, lead to meetings in the real world" (1997: 86). If shared virtual spaces are grounded to geography, then the kind of chance encounters discussed above will have a greater opportunity of themselves being grounded in a face-to-face meeting.

Thus, in the same way that teleworkers can be assisted in chance encounters with colleagues that they work closely to, one can image the situation in which each organisation within a city has a virtual space above its building. I can wander around the virtual spaces in my locality and meet users online who would have a greater likelihood of being physically present in the built city. For example, consider the case of a virtual bar, which are commonly found on the Internet, and aim to be places for informal conversation. In the approach proposed above, a physical bar (drinking establishment) would have a virtual extension sitting above it. I might drop into the virtual bar that is near to me geographically and chat to various people who are present. Due to the 'sited' nature of the design, I might then visit the physical bar and possibly meet others who I have met in the virtual space. My encounters have a greater potential of being grounded.

6. Conclusion

This paper has proposed two issues drawn from the field of architecture that can aid in the design and use of shared virtual environments: The management of chance encounters between users, and the re-siting of the virtual onto physical geographies. As the Internet migrates into everyday situations, these two become interwoven, as we seek to facilitate the encounters between individuals who then have a greater chance of meeting physically, grounding their online relationship. The literature indicates the importance of co-presence and co-awareness for the effective functioning of both the organisation and the larger community. Blanchard & Horan (n.d.) conclude that "civic engagement will be positively affected when virtual communities develop around physically-based communities".

Although still some years away, physical communities are beginning to move into the virtual. There are an ever increasing number of town and cities that are creating 'community networks'. One of the most ambitious of these virtual communities is the Helsinki Arena 2000 project[7] which aims to use a 3D model of the city as a gateway into telematic services. They are building a VRML model of the city allowing ordinary citizens to access telematic services. If this were a shared space, the opportunity for encounter between citizens would be facilitated, which may be of value if they are increasing able to access many services through their computers, rather than going out into the city. Of course, I would argue with the idea of recreating the city in VRML, constraining the forms that could be built. The use of video proposed above would give users a better feel for the part of the city they were visiting online, and free the world designers to exploit the affordances of the new technology.

For the design of shared virtual spaces is not simply a rebuilding of existing building forms, nor a purely abstract exercise in information design. It must instead draw upon the wider issues of architecture to create spaces that are places for social exchange, but at the same time respecting the essentially digital nature of its own content. The same spatial mechanisms above can support chance encounters and weak ties in both organisations, such as BT Labs, and communities, such as the city of Helsinki. This is not to say that the ideas described above are meant in any way to exclude alternative non-proximal communities. There are needs for global communities, but it is important to acknowledge that a significant role for the Internet will be in bringing people together to work and to play, and that these activities will have important, localised, face-to-face, components.

Acknowledgements

Much of the work described in this paper was undertaken as part of a Short-term Fellowship that was undertaken with the Shared Spaces Group at BT Laboratories, Martlesham Heath. He would like to acknowledge the Shared Spaces Group, and Tim Regan in particular, for their support during his time at the Labs.

Bibliography

Backhouse, A. & P. Drew (1992) The design implications of social interaction in a workplace setting. *Environment and Planning B: Planning and Design*, 19: 573-584.

De Bure, G. (1992) *Jean Nouvel, Emmanuel Cattani and Associates - Four projects*. Artemis.

Bélanger, F. & R. Webb Collins (1998) Distributed Work Arrangements: A Research Framework. *The Information Society*, 14: 137-152.

---

[7] http://www.helsinkiarena2000.fi/summary

Blanchard, A. & T. Horan (n.d.) Can we surf together if we're bowling alone? An examination into virtual community's impact on social capital. *Paper presented at The American Sociological Association Session on the Internet and Social Change.* Available online at http://www.cgs.edu/inst/cgsri/surfbowl.html

Broughton, T., Coates, P. & H. Jackson (1998) Evolutionary Models of Space. *Proc. Eurographics UK Conf.,* Leeds, UK, March 1998, 231-249.

Carlsson, C. & O. Hagsand (1993) DIVE - A Platform for Multi-User Virtual Environments. *Computers & Graphics,* 17(6): 663-669.

Fitzpatrick, G., Mansfield, T. & S. M. Kaplan (1996) Locales Framework: Exploring foundations for collaboration support. *IEEE Pro.c of the 6th Australian Conf. on Computer-Human Interaction (OZCHI'96),* Hamilton, NZ, pp. 34-41.

Greenhalgh, C. & S. Benford (1995) MASSIVE: A Collaborative Virtual Environment for Tele-Conferencing. *ACM Trans. On Computer-Human Interfaces,* 2(3): 239-261.

Hillier, B. (1996) *Space is the Machine: A configurational theory of architecture.* Cambridge: CUP.

Huxor, A. (1998) The Role of 3D Shared Worlds in Support of Chance Encounters in CSCW. *Proc. of "Digital Convergence: The Future of the Internet and World Wide Web" Conf.,* Bradford UK, April 1998.

Huxor, A. (1997) The Role of Virtual World Design in Collaborative Working". *Proc. Interactive Visualisation (IV'97),* London, August 1997.

Huxor, A. (1996) Virtual Realities, Media Landscapes, and Real Cityscapes. *Proc. 3rd UKVRSIG Conf.,* De Montfort University, July 1996.

Ingram, R., Bowers, J. & S. Benford (1996) Building Virtual Cities: Applying Urban Planning Principles to the Design of Virtual Environments. *Proceedings of ACM VRST'96,* Hong Kong, July 1996

Isaacs, E. A., Tang, J. C. & T. Morris (1996) Piazza: A Desktop Environment Supporting Impromptu and Planned Interactions. *Proc of the ACM Conf on Computer-Supported Co-operative Work,* Boston, MA.

Katz, J. E. & P. Aspden (1997) A Nation of Strangers? *Communications of the ACM* 40(12): 81-86.

Kraut, R. et al. (1998) Communication and Information: Alternative Uses of the Internet in Households. *Proceedings of the Computer-Human Interaction (CHI) Conference,* Los Angeles, April 1998, pp. 368-375.

Lewis, P. F. (1996) A Feasibility Study of Implementing a Telecommuting Program at Booz•Allen and Hamilton. In Watson, R. T. & Bostrom, R. P. (eds.) *Telecommuting'96.* Electronic Proceedings, http://www.cba.uga.edu/tc96/proceedings.html

Line, L. & Syvertsen, T. G. (1996) Virtual Engineering Teams: Strategy and Implementation. In Turk, Z. (ed.) *Construction on the Information Highway.* Electronic Proceedings, http://www.fagg.uni-lj/bled96/

Mayer, M. (1977) The Telephone and the Use of Time. In: de Sola Pool, I. (ed.) *The Social Impact of the Telephone.* Cambridge, MA: The MIT Press.

Rocco, E. (1998) Trust Breaks Down in Electronic Contexts but Can be Repaired by Some Initial Face-to-Face Contact. *Proceedings of the Computer-Human Interaction (CHI) Conference*, Los Angeles, April 1998, pp. 496-502.

Scholtz, J., Bellotti, V., Schirra, L. Erickson, T., DeGroot, J. & Lund, A. (1998) Telework: When Your Job is On the Line. *Interactions*, January + February, 44-54.

Weinreich, F. (1997) Establishing a point of view toward virtual communities. *CMC Magazine*, Feb. 1997.
Available online htpp://www.december.com/cmc/mag/1997/feb/wein.html

Remote Object Translation Methods for Immersive Virtual Environments

Jurriaan D. Mulder*

Abstract

In this paper, seven methods are described to perform remote object translations with a six degree-of-freedom input device in an immersive virtual environment. By manipulating objects remotely, a number of disadvantages of the real-world 'direct grab and drag' metaphor can be avoided. The different methods are evaluated with a pilot user experiment. From the results of the experiment, some initial recommendations are formulated on the use of the methods for different manipulation tasks.

1 Introduction

Virtual reality systems are designed to provide the effect of *immersion* in an *interactive* three-dimensional computer-generated environment [2]. Virtual environments in potential can provide more intuitive methods for viewing and user interaction. A wide variety of 3D graphics applications could benefit from these methods. However, whereas the viewing aspect of virtual environments is well understood, user input is still a current research issue.

User input in virtual environments is usually performed with multiple degree-of-freedom input devices. A survey of various research results in this area of *spatial input* was composed by Hinckley et al. [5]. More recent results on methods for 3D object manipulation with multiple degree-of-freedom input devices are for instance given by Zhai et al. [12] who report on human performance in six degree-of-freedom input, Cutler et al. [4] who report on two handed interaction, and Bowman et al. [1] who evaluated different techniques for grabbing and manipulating remote objects. Most of these methods however, are designed to incorporate multiple types of transformations, primarily combined rotation and translation.

In this paper, we describe seven different methods for object translations only, and present the results of a pilot user experiment conducted to evaluate the methods on the aspects of speed, accuracy, and user friendliness. Although we have focussed on the use of these methods in a CAVE [3] equipped with the hand-held six degree-of-freedom input device (the *wand*), the results are applicable to other immersive virtual environments with different input and display devices as well.

---

*Center for Mathematics and Computer Science CWI, P.O. Box 94079, 1090 GB Amsterdam, the Netherlands. mullie@cwi.nl

2   Why Remote?

As the CAVE is an immersive environment, an obvious manipulation scheme is the real-world metaphor: direct grab and drag. Here, the user moves his hand with the wand to the position of the object and 'grabs' the object by pushing a wand button. The user then drags the object to a new position as if he holds the object in his hand. This approach is both simple and intuitive. However, it does have four major disadvantages.

First of all, when the physical hand is moved onto the object, the hand and arm of the user are brought into the area onto which the user's view is focused. In the CAVE, this causes a disturbance of the correct view of the scene: objects that are (virtually) located in between the user's eyes and hand are no longer viewed correctly. As a result, the user has great difficulty determining whether his hand is at the same position as the object to be picked. Once the object is picked, exact positioning of the object becomes difficult for the same reason. A similar (albeit reverse) violation of the occlusion cue was reported by Schmandt [8] as a major factor for incorrect depth judgements.

The second disadvantage is that the device that tracks the wand's position must be very accurate. Small discrepancies between the physical and virtual position of the wand become very visible and disturbing as the user is directly watching the wand and the object and expects an absolute correspondence between the positions of the two. Such distortions become less of a problem when relative positioning can be used [10], e.g., when the wand and object are not at the same location and there is an indirect connection between the object and the user's hand.

The third disadvantage is that the user can only manipulate those objects that are within reach. The user's arms are of limited length, and the CAVE has only a limited space in which the user can maneuver, whereas the virtual world in principle can be infinitely large. To manipulate objects that are not within reach, or to position objects to locations that are out of reach, the user has to perform a navigation action to move himself through the virtual world. Bowman et al. [1] state that navigation is desirable, as it allows different visual perspectives, but it should not be required.

Finally, as also reported by Bowman et al. [1], a direct 'real-world' grab and drag is cumbersome for the manipulation of large objects. Frequent navigation is required as such objects occlude the user's view if they are within reach of the user's arm, thereby preventing the user from obtaining a proper perception of the current position of the object in the scene.

All of these disadvantages to a great extent are directly related to the real-world manipulation metaphor and can be avoided by the use of techniques for *remote* object translations, where the objects are not required to be within reach of the user.

3   Translation Methods

Before an object can be translated remotely it has to be picked. Bowman et al. [1] report that ray casting is a good method for distant object picking. With ray casting, the wand emits a visible ray. The user can point the ray such that it passes through an object. Pressing the left wand button picks the object hit by the ray (if the ray passes through multiple objects, the object closest to the user is picked). The object can now be manipulated. Releasing the wand button releases the object which then stays at its current position, i.e., the button serves as a clutch.

We have evaluated seven different methods for remote object translations. The methods can be classified into different categories according to two important characteristics: Which degrees of freedom of the wand are used to perform the object translations, and the mapping scheme from the wand motions to the actual object translations. For the first characteristic, a distinction is made between methods that are related to (changes in) the wand *position, orientation,* or a *combination* of both. For the second characteristic a distinction is made between methods that use object *position* control, object *velocity* control, or a *combination*. Table 1 depicts the classification of each method according to the forementioned characteristics.

| | | *Wand Parameters* | | |
		position	position + orientation	orientation
	position	Slave	Stick Crosshair	
Motion Control	position + velocity	Slave & Fly	Stick & Throttle	
	velocity	Fly		Throttle

Table 1: Classification of the manipulation methods according to their characteristics on degree of freedom dependency (horizontal) and object motion control (vertical).

A short description of each of the methods that were implemented is now given. Each method is also illustrated in a figure. This figure depicts how an example translation can be performed with the particular method. A sphere is to be translated from a start position to a goal position. The example translation is shown in figure 1 at the instant the sphere is picked for translation.

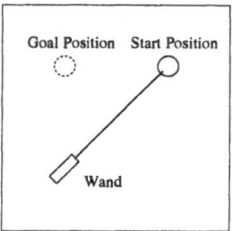

Figure 1: Example translation task at the instant the sphere is picked for translation.

3.1 Position Control

Three different methods were investigated that use position control as the mapping function from the wand's movements to the objects translations. The first method is solely based on the position (changes) of the wand, whereas the other two methods incorporate both the wand's position and orientation parameters.

Slave This method is based on a direct, one-to-one position mapping between the wand and the object: each translational movement of the wand is also applied to the object. This method is referred to as the 'Slave' method as the relation between the wand and the object can be seen as a master-slave relation: the object follows the exact (translational) movements of the wand. A disadvantage of this method is that the amount of translation is bounded by the reach of the user's arm. For larger translations, the concept of *ratchetting* has to be used, i.e., a series of grab-translate-release actions. The Slave method is illustrated in figure 2.

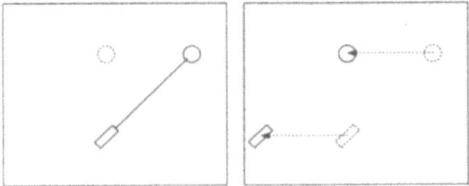

Figure 2: The Slave method. The sphere simply follows the wand movement.

Stick In this method the object is connected to the ray emitted by the wand upon the grab action. Then, each translational and rotational movement of the wand is also applied to the object, i.e., the wand is used as a pointer stick to position the object. Therefore this method is referred to as the 'Stick' method. Again, ratchetting has to be used for large translations, although in this case only for large object translations towards or away from the user. The Stick method is illustrated in figure 3.

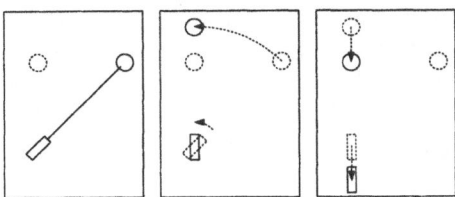

Figure 3: The Stick method. The sphere moves as if attached on a stick.

3D Crosshair This method is based on a crosshair cursor method that has been employed successfully in 3D graphics applications for desk-top computers where 3D positioning is performed with a conventional 2D mouse [7]. Here, a 3D crosshair cursor is projected on the 2D screen. The user can translate the crosshair by dragging the 2D mouse pointer along one of the projected axes of the 3D crosshair. The same scheme is employed in the CAVE version of this method: when the object is picked, a 3D crosshair cursor appears at the intersection point of the ray and the object. The user can now translate the object by dragging the ray of the wand along one of the crosshair axes. In this method, no ratchetting is needed to perform large object translations. However, disadvantages are that only translations along the crosshair's axes can be performed, and no translations can be performed along axes of the crosshair that are parallel to the wand's ray. The Crosshair method is illustrated in figure 4.

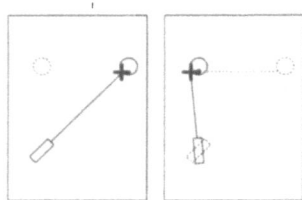

Figure 4: The Crosshair method. The crosshair (and the sphere) is moved by pointing the wand ray along one of the axes of the crosshair.

3.2 Velocity Control

Two methods were investigated that are based on velocity control. The first method is based solely upon the wand's position, while the other method is solely based on the wand's orientation.

Fly This method maps the change in position of the wand to a direction and velocity of a motion that is applied to the object. The position of the wand at the instant the object is picked is considered the rest position. When the wand is moved to a different position, the difference vector from this new position to the rest position indicates the direction of translation. The velocity of the object is derived from the length of the difference vector: the longer the vector, the faster the object moves. Below a certain threshold length no motion is applied to the object. To halt the object, the wand is brought back to the rest position. This method is referred to as the 'Fly' method as the user is in control of what can be regarded as the object's flight. The Fly method is illustrated in figure 5.

Throttle This method is based on the orientation of the wand. The user indicates the direction of the motion by pointing the wand (ray). To control the velocity of the object, a motorcycle throttle grip metaphor is used: by rotating the wand about the direction of the motion (i.e., the *roll* of the wand) the velocity of the motion is indicated. A counter clockwise rotation implies a forward motion along the indicated direction, a clockwise rotation a backward motion. In both directions, a threshold value on the amount of rotation applies below which no translations are performed. To halt the object, the wand is rotated back to the rest orientation. This method is referred to as the 'Throttle' method. It is illustrated in figure 6.

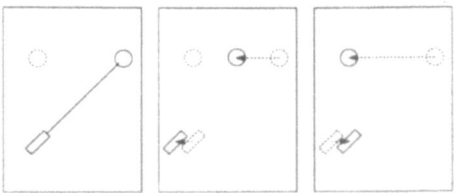

Figure 5: The Fly method. A motion is applied to the sphere by moving the wand away from its rest position. To stop the sphere the wand is brought back to the rest position.

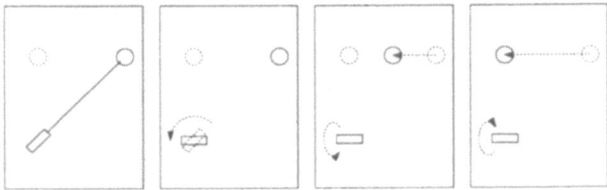

Figure 6: The Throttle method. The direction of movement is indicated by the wand. A velocity is implied on the sphere by rotating the wand about the direction of movement. To stop the sphere the wand is rotated back to its rest orientation.

3.3 Hybrid Control

Previous research results have shown that object positioning with velocity control is often less precise than with position control (e.g., [11, 6]). Therefore, two hybrid methods were created that use both velocity and position control. The intention of these methods is to combine the benefits of velocity control (facile large object translations) with the possibly more precise object positioning obtained with position control.

Slave & Fly In the Fly method, there is a spherical volume around the wand's rest position where no motions are applied to the object. The radius of this sphere equals the threshold value used for the derivation of the velocity from the length of the difference vector between the current wand position and the rest position. In this hybrid method, wand motions inside the sphere are directly coupled to the object position, i.e., the Slave method is used inside the sphere. The Slave & Fly method is illustrated in figure 7.

Stick & Throttle The second hybrid method is a mix of the Stick and Throttle methods. Actually, it is the same as the Stick method, only now the throttle metaphor has been added for translations along the stick, i.e., the object can be moved towards and away from the user by rotating the wand about the roll axis. In [1] such control over the distance from the object to the user is referred to as a *fishing reel* metaphor. The Stick & Throttle method is illustrated in figure 8.

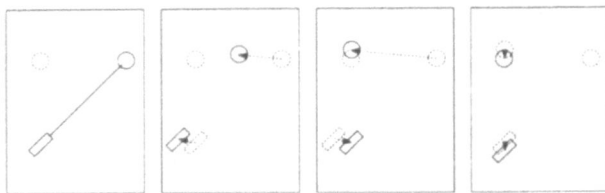

Figure 7: The Slave & Fly method. If the sphere is not translated to the exact desired location with the Fly method, small corrections can be made according to the Slave method.

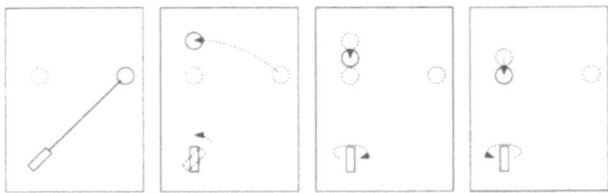

Figure 8: The Stick & Throttle method. The sphere can be translated towards and away from the wand with the throttle metaphor.

4 Evaluation

4.1 Experiments

To test the manipulation methods on their usability, a small pilot experiment was conducted. Four test subjects were asked to complete a number of object translation tasks. Each of these subjects was familiar with the CAVE, but none had previously used any of the object manipulation techniques. While standing in a square virtual work space of equal size as the physical CAVE, a sphere was to be translated from a start position onto a goal position inside a bounding box. The sphere was constrained to stay inside the workspace. To provide additional feedback on the 3D position of the objects, orthogonal shadow projections were depicted on each of the side planes of the working space (i.e. the walls of the CAVE).

First, the different methods were explained to the test subjects and they were given a practice session to get familiar with the methods. Then, for each method a session of eight diffrent translation tasks had to be completed. The subjects were asked to bring the sphere from its start position to the goal position.

The experiments were conducted to evaluate the manipulation methods on three criteria: accuracy, speed, and user friendliness. To be able to determine the accuracy and speed of a method, all movements of the sphere invoked by the test subjects were logged to file. In the analysis, the first trial position performed with each method was discarded. User friendliness is a subjective merit. It was evaluated by having the test subjects fill out a small questionnaire about the different methods, and by making observations of the subjects while performing the manipulation tasks.

4.2 Results

The number of subjects and the sample size is small. Therefore, a full statistical analysis is not appropriate. The tests are primarily intended as a pilot study to obtain indications on the usability of the techniques and to evaluate the current implementations and parameter settings of the techniques. The experiences obtained from these experiments can be used for the design and conduction of a more formal and extensive usability analysis. Nevertheless, several interesting observations can be made.

Figure 9 shows box and whisker plots [9] of the task completion times per method and per subject. The figure shows great variety among the different methods. From this figure, a ranking can be obtained where the Stick method is ranked best, followed by the Stick & Throttle method, the Slave, Slave & Fly, and Fly methods, and finally the Throttle and Crosshair methods. The Throttle and Crosshair methods perform really bad, and reveal some unacceptable outside and far outside measurements.

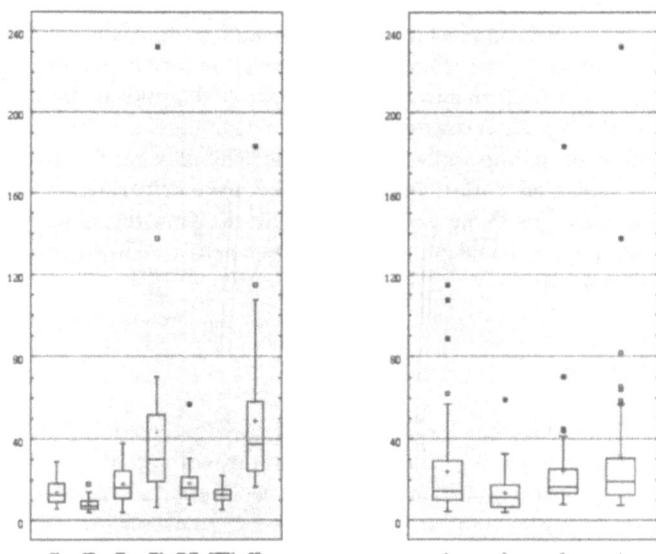

Figure 9: Box plots of the overall completion time in seconds of all trials. Left per method (SL = Slave, ST = Stick, FL = Fly, TH = Throttle, SLFL = Slave & Fly, STTH = Stick & Throttle, CR = Crosshair), right per subject.

Figure 9 also shows some variety among the subjects. If a ranking was to be made, subject 2 would score best, followed by subjects 3 and 1, and finally subject 4. Each of the subject plots reveal some outside or far outside scores. All of these scores were obtained with either the Throttle method or the Crosshair method.

To investigate the methods more thoroughly on the two aspects of speed and accuracy, the completion time was split in two components. The first is the time it took for the subjects to bring the sphere into the vicinity of the box, i.e. the point in time where the center of the sphere was located inside the box for the first time. This component can be regarded as a measurement for manipulation speed, i.e. how rapidly can the sphere be brought into the vicinity of the box with only limited accuracy. The second component is the time it took for the subjects to bring the sphere from that 'vicinity position' to the final position. This can be regarded as a measurement for accuracy, i.e. how easily can the final adjustments be made to accurately position the sphere inside the box. Besides looking at the final completion time of the trials as a measure for accuracy, the final distance of the sphere to the ideal end position was also considered.

4.3   Discussion

From the pilot user experiments it could be concluded that the Stick method performs best overall. The subjects perceived it as easy to use, intuitive, and not fatiguing. Furthermore, the obtained measurements indicated that the Stick method performs well for both fast and precise object placement. However, the object translation tasks as they were performed during these experiments did not require the sphere to be translated over large distances towards or away from the subjects. If a manipulation method is required to perform such large scale object translations, the Stick & Throttle method would be a better choice as far as fast object translations are concerned. However, precise object placement performance with the Stick & Throttle method might degrade as the object is located far away from the subject. In such a case, even small wand movements will result in large object translations. The Slave & Fly method might be a better choice in such a case. Further and more extensive experiments are needed to be conclusive about this. One thing was clear though: the Throttle and Crosshair methods performed by far the worst, and are not likely to be useful to perform object translations in a virtual environment.

5   Conclusion

User input is an underdeveloped aspect of the use of virtual environments. In particular, spatial input techniques for 3D object manipulations with the use of multiple degree-of-freedom devices is still a current research issue. We have evaluated seven different methods for remote object translations in immersive environments. The results of the pilot user experiments showed a wide variety among the different methods, and some initial recommendations could be formulated on the use of the methods for different tasks. We plan to perform more extensive user experiments to be conclusive about these recommendations.

Acknowledgements

The author would like to thank the test subjects for their cooperation, and R. van Liere (CWI) and J.J. van Wijk (Netherlands Research Foundation ECN) for their help during this work and their comments on the paper drafts. This work was partially funded by the National Computer Facilities Foundation NCF.

References

[1] D.A. Bowman and L.F. Hodges. An evaluation of techniques for grabbing and manipulating remote objects in immersive virtual environments. In S.N. Spencer, editor, *1997 Symposium on Interactive 3D Graphics*, pages 35–38, 1997.

[2] S. Bryson. Approaches to the successful design and implementation of VR applications. In R.A. Earnshaw, J.A. Vince, and H. Jones, editors, *Virtual Reality Applications*, pages 3–15. Academic Press, 1995.

[3] C. Cruz-Neira, D.J. Sandin, and T.A. DeFanti. Surround-screen projection-based virtual reality: The design and implementation of the CAVE. In *Computer Graphics (SIGGRAPH '93 Proceedings)*, volume 27, pages 135–142, 1993.

[4] L.D. Cutler, B. Fröhlich, and P. Hanrahan. Two-handed direct manipulation on the responsive workbench. In S.N. Spencer, editor, *Proceedings of the 1997 Symposium on Interactive 3D Graphics*, pages 107–114, 1997.

[5] K. Hinckley, R. Pausch, J.C. Goble, and N.F. Kassell. A survey of design issues in spatial input. In *Proceedings of the ACM Symposium on User Interface Software and Technology (UIST '94)*, pages 213–222, 1994.

[6] W.S. Kim, F. Tendick, S.R. Ellis, and L.W. Stark. A comparison of position and rate control for telemanipulators with consideration of manipulator dynamics. *IEEE Journal of Robotics and Automation*, RA-3(5):426–436, October 1987.

[7] J.D. Mulder and J.J. van Wijk. 3D computational steering with parametrized geometric objects. In G.M. Nielson and D. Silver, editors, *Visualization '95 (Proceedings of the 1995 Visualization Conference)*, pages 304–311, 1995.

[8] C. Schmandt. Spatial input/display correspondence in a stereoscopic computer graphic work station. *Computer Graphics*, 17(3):253–261, 1983.

[9] J.W. Tukey. *Exploratory Data Analysis*. Addison-Wesley, 1977.

[10] C. Ware. Using hand position for virtual object placement. *Visual Computer*, 6(5):245–253, 1990.

[11] S. Zhai and P. Milgram. Human performance evaluation of manipulation schemes in virtual environments. In *Proceedings of the 1993 IEEE Virtual Reality Annual International Symposium*, pages 155–161, 1993.

[12] S. Zhai, P. Milgram, and A. Rastogi. Anisotropic human performance in six degree-of-freedom tracking: An evaluation of three-dimensional display and control devices. *IEEE Transactions on Systems, Man, and Cybernetics Part A: Systems and Humans*, 27(4):518–528, 1997.

Meet.Me@Cyberstage: towards Immersive Telepresence

Vali Lalioti[1], Christophe Garcia[2] and Frank Hasenbrink[1]

[1] GMD - IMK

53754 Sankt Augustin

Germany

{Vali.lalioti, Frank.Hasenbrink}@gmd.de

[2] FORTH - ICS

GR 711 10 Heraklion

Crete GREECE

cgarcia@csi.forth.gr

1. Introduction

Virtual Reality is widely accepted as a promising approach to a better man-machine interface, overcoming the present limitations of desktop systems and adapting more closely to the user needs. Projective VR systems are using metaphors, such as the blackboard or the desk for creating shared working environments that provide a more natural man-machine communication[12][16]. However, today's technology and advances in telecommunication rapidly change the way the business is carried out, making it a globally distributed process, in which communication and collaboration of geographically dispersed groups is of vital importance. VR systems are adapting accordingly, by providing not only a better man-machine interface, but also by facilitating human to human interaction and collaboration over distance. New challenges are introduced in terms of distribution and interaction. It is not only a question of solving the technical problems of gathering and transmitting multimedia datastreams with sufficient quality and speed, but also a question of addressing the specific needs of human communication. For example, facial expression, body language and eye contact are an integral part of this communication.

Teleconferencing systems that provide high-degree of Telepresence, such as [2], and collaborative co-presence systems such as [11][17][18][19], give enough evidences that projective VR systems when combined with Telepresence facilities can greatly facilitate the communication and collaboration over distance in a variety of application areas. The approach presented in this paper, creates an environment where remote participants not only meet as if face-to-face, but also share the same virtual space and perform common tasks, in order to reach a common goal. In particular, live stereo-video of remote participants is integrated into the virtual space of another participant, allowing a geographically separated group of people to collaborate while maintaining eye-contact, gaze awareness and body language. Participants could be using a wide range of Projective VR systems [2][12][4], resulting symmetric or asymmetric collaboration scenarios. In the section that follows, we present some of these projective VR systems, while in section 3 the scientific approach is described. Section 4, summarizes the demonstration in Cyberstage[TM1], of a prototype environment for Immersive telepresence, which took place at GMD's open-house event 1997. Finally, section 5 concludes this paper with some of the open issues and future research directions.

2. Background

Projective Display Systems are the state of the art in high end Virtual Reality Environments [4]. Releasing the user from the heavy load and inconvenience related to head mounted displays, increasing resolution and rendering speed enables VR for serious applications [10]. Currently desk and room size installations are available, like the Responsive Workbench™, the CyberStage™ or the Teleport[2]. All of them extend the real space by a virtual space providing a common world coordinate system, where the local and the remote participants are part of Fig. 1.

Fig. 1 Projective VR Systems

In the RWB concept [12] the user no longer experiences simulations of interesting procedures on the computer, but the computer is (invisibly) integrated into the user's world, Fig. 2. The virtual objects and control tools, displayed as computer-generated stereoscopic images, are projected onto the surface of a table. The user interacts with the virtual objects and manipulates them as if there were real. Only one viewer is tracked at the moment, while several observers can watch the operations simultaneously, by the use of shutter glasses.

Fig. 2 Responsive Workbench

---

1. Cyberstage™ is a registered Trademark of the German National Research Center for Information Technology GMD

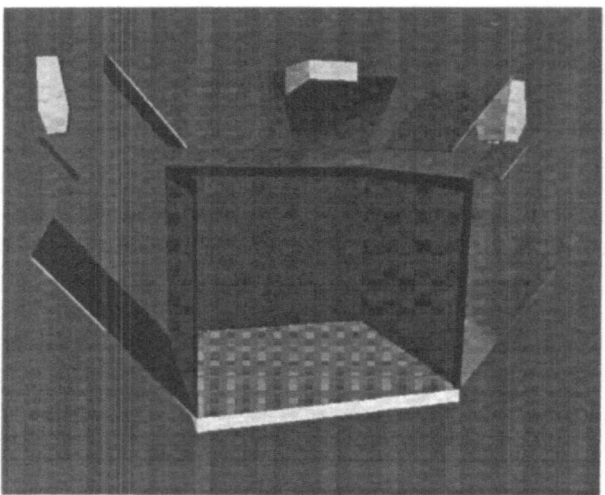

Fig. 3 Cyberstage installation

CyberStage^TM is a CAVE^TM1 like [3] four-side room-size stereo display system installed at GMD, which creates the illusion of immersion within a computer generated virtual environment, Fig. 3. Users see large virtual spaces and hear spatially distributed sound. Projection systems like CyberStage allow a direct and body centered human interaction within virtual worlds as well as team work. Users immersed in a virtual world are physically standing within the display system. Three wall size rear projection systems are installed orthogonal to the floor projection, each with a size of 3x3 meters. An SGI 4 pipe Onyx 2 Infinite Reality generates eight user controlled images. Each pipe generates 10 million shaded triangles per second (peak rate) and is equipped with 64 MB of texture memory. 12 Mips R1000 CPUs are used in combination with 1.5 GB of RAM to compute VR applications. The user position is tracked with Polhemus Fastrak sensors. Crystal Eyes shutter glasses are used for stereo image perception. The display resolution is 1024 x 768 pixels at 120 Hz for each of the four displays. The eight channel-surround-sound system is fed by IRCAM's room acoustic software Spatilisateur [5][13] and provides support for localized sound sources within the virtual environment. A significant characteristic of the Cyberstage is the acoustic floor which allows to generate the sense of vibrations. The two existing CyberStage^TM installations use a wooden skeleton to minimize noise for the electromagnetic tracking.

TELEPORT is a sychronous collaboration system that provides high degree of co-presence [2]. The system is based around special rooms, called display rooms, where one wall is a "view port" into a virtual extension. The geometry, surface characteristics, and lighting match the real room to which it is attached. When a teleconferencing

1. CAVE^TM is a registered Trademark of the University of Illinois

connection is established, video imagery of the remote participant (or participants) is composited with the rendered view of the virtual extension (see Fig. 4). The viewing position of the local participant is tracked, allowing imagery appearing on the wall display to be rendered from the participant's perspective. The combination of viewer tracking, a wall-sized display, and real-time rendering and compositing, give the illusion of the virtual extension being attached to the real room. The result is a natural and immersive teleconferencing environment where real and virtual environments are merged without the need for head-mounted displays or other encumbering devices. The current system uses a 3m x 2.25m rear-projected *video wall* attached to a 3m square room. A *camera* is placed on a stand or a table and set at approximately eye height. The field of view is wide enough to take in a full upper body shot of the local participant. Two techniques are used for *segmentation* (for determining the regions of the video signal where a participant appears) chroma-keying and delta-keying. For audio, each participant wears a small microphone. The audio signals from remote participants are mixed together and sent to speakers mounted on either side of the video wall.

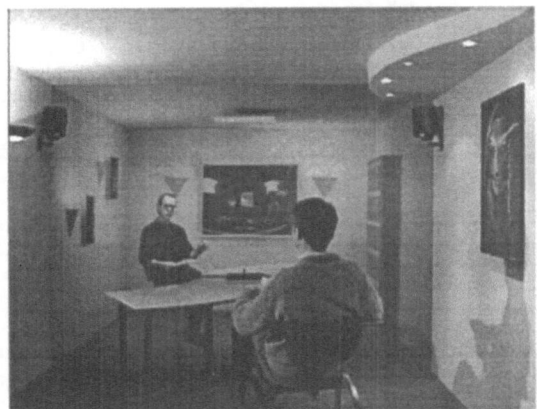

Fig. 4 Telepresence session in the TELEPORT room

3. Scientific Approach

In the approach presented in this paper, we merge the stereo video of a remote participant into Cyberstage using the texture based effects of our AVOCADO Software Framework. In particular, each image of the stereo camera is mapped onto a simple geometry representing a plane. The AVOCADO Software Framework then displays the right camera image to the right eye of the viewer and the left to the left eye respectively. However, these two planes have to be fully defined in terms of size, position, aspect ratio and orientation in order to provide the Cyberstage viewer with the best quality stereo-video and to respect the appearance of the remote person. In addition, the segmentation techniques of the TELEPORT system are also used in our approach. Therefore, we are able to determine the regions of the video signal that are of interest

94

(i.e. the image of the remote participant) and combine this information into the original video signal, thus making the background transparent.

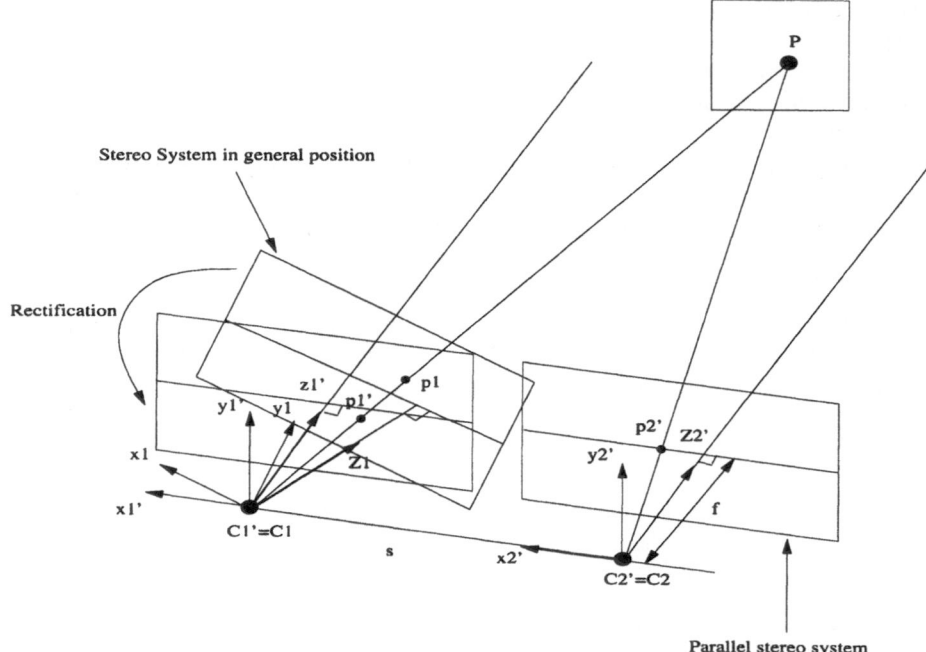

Fig. 5 Rectification of a stereo vision system

The Cyberstage viewer, should have the sensation of sharing the same virtual space with the remote participant. Therefore, when positioning the video planes we have to respect physical rules such as the size of the participants. In addition, when the image of a remote participant is positioned behind a virtual object the stereo impression for the Cyberstage viewer should confront to this (i.e. the stereo-effect should not result in the remote participant perceived as been within virtual objects). Thus, the stereo images have to be adjusted in terms of size, orientation and position, before being integrated into the virtual world. Automatic camera calibration and stereo image rectification are required to perform such a task. In this section, we describe the steps required to integrate the stereo-video image of a remote participant into Cyberstage, while preserving the perspective of the Cyberstage viewer.

3.1 Stereo image rectification

We choose to use an unrestricted stereo vision system, consisting of a rig of standard video cameras placed all over the observed scene. In the current implementation, two cameras are used with the only constraints that they share a large field of view. In most of the applications using stereo vision, a parallel stereo vision system like the one shown in Fig. 5 is required and especially in the present case, where the produced images should be comfortably viewed by a human visual system.

It is a difficult task to mechanically set up a parallel stereo vision system. A way to use a non-parallel stereo vision system is to perform image rectification. This process aims at transforming the images taken by such a non-parallel system into images taken by a virtual parallel stereo vision system. The rectified images can be thought of being acquired by a new stereo rig, obtained by rotating the original cameras. This is indeed the basis for computing the rectifying transformation, as well as the perspective projection matrices rectifying the images (rectifying projection matrices). Efficient methods for rectification may be found in [1],[8] and [14]. Our work improves and extends [1] given that we enforce explicitly all the constraints necessary and sufficient to derive a unique rectification matrix, and obtain the latter as the solution of a resulting system of 4 simultaneous linear equations. The resulting algorithm is quite simple. The correct behavior of the algorithm has been demonstrated with both synthetic and real images. The rectification transformation acts as shown in Fig. 5. We compute the transformation from (C_1, x_1, y_1, z_1) to (C_1, x_1', y_1', z_1'), which is the new coordinate system for camera 1 (symmetrically for camera 2).

The rectification algorithm performs in real time since it uses only the parameters gained by the cameras calibration and needs at least 6 operations per pixel. The images are rectified by projectively mapping all pixels of the virtual image plane into the original image plane and interpolating the intensity information using a lowpass filter.

In order to perform rectification and to position the resulting rectified images in the virtual world, a robust and full recovery of the camera parameters is required. The image rectification step can be avoided when a parallel stereo vision system is used. However, the calculation of the camera parameters is necessary since they are also used for integrating the stereo images into the virtual world. Camera calibration methods are designed to perform these parameter estimation.

3.2 Camera Calibration

Basically, there are two kinds of parameters associated with camera calibration [9],[15]: (i) the *intrinsic parameters* including optical and electronic properties of a camera, such as focal length, lens distortion coefficients, image center, scaling factors of the pixel array in both directions. Sometimes, manufacturers provide a partial set of these parameters, but they are not accurate enough. Also, some of these parameters may vary from time to time, while some of them may be calibrated once for all, depending on the stability of the mechanical and optical construction of the camera; (ii) the *extrinsic parameters* corresponding to the pose estimation (rotation and translation) of the camera system relative to a user-defined 3D world coordinate frame.

We take profit of our previous work [6] [7], consisting of the fully automatic and simultaneous estimation of both the intrinsic and extrinsic camera parameters. A non-linear optimization method [7] based on a quaternion formulation is derived from 2D to 3D point or line correspondences.

A special object has been constructed for camera calibration which is a white cube with black circular marks. These landmarks are precisely positioned and define a coordinate system attached to the object. Image points are extracted by segmenting the dark marks and by locating the center of gravity of each of these clusters. Then, pairs of 2D-3D

96

point coordinates are built automatically, establishing the 2D-3D correspondences. As mentioned above, at least 6 pairs of 2D-3D correspondences have to be used in our camera calibration algorithm.

After calibrating separately each of the camera, external parameters such as optical center position (which leads to intercamera distance estimation), image plane orientation are gained and are used as input for the stereo image rectification step together with internal parameters such as real focal length (and not the nominal one). These internal parameters are used then when positioning and scaling the stereo images into the cyberstage.

3.3 Stereo-video integration into Virtual World

In order to merge the stereo video of a remote participant into the Cyberstage, the rectified stereo images are mapped onto virtual planes. Fig. 6 shows the relation between Cyberstage, Camera and Virtual World coordinate systems. The world coordinate system (WC) is the coordinate system of the virtual world. We position the video planes, as well as any virtual objects, according to this coordinate system. The Cyberstage room is a 3x3x2.245m height cube. The (0,0,0) of this coordinate system (CC) is at the center of the room 1.5m from the floor. We call this the Cyberstage coordinate system (CC). The viewer's location is given according to the CC and we know the mapping from WC to CC at any given time (e.g. the Cyberstage is moving around the virtual world). On the other hand we have the stereo camera coordinate system (KC) which for matter of simplicity we assume that it is also the coordinate system of our real world.

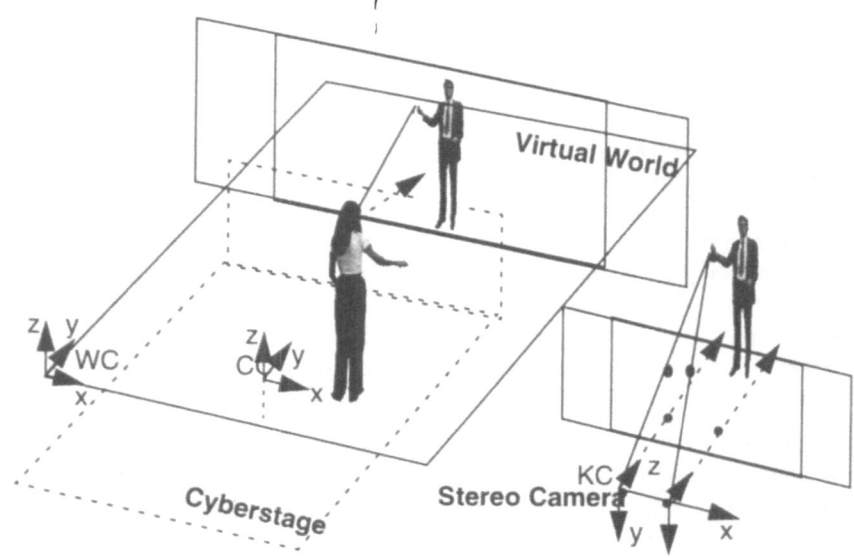

Fig. 6 Virtual, Camera and Real World Coordinate Systems

When the mapped planes are projected onto the Cyberstage, the viewer should have the sensation of seeing the 3D image of the remote participant together with the 3D scene of the virtual world. For this purpose the video planes should be centered around the corresponding eye of the viewer. There also have to be sized according to the distance of the viewer from the Cyberstage projection screens and to the distance of the video plane from the viewer. In the rest of the section we examine which are the parameters that determine the scaling and translation factors.

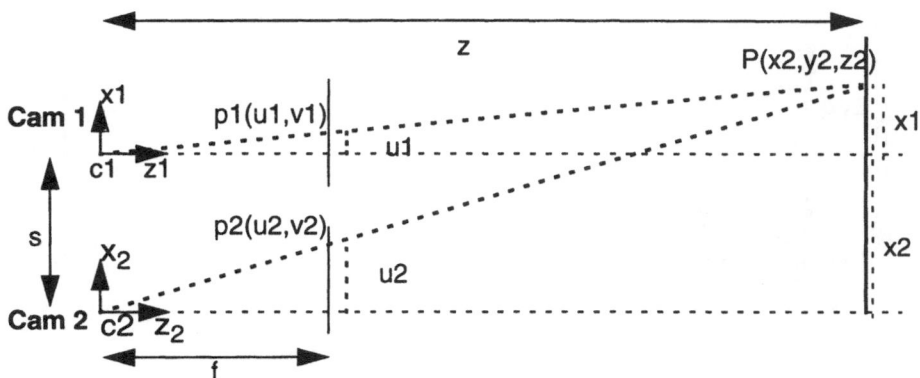

Fig. 7 Two Camera Coordinate System

In Fig. 7, the camera pair is shown after rectification. Let c2, the focal point of Cam2, be the center of the Camera coordinate system, f the focal length and (u,v) the image plane of the cameras.

A point $P(x,y,z) = P(x_2,y_2,z_2)$ would be projected on the image plane of camera 2 at $p_2(u_2,v_2)$ and on the image plane of camera 1 at $p_1(u_1,v_1)$ respectively. Let s be the distance between the focal point of the two cameras, then:

$$\left.\begin{array}{l} \frac{u_1}{x_1} = \frac{f}{z} \\[2mm] \frac{u_2}{x_2} = \frac{f}{z} \end{array}\right\} \Longrightarrow \begin{array}{l} x_1 = \frac{u_1}{f} \cdot z \\[2mm] x_2 = \frac{u_2}{f} \cdot z \end{array} \tag{1}$$

The disparity between the two images for point $P(x,y,z)$ is then:

$$d = u_1 - u_2 \Big\} \Longrightarrow d = \frac{f}{z} \cdot s \tag{2}$$

The same point $P(x,y,z)$ viewed by a person at distance Z, with eye-focal length F and distance S between the eyes, would appear at point $P_2(U_2,V_2)$ and $P_1(U_1,V_1)$ respectively. As shown in Fig. 8, let Z be the distance of the viewer's eyes. Let the distance s between the camera pair and the focal length f of the cameras be different from the distance S and focal length F of the eyes of the viewer.

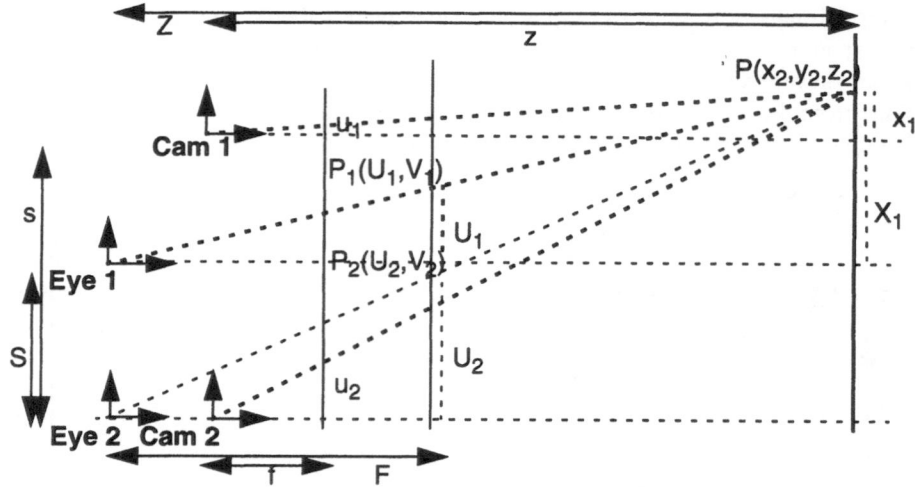

Fig. 8 Eye and Camera Coordinate Systems

Then the relationship between the projection of point P on the eye image plane with the projection on the camera image plane is as follows:

$$\left.\begin{array}{l} \frac{U_1}{X_1} = \frac{F}{Z} \\[2mm] \frac{U_2}{X_2} = \frac{F}{Z} \end{array}\right\} \Longrightarrow \quad \begin{array}{l} X_1 = \frac{U_1}{F} \cdot Z \\[2mm] X_2 = \frac{U_2}{F} \cdot Z \end{array} \tag{3}$$

From Fig. 8 we derive that $X_1 = x_1 + (s-S)$ and $X_2 = x_2$, and by substituting X_1 and x_1 from equation (3):

$$\left.\begin{array}{l} \frac{U_1}{F} \cdot Z = \frac{u_1}{f} \cdot z + (s-S) \\[2mm] \frac{U_2}{F} \cdot Z = \frac{u_2}{f} \cdot z \end{array}\right\} \Longrightarrow \quad \begin{array}{l} U_1 = u_1 \cdot \frac{F}{f} \cdot \frac{z}{Z} + \frac{(s-S)\cdot F}{Z} \\[2mm] U_2 = u_2 \cdot \frac{F}{f} \cdot \frac{z}{Z} \end{array} \tag{4}$$

According to the equations (3) and (4) if we would want to position the remote participant at an average distance of Z from the viewer and if the observed scene is located at an average distance of z from the stereo camera's optical centers, then we would perform the following operations:

- define two planes of size G multiplied by the size of the video image plane in u and v, where G=(F*z)/(f*Z)

- position them in front of each eye (each eye's optical axis passing through the center of each plane) at a distance Z into the virtual world

- translate the plane by T along the X-axis of the CC, where T=(F/Z)*(s-S)

4. Schlosstag '97

For our open-house event in October 1997 (Schlosstag'97) we demonstrated a step towards Immersive Telepresence in Projective VR systems, by connecting our virtual studio facilities with Cyberstage. In particular, a person captured by a stereo-camera was keyed and integrated into a 3-dimensional virtual environment, allowing a fully immersed 3D virtual teleconference. The real-time stereo video image from GMD's Blue Room, was merged into the virtual world shown in Cyberstage, allowing immersive telepresence on the Cyberstage site.

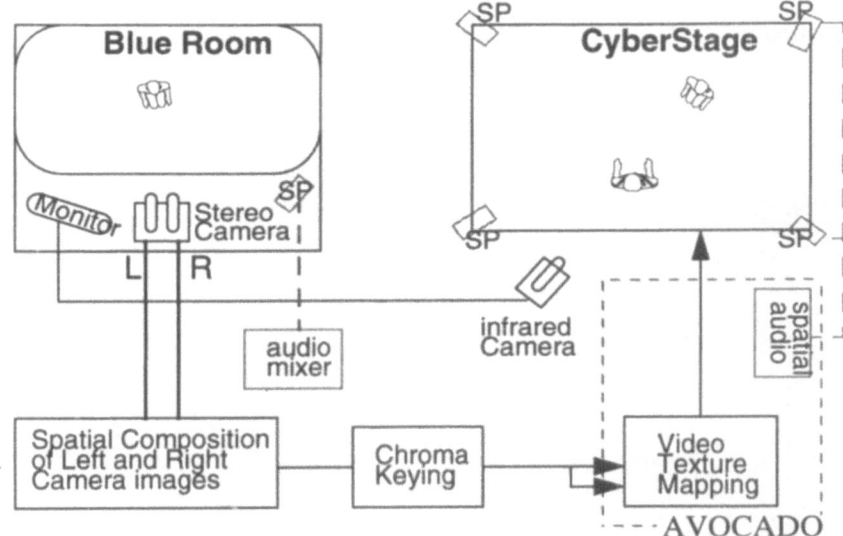

Fig. 9 Schlosstag'97 set-up for Immersive Telepresence

An overview of the set-up, is shown in Fig. 9. The stereo camera generated two video streams, one for the left and one for the right eye. These two streams were spatially combined. The resulting video stream, containing the even fields of each signal, was then send to an Ultimate keying system to be enhanced by an additional alpha channel, masking all background information. The resulting video stream was then send to an SGI Onyx with a 2 Pipe RE2 graphics subsystem, which is powering the Cyberstage installation. The Onyx has two Sirius boards which received the video stream as input and integrated it as a stereo video texture in the virtual scene.

As feedback information a video signal from an infra-red camera out of the Cyberstage room was send to a monitor in the Blue Room. Thus, the person in the blue room was able to have a view of the virtual objects in Cyberstage and also of his own video image which was included as video texture within the virtual world.

The audio connections and equipment are shown in Fig. 9 with dotted lines. For the blue room one speaker and one wireless-microphone were used connected via an audio mixer. In the Cyberstage room AVOCADO's spatial audio system in conjunction with the 8 channel audio display and one wireless-microphone were used. Two receiver/ trasmitter pairs were used for the wireless microphones.

Fig. 10 shows a reconstruction of the Cyberstage view during the Schlosstag scenario demonstration. We integrated the remote person into an operating theater. The remote participant was giving some information and advice to the group of visitors currently present in the Cyberstage installation. To show the possibilities of our software framework, this operating theater includes a large set of interactive elements according to a design study of the German Max Dellbrueck Center in Berlin. The way to interact with these elements was explained to the visitors by the remote participant. A virtual projection screen showed a prerecorded laparoscopic treatment for additional information.

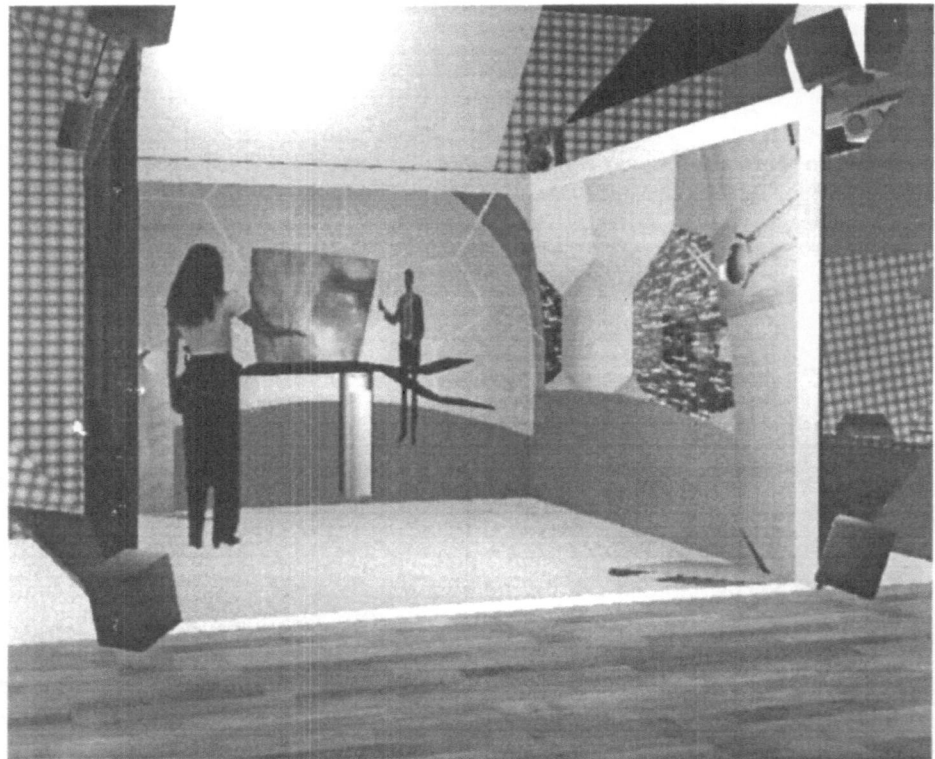

Fig. 10 Reconstruction of Schlosstag'97 Cyberstage View

5.   Conclusions and Future Work

We have presented an approach towards Immersive Telepresence in Projective Virtual Reality Systems. Our aim is to provide geographically dispersed groups of people the possib'lity to meet and work within Projective Virtually Reality systems as if face-to-face. For this purpose we integrate stereo video images from remote participants into the same virtual space. Participants could be located at sites having different Projective VR systems. A first prototype of the approach was presented in GMD's open house event in October'97. The scientific approach requires camera calibrated, in order to obtain the camera parameters, which are then used for integrating the stereo-video into the virtual space, while preserving the stereo-effect and the viewer's perspective. In addition, stereo image rectification is required when a nonparallel stereo camera system is used.

The results drawn by the use of this prototype have encourages us to continue our research towards Immersive Telepresence in a number of different directions. In particular, we working on solutions on a number of open issues such as the use of more than one camera-pair, the real-time rectification algorithm, and different usage scenarios for different projective VR systems and different application areas.

REFERENCES

[1]   Ayache N. Artificial Vision for Mobile Robots: Stereo Vision and Multisensory Perception. The MIT Press, 1991.

[2]   Breiteneder C., Gibbs S., Arapis C., TELEPORT- An Augmented Reality Teleconferencing Environment, Proc. 3rd Eurographics Workshop on Virtual Environments Coexistence & Collaboration, Monte Carlo, Monaco, February 1996

[3]   Cruz-Neira, C., Sandin, D.J., DeFanti, T.A., Kenyon, R., and Hart, J.C. The CAVE, Audio Visual Experience Automatic Virtual Environment. Communications of the ACM, June 1992.

[4]   Dai P., Eckel G., Gbel M., Hasenbrink F., Lalioti V., Lechner U., Strassner J., Tramberend H., Wesche G., Virtual Spaces - VR Projection System Technologies and Applications, Tutorial Notes of the 1997 Eurographics Conference, Budapest, 1997.

[5]   Dechelle, F., DeCecco, M., The IRCAM Real-Time Platform and Applications, Proceedings of the 1995 International Computer Music Conference, International Computer Music Association, San Francisco, 1995.

[6]   Dornaika F. and Garcia C., Pose estimation using point and line correspondences. To appear in International Journal of Real Time Imaging, New York, February 1998.

[7]   Dornaika F. and Garcia C., Robust camera calibration using 2D to 3D feature correspondences. In Proceedings of the International Symposium SPIE --Optical Science Engineering and Instrumentation, Videometrics V, Volume 3174, pages 123--133, San Diego, Ca., July 1997.

[8]   Faugeras O., Three-Dimensional Computer Vision: A Geometric Viewpoint. The MIT Press, Cambridge, 1993.

[9] Faugeras O. and Toscani G., Camera calibration for 3D computer vision. In Proceedings of the International Workshop on Machine Vision and Machine Intelligence, Tokyo, Japan, February 1987.

[10] Haase H., Dai F., Strassner J., Goebel M., Immersive Investigation of Scientific Data, Scientific Visualization, IEEE Press, 1997

[11] Ishii H.and Kobayashi M., ClearBoard: A Seamless Medium for Shared Drawing and Conversation with Eye Contact, CHI'92, May 3-7, 1992.

[12] Krueger W. and Bernd Froehlich B., The Responsive Workbench, IEEE Computer Graphics and Applications, May 1994

[13] Lindemann E., Starkier F., Dechelle F., The IRCAM Musical Workstation: Hardware Overview and Signal Processing Features, In: S. Arnold and G. Hair, eds. Proceedings of the1990 International Computer Music Conference. San Francisco: International Computer Music Association, 1990.

[14] Papadimitriou D.V. and Dennis T.J., Epipolar line estimation and rectification for stereo images pairs. IEEE Transactions on Image Processing, 3(4):672-676, April 1996.

[15] Tsai R., A versatile camera calibration technique for high-accuracy 3d machine vision metrology using off-the-shelf tv cameras and lenses. IEEE Journal of Robotics and Automation, 3(4):323-344, August 1987.

[16] Wellner P., DigitalDesk, Communications of the ACM, Vol. 36, No. 7, July 1993.

[17] Weatherall A., GroupSystems Electronic Meeting across the Enterprise and across the World, HICSS-30, January 97, Maui, Hawaii.

[18] http://www.xerox.fr/ats/br/livead.html

[19] http://www.xerox.fr/research/cms/eurocode_4.htm#HEADING3

[20] http://www.radnet.com

VR Geo - Planning Tool for the Redevelopment of Landscape

Bernd Lutz, Rolf Ziegler

Fraunhofer IGD, Rundeturmstr. 6, D-64283 Darmstadt,

Tel.: +49 6151 155 124, Fax: +49 6151 155 196,

email: <blutz, ziegler>@igd.fhg.de

http://www.igd.fhg.de

0 Abstract

This report describes in more detail a project applying VR as a planning tool for the redevelopment of landscape. The aim of the project was to visualize redevelopment projects of two sites of the company Wismut GmbH [4], a former mining company.

Applying VR technology, both the actual and the planning state of the landscape can be visualized interactively. The visualization of the planning state includes also the several processes (e.g., leveling and deposit) which will be carried out through the redevelopment.

With the VR Geo system the engineers of Wismut were able to plan these two redevelopment projects in a powerful manner. They visualized the various planning states and discussed them with decision-maker. Furthermore the results were presented to people who are living in this area. They got a first impression of how their region will look in future.

This report describes not just another VR application. It describes the realization of a project which provides the customer with a system to generate, to change, and to present a landscape in different states. In fact the most difficult problem was to generate, i.e. to model, the landscape based upon the different kind of original data: hard copies of 2D maps, a lot of textual information, color photos and some digital data (3D point and line data of the dumps, grey scale aerial photo of the landscape). All the remaining has been modeled during the project: topology of the landscapes, streets, trees, bushes, buildings, dumps, railway tracks, fences, pits, churches, a location line for the trucks to level one dump, etc.

The next difficulty was the different kind of user requirements. The system should be integrated into the daily work to support the engineers in planning redevelopment projects. Furthermore the redevelopment projects should be presented using a high end and a low end VR environment: high end VR workstation, VR interaction devices, stereo large screen projection, low end graphics workstation. Third, the system should be able to produce on demand videos and color images based on the requirements of the customer. And fourth, the system should be open for future extensions.

To sum up the VR Geo system enables the engineers of Wismut to visualize redevelopment projects in a scalable manner: snapshots of the planned landscape as color images, videos of a flight through the landscape, interim results for discussion on a low end workstation, and a highly immersive presentation using a high end VR system. All alternatives have been applied during the project described within this paper.

1 Introduction

This report describes in more detail a project applying VR as a planning tool for the redevelopment of landscape. The aim of the project was to visualize redevelopment projects of two sites of the company Wismut GmbH [4], a former mining company. These two sites are located in Saxony, Germany.

Applying VR technology, both the actual and the planning state of the landscape can be visualized interactively. The visualization of the planning state includes also the several processes (e.g., leveling and deposit) which will be carried out through the redevelopment.

One redevelopment project plans to level a dump and to deposit it to a second dump. This bigger dump will be plant with different kinds of trees and bushes. The second project contains the planting of several dumps and the planning of a spa garden.

With the VR Geo system the engineers of Wismut were able to plan these two redevelopment projects in a powerful manner. They visualized the various planning states and discussed them with decision-maker. Furthermore the results were presented to people who are living in this area. They got a first impression of how their region will look in future.

This report describes not just another VR application. It describes the realization of a project which provides the customer with a system to generate, to change, and to present a landscape in different states. In fact the most difficult problem was to generate, i.e. to model, the landscape based upon the different kind of original data: hard copies of 2D maps, a lot of textual information, color photos and some digital data (3D point and line data of the dumps, grey scale aerial photo of the landscape). All the remaining has been modeled during the project: topology of the landscapes, streets, trees, bushes, buildings, dumps, railway tracks, fences, pits, churches, a location line for the trucks to level one dump, etc.

The next difficulty was the different kind of user requirements. The system should be integrated into the daily work to support the engineers in planning redevelopment projects. Furthermore the redevelopment projects should be presented using a high end and a low end VR environment: high end VR workstation, VR interaction devices, stereo large screen projection, low end graphics workstation. Third, the system should be able to produce on demand videos and color images based on the requirements of the customer. And fourth, the system should be open for future extensions.

To sum up the VR Geo system enables the engineers of Wismut to visualize redevelopment projects in a scalable manner: snapshots of the planned landscape as color images, videos of a flight through the landscape, interim results for discussion on a low end workstation, and a highly immersive presentation using a high end VR system. All alternatives have been applied during the project described within this paper.

2 System structure

The VR Geo system is based on the VR system developed at Fraunhofer IGD [1]. The overall structure of the system is shown in Figure 1.

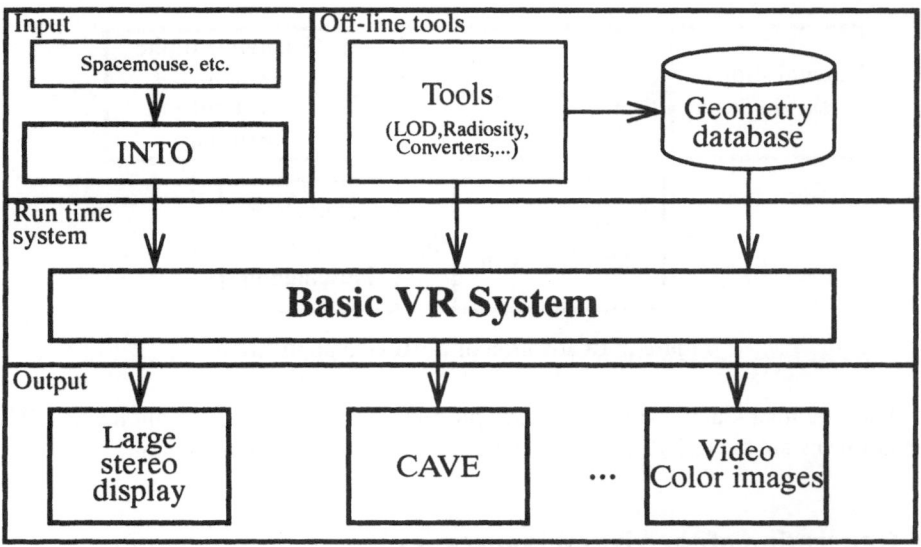

Figure 1: System structure

The system consists of several modules to execute off-line and on-line tools. The tools were developed to filter the data, to tile the terrain data and the aerial photo texture, to generate LODs of the terrain data and to map the texture data onto the terrain data automatically.

The interaction toolkit allows the integration of several VR input devices. We are mainly using a 6D spacemouse and function keys. In addition we have tested interaction using a data glove and voice input in combination with the CAVE projection. As output devices we are using large screen stereo projection and for testing purpose the CAVE system.

3 VR Geo system

The VR Geo system is a system to plan projects for the redevelopment of landscape and to visualize several planning processes interactively and in an immersive way using VR technology.

Actually two projects have been realized applying the system. In the first project the current and the planned state of the landscape had to be integrated into the system. In the second project the ancient state (year 1949) of another landscape, the current state and the planned state had to be realized.

As described in the previous chapter, the system contains of several modules. Some of these modules were developed specially for the VR Geo system. Other modules were implemented by adopting existing modules.

Applying the whole system the realization of a certain redevelopment project can be divided in five tasks (see Figure 2):

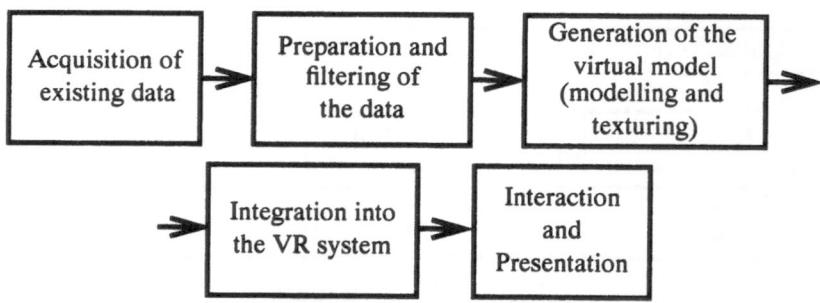

Figure 2: Realization of a VR Geo application

Tasks number 4 and 5 are well-known procedures in realizing a VR application. The major tasks are the tasks 1., 2. and 3. and will be described in more detail.

4 Generation of the virtual landscapes

4.1 Acquisition of existing data

The original data comprised 2D maps, color images, digital terrain data and digital height maps of the landscape. Furthermore detailed reports of the redevelopment projects were available. The first steps were to get an overview of all collected data, to sort out all the data which are not suitable for the project and to see if there is a sufficient amount of maps and photos for all the objects to be generated. To get an better impression of the landscape and to take missing pictures we visited both regions.

The next step was the generation of a digital representation of the landscape based upon the very detailed height map. To get a realistic impression of the landscape the 3D model had to be textured with digitized aerial photographs.

Then additional objects, like buildings or dumps, had to be modeled and integrated into the scene. For this modelling task we used plans, maps, CAD-data, photographs as well as textual informations. The textures for the objects were obtained by digitizing aerial photographs, photographs and from texture libraries.

The generation of the objects was split up in two parts. First of all the 3D geometry was generated. Then all the materials were defined and the geometry was textured.

For the modeling of the 3D geometries (houses, streets, dumps, etc.) two commercial tools had been applied. For the generation of the landscape special software tools had been developed.

Genesis 2, a tool developed by Fraunhofer IGD [2] had been used for the preparation of the models for the VR system (building up the scene hierarchy, applying object materials, mapping textures, light simulation).

4.2 Modeling and texturing of the landscapes

For the conversion of the height maps into a 3D model of the landscape a special converter has been developed. The height maps consisted of ASCII-Files with xyz-data. These data files consist of three or five values per 3D point. The first three values defined the coordinates and the height of the point. The next two values contained organizational data and were not evaluated by the converter. Due to the high resolution of the height data, the triangulation process resulted in more than 240.000 triangles for the digital 3D model of the landscape. This model was far to complex for real-time rendering. To reduce the complexity and to be able to use level of detail techniques, the model was first divided into tiles and than reduced using an algorithm developed by William Schroeder [3] (see Figure 3). The subdivision of the landscape into tiles gives us the possibility to use culling techniques to gain rendering speed.

The points at the edges of the tiles were not changed so that all the tiles will fit seamless with their neighbors, even if another level of detail is used. For the realized application the generation of two different levels of detail was sufficient (14.000 and 38.000 triangles).

Another advantage of the tiling was the possibility to use high resolution textures. The texture size of the high end workstation we are using is limited to 2048 by 2048 pixels. The textures also should have a size of 2^n x 2^m. So the aerial map had to be split to smaller images according to the

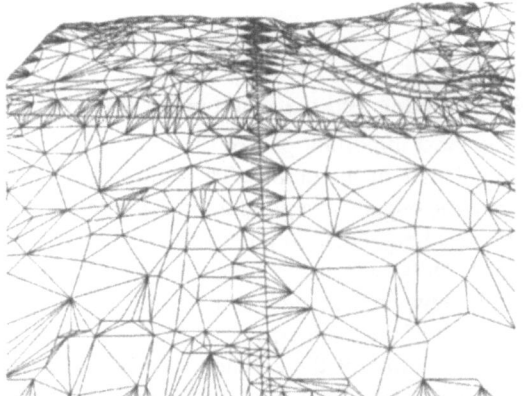

Figure 3: The tiled and reduced landscape (Courtesy of Wismut GmbH)

tiles of the landscape. A special tool was developed to automatically split the large textures into smaller textures fitting the tiles of the landscape and to texture these tiles. During this process the textures were scaled to 2^n x 2^m.

The available aerial photographs were greyscale images. Therefor we had to color the greyscale pictures to get a more realistic impression of the landscape. Only for the ancient state (about 1949) of the second landscape the greyscale images were used. In the ancient model also all additional objects were textured using greyscale textures to achieve the impression of viewing an old greyscale movie.

Due to the fact that most of the regions in the aerial photograph were structured (fields, streets, rivers, forests, etc.), the coloring had to be done manualy. The result of this process was a structured color image. This color image then was combined with the greyscale aerial photograph to get the colors as well as the details of the regions.

Because of the size and the complexity of the aerial image for the second project only a part of the image was colored manualy (see Figure 4 - Colorplate Lutz/Ziegler Figure 1). We managed to get an colored aerial photo, which then was used to texture the landscape (see Figure 5 - Colorplate Lutz/Ziegler Figure 2).

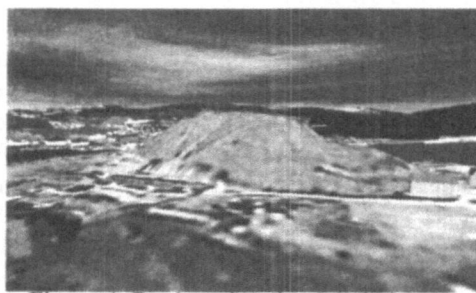 

Figure 4: Partly colored geyscale image (Courtesy of Wismut GmbH) Figure 5: Color image (Courtesy of Wismut GmbH)

4.3 Modeling and texturing of the dumps

The most important part of the project was the modeling of the actual state and the planned state of the dumps. The dumps had to be modeled very accurate and detailed to give the engineers a good impression of the dimension of the dumps.

The 3D height data of the landscape already contained the actual state of most of the dumps. Only two of the actual dumps had to be modeled in addition. To be able to switch between the actual and the planned state of the dumps the actual dumps had to be cut out of the landscape.

The modeling of the planned state was based on plans. An important aspect of the modeling was to get a very good impression of the berms, the pathes and the plants. Therefore special textures were generated for the gras, the pathes and the trees to match the planned planting.

Firstly we scanned the plans of the dump and used this scan as an underlay for the modeling process. The outlines of the dumps and of the berms and ways were traced using the underlaying image and the height information in the plans. A compromise had to be made between the accuracy of the tracing and the complexity of the resulting object. Then the generated lines were used to create the surface of the dump and the ways. If possible these models were compared with the existing 3D geometry of the dump and if necessary, the models were changed.

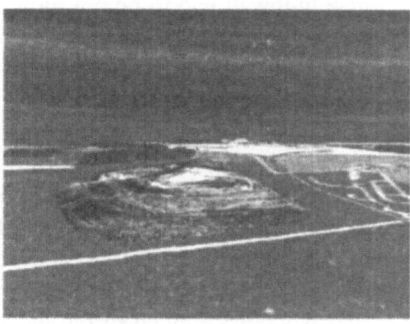 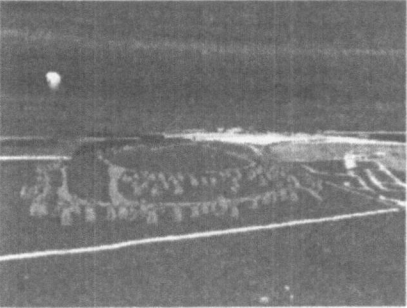

Figure 6: Dump Beerwalde (current state)　Figure 7: Dump Beerwalde (planned state)
(Courtesy of Wismut GmbH)　　　　　　(Courtesy of Wismut GmbH)

Another important aspect was the planned planting for the dumps. In some regions existing woods should be preserved, in others new trees and bushes will be planted. For that reason trees and bushes were placed on the dumps according to the plans.

Figure 6 (Colorplate Lutz/Ziegler Figure 3) and Figure 7 (Colorplate Lutz/Ziegler Figure 4) show one of the dumps with ways and trees in the current and the planned state.

4.4 Modeling and texturing of additional objects

To get an realistic impression of the whole landscape and to give the user additional hints for his orientation, additional objects have been modelled. All the pits and the company buildings were modelled, as well as most of the buildings in the villages nearby. To achieve the right position, size and form of the buildings the aerial photographs as well as maps and additional photographs were used. Because of the huge amount of buildings most of them were modelled very simple and just colored according to the images. However, to increase the realistic impression and to guarantee the re-perceptibility of important buildings they were modeled very detailed. The textures for these buildings were created using photographs.

The second project includes more than 500 simple buildings and 8 detailed spots, such as pits or a church, with about 60 textured buildings.

Beside buildings and trees, a river, railway lines and some important streets also had to be included. For the river, the contours of the river were traced according to the aerial photograph and then the river was integrated into the landscape.

110

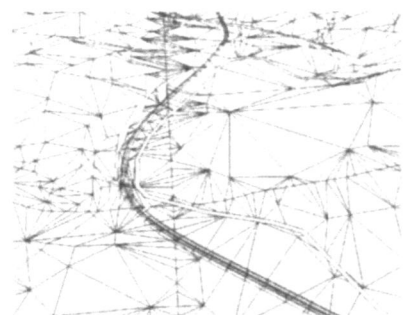

Figure 8: Wireframe image of the landscape
(Courtesy of Wismut GmbH)

The railway lines as well as the location line for the trucks and a part of a new highway had to be put on top of the landscape. The problem was to model these objects so that they follow the contours of the landscape. We used a 3D modelling system to generate a freeform model of the railway line. This model than was deformed by the surface of the landscape. Than the freeform model was converted into a faceted model.The same process has been applied to the location line for the trucks and the highway.

In Figure 8 a wireframe image of the landscape with the railway line and the river is shown.

To overcome the ficitiousness of virtual environments and to get a better depth perception fog was integrated to simulate haze.

4.5 Interaction and presentation

Virtual Design II, the VR system developed by Fraunhofer IGD [1] was applied for the real-time presentation.

To change between the ancient, the actual and the planned state different interaction mechanism have been realized.

Figure 9: Current state
(Courtesy of Wismut GmbH)

Figure 10: In construction
(Courtesy of Wismut GmbH)

Figure 11: Planned state
(Courtesy of Wismut GmbH)

In the first redevelopment project, the whole process of the landscape reconstruction has been presented. Starting with the current state of the dumps (Figure 9 - Colorplate Lutz/Ziegler Figure 5), one could see the leveling of one of the dumps, the construction of a street for the trucks (Figure 10 - Colorplate Lutz/Ziegler Figure 6), a truck transporting material from one dump to the other leaving an empty space (Figure 11 - Colorplate Lutz/Ziegler Figure 7). The transported material will be used for the extension of another dump. When the dump is removed the construction line will also be removed and the other dump will be planted (Figure 7 - Colorplate Lutz/Ziegler Figure 4).

In the second redevelopment project the ancient (Figure 12), the actual (Figure 13 / Colorplate 8) and the planned landscapes (Figure 14 - Colorplate Lutz/Ziegler Figure 9) have been realized. This landscape contains much more details; three dumps, a dam and its water basin, a huge amount of buildings, streets, a retaining wall, a house colony and a planned spa garden.

Figure 12: Ancient landscape
(Courtesy of Wismut GmbH)

Figure 13: Actual landscape
(Courtesy of Wismut GmbH)

Figure 14: Planned landscape
(Courtesy of Wismut GmbH)

The user can move around the scene in different ways. First it is possible to navigate freely using the mouse or the spacemouse. Then he can "jump" directly to different viewpoints and see the landscape in the different states. Also some animation pathes were defined. It is possible to sit in one of the trucks moving from one dump to the other

5 Results and Future Work

The realized VR Geo system enables the engineers to prepare their original data (converter, tiling tool, texture mapping tool, etc.) and to model landscapes and additional objects. Furthermore VR Geo provides an interactive visualization system and a VR system to interact and to present the planning results in an immersive way. Even the very complex scene with over 60.000 triangles and 40 MB of textures can be presented on a low end graphic workstation with a frame rate of 5 - 10 frames per second.

The system has been integrated into the daily work of the engineers to support them in planning redevelopment projects. They use it to present the results and to discuss them with colleagues and decision-maker. Furthermore they generate high quality video and color images for presentation and documentation. Wismut is planning to present the redevelopment projects at the EXPO 2000 using the VR Geo system.

Several extensions of the system have been discussed. For example the integration of an object data base to be able to visualize different variations of the planned landscape. A visualization of the measurement data of the contaminated ground superimposed to the landscape would be possible. Furthermore the engineers require additional modeling functionality. This can be described, more or less, as a feature based modeling technique of the landscape. For instance changing the shape of a dump interactively without changing the overall volume.

Figure 15: Spa garden, actual state (Courtesy of Wismut GmbH) Figure 16: Spa garden, planned state (Courtesy of Wismut GmbH)

6 Acknowledgment

The presented work is the result of a project funded by the Wismut GmbH. Without the help and cooperation of the responsible engineers the successful realization of the system and the two projects would not have been achieved. In particular we thank Dr. Haase, Stefan Knopf and Manfred Hauschild.

Furthermore we thank our colleagues and students who implemented the tools and modelled parts of the virtual landscapes. In alphabetical order this is:

Christian Knöpfle, Henry Kohtz, Claudia Pilo, Matthias Unbescheiden, Mike Weintke.

7 References

[1] Astheimer, P., Dai, F., Felger, W., Göbel, M., Haase, H., Müller, S., Ziegler, R.: "Virtual Design II - An Advanced VR System for Industrial Applications.", In Proc. Virtual Reality World '95, Stuttgart, Februray 1995.

[2] Müller, S., Schöffel, F., Gatenby, N., Grosch, T., Krake, S., Kresse, W., Liesenfeld, O., Pomi, A., Reiners, D., Unbescheiden, M.: "Genesis Manual Version 2.4", 1997.

[3] William Schroeder et al.:"Decimation of Triangle Meshes", SIGGRAPH92, pp. 65-69.

[4] Gatzweiler, R., Marski, R.: "Haldensanierung - eine interdisziplinäre Herausforderung", In Geowissenschaften, Nr. 11, 14.Jahrgang, 1996, pp. 461 - 465.

Editors' Note: see Appendix, p. 331 f. for colored figures of this paper

Design of A Virtual Environment That Employs Attention-Driven Interaction and Prioritization

Doreen Y. Cheng
Philips Multimedia Center
1070 Arastradero Rd
Palo Alto, CA 94304-1336 USA
dcheng@pmc.philips.com

This paper presents the design of a virtual environment that enhances immersive feeling and provides natural interaction experience while reducing resource requirements. The enabling mechanism is encapsulated in an attention model, its interaction control engine, and attention-driven object prioritization. Attention for a particular sense is modeled using an attention space that comprises attention cones and attention vectors. The model applies to multiple senses such as sight and hearing. The interaction control engine accounts for sensing, focusing, drift and lock-in phases of attention, and allows users to interact with avatar and non-avatar objects through gaze intermixed with explicit activation of interaction-control UI objects. The priority computation first generates basic priorities using the attention model. It can then selectively take into account participants' profiles, needs raised from social interaction, the cost structure of an application, and specification from content development. As a result, it generates higher priorities for the objects that are more important to the user and to the application. The priorities can be used to determine which objects to be communicated over the network at which levels of quality and to determine which objects to render at which levels of quality. This in turn may increase scalability of the system in addition to enhancing immersive and natural user experience in virtual environments.

1 Introduction

Multimedia virtual environments have been used for social interaction [1,2,3]. However, they provide limited support for it. For example, interaction between users is usually text based, avatars' very limited facial expressions and body gestures in 3D worlds usually bear little relationship to the social context of communication. In case of pair-wise interaction in a group social setting, text chat messages from all participants are displayed in the same screen area. As a result, messages often appear out of context and confusing. In some environments, two interacting partners must leave the group and go to a place like private chat rooms for less confusing communication. Supporting gesture, facial expression, and believable multi-modal human-figure animation in virtual worlds is expected to dramatically increase computation and communication requirements, which will leave most consumers further behind due to inadequate computer and network access from their homes.

Prioritization schemes that determine which media objects should be sent over the network and rendered at the destinations, and the levels of quality at which an object should be sent and rendered can help to alleviate the problem. However, current priority schemes are mostly at network and operating system levels, and there is no convenient ways for applications to specify their requirements to the underlying systems and to the rendering engines. As a result, application intentions are often compromised. Some applications, e.g. [1, 2, 3,] use proximity sphere to cut off the objects that are too far away from the observing user's avatar. However, they do not account for the importance of an object to the user, and lack a uniform frame for computing priorities.

This paper describes the design of a virtual environment that addresses the above problems by employing *the attention model* [4] and *the attention-based object prioritization scheme* [5]. The priorities can then be passed to system software and rendering engines to enhance scalability. The rest of this paper will first introduce the attention model and the prioritization scheme, and then present the design of a virtual environment using these components.

2 The attention model

In the real world, social interaction can be a result of either *intentional* activation, e.g. shoulder tapping (waving good-bye) or be a consequence of *spontaneous* events, e.g. mutually locked (separated) gaze. The attention model and its interaction control engine are designed to support this interweaving intentional and spontaneous interaction in a virtual world. The model is based on extracting features from human attention that are important in conducting interaction yet simple enough to compute. This section describes the model and its associated interaction control engine.

2.1 Attention space

Attention for a particular sense (e.g. sight) is modeled using an *attention space* that comprises two subspaces: a *sense space* and a *focus space*. An avatar can have multiple attention spaces, one for each sense. Figure 1 shows an example of an attention space of avatar A.

Fig. 1: An example of an attention space

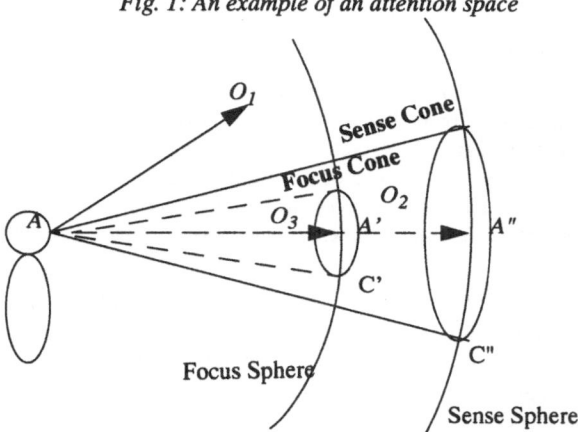

As shown in the figure, a sense space is bounded by a *sense sphere*, e.g. the sphere centered at point A with radius AA ". It is defined by a *sense cone* and a *sense vector*. The vertex of the cone shares the center of the sphere, A, and it is attached at a selected sensing point, e.g. the center of the avatars face or a camera point. The sense vector $\overline{AA}$" originates from the center of the sphere and is collinear with the axis of the cone. Its direction indicates the center of the attention and its length limits the distance within which attention can be directed.

A focus space is contained in a sense space. It is bounded by a *focus sphere*, e.g. the sphere centered at A with radius AA '. It is defined by a *focus cone* and a *focus vector*. The focus cone shares the vertex A and axis AA" with the enclosing sense cone. The focus vector $\overline{AA}$' is generally collinear with the sense vector $\overline{AA}$". Its direction defines the center of the focus and its length limits the distance within which attention can be focused. The angle of rotation of the focus (sense) cone, *C'AA' (C"AA")*, ranges from *0* to *180* degrees.

2.2 The sense condition and focus condition

The *sense condition* is evaluated to determine whether or not an object, e.g. *O*, is in an avatar's, e.g. *A's*, sense space, and therefore determines whether or not the avatar can perceive the signals emitted from the object. The sense condition computed using Equation (1) becomes true if the object is in the sense cone. In the example, avatar A can sense O_2 and O_3, but not O_1. In the equation, $|\overline{AO}|$ is the length of the vector connecting avatar A and object O, L_{as} and $\overline{u}_{as}$ are the length and the unit vector of the sense vector $\overline{AA}$", and C_{as} is the cosine of the angle of rotation of the sense cone.

$$(|\overline{AO}| < L_{as}) \, AND \, (\overline{AO} \bullet \bar{u}_{as} > C_{as} |AO|) \qquad (1)$$

The *focus condition* is evaluated to determine whether or not an object, e.g. O, is in an avatar's, e.g. A's, focus space, and therefore determines whether or not the avatar can spontaneously interact with the object. The focus condition computed using Equation 2 becomes true if the object is in the focus cone. For example, avatar A in Figure 1 can interact with O_3 but not with O_2 and O_1. In the equation, L_{af} and $\bar{u}_{af}$ are the length and the unit vector of the focus vector $\overline{AA}'$, and C_{af} is the cosine of the angle of rotation of the focus cone. *Mutual gaze* between A and B is established when the focus condition is true for both AB and BA.

$$(|\overline{AO}| < L_{af}) \, AND \, (\overline{AO} \bullet \bar{u}_{af} > C_{af} |AO|) \qquad (2)$$

2.3 The interaction control engine

During interaction, participant's attention may shift. For example, a newly arrived avatar has requested attention from a participant. The participant can examine whether it is worthwhile to leave the current group and establish interaction with the new partner. A participant can also shift attention to a signal source, e.g. an explosion. Attention drift may or may not indicate the termination of an interaction. The interaction control engine accounts for this kind of *attention drift and lock-in* and therefore can make the experience more natural, especially in immersive virtual environments.

The interaction control engine implements a finite state machine with eight states as shown in Figure 2. Detailed state transitions are described in [4]. Only the main ones are described here. The unshaded states (*base, gazing, interacting,* and two *wait* states) are for interactions without attention drift. An avatar is not related to any other avatars when it is in the *base* state. When it has sent (received) an explicit invitation for interaction, it will go to the *wait* state waiting for the remote (local) user to grant attention. When two avatars have established mutual gaze, they will enter the *gazing* state. When either the waited attention grant is received or the mutual gaze lasted longer than the time threshold associated with the *gazing* state, the avatar goes to the *interacting* state. Explicitly ending attention will bring the avatar to the *base* state.

Fig. 2 The finite state machine for the interaction control engine

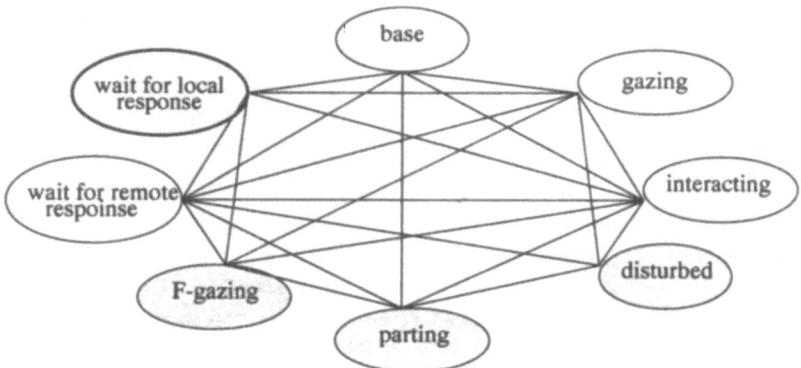

The three shaded states (*disturbed, parting,* and *F-gazing*) account for attention drift. When the mutual gaze fails due to an attention grabbing event, e.g. a tiger appears, the avatar will enter the *parting* state. If mutual gaze is reestablished before a timer associated with the *parting* state expires, the interaction continues. Otherwise, the avatar goes to the *base* state. When an interacting avatar receives an attention request from a third party, the avatar enters the *disturbed* state. If mutual gaze with a third party becomes true during attention drift, the avatar goes to the *F-gaze* state. In these states, if the user explicitly chooses to continue the original interaction, his avatar will return to the *interacting* state with the old partner. He can also choose to interact with the new partner and return to the *interacting* state. The time threshold in each of the states can be adjusted to create attention lock-in effect. For example, mutual gaze with the third party must last longer than the threshold of the *F-gazing* state for interaction with the new partner to occur. Otherwise, interaction with the old partner continues.

2.4 Third-person view

The attention model can be applied to both first and third person views. First person view enables a user to experience a virtual environment through the senses of his avatar (e.g., seeing the environment through the avatars' eyes). Third person view enables the user to experience a virtual environment at a selected sensing point, e.g., observing the avatars encounters, via a camera mounted at a selected point. When an attention space is applied in third-person view, the center of the sense sphere is attached to the sensing point and the semantics of other components may depend on the application. One scenario is to have the third-person-view sense space to enclose the first-person-view sense space, and to have the third-person-view focus vector to point at the avatar representing the user. Another scenario is to have the third-person-view focus vector to point at the avatar with which A is interacting. Users can dynamically change the parameters of these vectors using UI controls. These controls may be the same as the UI objects that control avatar movement and orientation.

2.5 Use the attention model for interaction

A user can modify the parameters of his attention spaces to express his interest in social interaction, e.g. he can set the sense cone large and focus cone small to sense around but be left alone, or he can set the focus cone large to be social. Group interaction can occur by including multiple avatars in one's focus cone. Users can use explicit controls to initiate pair-wise interaction within the group. Parameters for priority computation can be set to give a pair-wise interaction partner the highest priority, and to give group members priorities higher than objects outside the group (see Section 3.2). As a result, the user can perceive the signals from the group members better than non-group members while best perceiving the interacting partner. A user can join the group by moving into the focus space. A user can also use controls to ignore selected members. Consequently, each member of a group can have different participants in the group he interacts.

The attention-based interaction mechanisms also apply to objects other than avatars or the objects that are part of an avatar. If vision space is used to control interaction, when an avatar gazes at an object for long enough time, the gaze can trigger an on-behavior defined for the object. For example, when an avatar has gazed at a door for long enough time, the door opens and the objects behind the door become visible. If an avatar has gazed at a picture for long enough time and the picture is a link, the content (e.g. a web page) will be fetched and displayed. Application developers can also choose to activate a different behavior based on different duration of the gaze. For example, if the gaze at a dog lasts long enough the dog starts barking happily and wagging its tail. If the user continue to gaze at the dog for a time period longer than a second threshold, it starts rolling and running towards the user's avatar. Similarly when the gaze moves away from the object and stays away for long enough time, the off-behavior defined for the object can be triggered. For example, the door closes, the dog barks in a sad tune and its tail falls.

3 Attention-based object prioritization

The goal of prioritizing objects in virtual environments is to enhance user experiences while lowering computation and communication requirements. To achieve this, the computation assigns higher priorities to the objects closer to an avatar's center of attention. For this reason, the computation divides a sense sphere into regions, and assigns a priority number to each region. Higher priorities are assigned to the regions that are closer to the center of the sense sphere and closer to the sense vector. The priority of an object is the same as the priority of the region it resides. The division can be done along either or both radial and angular dimensions. Each dimension can be divided either linearly or nonlinearly. The priority numbers assigned can then be modified using selected factors such as participants' profiles, social interaction, economic cost structures, and specification in content. For an application intended to facilitate social interaction, the computation guarantees that the object with which the avatar is interacting will have the highest priority, and the objects in an interacting group will have priorities higher than those outside the group. More details of the computation can be found in [5]. A summary is provided here.

Table 1: Ways of dividing a sense sphere into priority regions

	radial dimension	angular dimension
linear division	R: $P_r = D / d$	A: $P_\alpha = cos^{-1}\beta / \alpha$
non-linear division	R^2: $P_{r2} = D^2 / d_2$	C: $P_c = (1 - cos\beta) / c$

3.1 The basic computation

The basic priority computation is based on sense sphere division. Table 1 shows the computation of the priorities. The symbols before ':' are for easy reference to the division. Smaller priority numbers (P in the table) correspond to higher priorities. The subscripts indicate the method of division. D is the distance between the guest avatar and the local avatar and d and d_2 are the units used to divide the sense sphere in radial dimension. β is the angle formed by the guest avatar with respect to the local avatar's sense vector, e.g. *angle O_lAA"* in Figure 1, and α and c are the dividing constants.

An application can choose from four possible ways (R, R^2, A, or C) to divide a sense sphere along a single dimension, and can choose from four possible ways (RA, RC, R^2A, or R^2C) to divide the sphere in both dimensions. Among the latter choices, R^2C follows more closely the physics of senses such as vision and hearing, and omputes more efficiently. When a sense sphere is divided in both dimensions, the composite priority number is a weighted sum of the numbers in each dimension, e.g. in case of R^2C, the result is given by Equation (3), where non-negative valued w_r (w_a) is the weight for the contribution from radial (ngular) dimension.

$$P = w_r P_{r2} + w_a P_c \qquad (3)$$

Computing priorities for objects of different media types can use attention spaces for different senses, e.g. vision spaces for video objects and hearing spaces for audio objects. Different attention spaces for different senses can have different parameters. The radius of the sense (focus) sphere and the angle of rotation of the sense (focus) cone can be adjusted to reflect the perception range of the sense (focus). Sensitivity to the direction of attention vectors can also be adjusted to create desired effect. For example, an application can decide that vision is sensitive to the orientation of eyes, whereas hearing is not so sensitive to the orientation of the ears. As a result, a vision cone only covers a smaller portion of the vision sphere and a hearing sense cone covers most or entire hearing sense sphere.

In order to be able to modify basic priorities in a flexible fashion, objects in a virtual environment are classified to be source objects or media objects. Source objects are those with which a user can interact (e.g. avatars, TVs). Media objects are those that stimulate users' sensors when rendered (e.g. animation files, video streams). In other words, a virtual environment comprises source objects and a user perceives them through associated media objects. A source object can have one or more associated media objects. Source objects are denoted using capital letters, e.g. A, and media objects are represented using an extension ".m" to its source object. When a single attention space is used for priority computation, the basic priorities of a media object is the same as its source object. When multiple attention spaces of different senses are used in the computation, all media objects of the same type have the same priority as their source object in the corresponding attention space.

The output of the basic computation takes the form of a list: {type-of-division $(A_i.m_l\ p_{il})^*$ $(A_j$ $p_j)^*$}, where type-of-division takes the value R, R^2, A, C, RA, RC, R^2A, or R^2C. A_j represents a source object and p_j is the priority number for all its media objects. $A_i.m_l$ represents a media object m_l associated with the source object A_i, and p_{il} is its priority number.

3.2 Modifying the basic priorities

The basic priorities can be modified by various factors. An application can choose to use none, some, or all of the modifiers. It can also adjust the weights to create desired effect.

User profiles. Object priorities can be modified based on user profiles. Let Wanted = {(W_i, $w_i)^*$} be a list of objects W_i that the user likes to the degree of w_i and Unwanted = {(U_j, $u_j)^*$} be a list of objects U_j that the user dislikes to the degree of u_j. In the lists w_i and u_j are referred to as *blocking factors* and they have positive values. When W_i (U_j) is a source object, the blocking factor applies to all of its media objects. When it is a media object, the blocking factor applies only to the object. Words and phrases can also appear in these lists. They are referred to as *concept objects* and can be used for content-based rendering.

For priority computation, the Wanted and Unwanted lists are merged into a single profile list, Profile = {(A_j, $b_j)^*$ $(A_i.m_l$, $b_i)^*$}, where A is either a source object or a concept object and $A.m$ is a media object associated with source object A. The blocking factor b is -w if the object is in the Wanted list, and u if it is in the Unwanted list. If an object appears in both lists, b is u-w. When an object A_k in the Profile list also appears in the output list of priority computation as A_i, its priority can be modified as p_j +b_k in favor of objects in the Wanted list (p_j - b_k in favor of objects in the Unwanted list).

Matching interests. Avatar priorities can be modified by similarity between profiles of two users. Similarity between the local user A and visitor B, sim_{AB}, is computed in following steps.

- Compute the union of the objects in the profile of A and the objects in the profiles of all users in consideration, U_A = {($O_i)^*$}.
- Construct the profile vector $\overline{V}_A$ for A. If O_i in U_A is also in A's profile, the value of the vector component is the blocking factor for O_i. Otherwise the value is 0.
- Similarly, construct a profile vector $\overline{V}_B$ for B.
- Calculate the similarity between A and B by computing $cos\theta$ of vectors $\overline{V}_A$ and $\overline{V}_B$. sim_{AB} = ($\overline{V}_A \cdot \overline{V}_B$) / $|\overline{V}_A|\ |\overline{V}_B|$, where '.' is dot product and $|\ |$ is the size of the vector.

The values of similarity runs from -1 (opposite profiles) to 1 (identical profiles). To increase the priority of an avatar B whose user shares more interests with A, B's priority can be modified as $p_B = p_B - w_s s_{sim} sim_{AB}$, where $w_s > 0$ is the weight and s_{sim} is a positive scaling factor to bring the value of similarity to the range of priority values. To decrease B's priority. $p_B = p_B + w_s s_{sim} sim_{AB}$ can be used. When profiles are available for objects other than users, e.g. TV channels, similarity can also be computed and used to degrade or enhance the rendering quality of the media objects.

Since the accuracy of similarity is not critical in many applications, old similarity values may be used when computation resources are tight. Old union can also be used to compute similarities. The union and/or similarities can be updated when resources become available later. To reduce the computation, union can be computed over only the users who has recently presented in the local user's attention space, instead of all users who have visited.

Interaction. A sense cone can be used to exclude objects outside the core since the user cannot sense them. A focus cone can be used to increase the priorities of the enclosed objects. If interaction is important in an application, it can be ensured that the object with which the user is interacting receives the highest priority. Based on Equation (3), Equation (4) shows the result, where P_f is the priority for the regions within the focus cone and M_{max} is the maximum modifier. If an application chooses to use all modifiers, M_{max} can be expressed as $M_{max} = M_r + M_c + M_w + M_s$, where M_r is the maximum priority number that can be generated from dividing the radial dimension, M_c is the maximum priority number that can be generated from dividing the angular dimension, M_w is the maximum blocking factor that can be specified in user profiles, and M_s is the maximum modifying factor from similarity measure.

$$P = w_d P_{r2} + w_a P_c - w_f P_f - M_{max} \qquad (4)$$

Cost structure. An application may have a cost structure that allows information providers (e.g. ad agencies) to raise the priority of their information sources. On the other hand, it can also allow information consumers to pay more to increase their blocking power. Let's assume that the cost structure provides n levels of pricing, represented by two lists: $\{c_1, c_2, \dots c_n\}$ and $\{e_1, e_2, \dots e_n\}$, where c and e are monotonically increasing positive numbers. The first list is used to assign a c to an information source based on how much the provider has paid for advertising it; the more a provider pays, the higher the value of c. The second list is used to assign an e to a user; the more the user pays, the larger the value of e. Typically, the values of c are much larger than the values of e.

For information providers, $-c$ becomes the initial priority of the information source or media objects. An application can have an initial priority, e.g. c_k, $(1 <= k <= n)$ be higher than the highest blocking factor any user can have without paying. For information consumers, the blocking factors can be multiplied by e before being used in priority modification. For example, $e=1$ results in the use of the base factors, $e=1.2$ increases the user's blocking factors by 20%, and $e_1=0$ makes users to pay if they want any blocking power at all.

Specification in content. Sometimes, content developers may need to give different priorities to different media objects associated with the same source object. For instance, when a robot is designed to talk, play music, and move with mechanical noises at the same time, the author may want to indicate that talking takes precedence over music, mechanical noise, and animation. This kind of needs can be taken care of by allowing developers to specify relationships between media objects of the same source object. In the robot example, the author can specify, for instance, the robot's speech is twice more important than mechanical sound, 4 times important than music, and 3 time more important than animation. If the robot's entry in the R^2C structure is *(R p_R)*, The priority of mechanical sound becomes *0.5 p_R*, the priority of music becomes *0.25p_R*, and the priority of animation becomes *0.33p_R*. After the modification, the entry is replaced by *(R.speech p_R) (R.mech 0.5 p_R) (R.music 0.25p_R) (R.animation 0.33p_R)*.

3.3 The final output

The final output of the priority computation contains one or more of the following structures, A concept profile can be used for content-based rendering, where O_i represents words or phrases and b_i is the corresponding blocking factor assigned to the concept. One scenario is that when b_i is positive, the strength and quality of the signal relevant to the concept will be reduced, and they will be enhanced when b_i is negative. The raw structure contains data that can be used for generating 3D sound, where R_i is the distance between object A_i and avatar A, $\bar{u}_i$ is the unit focus vector of A_i, β is the angle between vector $\overline{AA_i}$ and $\bar{u}_i$.

- Priority structures: $\{$*type-of-division* $\{(A_i.m_l p_{il})^*\}\}$
- Concept profiles: $\{$CON $(O_i, b_i)^*\}$
- A raw structure: $\{$RAW $(A_i, R_i, \cos\beta_i, \sin\beta_i, \bar{u}_i)\}$

3.4 Sample usage of priorities

As an example of the usage of priorities, Figure 3 shows five avatars in avatar A's attention sphere. A_3 and A_5 are in A's gaze cone, A_1, A_2, A_3 and A_5, are in A's vision cone. A and A_3 are interacting (as depict by the double-arrow line). In the calculation, the radial dimension of the sense sphere is divided into three regions and the angular dimension is divide into 8 regions. The composite priority is $\{R^2C (A_1$ 2$) (A_2$ 3$) (A_3$ -10$) (A_4$ 6$) (A_5$ 1$)\}$, where the numbers are truncated into integers, and smaller values mean higher priorities. The priorities are computed using $d_2 = r^2/3$ (*r* is the radius of the sense sphere.) and *c = 0.25* (see Table 1).

Fig. 3 An example of avatars in relation with avatar A's attention space

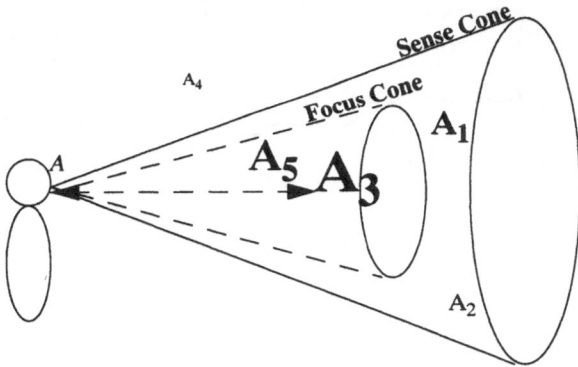

For a four-level animation, *A*'s vision cone is first used to eliminate the avatars that are outside (A_4). The remaining structure sorted by decreasing priority, $\{R2C (A_3$ -10$) (A_5$ 1$) (A_1$ 2$) (A_2$ 3$)\}$, is then used to guide rendering. The most detailed animation, level 4, is assigned to avatar A_3, level 3 for A_5, level 2 for A_1, and the least detailed level is assigned to A_2. For audio, the sense cone in this example encompasses entire sense sphere, i.e. all sound sources in the sphere are perceivable and the amplitude is attenuated 3dB every time the priority decreases by 1. While A_3's signals are not attenuated, signals from A_1, A_2, A_4, A_5 are attenuated by 36dB 39dB, 48dB, 33dB accordingly. This example shows that parameters can be adjusted so that the user can perceive the signals from the group members (A_3 and A_5) better than the signals from non-group members (A_1 and A_2) while perceiving the signals from the interacting partner (A_3) the best. As a result, experience in interaction can be more natural.

4 The architecture

As shown in Figure 4, the algorithms described above are encapsulated in three components: *the attention module, the interaction control engine,* and *the prioritization module* as highlighted boxes. Each component has related UI objects. UI objects for the attention module enable users to examine and modify the parameters of their attention spaces (e.g. the length of the sense and focus vectors and the angle of rotation of the sense and focus cones). UI objects for the interaction control engine give means for users to intentionally initiate and terminate interaction. They also allow users to change the parameters that control interaction, e.g. time tolerances to create attention drift and lock-in effect. UI objects for prioritization module enable users to tune the parameters used in the computation, e.g. relative importance of social interaction, user profiles, cost structures, etc. Users can also use these UI objects to specify their interests and assign priorities directly to objects. Data of longer-term use is stored in the *user info*, e.g. preferences of the local user and profiles of users who have recently visited the local user's attention spaces (Section 3.2). Inclusion of non-avatar objects in an avatar object in the world model illustrates that an avatar object can have non-avatar objects as parts, and another avatar can interact with these part objects.

Fig. 4 Architecture of a virtual environment using attention-guided interaction and object prioritization

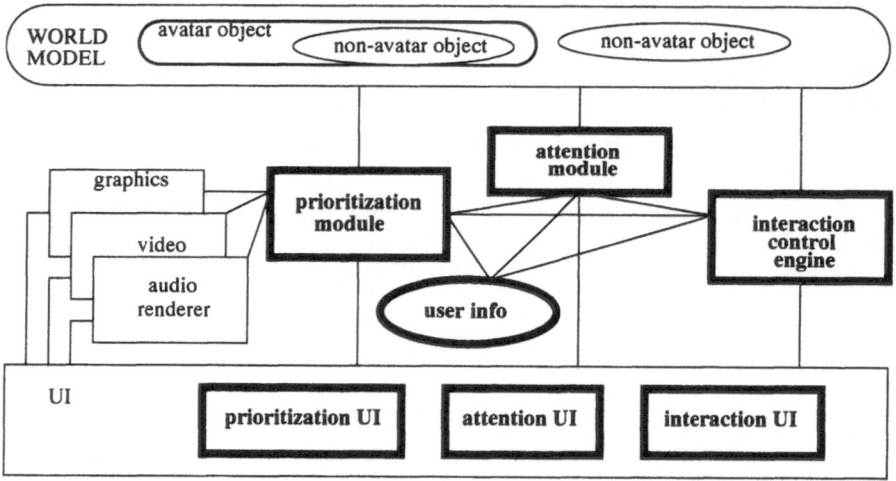

The attention module takes input from the world model, and evaluates whether a world object satisfies the sense condition and the focus condition of the local user's avatar. The results are communicated to the prioritization and interaction components. The interaction control engine implements a finite state machine. An avatar can be in one of eight states: *base, gazing, interacting, disturbed, parting, f-gazing,* and two *wait* states (see Section 2.3). A transition between states can be triggered by explicit user activation of relevant UI controls, by object position changes or avatar attention space changes, or by occurrence of attention grabbing events. The output of the interaction control engine can be used in priority computation and may change states of the objects in the world. Moreover, the output may trigger behaviors of objects defined for gaze-based interaction, e.g. a music box opens up and starts playing music.

The prioritization module computes priorities of world objects based on their relation with the attention spaces of the local user's avatar. It takes into account the modifying factors selected by an application developer and/or a user, and converts the results to a format acceptable to the next stage software. When applied to rendering and multiple senses are supported, the module sends the computation results with respect to a particular attention space to the corresponding rendering software. For example, it sends the results from auditory attention space to audio renderer and the results from vision space to video and graphics renderers. The application can also choose to use priority structures of different division types to guide different aspects of rendering of the same object. For example, it can use the priorities generated from the radial division to determine the resolution of a video object, and use the priorities generated from the angular division to determine the frame rate of the object, while using the composite priorities to decide which objects are to be rendered.

5 Conclusions

In summary, this paper has described the design of a virtual environment that uses an attention model and associated interaction-control engine to enable users to select partners, and to initiate, conduct, and terminate interactions. The model also enables avatars to interact with avatar or non-avatar objects through gaze. It accounts for sensing, focusing, drift and lock-in phases of attention, and can be applied to multiple senses including sight, hearing, and smell. The interaction control engine supports interweaving intentional and spontaneous interactions. As a result, the experience in the virtual world can be more natural.

The design also uses the attention model to guide the computation of object priorities. The computation can selectively take into account participants' profiles, needs raised from social interaction, the cost structure of an application, and specification from content development. It generates higher priorities for the objects that are more important and/or more interesting to the user and/or to the application. The priorities can be used in making the decision of which objects to be communicated over the network at which levels of quality, and the decision of which objects to be rendered at which levels of quality. In addition to increasing scalability, the attention-guided rendering may enhance immersive feelings.

References

1. http://www.activeworlds.com, Feb. 1998.
2. http://www.oz.com, Feb. 1998.
3. http://www.worldsawy.com/press, Feb. 1998.
4. D. Y. Cheng, "An Attention Model for Interactions and Object Prioritization in Virtual Environments", to be presented in the Computer Graphics Workshop of VRST, Nov. 1998.
5. D. Y. Cheng, "An Object Prioritization Scheme for Scalable Multimedia Data Communication and Rendering in Virtual Environments", Computer Graphics Workshop of VRST, Nov. 1998.

Acknowledgement

I would like to thank N. Ismail, P. da Costa, R. Allen, P. Verdonk, M. Schmitt, and P. Rankin of Philips for helpful discussions.

Navigation in real and virtual environments:
Judging orientation and distance in a large-scale landscape

H.K. Distler, H.A.H.C. Van Veen, S.J. Braun, W. Heinz, M.O. Franz & H.H. Bülthoff
Max-Planck-Institute for Biological Cybernetics
Spemannstraße 38, 72076 Tübingen, Germany

Abstract

Virtual environments (VE) provide an almost optimal setting for studying human navigation behaviour. The current study compares the ability of human subjects to judge the distance and orientation of places in a natural landscape and in its corresponding virtual 3D model. The results of the Euclidean distance judgements confirm that spatial knowledge acquired in VEs is less accurate than that acquired in the real world. However, distance judgements performed by subjects using a VRbicycle to actively move in the scene (active observer) were more accurate than those of subjects who were automatically driven through the landscape (passive observer). The accuracy of the orientation judgements was the same in both environments and independent of the use of the VRbicycle. The results suggest that the VRbicycle can facilitate the perception of spatial dimensions but that additional improvements of the man-machine interface of our VE are needed to improve the subjects' sense of orientation.

1 Introduction

1.1 Using virtual environments for studying human navigation behaviour

The introduction of 3D computer graphics and, more recently, virtual environments (VE) technology to the study of human perception and behaviour has provided scientists with the appropriate means to study complex human behaviour in laboratory settings. The enormous progress in high performance computing, projection technology, and man-machine interfaces in recent years, allows one to create highly realistic scenes with which the user can interact in real-time. Scientists investigating navigation and orientation behaviour in large-scale environments have been among the first to take advantage of VEs in their research (Darken, Sibert, 1993; May, Peruch, Savoyant, 1995; Distler, 1996; Peruch, Gaunet, 1997; Van Veen, Distler, Braun, Bülthoff, 1998). Until very recently most experiments studying human navigation behaviour in large-scale environments were performed in the natural environment (e.g. Okabe, Aoki, Hamamoto, 1986). Although the natural environment provides the optimal stimulation for the sensory systems it lacks experimental control. Given that navigation experiments often last one hour or longer, it is usually difficult to guarantee that all subjects perform the experiment under the same conditions. VEs, however, are simultaneously capable of providing multisensory simulation of complex environments and precise control over the experimental conditions.

Moreover, VEs facilitate the manipulation of various features of the simulated scene that cannot easily be accomplished in the real world. Examples are:

- changing the position, size and orientation of objects such as moving buildings in an urban environment
- modifying the appearance of objects by changing their colour, texture and shape
- adding and/or removing objects to/from the scene, e.g. roads, places, buildings
- manipulating the layout of the scene like changing the course of roads
- switching from one scene to another in a few milliseconds
- changing visibility conditions by manipulating the field of view, by introducing fog, or by changing the time of day
- adding and/or removing sensory cues to test the influence of a particular type of sensory information such as vestibular and auditory cues
- using different metaphors for subject interaction with the environment, e.g. subjects driving a car, riding a bicycle, walking or simply being driven around passively

To summarise, VEs provide scientists investigating human navigation behaviour with an experimental setting that enables them to perform their studies in naturalistic environments under well-controlled laboratory conditions.

1.2 Navigation in real and virtual worlds

One of several long-term projects in our laboratory studies human navigation and orientation behaviour (Gillner, Mallot, 1998; Van Veen, Distler, Braun, Bülthoff, 1998). So far, we have been using several artifical scenes for our navigation studies. "Hexatown", for instance, is an artificial town with a hexagonal roadmap which was designed specifically to study navigation behaviour (Gillner, Mallot, 1998). The question is whether the results obtained using such VEs can explain human navigation behaviour in natural environments. One way to test this is by performing the same experiment in parallel in the real and virtual world.

When performing comparative navigation studies we might learn that navigation behaviour in the real and virtual world is different. Although some people consider that as being a disadvantage, we think that we can actually learn something from such differences. By using the advanced features of VEs listed above, we can easily change several aspects of the virtual world in order to figure out which features of a VE are essential to obtain the same navigation behaviour as in the natural environment. Therefore, what initially might be considered as a negative result can turn out to be very instrumental in explaining navigation behaviour in natural and virtual environments.

Comparative studies of navigation behaviour have already been conducted in the context of applications that focus on the utilisation of VEs for familiarising people with unknown terrain. Such applications include terrain appreciation by soldiers (United States Army Research Institute for the Behavioural and Social Sciences, e.g., Singer, Allen, McDonald, Gildea, 1997) and training of fire-fighters (Bliss, Tidwell, Guest, 1997). The idea in the latter case is that fire-fighters learn the spatial layout of a complex building in a VE before they actually enter the real building in an emergency case. Bliss et al. (1997) could indeed show that some of the skills and knowledge acquired in the VE do transfer to the real world.

The results of these and other comparative studies (e.g., Witmer, Bailey, Knerr, 1996; Ruddle, Payne, Jones, 1997 based on Thorndyke, Hayes-Roth, 1982; Richardson, Montello, Hegarty, 1998; Waller, Hunt, Knapp, 1998) show that spatial knowledge acquired in VEs can be quite similar to that obtained in real world settings. However, in most cases it takes subjects in VEs longer to acquire spatial knowledge and the respective knowledge is often less accurate. This might be related to the fact that users of VEs (including the experts) obviously have much less experience with acquiring spatial knowledge in VEs than in natural environments. In the real world we can rely on highly trained and tuned strategies in processing sensory information to extract information about the environment, but we still have to develop those skills in VEs.

In general, the interaction between the human being and environment is rather different in real and virtual worlds. In most navigation experiments subjects performing in VEs barely change their physical position in the real world. Often subjects just use a computer mouse to navigate through the virtual environment, which means that proprioceptive and vestibular input are wrong or missing at all. Some studies make use of a treadmill (Darken, Carmein, 1997) or a virtual bicycle (current study) for simulating locomotion. Although these devices require the subjects to spend effort in order to move (proprioceptive input), they still do not provide any appropriate feedback for the vestibular system.

The question to answer is how a particular VE should to be designed so that navigation behaviour of subjects in the real and virtual world is identical. In this context Waller et al. have introduced the concept of fidelity which is '*the extent to which the VE and interactions with it are indistinguishable from the participant's observations of and interactions with a real environment*' (Waller, Hunt, Knapp, 1998). Waller et al. distinguish between environmental and interface fidelity factors. Environmental factors are those that define the resemblance between the virtual and the real world. For instance, a common approach to increase the environmental fidelity of virtual worlds is to use high-resolution texture maps. Environmental fidelity can also be improved by using information sources that are not available in the real world. For instance, Darken and Sibert (1996) have shown that adding a grid and/or a 'you are here map' to the VE considerably improved subjects navigation performance. Interface fidelity factors are responsible for the '*degree to which the input and output devices associated with the VE function similarly to the way in which the trainee would interact with the real world*' (Waller, Hunt, Knapp, 1998). In other words, interface fidelity factors are concerned about the suitability of input and output devices.

Yet, before we can optimise environmental and interface fidelity factors in VEs we need to know the differences between human behaviour in real and virtual worlds. As was pointed out above, one way to learn about these differences is by performing comparative studies of wayfinding in the real and virtual world. Depending on the nature of the differences subsequent experiments can vary environmental and interface fidelity factors in the VE in order to figure out which information has to be provided by the VE and how the particular information has to be mediated. This approach is relatively new and most studies so far, including the current one, are not matured to the stage where they can point at the most optimal design parameters for VEs. At this stage it is more feasible to try to identify which the important environmental and interface fidelity factors are.

2 Judging orientation and distance in a real and virtual landscape

2.1 Introduction

To test whether our simulation environment provides (1) sufficient and (2) appropriate information to guarantee proper acquisition of spatial knowledge in large-scale environments, the current study compares the ability of subjects to judge the distance and orientation of places in a natural and in its corresponding virtual environment. We pay special attention to the potential influence of interface fidelity factors such as field of view and movement type on the performance of subjects in our VE.

2.2 Experiment in the natural environment (NE)

In the course of the experiment the subjects were guided along a predefined path on a landscape on the Swabian Alb in the neighborhood of Blaubeuren, Germany (Fig. 1., top image). Although most of the landscape consisted of forest, it contained some open field areas as well. The forest prevents the subjects from getting a global overview of the area, whereas the open fields allow them to obtain some information about the structural layout of parts of the environment.

The subjects were driven by car to the starting point (S) of the experiment, which was located on the border of the forest. We told the subjects that the experiment was designed to study navigation and orientation behaviour, but we did not inform them about the task they had to complete during the experiment. That the subjects were not familiar with the purpose of the experiment is relevant, because it prevented them from selectively attending to information that could facilitate their orientation and distance judgements. Guided by the experimenter the subjects walked at a comfortable speed from the starting point (S) to the first control point (C1). Once they arrived at the first control point, each subject was separated from the group and was asked to judge the orientation and distance of the starting point. Subjects indicated the direction of the starting point by making a mark on the arc of a circle, which was drawn on a piece of paper. To perform their judgement subjects had to imagine themselves as being in the centre of the circle. The distance judgement task required the subjects to make verbal estimates of the Euclidean ('as the crow flies') distance. They were free to make the judgement in their preferred unit (m, km or miles) and with the accuracy that fitted their comfort. Having finished the task the subject was not allowed to join the other members of the group who had not yet delivered their judgements. After all subjects had finished the task, the group moved on to the second control point (C2), where the same procedure was repeated. At this place the subjects had to indicate the direction and distance of the starting point as well as the first control point.

Fig. 1.   Top image: Map of the landscape near Blaubeuren (Southwest Germany) where the experiment was conducted. The real world dimensions of the depicted area are approximately 3.5x2.5 km. S marks the starting point of the experiment, C1 and C2 are the respective control points. The black line shows the path along which the subjects were guided in the experiment. Bottom image: Screen snapshot of the 3D model of the area on the Swabian Alb. The small hut and the block to the left constitute the first control point (C1) where subjects had to judge the orientation and distance of the starting point (S).

2.3 Experiments in the virtual environment (VE)

Simulation environment

The experiments in the VE were performed in a large-scale simulation environment featuring a 3-pipe Silicon Graphics™ Onyx2 InfiniteReality, which computes highly detailed images of the virtual world (simulation environment I). These images are front-projected on a half-cylindrical projection screen by three Electrohome™ Marquee 8000 CRT-projectors (Fig. 2. , left; see Van Veen, Distler, Braun, Bülthoff, 1998). One condition of the experiment, designed to study the influence of field of view size on subject performance, was conducted in a small-scale version of the simulator (simulation environment II) using a Silicon Graphics™ Onyx RealityEngine2 and a smaller projection screen (Fig. 2. , right; see Distler, 1996).

The most important difference between the two simulation environments concerns the size of the field of view which is 180x50° in simulation environment I and 50x40° in simulation environment II. Additionally, subjects performing in simulation environment I wore active LCD-shutterglasses (Stereographics™) to enable stereoscopic viewing of the simulated scene. In both simulation environments subjects used a Virtual Bicycle (VRbicycle, CyberGear™) to move through the virtual world. The VRbicycle requires the subjects to actively steer and pedal (Distler, 1996). Simulations of going up- or downhill, or cycling on grounds with different friction coefficients are obtained by computer-controlled changes of the pedalling resistance.

Fig. 2. The photographs show two versions of the simulation environment we used in our experiment. Left image: simulation environment I, right image: simulation environment II. Note that the images that can be seen on the respective projection surfaces are not related to the current experiment.

Modelling the virtual landscape

To be able to perform the experiments in the VE we developed a 3D-computer graphics model of the landscape on the Swabian Alb (Fig. 1. , bottom image). The model encompassed the rectangular area of 3.5 by 2.5 km shown in the map (Fig. 1. , top image) and was designed such that subjects never saw the end of the simulated world. The trajectories of the roads and paths were modelled on the basis of a high-resolution map of the area. This map was scanned and the resulting image was mapped as a texture on a polygon sized to the real world dimensions of the map. Using a commercial 3D-modeller we manually fitted B-Splines to the trajectory of the paths. These B-Splines were subsequently converted into polygons by a purpose-developed software tool, which also filled the open space between the roads with polygons. The ground floor was manually textured using Medit™ Modeller. Since no commercial software tool was available which allowed us to position a large amount of trees in a 3D database we developed a software tool for building virtual forests. In its final version the database contained approximately 10.000 trees. Although this number appears to be relatively high, it constitutes only a fraction of the trees in the natural environment. In general, however, it was guaranteed that those parts of the terrain, which were occluded by trees in the natural environment were also occluded in the 3D model. Since the height differences in the natural environment were relatively small, we did not implement any height differences in the 3D model.

Experimental procedure in the VE

The subjects in the VE performed the same task as the subjects in the natural environment: they had to judge the orientation and Euclidean distance of the same places as in the real world. In addition, we also asked subjects to judge the distance

130

they actually traversed. Again, distance judgements were performed verbally. The influence of interface fidelity factors on subject performance was studied using four different conditions of the experiment in the VE (VE1-VE4):

- Field of view: The size of the subjects' field of view in VE1 was 50x40° and 180x50° in VE2-VE4.

- Instruction: Subjects performing in conditions VE1-VE2 did not receive any instructions, whereas in conditions VE3-VE4 they were informed about the purpose of the experiment before it started. Thus, subjects in these conditions could selectively attend to information of importance for orientation and distance estimates.

- Type of movement: In VE4 subjects were passively driven (passive observer) through the landscape, whereas in VE1-VE3 they had to pedal on the VRbicycle to move through the virtual world (active observer). We included this parameter to test whether the effort subjects spent on riding the bicycle improved their distance judgements and whether steering improved the quality of orientation estimates.

Condition VE1 was performed in simulation environment II, whereas the other conditions were conducted in simulation environment I. Eight subjects participated in each of the five conditions of the experiment. None of the subjects participated in more than one condition.

2.4 Results

The orientation estimates of the subjects were analysed using circular statistics (Batschelet, 1980). The distance judgements of the subjects will be presented as absolute and signed errors. The absolute error is a measure for the accuracy of the subjects distance judgements, whereas the signed error is useful to get an idea about the general direction (under- or overestimation) of the distance estimates.

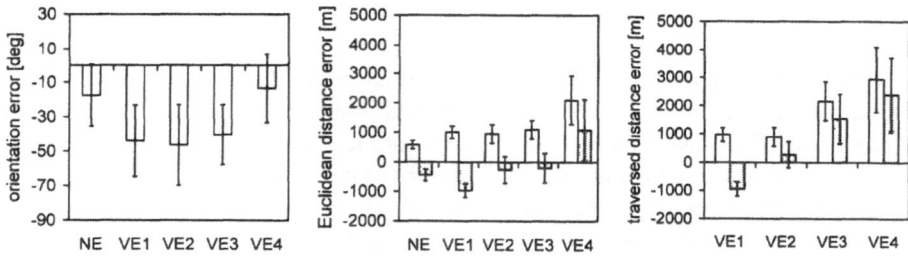

Fig. 3. The graphs depict the mean error of subjects' estimates of orientation (left graph), Euclidean distance (middle graph) and traversed distance (right graph) as a function of the experimental condition. Distance judgements are plotted as absolute (empty bars) and signed (filled bars) errors. Each bar constitutes the mean of 8 subjects, 3 orientation judgements per subject. The error bars correspond to one standard error of the mean.

Orientation judgements

Fig. 3. (left graph) depicts the mean error of the subjects' orientation estimates. There is no significant difference between the subjects accuracy in the NE and the four conditions performed in the VE. If we consider only the first three conditions of the VE it seems that the accuracy in the NE is slightly better. The results also show that there is no significant difference in the accuracy of the subjects' orientation judgements in the different VE conditions.

Euclidean distance judgements

It can be seen from the middle graph of Fig. 3. that the absolute error of the subjects' estimates of Euclidean distance in the NE is significantly smaller than the respective errors in the VE conditions. We found no significant difference for the instruction (VE2 vs. VE3) and the field of view (VE1 vs. VE2) conditions. However, we observed a significant effect of movement type on the subjects' judgements of Euclidean distance. The distance error made by subjects pedalling actively was significantly smaller than the error made by subjects driven passively (VE3 vs. VE4). The signed error reveals that subjects in condition VE4 (passive observers) overestimated the Euclidean distance, whereas in the other four conditions (active observers) they underestimated the distance.

Traversed distance judgements

The absolute and signed errors made by subjects when judging the traversed distance are plotted in the right graph of Fig. 3. . Note that the judgements of traversed distance were only performed in the VE conditions. It can be seen that field of view size has no significant influence on the accuracy of the subjects' estimates of traversed distance (VE1 vs. VE2). We furthermore found no significant difference between VE3 and VE4 indicating that the accuracy of distance judgements made by active observers was not better than that of passive observers. We did find a significant effect of instruction (VE2 vs. VE3). However, the effect is rather unexpected, since the distance estimates of the instructed subjects were less accurate.
The values of the signed error show that subjects underestimated the traversed distance in condition VE1, whereas they overestimated the distance in the other conditions.

2.5 Discussion

In general, the accuracy of subjects' estimates of orientation and distance is higher in the natural than in the virtual environment. This confirms the results of previous experiments comparing the acquisition of spatial knowledge in large-scale environments. However, whereas the difference is highly significant for the distance estimates, there is only a trend for the orientation judgements.
Although we expected that the larger field of view in conditions VE2-4 would increase the accuracy of subjects' judgements of distance and orientation, we did not find such an effect. This is somehow surprising, since previous results of real world

132

experiments (Alfano, Michel, 1990) have indicated that subject performance in several different tasks is improved by increasing the size of the field of view from 9° to 60°. This result might be task-dependent though. Whereas the reduced field of view in a navigation task might after a while be compensated by a change in the information processing strategy, the situation is somehow different when subjects have to avoid collisions with other objects or have to manoeuvre a difficult track. The latter behaviours require the availability of peripheral information and therefore the size of the field of view might be more critical in such tasks. Although we did not find a significant effect of field of view size on the accuracy of the distance judgements, a significant influence is obtained for the signed error of subjects' estimates of traversed distance.

Type of movement, the second interface fidelity factor considered, has a differentiated impact on the performance of subjects. Whereas active pedalling significantly improved the subjects' estimates of Euclidean distance, the effect was much less pronounced for the judgements of traversed distance. Active steering did not improve the accuracy of the subjects' orientation judgements. The results of a recent study by Chance, Gaunet, Beall, and Loomis (1998) indicate that orientation judgements in VEs are more accurate when visually simulated orientation changes are triggered by the subject actually performing the orientation change. By using the VRbicycle the subjects in our experiment have proprioceptive information (muscular effort) about their orientation changes, however, the subjects lack vestibular information.

3 Conclusion

Virtual environments provide scientists studying human navigation behaviour with the means to significantly facilitate and accelerate their research. The current article shows that performing comparative studies of navigation behaviour in the real and virtual world has a double benefit: First, comparative studies allow us to validate whether the results that we obtained in virtual worlds can explain navigation behaviour in the real world. Second, if it turns out that navigation behaviour is different in the real and virtual world, we can selectively change aspects of the virtual world in order to obtain the same navigation behaviour as in the real world and thus develop a better understanding of the mechanisms that drive navigation in general.

Our results suggest that the VRbicycle, which requires the subjects to actively steer and pedal facilitates the perception of spatial dimensions (distance) in a large-scale environment. However, the VRbicycle does not help to improve the sense of orientation in the VE. Thus, further changes of the man-machine interface in our virtual environment are required to provide subjects with a better sense of orientation.

Acknowledgement

We are grateful to Scott Yu for providing us the 3D model of our simulation environment (Fig. 2. , left image). Fig. 2. (right image) is reprinted with permission of the Deutsche Verlags-Anstalt GmbH, Redaktion Bild der Wissenschaft.

References

Alfano, P.L, Michel, G.E. (1990). Restricting the field of view: Perceptual and performance effects. Perceptual and Motor Skills, 70, 35-45

Batschelet, E. (1980). Einführung in die Mathematik für Biologen. [translation: Introductory Mathematics for Biologists] Springer Verlag, Berlin, Heidelberg.

Bliss, J.P., Tidwell, P.D., Guest, M.A. (1997). The effectiveness of virtual reality for administering spatial navigation training to firefighters. Presence, 6(1), 73-86

Chance, S.S., Gaunet, F., Beall, A.C. Loomis, J.M. (1998). Locomotion mode affects updating of objects encountered during travel: The contribution of vestibular and proprioceptive inputs to path integration. Presence, 7(2), 168-178

Darken, R.P, Sibert, J.L. (1993). A toolset for navigation in virtual environments. Proceedings of the ACM User Interface Software & Technology, 157-165

Darken, R.P, Sibert, J.L. (1996). Wayfinding strategies and behaviors in large virtual worlds. Proceedings of ACM SIGCHI 96, 142-149

Darken, R.P., Carmein, D. (1997). The omni-directional treadmill: A locomotion device for virtual worlds. Proceedings of UIST '97, 213-221

Distler, H.K. (1996). Psychophysical experiments in virtual environments. In: Virtual Reality World 96 Conference Documentation, München 1996: Computerwoche Verlag AG.

Gillner, S., Mallot, H. A. (1998). Navigation and acquisition of spatial knowledge in a virtual maze. Journal of Cognitive Neuroscience (in press). Also: Technical Report No. 45, 1997, Max-Planck-Institut für biologische Kybernetik, Tübingen.

May, M., Peruch, P., Savoyant, A. (1995). Navigating in a virtual environment with map-acquired knowledge: Encoding and alignment effects. Ecological Psychology, 7(1), 21-36

Okabe, A., Aoki, K., Hamamoto, W. (1986). Distance and direction judgement in a large-scale natural environment. Effects of slope and winding trail. Environment and Behaviour, 18(6), 755-772

Peruch, P., Gaunet, F. (1997). Virtual environments as a promising tool for investigating human spatial cognition. Accepted for publication in Current Psychology of Cognition.

Richardson, A.E., Montello, D.R., Hegarty, M. (1998). Spatial knowledge acquisition from maps, and from navigation in real and virtual environments. Submitted to Memory and Cognition

Ruddle, R.A., Payne, S.J., Jones, D.M. (1997). Navigating buildings in „Desk-Top" virtual environments: Experimental investigations using extended navigational experience. Journal of Experimental Psychology: Applied, 3, 143-159

Singer, M.J., Allen, R.C., McDonald, D.P., Gildea, J.P. (1997). Terrain Appreciation in virtual environments: Spatial knowledge acquisition. Technical Report 1056, United States Army Research Institute for the Behavioral and Social Sciences.

Thorndyke, P.W., Hayes-Roth, B. (1982). Differences in spatial knowledge acquired from maps and navigation. Cognitive Psychology, 14, 560-589

Van Veen, H.A.H.C, Distler, H.K., Braun, S.J., Bülthoff, H.H. (1998). Navigating through a virtual city: Using virtual reality technology to study human action and perception. Accepted for publication in Future Generation Computer Systems.

Waller, D., Hunt, E., Knapp, D. (1998). The transfer of spatial knowledge in virtual environment training. Presence, 7(2), 129-143

Witmer, B.G., Bailey, J.H., Knerr, B.W. (1996). Virtual spaces and real world places: Transfer of route knowledge. International Journal of Human-Computer Studies, 45, 413-428

Analyzing draft tube characteristics for hydraulic turbines in a VR environment

R. Eisinger[1], E. Göde[1], D. Rantzau[2], A. Ruprecht[1], U. Wössner[2]

[1] Institute for Fluid Mechanics and Hydraulic Machinery, University of Stuttgart
   Pfaffenwaldring 10, D-70550 Stuttgart, Germany (IHS)
[2] Computing Center, University of Stuttgart
   Allmandring 30, D-70550 Stuttgart, Germany (RUS)

1 Introduction

Usually hydraulic turbines have to be designed individually according to the local discharge, head and the given geometrical situation. This requires the detailed knowledge of the flow for different points of operation, since the head and especially the discharge of the turbine vary during the year. In order to be competitive the design process must be fast and cheap. This is particularly the case for smaller low head turbines, which are frequently installed in brooks and rivers. A typical turbine is shown in fig. 1. In order to obtain efficient shapes for the components in a short time the designer needs a qualified tool for flow analysis. Since the designer is an expert in turbines and not in computers as well as simulation techniques, the tool should allow an „intuitive design" in a virtual reality environment with a nearly on-line response of the simulation results.

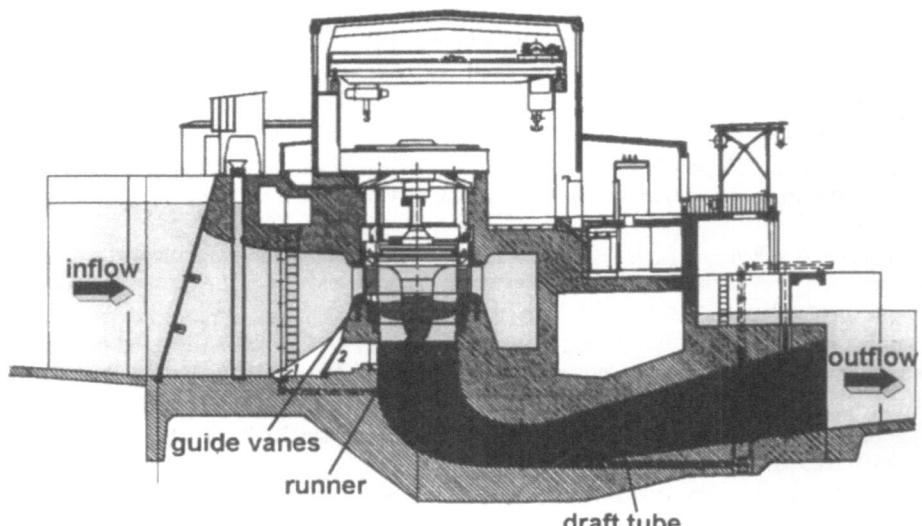

Fig. 1. Hydraulic power plant with Kaplan type turbine

In the ever increasing business for refurbishing as well as upgrading of existing power plants the analysis of the characteristics of the turbine or components of the turbine is even more crucial. For the low head plant described above, the stability of the draft tube flows depends strongly on the flow field at draft tube inlet, that is produced by the runner. In case of a Kaplan turbine the runner blade pitch can be adjusted to changes in head and discharge. Normally, in order to increase the power output of an existing plant, the old runner is replaced by a new one with higher efficiency and increased capacity. To cut costs the intention is to let the other components of the turbine be unchanged, as far as possible. To make sure that the new runner design is successful, the influence on the downstream flow characteristics must be analyzed carefully.

The draft tube has the role to convert the kinetic energy behind the runner into a rise of static pressure which leads to an improvement of the performance of the machine. For low head turbines the kinetic energy can be more than 50% of the total energy. In this case the draft tube efficiency strongly influences the total efficiency and the output of the power plant. A typical draft tube geometry is shown in fig. 2. Important for the shape of the draft tube is to obtain a compact form. Otherwise the civil engineering costs increase dramatically. To fasten the design cycle, a VR environment is used for performing the simulation and analysis tasks in an intuitive way.

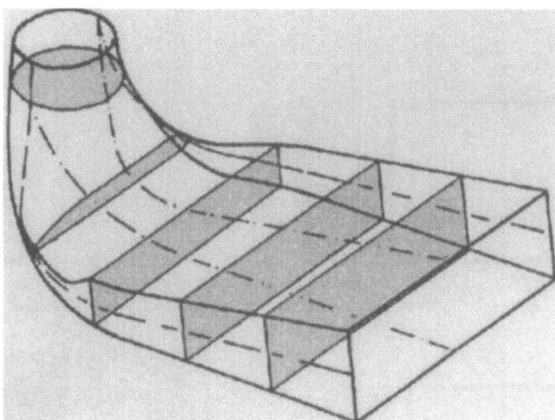

Fig. 2. Typical draft tube

2 Case description

The location and the season defines the two values: head H and discharge Q. Knowing these values, the main geometry and type of the runner can be selected. Normally for H < 20 m Kaplan turbines are used. For this type of turbine it is possible to change the guide vane and the runner blade angle during operation, to react on changes of H and Q.

For every combination of H and Q an optimal blade angle for the guide vanes and the runner exists, where the flow leaves the runner without swirl, only with a transport component. This is the design point of the runner. In this case in the draft tube an unwished reverse flow region occurs in the middle top of the draft tube end. This reduces the pressure recovery strongly. To avoid this reverse flow, a little bit of swirl can be allowed, so the blade angles differ from the design point. By that the performance of the runner decreases whereas the performance of the draft tube increases. The designer have to make a trade-off and choose the optimal point of operation for both components. To find the optimum angle it should be easily adjustable in the simulation phase to allow fast parameter studies. This is realized by an intuitive user interface in the VR environment. By running the on-line simulation on a high performance computer the reaction of the flow can be seen nearly immediately.

3 Environment

For the VR based visualization two different environments are used, one at IHS and one at RUS. In both environments the visualization runs on local SGI workstations, the on-line flow simulation program runs on the super-computers of HLRS (Höchstleistungsrechenzentrum Stuttgart) either on a NEC SX-4 vector computer or on a CRAY T3E computer in parallel. The workstations and the super-computers are connected either by a high speed network (HIPPI, ATM) or by FDDI. The environment is schematically shown in fig. 3.

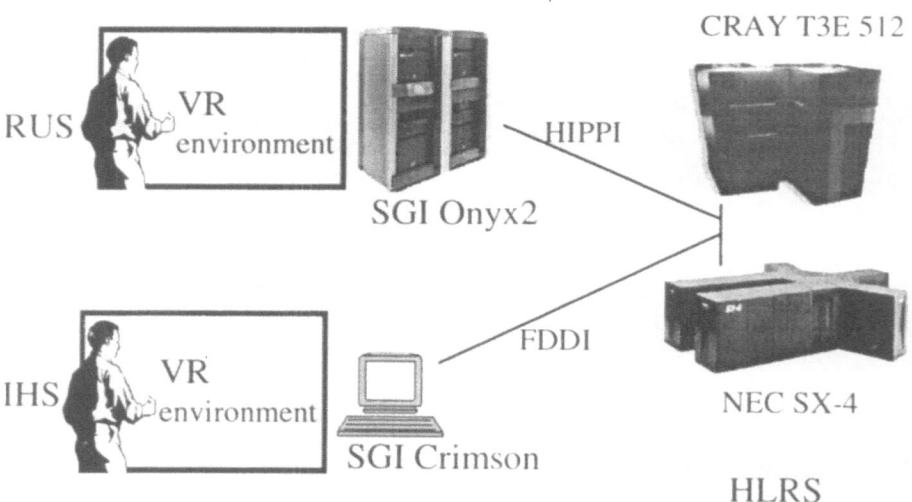

Fig. 3. Working environment

3.1 VR Hardware

The currently installed hardware are one single wall back projection system at IHS driven by a SGI RealityEngine system and a four side back projection system called the CUBE at RUS. The CUBE is connected to a Silicon Graphics Onyx2 double rack system with 14 R10000 CPUs and 4GB of main memory. The Onyx2 has three InfiniteReality pipes each equipped with two raster managers. Several magnetic tracking systems such as Polhemus Fastrack with Stylus pen and the Ascension Motionstar with 3D mouse are supported for the interaction of the user with the virtual environment.

3.2 Software

COVISE

COVISE is a software environment which tries to integrate visualization and simulation tasks across heterogeneous hardware platforms in a seamless manner. It has been optimized especially for efficient network transfer and high performance computing environments. The user interface is based on the visual programming paradigm as used also in other visualization packages such as e.g. AVS or SCIRun. Distributed applications can be built by combining modules (modeled as processes) from different application categories on different hosts to form more or less complex module networks. At the end of such networks usually the rendering step does the final visualization. This application building step is done in the Mapeditor module, the central user interface and visual application builder of COVISE. Session management for adding new hosts and synchronizing the tasks in the module network is done by a central controller which has the only knowledge about the whole application topology. The data management and efficient network transfer including conversion is done by request brokers which are running on each host in a session. On a single host a shared data space (SDS) is used to exchange of data objects between locally running modules to minimize copying overhead. On most platforms this is realized as shared memory communication. A special feature of COVISE is that it allows several users to work in a collaborative way which allows to provide online consulting to end users at remote sites. For the visualization COVISE supports desktop as well as VR oriented renderer modules.

FENFLOSS

FENFLOSS is a finite element flow simulation program. It is based on the Reynolds averaged Navier-Stokes equations with various models of turbulence. For the draft tube calculation the k-ϵ model is used. FENFLOSS uses a segregated solution algorithm, in which the individual momentum equations are solved separately. The pressure is calculated by a modified Uzawa-pressure correction algorithm. The time discretisation is done with an implicit 3-level scheme of 2nd order. For the solution

138

of the linear equation systems a conjugated gradient method is used for non-symmetrical matrices (BICGSTAB2) with a ILU-preconditioning. FENFLOSS runs on various platforms ranging from PC to vector-supercomputers and parallel machines. The parallelization is obtained by a domain decomposition algorithm with overlapping meshes. For the on-line simulation FENFLOSS has been integrated into COVISE.as a module.

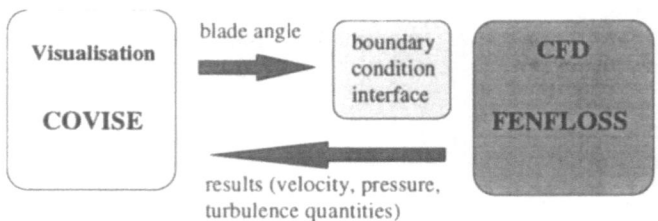

Fig. 4. Date flow between COVISE and FENFLOSS

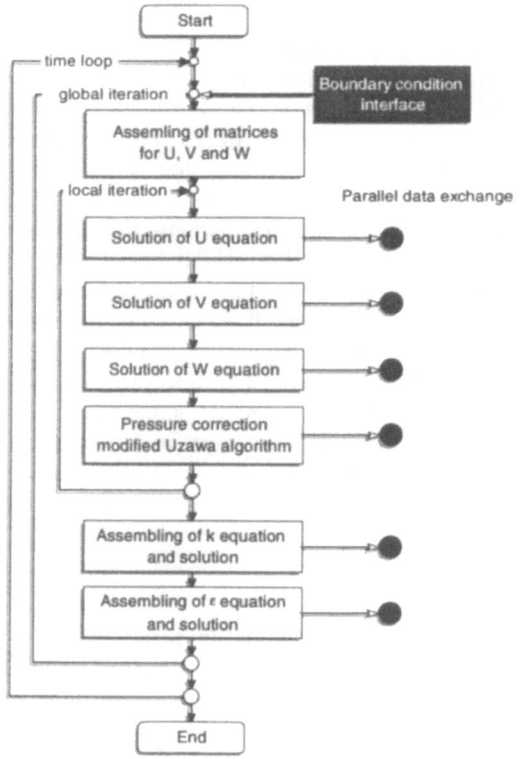

Fig. 5. Flow chart of FENFLOSS

VR driven Boundary-Condition-Interface

As mentioned before, changing of the runner blade angle results in changing of the flow through the draft tube. In the simulation the blade angle can be changed interactively either by entering a value in the 2D user interface or in VR by grabbing one of the rotor blades and rotating it to the desired position, fig. 6. After the user has released the blade, COVISE informs FENFLOSS of the new angle, and then the boundary conditions interface is activated. This interface calculates and sets the new boundary conditions. The following steps are needed:

- Calculation of the velocity distribution behind the runner (transport and the swirl component) by the Euler turbine equation in the relative coordinate system of the runner (polar coordinates).
- Transfer of the velocities from the rotating coordinate system to the absolute system of the draft tube.
- Change the coordinate system from polar to Cartesian coordinates.

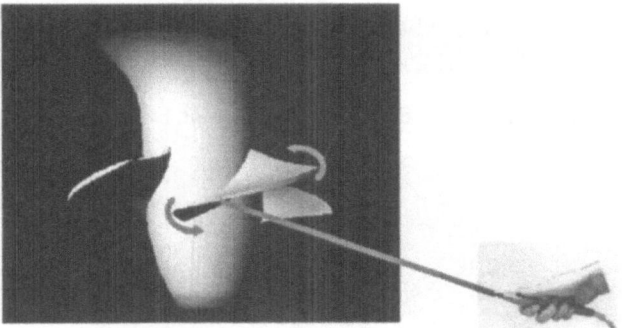

Fig. 6. Intuitive user interaction

4 Results

Fig. 7 shows the runner in the design point. The runner works in its optimum. There is no swirl component at the runner outlet. This results in a big reverse flow in the upper part of the tube end. The reverse flow reduce the efficiency dramatically.

In fig. 8. the runner is opened by 20 degrees. Therefore one obtains a swirling inflow in the draft tube. This reduce the efficiency of the runner, but the results of the draft tube are better. The area of reverse flow is clearly smaller and so the efficiency is higher. In praxis the engineer have to choose a trade-off between runner and draft tube efficiency, so that the total efficiency of the power plant reaches an optimum.

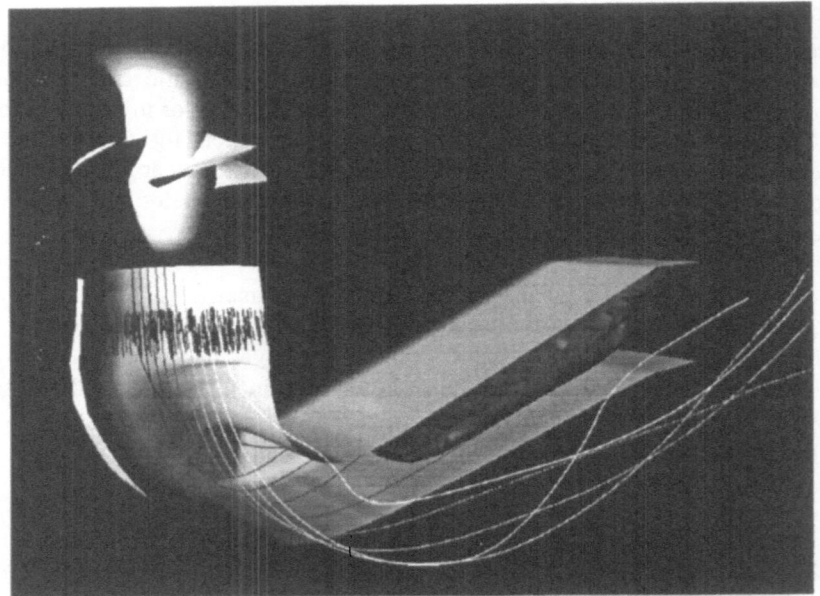

Fig. 7. Flow in the draft tube, design point, blade angle 0°

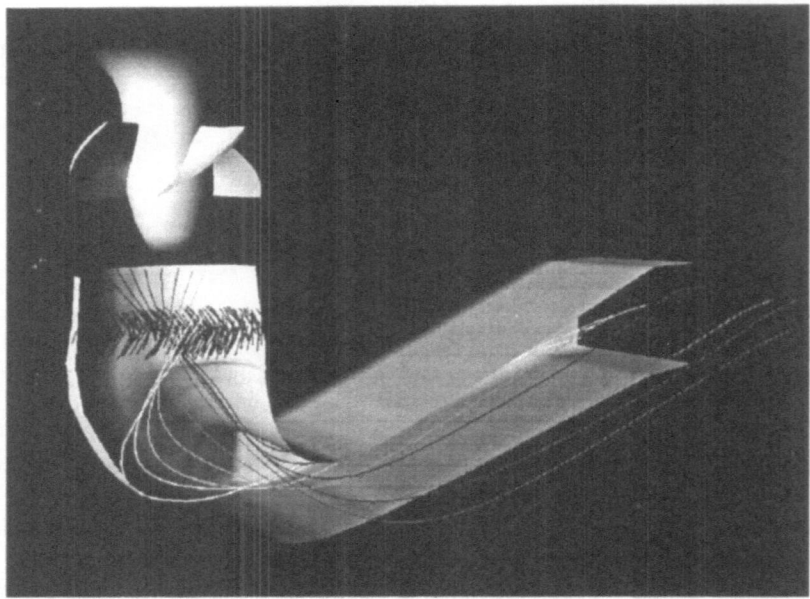

Fig. 8. Flow in the draft tube, blade angle 20°

5 Conclusion

A tool has been described which allows the analysis of the flow in a draft tube of a hydro turbine in a virtual reality environment. By using intuitive interaction techniques the designer can use the tool without great computer knowledge. Running the simulation on a high performance computer leads to very short response times and therefore to a fast and very efficient design cycle. For an existing draft tube an optimum point of operation can be selected very fast and very cheap with this tool.

In a further step it is intended to integrate a geometry and grid generator into the system which then also allows modification of the geometry. During development of a new power plant a lot of parameters of the draft tube should be investigated, in order to obtain a good shape with high efficiency and cheap costs of civil engineering work. For this the draft tube geometry will be represented by a set of parameters, e. g. defined cross-sections with shape and location, bending radius etc.

The designer can modify these geometrical parameters interactively using an intuitive VR user interface, fig. 9. According to the parameters the surface of the tube will be generated and immediately displayed by COVISE. In this way the complete geometry can be designed and changed.

After finishing the shape modification an automatic grid generator will be activated to generate a computational mesh and the necessary boundary conditions and FENFLOSS will calculate the flow on the new mesh.

This intuitive working environment will allow a very fast and therefore cost effective design.

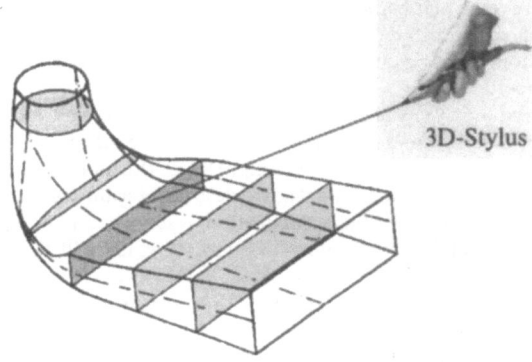

draft tube geometry
Fig. 9. Interactive change of a draft tube geometry

Collaborative Volume Rendering in a Distributed Virtual Reality Environment

P. Benölken, R. Niemeier, U. Lang

University of Stuttgart, RUS/ ICA II, Dept. of Visualization and Computer Simulation
Allmandring 30, D-70550 Stuttgart, Germany

Abstract. This paper presents the integration of direct volume rendering algorithms into a collaborative working environment. The integration allows not only to share the same viewings on separated workstations and to use telepointers for communication, but also to classify volume elements during a collaborative session. The assignment of opacities and other material properties is updated for all participants. Furthermore it is possible to modify light sources, to switch on or off depth cueing and to change the current direct volume rendering algorithm during the collaborative session. Based on a distributed and load balanced implementation, navigation in a virtual reality environment is possible. Results of performance measurements with different settings are reported.

1 Introduction

In the recent years collaborative working with remote cooperation partners has evolved in different domains of engineering and science. The objective of this new working technique is that spatial distributed experts solve their problems in a cooperative way. For this reason, different tools for computer supported collaborative working (CSCW) like video and audio-conferencing or shared whiteboard have been developed for several platforms. An important field in CSCW is the collaborative visualization of complex data, e.g. from CAD or numerical simulations. This means that visualization results can be seen and modified by all cooperation partners in different locations.
COVISE (**Co**llaborative **Vi**sualization and **S**imulation **E**nvironment) is a distributed visualization system that supports this functionality and includes different modules for polygon based surface rendering. Beside this polygon based surface rendering, direct volume rendering is another widespread technique for the visualization of 3D-scalar fields. Therefore the visualization system has now been extended by a new module for collaborative volume rendering, which will be presented in this paper.
Another aspect that will be described here is the integration of direct volume rendering into a virtual reality environment. Virtual Reality (VR) offers new possibilities for interactive exploration of 3D-scalar data and hence it is an important technique for getting better insight and comprehension of complex structures. In the following section we first give a short summary on the design of the COVISE system and its collaborative functionality. Afterwards the integration of direct volume rendering into a VR environment is described. In section 4 we present the design and the features of the new volume renderer module.
The performance of this renderer was measured on different computers at the Computing Center of the University Stuttgart. In the last section we finally present the results of these measurements.

2   Collaborative working with COVISE

The COVISE system was developed in several projects at the Computing Center of the University Stuttgart. It is described in [1], [2] and its usage in [3]. As in other visualization systems known as application builders (e.g. AVS, IBM Data Explorer or IRIS Explorer), the visualization process is split into several subprocesses (modules). Each of these subprocesses receives its input data from dedicated input ports, while the computed output data is transmitted via output ports. The visualization pipeline is built by choosing several modules and connecting their input and output ports. These modules can be spread across different hosts to make optimal use of the varying hardware characteristics in a heterogenous network. The COVISE user interface is presented in figure 1.

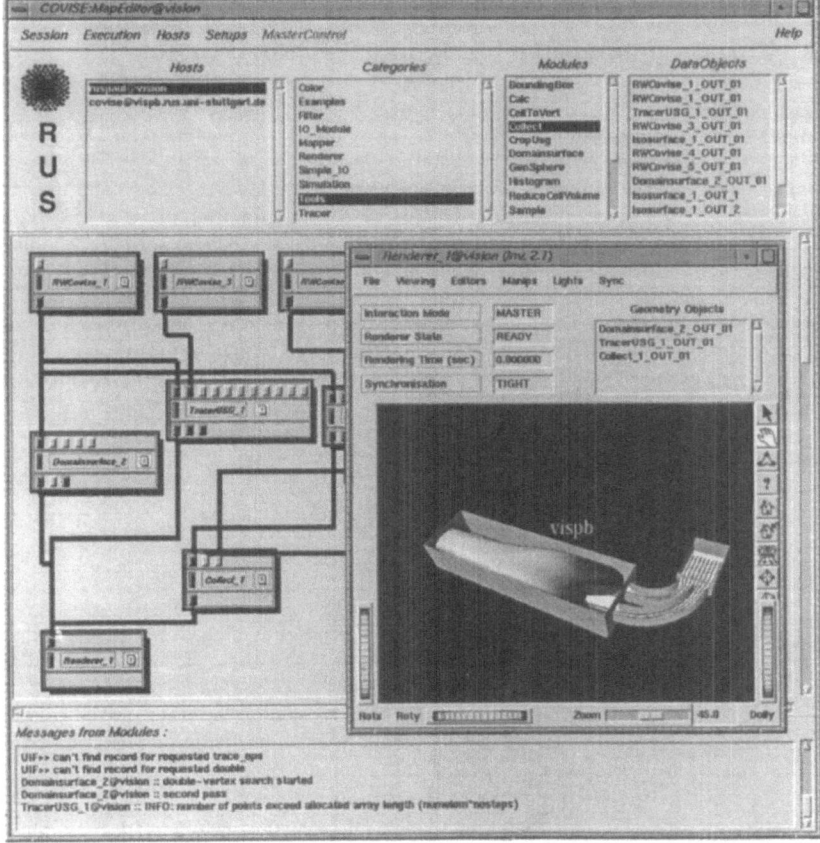

Fig. 1. The COVISE user interface.

A key feature of the COVISE system is the support of collaborative working. This allows spatially separated scientists or engineers to share the same viewings of a rendered scene. In detail this is done by inviting remote partners to participate in an existing COVISE session. A master/slave configuration is applied among these cooperating partners. This means that changes on the master host will be seen by all other participants, whereas changes on the slave hosts only have local effects. The user on a slave host can get control over the session by requesting the master status.

Unlike many other CSCW tools, COVISE does not transmit the graphics output to all remote partners. COVISE supports alternative modes with different types of data to be duplicated for sharing. Depending on the mode there are also different points in the visualization pipeline, where data is shared. This gives the required flexibility to optimize the network usage. In the given case, at the beginning of a collaborative session the data itself is duplicated. This is more efficient as duplicating the graphics output, because after once the data has been duplicated, the rendering pipeline is executed on the local host. The only information send across the network are the new viewing parameters. Finally the collaborative working partners can point on regions of interest in a rendered scene using the telepointer.

3 Direct Volume Rendering in a VR Environment

Visualization of 3D-scalar fields is in general done by either surface rendering which requires the computation of an isosurface, or by direct volume rendering. One problem with surface rendering is, that interesting isovalues are often unknown in advance. Here surface rendering may fail or some expensive precalculations may be required. In contrast to this direct volume rendering supports the visualization of semi-transparent voxels. The advantage of this rendering technique is that the user can get more information from a single image.

In general the 3D scalar data is either defined on an arbitrarily defined grid or scattered in 3D space. Depending on the selected rendering algorithm and data representation a resampling step might be required. Another important step is the assignment of opacity and color to different scalar values (classification) which can be achieved by a user defined transfer function.

For our module the following steps are required for visualizing unclassified 3D scalar data:

- Data acquisition (*resampling on regular grid, if necessary*)
- Classification (*mapping from scalar values to opacities and colors*)
- Choice of shading parameters (*choose light source*)
- Define viewing parameters

A well known disadvantage of direct volume rendering algorithms is the higher computational cost compared to surface rendering algorithms. Therefore several algorithms have been developed for achieving better performance results. Most of them make high demands on hardware like texture memory or other special custom hardware as described in [4]. A fast hardware independent volume rendering algorithm has been developed by Lacroute [5]. This algorithm requires a few seconds for the classification step. Shading of the volume data is done "on the fly" so that a frame rate of $\sim 1Hz$ for a volume of size 256^3 voxels is achieved on a 150 MHz R4400-based workstation. This performance is achieved by:

- restriction on volume data represented on regular grids,
- shear-warp factorization of the viewing transformation,
- run length encoding of the volume,
- lookup-tables for fast shading.

Our aim is the integration of direct volume rendering into a distributed VR-environment. To achieve this aim rendering of stereoscopic images at high frame rates ($\geq 10Hz$) is required. During the last years several parallel rendering algorithm have been developed, which optimize the partitioning of the volume data for fast calculation of a single image [6], [7] and [8]. In the context of the requirements in a VR-environment emphasis is laid on small latency times on user interactions, which in turn requires a rapid sequence of images, not only the fast calculation of a single image.

For this reason Niemeier et al [9] developed a new algorithm for distributed volume rendering, which is based on the VolPack [10] volume rendering library. In this distributed approach different viewing matrices are given to different processes. Each of these processes is executed on a processor node which has the task to calculate the complete image. Dynamic load balancing is enabled by simply distributing new viewing matrices to idle render processes. This method has the advantage, that compared to the parallel algorithm described in [6], [7] and [8] the interprocess communication is kept minimal.

The algorithm is based on the assumption, that for a "uniform" (constant angular velocity) motion of an input device, the subsequent view matrices can be linearly extrapolated. This allows the calculation of images in advance and the reduction of latency times. The following paramaters are used to control the extrapolation of the view matrices:

- $\Delta_{position}$ is the distance between the predicted and current position
- Δ_{angle} is the difference between the orientation of the main axes.

A prototype, implementing these algorithms (VolVR) has been tested in the environment of our VR laboratory, where it achieved frame rates of $\sim 10Hz$ for a volume of size 128^3.

4 Design of the collaborative Volume Renderer

The priority for the implementation of the VolVR prototype was on the interactive working in a VR-environment. Therefore computation was restricted to rendering of run length encoded volume data, where the volume data was loaded by each render process from a given file.

Currently our aim is the extension of the described VolVR prototype to a fully interactive volume rendering system. This means that interactive classification is supported as well as manipulation of light, material, depth-cueing or any other rendering parameter. Figure 2 shows the userinterface and the display window of the new VolVR system, displaying an MRI scan of size 256 x 256 x 128 voxels. The 2D-plots are used to define transfer functions for assignment of classification and material properties.

Another important point is the integration of direct volume rendering into our collaborative working environment COVISE. In a first approach a collaborative volume renderer, running completely in a single process, was integrated into the COVISE environment. Beside the mentioned facilities for collaborative manipulation of the viewing parameters and the use of telepointers, this renderer supports collaborative classification and assignment of material, light and other parameters. This is done by transmitting these parameters via TCP/IP sockets, using the message passing mechanismn of the COVISE environment. Thus changes of classification- or any other parameter, initiated by a user, will be seen by all partners participating in a collaborative session.

In a second step the collaborative volume renderer was extended for rendering sterecscopic images and for interaction with VR tracking devices. For achieving better frame rates the render process is currently distributed on several processor nodes.

146

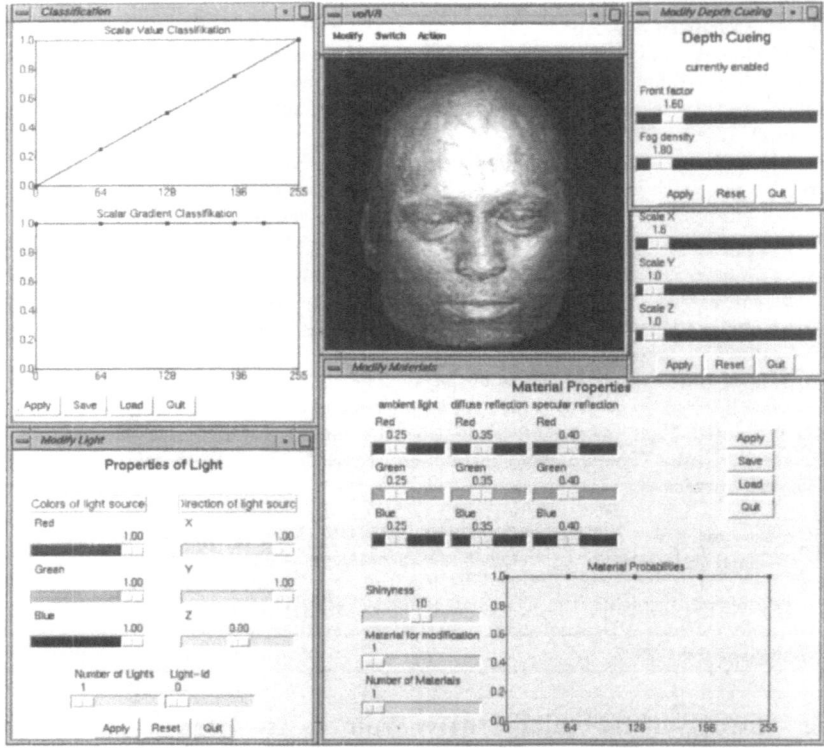

Fig. 2. The VolVR display window and user interface.

The functionality of the VolVR system has been grouped into three processes:

- control process and user interface (Controller)
    - starts the Display and Renderer processes
    - transfers new volume data to all renderer
    - distributes new matrices and parameter changes to Renderer
    - receives new images from Renderer
    - updates shared memory segments
- rendering (Renderer)
    - classifies new volume
    - applies new parameters
    - computes new images
- 3D user interface (Display)
    - Interpretation of user interaction (Mouse/Tracking System)
    - Generation of new viewing and model matrices
    - Lookup for new images in shared memory

The integration of the distributed volume renderer into the COVISE environment required a different design of the modules described in [9]. For reducing overhead in interprocess communication the user interface (Console process) shown in figure 2 was completely integrated into the Controller process.

Figure 3 shows, that the VolVR module running on the local workstation and the remote VolVR modul get the unclassified volume data from the COVISE-Controller.

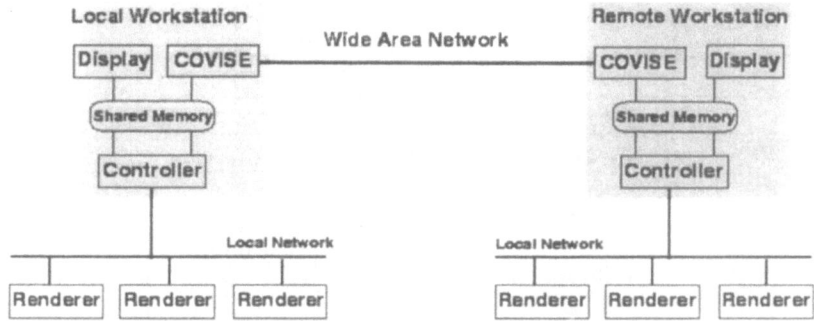

Fig. 3. Architecture of the collaborative, virtual reality volume renderer.

The figure indicates that the number of render processes on the local host may differ from those on the remote workstation. These render processes might be distributed either on several processor nodes in a multiprocessor environment or on several workstations in a fast, heterogenous network. After receiving the volume data from the COVISE-Controller, it is transferred together with a set of parameters (viewing, materials, lights etc.) to the different render processes. Each render process computes a new image, which is finally made visible by the Display process. A run length encoded volume is computed in a classification step, using the raw volume data. This is done if a new raw volume or a new set of classification parameters is transferred to the render process. For making optimal use of varying hardware characteristics we developed alternative modes (local, remote) for exchanging the computed images between Display and Renderer processes. In local mode images and matrices are exchanged via shared memory, which results in a significant performance improvement on multiprocessor hosts. The remote mode is used in a network environment, where the images are transferred via TCP/IP sockets.

5 Performance Results

The performance of the VolVR system has been studied in our Virtual Environments Lab (VE Lab). The center of the VE Lab is the CUBE [11], a stereoscopic back-projection system consisting of three walls and a floor. It is driven by a Silicon Graphics Onyx2 system with 14 R10000 CPUs running at 195 MHz and 4096 Mbyte main memory. For interacting in the CUBE we used an Ascension Ethernet-Motionstar magnetic tracking systems with a 3D mouse. Beside the SGI Onyx2 sytem we used an SGI Octane (2 R10000 Processors, 195 MHz, 1024 Mbytes main memory) and an SGI Indigo2 computer (1 x R10000, 195 MHz, 640 Mbytes main memory). We used the brainsmall data set [5] as a test volume for our application. These data are from an MRI scan reduced to a size of 128 x 128 x 84 voxels. To display the information of this data set, an image resolution of 256×256 pixel would be sufficient. For an immersive environment however the images have to be displayed with maximum size. Since the costs of the 2D warp increase with the image size, we have executed the tests with different scalings (blow ups) of the images.

The tables 1 and 2 show the frame rates on a SGI Octane and on a SGI Indigo2 computer with different image sizes and blow up factors. Table 3 and 4 show the influence of processors numbers on stereoscopic frame rates with a fixed image size of 1024×984 in remote- and local-mode. Figure 4 shows the frame rates achieved by automatic rotation and with enabled tracking device with image size 1024×984

image size	blow up factor		
	1	2	4
256 × 256	5.1	6.9	10.0
512 × 512	2.5	4.9	6.8
1264 × 984	1.3	2.5	5.0

Table 1. Frame rates: Renderer on SGI Indigo2.

	Remote Mode		Local Mode	
	blow up factor		blow up factor	
image size	1	2	1	2
256 × 256	7.1	7.9	9.7	12.1
512 × 512	4.9	6.9	6.9	9.3
1264 × 984	2.4	6.2	2.5	6.2

Table 2. Frame rates: Renderer on SGI Octane.

	Auto Rotate		Tracking	
	blow up factor		blow up factor	
#processors	1	2	1	2
1	0.8	1.6	0.8	1.6
2	1.3	2.4	1.2	2.4
4	2.4	4.7	2.3	4.8
6	3.6	7.0	3.5	6.5
8	4.2	9.6	4.1	9.4
10	4.9	11.8	5.0	11.5
12	5.8	14.0	5.5	13.9
14	6.5	15.9	5.8	15.0

Table 3. Stereoscopic frame rates: Renderer on SGI Onyx2 in remote mode.

	Auto Rotate		Tracking	
	blow up factor		blow up factor	
#processors	1	2	1	2
1	1.2	2.3	1.2	2.3
2	2.2	4.5	2.2	4.5
4	4.5	9.0	4.5	9.1
6	6.1	11.2	6.2	10.6
8	8.1	13.4	7.9	13.9
10	9.4	15.9	9.3	15.6
12	10.0	16.9	10.2	16.9
14	11.0	19.2	10.9	18.7

Table 4. Stereoscopic frame rates: Renderer on SGI Onyx2 in local mode.

	Auto Rotate		Tracking	
	blow up factor		blow up factor	
volume size	1	2	1	2
64x64x64	12.1	19.8	11.9	19.7
128x128x128	11.3	18.9	11.4	18.9
256x256x256	9.6	15.8	9.1	15.7

Table 5. Frame rates: Renderer on SGI Onyx2 with 12 R10000 CPU.

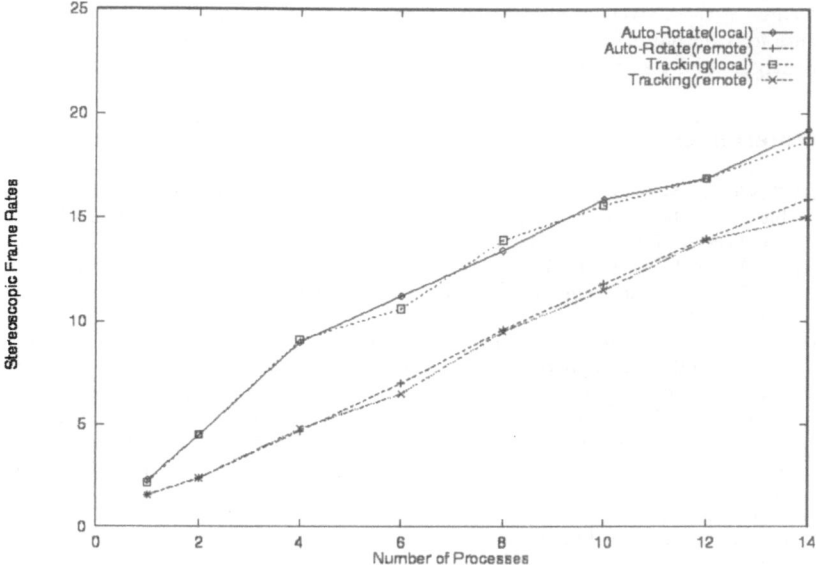

Fig. 4. Influence of processor numbers on frame rates with and without tracking.

and a blow up factor of 2. The figure indicates a linear growth of the frame rate for the automatic rotation and a slow decrease when tracking is enabled. Compared to the results presented in [9] this is an improvement of the frame rates achieved with a tracking device.

In our final experiment we measured the performance of the Renderer with different volume sizes. As mentioned in chapter 3, the performance of the fast shear warp algorithm [5] is achieved by a run-length encoding of the classified volume. The efficiency of the run-length encoding is in turn correlated with the fraction of transparent and non-transparent voxels of a classified volume. For this reason we generated some spheric data sets using a constant fraction of non-tranparent voxels. The results of this experiment are shown in table 5.

6 Conclusion

We developed a module for collaborative volume rendering, which was integrated into the COVISE environment. For the integration of direct volume rendering into a VR environment, we used a distributed approach, based on image precalculation. Starting from a prototype system we developed a full interactive and collaborative volume rendering system supporting the functionality of a VR environment. The performance of the distributed volume renderer has been improved by using shared memory for interchanging the computed images on a multiprocessor host. The number of frames is no longer limited by the VR input device.

7 Acknowledgements

This work was supported by DFN and Sonderforschungsbereich 382. We like to thank all COVISE developers at the visualization department of the Computing

Center at the University of Stuttgart as well as our project partners from the Institute for Computer Applications I, the Institute of Theoretical and Applied Physics Stuttgart and the Institute of Theoretical Astrophysics Tübingen.

References

[1] A.Wierse, M.Arya, D.Swanberg, V.Vasudevan: Database and Visualization: System Integration Issues. Proceedings of the IEEE Workshop on Database for Data Visualization,Lecture Notes in Computer Science, Volume 871, Lee, Grinstein (Eds.), Springer

[2] A. Wierse: Performance of the COVISE visualization system under different conditions. IS&T/SPIE Symposium on Electronic Imaging: Science & Technology, San Jose, 4-10 February 1995

[3] U. Lang, J. P. Peltier, P. Christ, Stefan Rill, Dirk Rantzau, Harald Nebel, Andreas Wierse, Ruth Lang, Sylvain Causse, Frédéric Juaneda, Michel Grave, Peter Haas: Perspectives of collaborative supercomputing and networking in European Aerospace research and industry. Future Generation Computer Systems 11 (1995) pp. 419-430.

[4] T. Günther et. al.: VIRIM: A Massively Parallel Processor for Real-Time Volume Visualization in Medicine. Proceedings Eurographics Workshop 94, pp. 103-108, Oslo, Norway 1994.

[5] P. G. Lacroute: Fast Volume Rendering using a Shear-Warp Factorization of the Viewing Transformation. PhD thesis, technical report CSL-TR-95-678, Computer Systems Laboratory, Stanford University, 9/95.

[6] P. G. Lacroute: Real Time Volume Rendering on Shared Memory Multiprocessor Using the Shear-Warp Factorization. Proceedings of the Parallel Rendering Symposium 95, pp. 15-22, Atlanta GA, USA 1995.

[7] M. B. Amin, A. Grama, V. Singh: Fast Volume Rendering Using an Efficient, Scalable Parallel Formulation of the Shear-Warp Algorithm. Proceedings of the Parallel Rendering Symposium 95, pp. 7-14, Atlanta GA, USA 1995.

[8] A. Koning, Parallel Volume Visualization, PhD thesis University of Utrecht, 1996.

[9] R. Niemeier, V. Schulze, D. Rantzau: Direct Volume Visualization in a Virtual Reality Environment Using a Distributed Volume Rendering Algorithm. Proceedings of 3D Image Analysis and Synthesis '96, pp. 133-138, Erlangen (Germany) 1996.

[10] http://graphics.stanford.edu:80/software/volpack

[11] Dirk Rantzau, Karin Frank, Ulrich Lang, Daniela Rainer, Uwe W"ossner An Environment for Analyzing Large and Complex Simulation Data
Proceedings of the 2nd Workshop on Immersive Projection Technology (IPT '98), Ames, Iowa 11.-12. May 1998, published on CDROM by ICEMT.

Sharing virtual environments over a transatlantic ATM network in support of distant collaboration in vehicle design

Volodymyr Kindratenko[1] and Berthold Kirsch[2]

[1] National Center for Supercomputing Applications (NCSA), University of Illinois.
[2] GMD - German National Research Center for Information Technology, Sankt Augustin.
E-mails: kindr@ncsa.uiuc.edu, kirsch@gmd.de

Abstract

Research in Virtual Reality no longer is focused only on computer graphics, it has become an interdisciplinary, involving new fields such as teleconferencing, networking, and distributed computing. This article presents results of a research project in the Distributed Virtual Reality. The goal of the projects was to evaluate the capabilities, practicality, performance, and cost of this technology for performing collaborative product design review on an industrial showcase application. In the course of the project a dedicated network between two virtual reality visualization systems was established across the North Atlantic. Tele-conferencing applications were integrated with a virtual reality system allowing users from geographically remote locations to see and talk to each other in the shared virtual environment while performing collaborative product design review.

Keywords: distributed virtual reality, teleconferencing, asynchronous transfer mode, IP multicast, collaborative product design review.

1 Introduction

As virtual environments become a part of industrial research programs, their applicability to machine design becomes increasingly apparent. Engineering is an iterative process whereby designs are created, analyzed, tested and modified until the very best design emerges. This process is inherently time consuming and expensive. Virtual prototyping is a method of decreasing the amount of time between the design phase and the time of introduction of a new product into the marketplace, allowing simultaneously for improved quality. A virtual environment (VE) allows engineers to interact with their designs (i.e. a vehicle model) in three dimensions in real time. Extending the virtual environment to several geographically remote sites, where each site is looking at the same model, allows interactive communication of design information. The challenge is determining how complex virtual environments can be shared between geographically remote sites involving large distances, and how real-time live video and audio can become an integrated part of such environments.

The Distributed Virtual Reality (DVR) project was an experiment to address these issues. The goal of the project was to establish an Asynchronous Transfer Mode (ATM) network between two virtual reality visualization systems across the North Atlantic and evaluate the capabilities, practicality, performance and cost of Distributed Virtual Reality technology for performing collaborative product design review on an industrial showcase application. The project started in September 1995. Functional specification [1] of the DVR system was finalized in December 1995. Development of the technical specification [2] continued through February 1996. The first implementation of the system and tests over local area network at NCSA [3, 4] were finished in September 1996. Since that time several major software components were redesigned [5] and some preliminary tests of the system between NCSA and GMD were performed over the Internet. ATM network between NCSA and GMD was established in the end of August 1997 and 19 transatlantic trials of the system took place in September – December 1997 [6, 7]. Two trials were solely dedicated to the system evaluation by Caterpillar engineers from the US and Belgium. This work describes the final implementation of the DVR system, transatlantic ATM network setup, trials, and their results.

2 Requirements for the DVR system

The system needed to be designed for engineers, located at geographically remote sites, to interact with virtual vehicle models in real time and to communicate design information to each other. Therefore, the following concept, functionality, and performance requirements to the system were defined:

Concept requirements. *Portability* implies that the system can be ported to different virtual reality (VR) platforms. *Scalability* means that an unlimited number of remotely located sites can join the shared VE. *Security* addresses the concern for protection of proprietary information in a DVR application.

Functionality requirements. *Ability to interact* with vehicle models in the shared VE. Each participating site should have a *virtual pointer* enhancing collaboration with other sites by pointing to an object of interest. Although, avatars are frequently used, we chose to investigate the applicability and usability of another type of representation - *live video* coming from a video camera located in front of the participants at each site, and seen in the shared VE. *Natural audio communication* should be a part of the shared environment.

Performance requirements. Delays in object modification, animation or motion data transmittals are unavoidable due to the long distances and heavy computations involved, but they should be minimized. The network performance should be such that the object manipulation looks smooth and natural. Voice transmission delays are expected to be equal to or less than those of conventional teleconferencing. Synchronization of voice and speaker image appearance is an essential feature.

3 Development of the DVR system

The model, selected for implementation, is a real-time vehicle simulation computation linked with a VR rendering process allowing one participant to control and drive a virtual model of a vehicle in a shared virtual environment whereas participants at geographically remote sites evaluate it communicating with each other using video and audio integrated with the shared VE.

3.1 VR visualization hardware

The display of the system at GMD is on the Responsive Workbench™ [8], a tracked, stereo, table-like display (Fig. 1a). The Responsive Workbench operates by projecting a computer-generated stereoscopic image off a mirror and through a table surface. Users observe a 3D image displayed above the tabletop by using stereoscopic shutter glasses. The group leader's head is tracked allowing to change the view angle according to his movement. Other group members observe the scene as the group leader manipulates it by using a fastrak stylus.

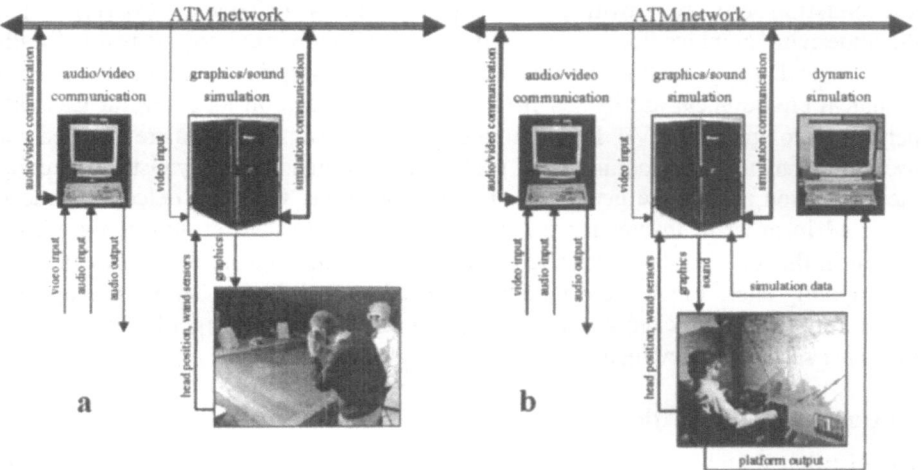

Fig. 1. System setup at **a**) GMD and **b**) NCSA. The display of the system at GMD is on the Responsive Workbench™; the display of the system at NCSA is in the CAVE™.

The display of the system at NCSA is in the Cave Automated Virtual Environment (CAVE™) [9] (Fig. 1b). The CAVE is a projection-based VR system that surrounds the viewer with 4 screens in a 10-foot by 10-foot by 9-foot surround-screen surround-sound cube with three rear-projection screens for walls and a down-projection screen for the floor. A viewer wears stereo shutter glasses and a six-degree-of-freedom head-tracking device, just like in the case of the Responsive Workbench. As the viewer moves inside of the CAVE, the corresponding stereoscopic perspective projections are calculated for each wall. A second sensor and buttons in a wand, held by the viewer, provide interaction with the virtual environment.

At each site SGI Onyxes with Infinite Reality graphics pipelines generate the projected images and SGI Indys with built-in video/audio board take microphone and video camera inputs and give speaker outputs. Wide-angle, low-light cameras and hands-free tie-clip omnidirectional microphones are used.

3.2 Vehicle simulation

The vehicle model implemented is a Caterpillar 990 wheel loader. Virtual prototype of the vehicle was created from the same Pro/Engineering CAD designs used throughout Caterpillar's design process. Caterpillar's proprietary dynamic simulation package Dynasty is used to perform real-time vehicle simulation. A vehicle mock-up platform, installed in the CAVE, is the main user interface in the simulation. It takes real-time operator inputs to the system including steering, throttle, gears, brake, lift, and tilt and communicates it to Dynasty which performs computations and sends results to the VR rendering process to update the position and orientation of the vehicle body in the shared virtual environment.

3.3 VR rendering

VR rendering software is written in C using Sense8's WorldToolKit® (WTK) [10] as the underlying graphics library. The software and all the virtual objects reside locally at each site. During initial set-up time the geometric description of the vehicle and the graphical environment are loaded from files. In a simulation loop several tasks are performed to update the VE. Inputs from the head and wand trackers are detected and used to calculate new head and hand position and orientation. If Dynasty is running, the simulation at that site gets updated vehicle position. Collision detection code is executed in order to insure that the vehicle is always located on top of the virtual terrain in the VE. Networking code is executed to communicate data between other participating sites. Finally, the rendering procedure is called to render the updated scene from the headtracked viewpoint. The simulation runs at a target frame rate of 15 times per second, achieving a relatively high degree of realism.

3.4 Communication with remote sites

The distributed architecture, that has been selected, is peer-to-peer rather than client-to-server. In the implemented model any site can begin first, and as long as there is more than one site participating, a shared environment is possible. Any site can join or leave the shared VE at any time. A new site that joins is immediately synchronized with the other participating sites. Each site maintains its own viewpoint and a virtual pointer. The communication with other sites is built using IP multicast protocol.

Communication with remote sites is a part of the main simulation loop. It is built using WTK network communication API. Network communications in WTK are established using the concept of individual *message items* that are assembled into IP/UDP packets that are than sent to a specific port number on the network. Only simulations that are "listening" to the particular port will be able to receive the packet. During the initial setup time the simulation sends out a packet containing a message having a unique integer identifier (ID) and the name of the computer running the site's simulation. Other sites listen on the same multicast address and port and respond by sending similar packets with their unique IDs and names. When a site leaves, it sends a message communicating this to the other sites. During each simulation loop, just before the actual rendering procedure is called, each site communicates all the pieces of information required to maintain the synchronization of the shared VE. These include the site's viewpoint and virtual pointer coordinates and orientation, and vehicle body coordinates and orientation. Within the time period of the network latency, changes in the vehicle position at one site are visible to all other participating sites. All positions and orientations are absolute, so any lost packets do not destroy the synchronization.

3.5 Integrated video and audio

Video conferencing application VIC [11], developed by the Network Research Group at the Lawrence Berkeley National Laboratory, is used for video communication. Source code of VIC is available making any particular customization possible. Each site runs two copies of the VIC tool, one has been modified the other not. Video input from a camera, located in front of participants, is digitized on the Indy workstation and sent by the unmodified copy of VIC over the network. At the other site the modified version of VIC, running on the same workstation with the VR rendering software, picks up the video from the network. This video is written frame-by-frame from the VIC process, via shared memory, to the graphics rendering process where it is converted to RGB format and placed into texture memory. The texture then is applied to a polygon located at the viewpoint of the corresponding remote site. This results in a dynamic texture displaying the incoming video in the VE (Fig. 2).

Fig. 2. Two video avatars inside of the shared virtual environment.

The audio conferencing application VAT [12], also available from the Lawrence Berkeley National Laboratory, is used for audio communication. The audio input from a microphone, attached to a participant, is digitized on the Indy workstation and sent by VAT over the network. Both VIC and VAT use Real-time Transport Protocol (RTP) for data communication and they can both send and receive transmissions from any number of remote sites.

4 Transatlantic ATM network

For real-time interaction and digital communication remote sites ideally should be

156

connected by a network possessing the following properties: bandwidth of the order of a few megabits per site, low latency, ability to run IP multicast, and be available and affordable. ATM network is a good choice. With ISDN network we eventually run in some bandwidth-related problems since it is commonly referred to as a technology used to handle connections below 2 Mbps.

Connectivity between NCSA and GMD was established across several ATM-based networks (Fig. 3) including the very-high Backbone Network Service (vBNS), CA*net II, ATM services provided by Teleglobe Canada under the Multimedia Applications on Intercontinental Highways (MAY) project, and Deutsche Telecom's ATM network in Germany. The vBNS and CA*net II interconnect in Chicago at the STAR TAP, an interconnection point for international high-performance research and education networks. To complete the connectivity, a permanent virtual circuit (PVC) was established between vBNS router in Chicago and router at GMD. This PVC traversed CA*net II to Nova Scotia where it was switched to the Teleglobe ATM network to cross the Atlantic (via CANTAT-3) into Sylt, Germany. From Sylt ATM cells were forwarded to GMD in Sankt Augustin via Deutsche Telecom's ATM network. Since all communications in the application are built on top of IP multicast, a multicasting tunnel was installed over the ATM network.

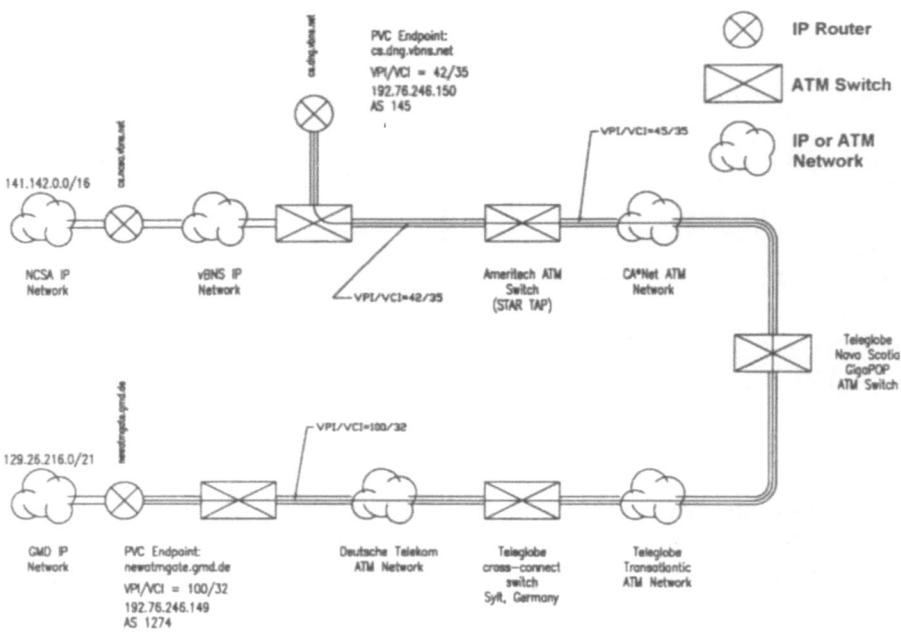

Fig. 3. Transatlantic ATM network.

Bandwidth use per sending site using H.261 encoding technique and sending 30 fps of a good quality low-motion color video is approximately 300 Kbps. For a higher quality or a high-motion video it might require a bandwidth over 500 Kbps. For the same video using NV encoding technique the bandwidth is of the order of 900 Kbps. The frequency used for audio communication is 8 kHz, resulting in a per-site bandwidth of 64 Kbps. Bandwidth, required to exchange position information in the shared VE, is 40 Kbps. In total, a bandwidth up to 1 Mbps per sending site is required. Therefore, the transatlantic ATM circuit was configured for 5000 cells (2 Mbps).

5 Trials

Nineteen transatlantic trials of the DVR system were performed from September to December 1997. Two trials were solely dedicated to the system evaluation by Caterpillar engineers from the factories in Aurora (US) and Gosselies (Belgium). Participants shared a virtual environment and communicated using digitized audio and video. They saw the real-time video of the other participants integrated with the virtual environment. Participants at GMD could see the vehicle move as the engineer drove it at NCSA.

5.1 Measurements

Numerous performance parameters were measured during the trials. *Round-trip time* was measured both by *ping* and *traceroute* utilities. For example, a typical output of *traceroute*, tracing network route from NCSA to GMD, was

```
traceroute to geier-a1.gmd.de (129.26.216.86), 30 hops max, 40 byte packets
1 pigpen.ncsa.uiuc.edu (141.142.223.120) 2 ms 2 ms 2 ms
2 141.142.11.150 (141.142.11.150) 2 ms 3 ms 3 ms
3 cs-atm0-0-12.ncsa.vbns.net (141.142.11.1) 3 ms 4 ms 2 ms
4 cs-atm0-0-6.dng.vbns.net (204.147.129.246) 5 ms 5 ms 5 ms
5 192.76.246.149 (192.76.246.149) 125 ms 125 ms 125 ms
6 geier.gmd.de (129.26.216.86) 125 ms 125 ms 131 ms
```

Results show the round-trip time in the range of 125 to 130 ms.

ATM cells measurements were performed at GMD's ATM switch. Measurements, performed on December 12th, 1997 during the evaluation of the DVR system by engineers from Caterpillar, are shown in Fig. 4. During the test we used NV video encoding sending 8 fps by each site and PCM2 audio encoding. Results show that the actual load of NCSA-GMD ATM network was below 1 Mbps.

Both VIC and VAT tools have built-in measurement capabilities based on analysis of data from Sender Report Packets and Receiver Report Packets defined in RTP. The following parameters were measured during the trials: 1) Amount of data sent/received (Kbps). This parameter is both a quantitative (defines the bandwidth use per sending site) and qualitative (comparison of amount of data sent at one site with amount of data received at another site gives a delivery quality) measure. 2) Number of packets sent/received (packets/sec). This parameter defines the number of RTP packets containing payload data sent/received at one site. 3) Number of missing packets (packets/sec) and cumulative number of packets lost. 4) In video conferencing the number of video frames per second sent/received was counted. 5) In audio conferencing playout time (ms) was measured. This measure corresponds to the time difference between when a sound was digitized at the sending site and played back at the receiving site.

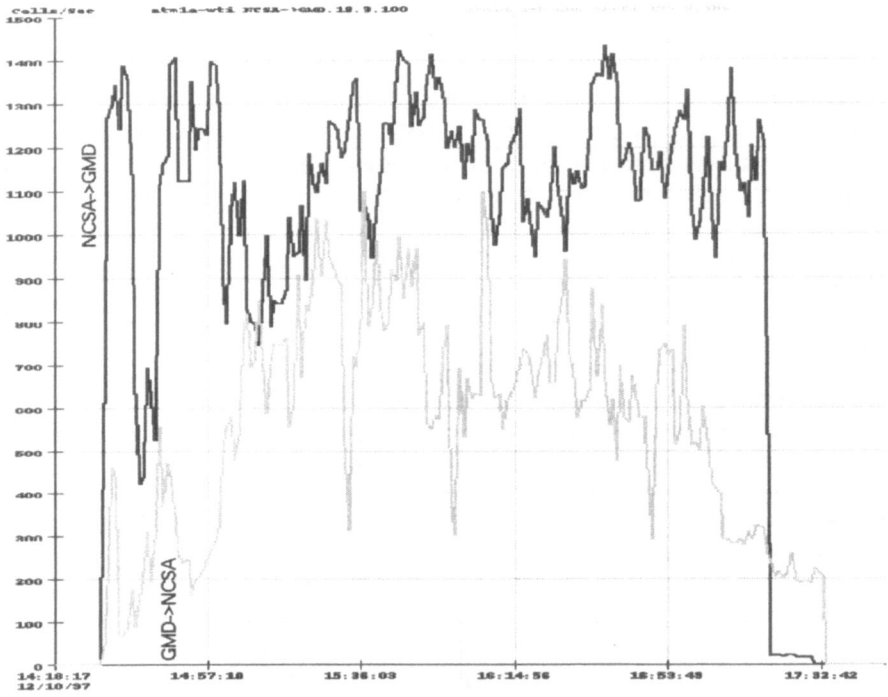

Fig. 4. ATM cells measured on December 12th, 1997 at GMD's ATM switch during one of the transatlantic trials.

The following results were obtained for VAT (Fig. 5). Typical bandwidth per sending site using PCM2 encoding at 8 kHz was 60-70 Kbps. Number of packets per sending site varied from 7 packets/sec for low intensity talk to 16-20 packets/second for high intensity talk. Usually there were no packets missing using unicast, but a considerable amount of packets was missing using multicast. Playout time typically varied between 80 and 150 ms, comparing to the one-way trip time of 62-65 ms.

The following results were obtained for VIC (Fig. 6) using NV encoding. Bandwidth per sending site using NV encoding and sending 8 fps varied between 10 - 20 Kbps for low-motion, almost still video, and up to 400 – 600 Kbps for high-motion video. Typically it was between 150 and 250 Kbps during system evaluation by Caterpillar engineers. Amount of sent/received packets varied proportionally to the bandwidth used and was in the range of 20 to 40 packets/second during system evaluation by Caterpillar engineers. From time to time some packets were missed introducing distortions in received video. We did not succeed to correlate missing packets with any of the set-up parameters that we could control.

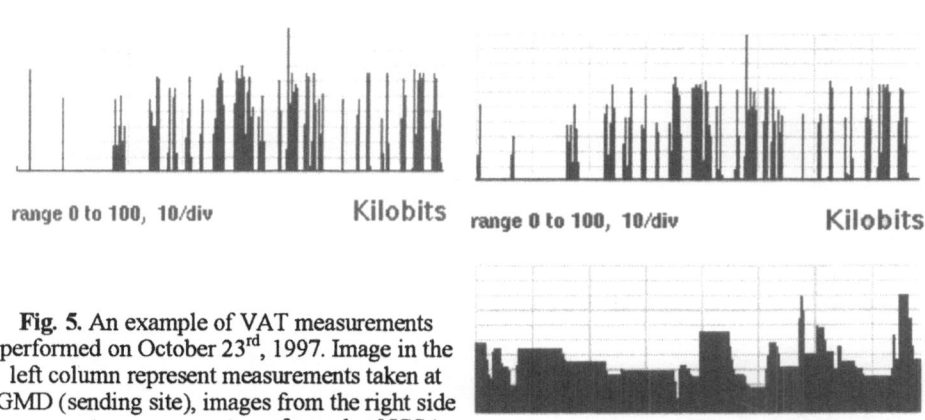

Fig. 5. An example of VAT measurements performed on October 23rd, 1997. Image in the left column represent measurements taken at GMD (sending site), images from the right side represent measurements performed at NCSA (receiving site) at the same time.

5.2 Lessons learned

The major lessons learned involved the use of IP multicast. It was found that multicasting packets were periodically missed resulting in a distortion of data communication. We found it more appropriate to use unicast instead of multicast for the audio transmissions. A problem also was discovered in our DVR software. Time, needed to copy and convert video from VIC process to graphics rendering process, was relatively long resulting in skipping a considerable amount of incoming video frames. There were some difficulties with handling more than 8 fps of video integrated into the VE. We see a solution of this problem in optimization of the video updating procedure.

An interesting synchronization problem due to the network latency was observed for events depending on other events. For example, participants at GMD could attach their viewpoint to the cab of the virtual vehicle driven at NCSA. The position and orientation of their viewpoint in this case dependent on the position of the vehicle calculated at NCSA. The system, running at GMD, updated it each time a new data arrived from NCSA, thus, keeping it a few frames behind the frames currently rendered at NCSA, but in sync with GMD's rendering. In its turn, the new GMD's viewpoint position was immediately communicated back to NCSA and updated at NCSA as soon as it arrived, a few frames, relatively to GMD's simulation, after it was sent. So, the new position of GMD's viewpoint in NCSA's VE was the position expected at the time when NCSA's simulation sent cab's position to GMD, or a few frames ago at NCSA. In practice it resulted in the GMD's viewpoint to be visible behind the cab of the forward driving vehicle and in the front of the cab of the backward driving vehicle as seen at NCSA. We see a solution for this problem in illuminating the need for the second-order event dependencies.

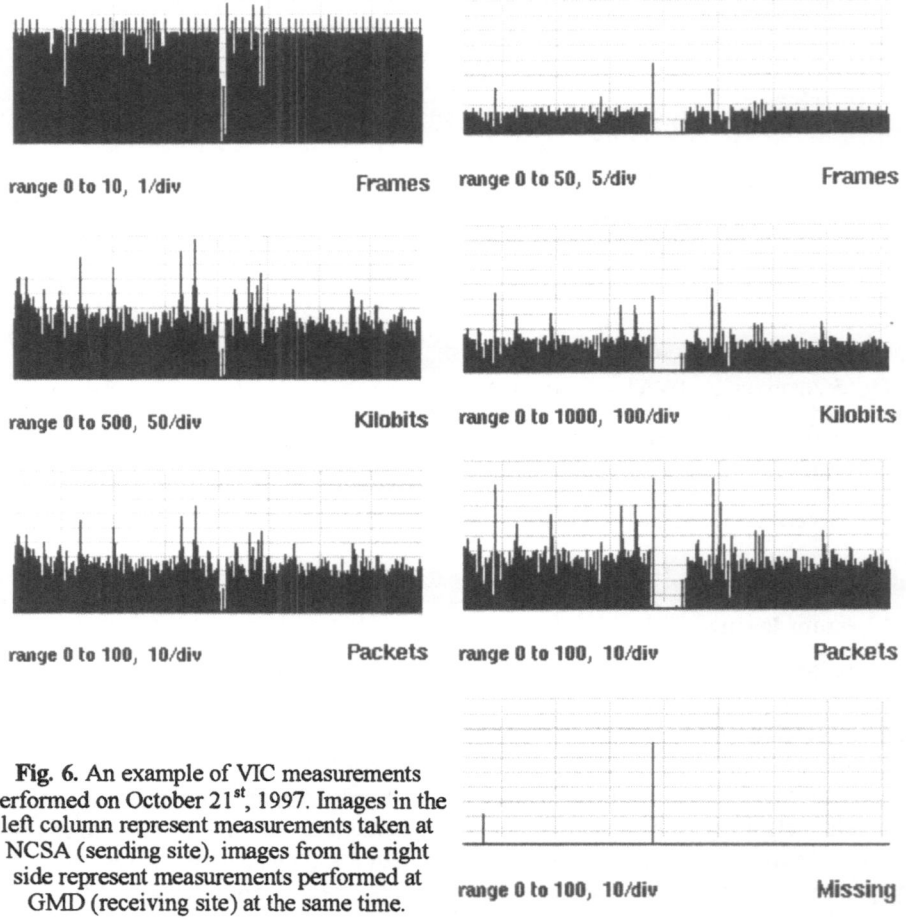

Fig. 6. An example of VIC measurements performed on October 21st, 1997. Images in the left column represent measurements taken at NCSA (sending site), images from the right side represent measurements performed at GMD (receiving site) at the same time.

6 Conclusions and future research

The system was designed for engineers located at geographically remote sites to interact with their models in the three dimensions in real time and to communicate design information to each other. It supports collaborative design review. Integrated real-time video transmissions let engineers see each other in a shared virtual environment. Audio transmissions provide natural voice communication. The current version of the DVR system may be considered as a prototype for future engineering development tools. Transatlantic trials of the system have shown a number of problems pointing network reliability and performance issues as well as some drawbacks in the developed software. Therefore, current work is focused on eliminating found problems and redesigning some components of the system.

7 Acknowledgments

The project is supported by Caterpillar Belgium S.A. and is a part of the Distributed Video Production (DVP) project sponsored by The European Union under the Advanced Communications & Technologies research and technological development program as project AC089. The partners involved into DVR project are GMD - German National Research Center for Information Technology and the National Center for Supercomputing Applications, University of Illinois, in the USA.

We are grateful for everyone who contributed to this project, in particular, Robert Fenwick (Caterpillar, Inc.), Jean-Paul Emond (Caterpillar Belgium S.A.), Dr. Manfred Kaul (GMD), Dr. Wolfgang Heiden (GMD), and Dr. Thomas DeFanty (NCSA). For Lance Arsenault and Jason Wessel (both from NCSA) for their contribution in software development. We are thankful for Paul Zawada, Randy Butler, David Mitchel, and Tony Rimovsky (networking group from NCSA), Wolfgang Ziegler, Lothar Zier, and Ferdinand Hommes (networking group from GMD), Randolph Nicklas (vBNS), Bill Arnaud (CANARIE), Alain Lechasseur (Teleglobe), and Peter Feil (DeTeBerkom) for their contribution in establishment of the transatlantic ATM link.

References

[1] J.-P. Emond, *CEC Deliverable A089.CAT.WLP.DS.L.441.b1: Distributed Virtual Reality - Functional Specification*, December 1995.

[2] V. Lehner, *CEC Deliverable A089.CAT.WLP.DS.L.442.b1: Distributed Virtual Reality - Technical Specification*, March 1996.

[3] V. Lehner, *CEC Deliverable A089.CAT.WLP.DS.I.443.b1: Distributed Virtual Reality - First Implementation*, September 1996.

[4]. V. Lehner, and T. DeFanti, *Distributed virtual reality: supporting remote collaboration in vehicle design*, IEEE Computer Graphics and Applications, 1997, vol. 17, no. 2, pp. 13-17.

[5] V. Kindratenko, and B. Kirsch, *CEC Deliverable A089.CAT.CAT.DS.I.444.b0: Distributed Virtual Reality – Implementation*, March 1998.

[6] V. Kindratenko, and B. Kirsch, *CEC Deliverable A089.CAT.CAT.DS.P.445.b0: Distributed Virtual Reality – Evaluation Report*, March 1998.

[7] V. Kindratenko, and B. Kirsch, *CEC Deliverable A089.CAT.CAT.DS.P.54.b0: Distributed Virtual Reality – Evaluation Report*, March 1998.

[8] W. Krueger and B. Froehlich, *The Responsive Workbench: A Virtual Work Environment*, IEEE Computer Graphics and Applications, 1994, vol. 14, no. 3, pp. 12-15.

[9] C. Cruz-Neira, D. Sandin, and T. DeFanty, *Surround-Screen Projection-Based Virtual Reality: The Design and Implementation of the CAVE*, in Proc. Siggraph 93, ACM Press, New York, pp. 135-142.

[10] *WorldToolKit®, the Industry's Chosen 3D Real-Time Software ToolKit*, SENSE8 Corporation, Mill Valley, CA. http://www.sense8.com/products/worldtoolkit.html.

[11] S. McCanne and V. Jacobson, *vic: A Flexible Framework for Packet Video*, in Proc. ACM Multimedia 95, ACM Press, New York, pp. 511-522.

[12] V. Jacobson and S. McCanne, *vat - LBNL Audio Conferencing Tool*, Lawrence Berkeley National Laboratory, Berkeley, CA. http://www-nrg.ee.lbl.gov/vat/.

ARCHITECTURE AND DIGITAL EXHIBITIONS THE EINSTEIN TOWER WORLD

Fabio Pittarello, Mauro Pittarello, Giuseppe F. Italiano
Ca' Foscari University of Venice - Computer Science Department
Via Torino, 155 – 30173 Mestre (Venice), ITALY
phone +39 41 2577126
fax +39 41 2577122
e-mail pitt@unive.it

This work is part of a general research about three-dimensional worlds usability issues, aimed at analysing the current points of strength and weakness of immersive navigation in virtual worlds on the net and at developing new cognitive artefacts to improve the quality of these experiences. The Einstein Tower World, a system conceived in occasion of the German Expressionism exhibition held in 1997 at Palazzo Grassi in Venice, can be seen as a first implementation of the results achieved so far by our research.

The Einstein Tower, a sun observatory built in Potsdam from 1919 to 1923 by Erich Mendelsohn and chosen as a symbol of the real exhibition in Venice, becomes the focus of a virtual exhibition where architecture, paintings, manifestos, cinema fragments and music melt into a unique composition, a small account of *gesamtkunstwerk* (an integrated esthetical experience achieved by eliminating the divisions between architecture, music and visual arts) proposed by expressionist artists.

Keywords: architecture, digital exhibitions, vrml, hypermedia, guided tour, locus, earcons, multimodality

1. Introduction

The Einstein Tower World is part of the official web site of Palazzo Grassi in Venice [5], the world-wide known cultural institution promoting exhibitions ranging from Archaeology to Modern Arts. Starting from 1995, the web site of Palazzo Grassi hosts detailed information about its current exhibition, about all the exhibitions held starting from 1986 and the history of the palace itself, a Venetian 18th century building conceived by Giorgio Massari.

The last exhibition held in 1997 was about German Expressionism, the artistic movement that developed in Germany early in this century, promoting a synesthetic union of all arts; thus, the main themes of this exhibition suggested to compose a full multimodal representation of what expressionism really meant: fusion of visual art, music and architecture.

A selection of the expressionist works of the real exhibition are displayed in the frame of the Einstein Tower, an expressionist work itself conceived by Erich Mendelsohn, one of the most significant architects involved in the artistic movement (see Appendix A for a detailed view of the model); the research rooms and the laboratories of the building are converted into exhibition rooms by exploring the different themes and the different phases of the artistic movement: at last, the visitor is guided through the inner tower to the observatory dome, ideally reconnecting the world of scientific exploration to the expressionist cosmo.

As pointed out before, the Einstein Tower World has been the first implementation of the ideas developed in our research about three-dimensional worlds usability issues. It is important to say that the expressionist world has been not only a great field to experiment our concepts, but also it provided us with some new suggestions as well; in fact we found some significant points of contact between the expressionist synesthetic ideals (meant to achieve a global esthetical experience) and our more practical needs to provide a more usable 3d experience: the auditorial artefacts (the so called *ear-cons* [1]) we have implemented in our virtual world are partly originated by this suggestion.

For the practical implementation, we had some constraints: the main goal was to produce a full multimodal experience; yet, this virtual world had to be accessible to a lot of people and to be compatible with low-bandwidth network constraints; so we chose for building the core of the project the second version of VRML, the language conceived to create and distribute 3D interactive worlds on the net [3].

2. The guided tour

Someone could say that in everyday life the maximum freedom consists of having the chance to move without any constraint; however, this is likely to yield highly inefficient and expensive tours.

We need guided tours in real life. We use cognitive artefacts [4] to go to work, to move through a complex building, to visit an exhibition; in other words we give a structure to space (or, more often, someone does this work for us) to move efficiently and perform our tasks.

Moreover, a lot of people would find unpleasant to move with their head in a box limiting the optical cone; but that is the way usually offered to move through virtual worlds on the net. And, with regard to VRML worlds, it is often more difficult to move the camera in the 3d scene than our head in the real life.

So it was an obvious decision for us to complement the opportunity for the user to move in three-dimensional space without constraints with the implementation of a preferential path to visit the virtual exhibition: a simple mechanism gives the visitor the chance to be guided through the rooms of the tower; yet, at any time, the visitor has the chance to choose a particular point of view to re-start exploration or to freely move in the 3d world.

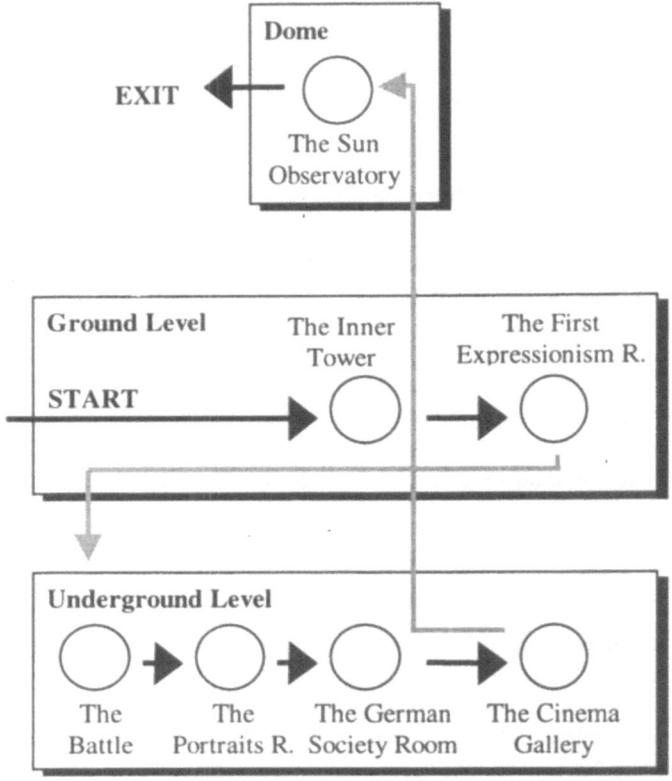

Fig. 1. The Einstein Tower World: a guided tour through an ordered collection of *loci*

3. Hypertext and vrml: integration vs. full immersion

Anyone who has tried the sensation of being in a foreign country without knowing its language will probably describe this situation as either unpleasant or uncomfortable; true 3D reality has not the strength to counterbalance lack of alphabetisation.

One of the main points of the Einstein Tower exhibition is to be an hybrid hypertext-vrml world; we tried to conjugate the strength of 3D representations offered by the VRML language, with the cognitive richness of hypertext; at any time, for each piece of art exposed in the tower, the visitor has the chance to ask for information, just clicking the mouse over the corresponding image movement (see Appendix B); moreover, textual information links to other information, in the usual way provided by hypertextual instruments.

The first version of the Einstein Tower World did not offer hypertextual information about the point of view on the scene corresponding to the visitor position; the second version automatically activates a link to information about the room currently occupied by the visitor movement (see Appendix B).

An usability test was informally proposed to some users, giving them the chance to experiment both the first vrml-only version and the subsequent html-vrml integration; all the people appreciated additional textual information; again this (perhaps obvious) observation is related to the fact that we live into an alphabetised world; so usually not only we need to know where we are, but also we wish (for need or pleasure) to have some qualitative information about the place we are in.

In conclusion, giving a pure experiential, illiterate immersion in a 3d world seems to have more drawbacks than points of strength. For this reason, we decided to integrate html and vrml; naturally someone could point out that some instruments offer the possibility to achieve a tighter integration, using text inside the virtual world; of course this is true, but it was well beyond our target (users connected to Internet using an average personal computer) because it would have requested a considerable amount of computing power to be devoted to text rendering in the scene with similar practical results.

4. Redundancy vs. single information

One of the keywords of this project was multimodality, that is to give the user multiple simultaneous information; we tried to implement it not only because of the peculiar nature of the exhibition, but as a general approach to render a synthetical experience more similar to real world experience, where often information regarding a particular situation comes simultaneously to different senses; in other words, we have tried to conjugate redundancy with efficiency; this apparently contradictory conjugation is often essential in real world, especially when a sudden reaction to outer events is requested.

Following this guideline we have tried to implement the whole virtual world as an ordered collection of *loci*, each of them defined as a co-ordinated set of three-dimensional, textual and auditorial information; for example the *locus* First Impressionism Room is defined as the summa of the three-dimensional representation, the hypertext automatically linked to describe the contents of the room and the Schönberg music audible only when the visitor walks inside it.

To be more precise, the music chosen to characterise Einstein Tower has an additional semantic link with artistic works contained inside; for example there is a strong correspondence between Schönberg music and Kandinsky paintings; they were both strongly involved in Blaue Reiter, the artistic association promoting synesthesia among arts.

Naturally we cannot expect to use this kind of semantic correspondence in any situation; in any case there are some considerations that can be generally applicable to virtual worlds.

5. Sounds as memoria loci

In particular the background music associated to places has a role similar to the earcons proposed by Meera Blattner et al. in 1989 [1]; which are defined as *the non-verbal audio messages used in the computer/user interfaces to provide information to users about some computer object, operation or interaction.* Soon afterwards, Stephen Brewster [2] investigated the use of earcons in different situations.

We tried to extend the use of this auditory interface to three-dimensional worlds. In this particular case, we associated specific earcons to a particular class of events: the presence of the visitor into a particular place. In the Einstein Tower World, earcons work as *memoria loci*, an auditorial reminder of the place the visitor is walking in.

This is particularly useful for VRML worlds on the net, where often the simplified morphology of the virtual environment and the limited optical cone don't permit a sudden visual recognition of locations. In this situation earcons integrate the role of vision, giving the user concurrent additional information about the place and thus permitting a more efficient navigation.

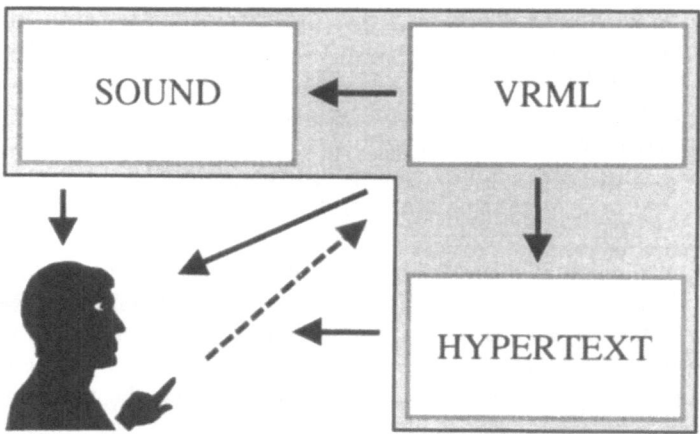

Fig. 2. Interactions between the user and a generic node (*locus*)
of the Einstein Tower World: information comes simultaneously to different senses

6. An exhibition in a floppy disk

As we pointed out in the introduction, one of the main goals of the project was to develop a virtual exhibition compatible with low bandwidth network; the first result obtained was a no-sound 500 kbyte version, including the Einstein Tower model, 30 artistic works and 50 hypertextual cards.

For sounds, we chose not to use MIDI because, although this system is a very efficient way to transmit information about sounds over the network, it doesn't guarantee the homogeneity of results using different sound cards: Schönberg music transformed in a game console melody would not have been compatible with the quality of the whole exhibition.

We worked hard to obtain 10 sound fragments long enough to avoid obsessive loops, but the result was a huge 5.5 Mbyte version with 8 bit 22 Khz WAV sounds; we were naturally eager to test the MPEG capabilities promised by the VRML 2.0 standard, but we had to wait for the availability of a browser.

At last, we could obtain satisfactory results only using the last version of Cosmo Player (the SGI VRML 2.0 browser): a 1.5 Mbyte version was obtained using 16 bit 44 Khz sounds coded with the mpeg layer 2 algorithm; so, thanks to the mpeg sound capabilities, we were able to obtain both higher quality and reduction of size: a whole exhibition in a floppy disk.

7. Future developments

Future development includes a simpler interface for guided tours in virtual worlds: the standard browser interface has too many options; we should be able to define a simpler set of widgets for navigation to augment interactivity.

Besides, we need to augment redundancy of information; in particular we should refine the use of earcons, extending the range of events to associate with sounds: the next step to be performed, in occasion of the fore coming Picasso exhibition again in Palazzo Grassi, will be the introduction of an improved auditorial interface with a larger set of earcons to help navigation and localisation of classes of objects.

8. Conclusions

The Einstein Tower is a work in progress; we conceived this world using beta version instruments, and in many cases we had to write the vrml files using simple text editors, because no tool seemed to be smart enough to automatically code our work; a lot of time was devoted to measure the distance between the VRML 2.0 standard and the software tools (editors, modellers, browsers) available; so we devoted a considerable part of our efforts to solve technical issues rather than concentrating exclusively on interface and in the virtual world contents.

Anyway there are some lessons that we learned and some partial results. The main lesson that we learned from our work is that it is extremely important to learn directly from life. Certainly 3d worlds offer the chance to build experiential situations that are too hard or too expensive to be built in real world and a considerable amount of efforts should be devoted to imagine and to test the potentiality of this issue; however, we should not forget real-life experience and one of our efforts should be to extrapolate the core of real world immersion to build richer, and more usable experiences in virtual worlds.

9. Acknowledgements

We would like to acknowledge the Palazzo Grassi management for their willingness to explore new frontiers of representation and new methods of communication. Special thanks to Otello Martin, director of the Interdepartmental Computer Centre for Scientific and Didactic Applications of Ca' Foscari University, that constantly supported our willingness to experiment new models of interactivity during the design of the Einstein Tower World.

References

[1] Blattner, M., Sumikawa, D., Greenberg, R. (1989). Earcons and icons: their structure and common design principles. Human Computer Interaction vol. 4, pp. 11-44
[2] Brewster, S.A. (1994). Providing a structured method for integrating non-speech audio into human-computer interfaces. PhD. Thesis, University of York, UK
[3] Hartman, J., Wernecke, J. (1996). The VRML 2.0 Handbook: Building Moving Worlds on the Web. Addison-Wesley, Reading (MA)
[4] Norman, D. A. (1993). Things that make us smart - Defending human attributes in the age of the machine. Addison-Wesley, Reading (MA)
[5] Pittarello, F. (1997). Palazzo Grassi web site. (http://www.palazzograssi.it)

Appendix A: The 3D Model

Fig. 1. External view

Fig. 2. Vertical section

170

Appendix B: Snapshots from the Einstein Tower World

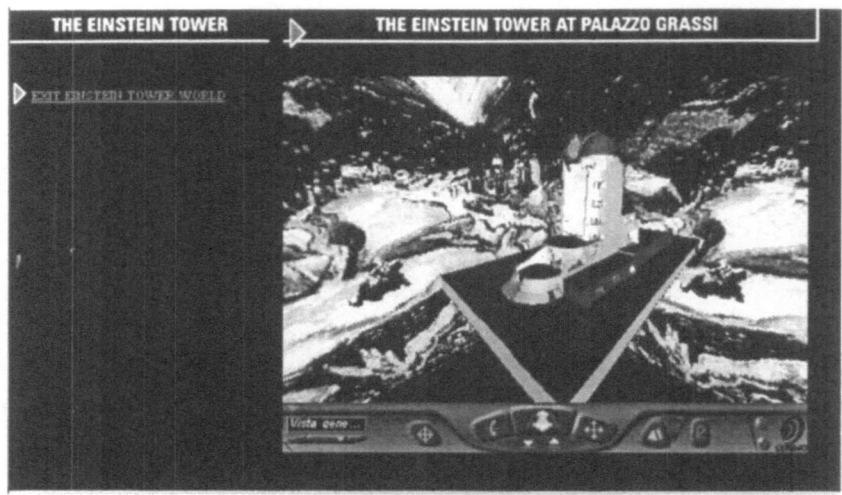

Fig. 1. The Einstein Tower landscape

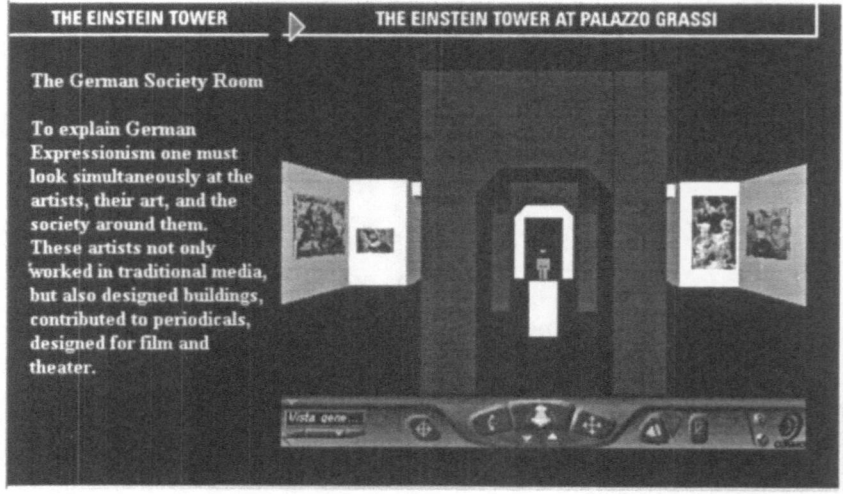

Fig. 2. Inside the Einstein Tower: the German Society Room

Fig. 3. The German Society Room: a painting by George Grosz

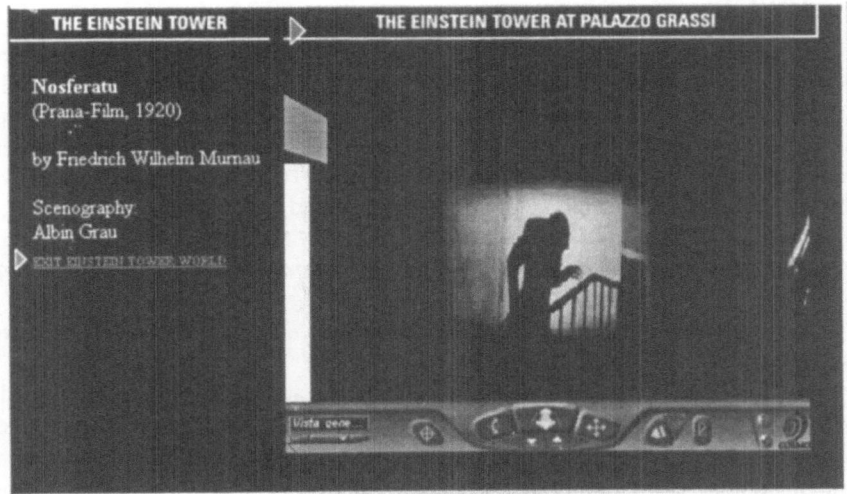

Fig. 4. The Cinema Gallery: a photo clipping from the film *Nosferatu*

Hybrid Approaches to Interactions between Real and Virtual Humans in Mixed Environments

Selim Balcisoy and Daniel Thalmann

Computer Graphics Laboratory, Swiss Federal Institute of Technology

EPFL, DI-LIG, CH-1015 Lausanne, Switzerland

{ssbalcis, thalmann}@lig.di.epfl.ch

Abstract

In this paper we analyse use of real-time video in Virtual Environments in interaction between real and virtual humans. We implemented our ideas in a Networked Collaborative Virtual Environment system, VLNET and in an Augmented Reality set-up. This paper presents three distinct case studies. The first one is a transatlantic demonstration, where distant users interact with virtual humans through several video tools. Our second case study is development of an Augmented Reality test bed. The third one presents a distributed Augmented Reality application, where participants share a mixed environment with real and virtual elements.

Keywords: Interaction, Virtual Environments, Distributed Augmented Reality, Real-time Video, and Virtual Humans.

1 Introduction

Virtual Environments are enjoying a large attention in recent years. Several shared virtual environment platforms are emerging. All these environments are mainly focused on 3D computer generated models and sometimes populated with virtual humans or simple avatars. State of the art virtual environments are human designed environments and less detailed compared to real world. To achieve higher immersive experiences and new ways of interaction between real and virtual humans, we need to reduce some basic limitations of the current virtual reality technology [BT97]:

Rendering of photo realistic, detailed and interactive environments in real time

Usage of restrictive human machine interfaces like magnetic trackers, head mounted displays.

In this paper we analyse these problems to some extent and propose several methods as possible solutions. In interaction our central concern is to let real humans to interact with virtual elements in a mixed environment in a natural way. We designed an Augmented Reality test set-up and realised a hardware and software platform. Computer vision techniques enabled us to perform correct mixing of real and synthetic worlds in real-time.

In our research we investigated several levels of interactivity in various mixed environments. Apart from our AR test environment, we investigated new ways of communication and interaction using Networked Collaborative Virtual Environments, NCVE, and live video streams. Live video stream can be used for several purposes. One typical example is a static video panel as a 'reality' window inside a virtual environment. We extended this basic idea to hybrid participant embodiments and hybrid networked environments.

This following section addresses interaction between real and virtual elements in detail. The subsequent section describes our Augmented Reality test environment briefly; it also demonstrates some research results. Afterwards we present our ideas on NCVEs and hybrid approaches to enhance them. We present our research results ranging from basic interactions in a homogenous NCVE to complex interaction in distributed Augmented Reality. The last section discusses our results and concludes the paper.

2 Interaction between Real and Virtual Elements

Interaction with surrounding environment means triggering some meaningful reaction in the environment in response actions such as body, social gestures or verbal output from a participant. In a mixed environment reacting elements can be real or virtual humans or other objects. In this section we will investigate interactions among all the elements of a mixed environment.

Object interactions in a homogenous environment is a well-studied problem. Virtual humans are able to interact with virtual elements by using sensors and autonomous agent technology [NT97]. A possible way of letting virtual humans to interact with real elements is to let them interact with virtual representatives of real elements. Considering trivial fact that a virtual human cannot move or deform a real object, interaction between real elements and virtual humans have some limitations. For static or 3D tracked real objects a virtual human can perform complex tasks like sitting on a real chair or following a real ball.

Real humans have similar limitations like their virtual counterparts. Their interaction is limited touching a virtual object using haptic VR devices or getting an immersive 3D visual feedback using head mounted displays (HMD). But such restrictive interfaces are not suitable for large scale mixed environments where several real participants are involved. Esthetics is an issue also. Tracker cables and HMDs are not suitable for design concerned application fields like broadcasting. A possible broadcasting application with HMDs and magnetic trackers is not suitable for production.

Interaction between real and virtual humans should be similar to interaction between real humans. In this paper we are interested in non-verbal interactions between real and virtual humans. This subset of interactions is concerned with body postures and their effects on other peoples' feelings. Virtual humans can perform pre-recorded body gestures as a combination of postures to express a specific state of mind. With a large repertoire of such gestures virtual humans can have a personalised body language [BT96]. The management of this repertoire can be done by different techniques: Autonomous agents, human operator or time-based sequential scripts.

Autonomous agents technique involves management of rule-based triggering of gestures. Balcisoy [BT97] proposed task oriented software architecture to handle such autonomous agents. Events can be triggered in context of a task and a task is activated by changes in a mixed environment. A major difficulty is indication of these changes in a mixed environment. A possible way of activating gestures is by a human operator. In this case virtual humans are guided by real persons in a mixed environment. This method is suitable for broadcasting and networked applications. Given a large set of gestures and some other motion generators, walking and grasping, participants guide virtual humans and let them interact with real humans.

Time –based sequential scripting is only interesting for some applications where all elements of real and virtual environments should follow a predefined script. Time-based event triggering can be useful for managing meta-tasks like drinking from a cup: grasping the cup, taking this cup to mouth and leaving it back.

3 Augmented Reality System Set-up

This section briefly presents system configurations and an overview of techniques used in our Augmented Reality set-up. We designed and realised a mixed environment to experiment on interactions between real and virtual elements. Our system, Figure 1, is implemented using off the shelf commercial equipment. Principal hardware platform is a Silicon Graphics Onyx RE2 graphics workstation, and a Sirius Video real-time video capture device.

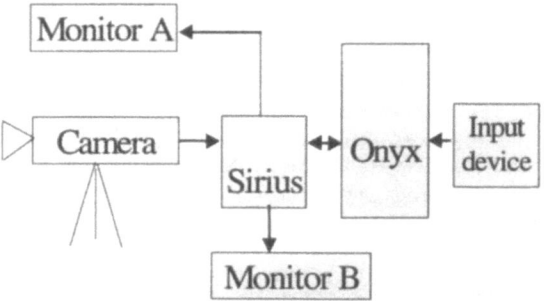

Fig. 1. Augmented Reality Setup

Correct occlusion of real and virtual elements is key issue to give the illusion of a mixed environment. We used a model-based approach where several real elements are represented by their 3D models in the virtual environment. Real camera parameters and positions of real objects are acquired by computer vision techniques to perform correct occlusion. Compositing is based on chroma-keying, where the virtual environment is treated as a 'blue room'. Participants in the mixed environment are getting the visual feedback from Monitor A. The mixed image is displayed on a large monitor to give a magic mirror illusion.

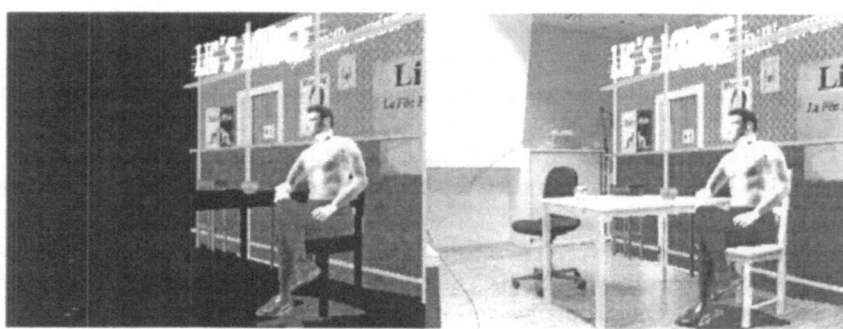

Fig. 2. Synthetic and Mixed Images

4 Networked Hybrid Environments

Networked collaborative virtual environments (NCVE) are enjoying a large attention in recent years. An example NCVE system, Virtual Life Network (VLNET) [CPNMTT97], is partly developed at LIG-EPFL.

VLNET is a client-server architecture based NCVE. A VLNET server includes a HTTP server for distribution of common files, a VLNET Connection Server, which manages new VLNET Clients entries and World Server initialisation issues and several World Servers managing distribution and world update, avatar update and live video steaming.

VLNET Clients are highly modular with several processes; Draw, Cull, Database, Communication and Main Process. Main Process includes several logical engines covering different functionality of VLNET system: Facial Representation, Body Representation, Navigation and Object Manipulation, Object Behaviour and Video Engines. In our case studies we used the following setup, Figure 3, to develop a Hybrid Avatar Controller.

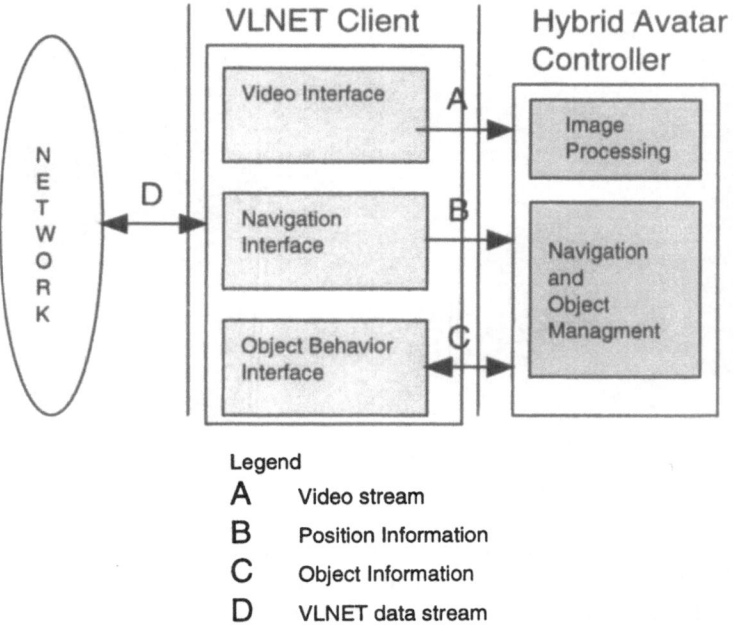

Fig. 3. VLNET and Hybrid Avatar Controller

5 Case Studies

We investigated several possible methods to use live video as an interaction tool between real humans and avatars in an NCVE.

Our first example is based on a homogenous NCVE with a 'window' into the real world. EPFL-LIG is partner of VISTA and VISINET projects and at Madeira'97 Conference on Global Networking European Project VISTA had made a joint demonstration with VISINET (TEN_IBC) and NICE project on NCVE topic. In this demonstration the objective was to present a virtual building created by the VISINET project in an interactive way. On the other hand more than ten different locations around Europe and North America were connected through ATM lines provided by NICE project. NICE project also provided a video conferencing application, ISABEL, which connects these sites with live video and audio stream. We used VLNET platform to integrate the virtual building and several virtual humans and a virtual camera. Virtual Humans were guided by remote users in Calgary (Canada) and Lausanne (Switzerland), the virtual camera was guided in Madeira (Portugal). Figure 4 presents network diagram of Madeira'97 demonstration. For the simplicity only ISABEL nodes at three VLNET clients shown. The video connection between ISABEL and VLNET was situated in Lausanne.

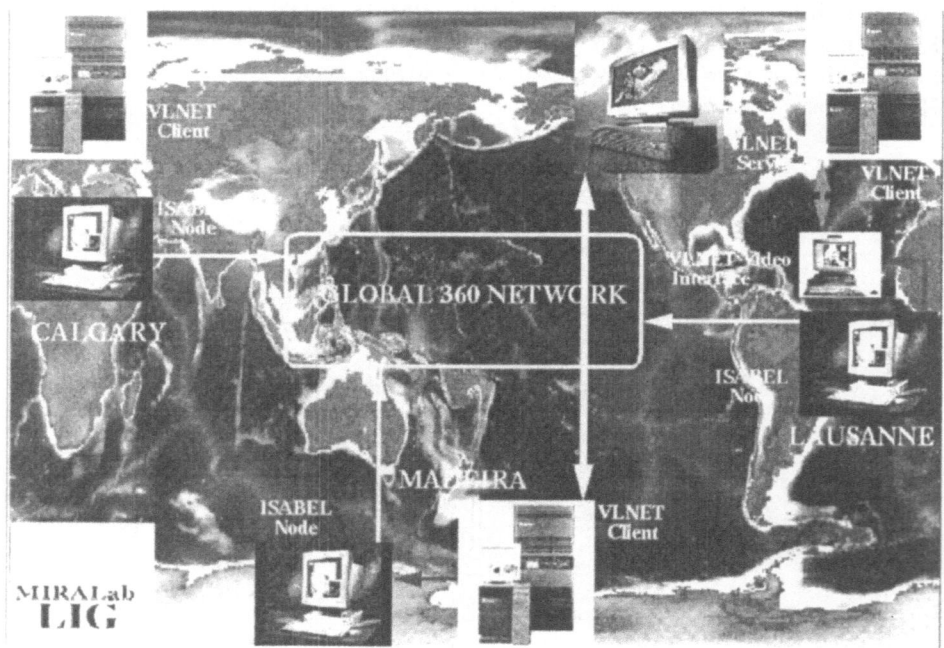

Fig. 4. Madeira'97 Network diagram

Our virtual camera output was distributed to all ISABEL sites over the ATM connections. In order to have interaction with some selected ISABEL sites we included a live video panel into our virtual environment, where we can have several videoconference nodes to be displayed and represented into our virtual environment. This video panel is a simple 3D object where live video stream is texture mapped on front panel. Texture mapped ISABEL node participants were able to see themselves and virtual characters, sharing the same environment. Guided virtual humans reacted to ISABEL participant's sentences with body animations, e.g. waving, dancing. Even in such a simple interaction, participants had the illusion of being in the virtual environment or in other words going one step further than just watching the event. Figure 4 display a snapshot from Madeira event, where the two virtual humans were interacting with ISABEL participants from Brussels.

Fig. 5. Interactions between virtual humans and video panels

Positive feedback from this demonstration inspired us to continue to work and experiment on Networked Hybrid Environments. We developed two distinct approaches to let participants interact in a NCVE.

Our first approach is to have hybrid embodiments in homogenous virtual environments. Hybrid embodiments are similar to primitive avatars, where a user is represented as a rigid 'body' and a 'hand'. In our implementation the rigid body is a texture mapped 3D object, namely a panel. The texture is live video stream from participants' camera.

Fig. 6. A Hybrid Embodiment

In our approach an avatar is characterised directly by participants' live video stream. Such a hybrid embodiment enables instant avatar personification. On the other hand there are several application fields like distant learning, where tens of participants is expected to interact with a lecturer on time-shared basis. In such case personification of avatars is an important interaction issue. Design of articulated 3D objects, as avatars is a time consuming process. On the other hand using a single video panel as avatar reduces interactivity in a 3D environment. Our hybrid solution is to extend a video panel with a hand as pointing and picking tool, which will enable participants to interact with the environment. Figure 6 displays a participant picking a box with virtual hand.

Our test hybrid embodiment is open to improvement. An immersive embodiment can be achieved by extracting participant from background image partially. Another approach is to improve design of the virtual panel. Several 3D objects can be texture mapped to increase perception and representation problems.

We tested our ideas in an experimental distant learning environment. Two students represented as hybrid avatars and one lecturer represented as a virtual human. Figure 7 presents a snapshot from this experiment. The goal was to introduce participants into a NCVE and let them interact with the Virtual Environment under guidance of a lecturer. The lecturer was able to perceive student's facial and upper body gestures on video panels in a natural way.

Fig. 7. Virtual Humans and Hybrid Avatars

Our second approach is to mix remote real persons in a real environment with real and virtual elements. Ahlers [AK95] proposed a Distributed Augmented Reality platform for collaborative design where users were interacting with real and virtual objects within a mixed environment. To have user representation and interaction we build our platform on VLNET system together with Augmented Reality modules. In this case a modified version of our Augmented Reality system, described in section 3, is being used. Main goal of this experiment was to study a possible distributed Augmented Reality platform. Our experiments concluded into a possible system design as presented in Figure 8.

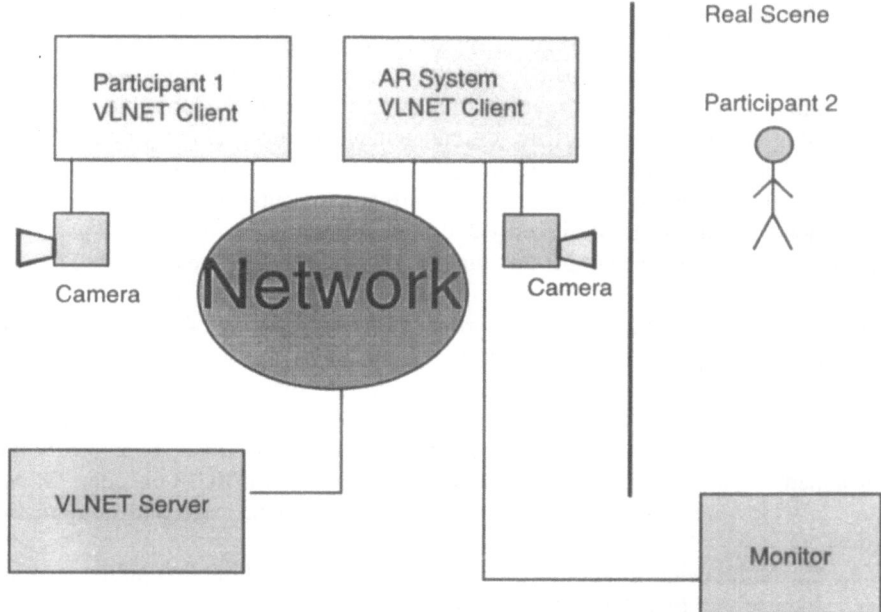

Fig. 8. Distributed Augmented Reality system.

In this system a remote participant, participant 1 is mixed into a real environment. To increase visual impact we extracted participant 1 from his VLNET client's video stream and performed transparent texture mapping.

The mixed image, Figure 9, contains one local participant, participant 2, with one remote participant, participant 1. In this setup both participant will have the same camera viewpoint. This Distributed Augmented Reality system is capable to let distant users share a real environment, and give illusions of being there to third party viewers.

Fig. 9. Interactions between real persons in a distributed environment.

5 Discussion and Conclusion

Our research in using video as an interaction medium between real and virtual humans is focused on two different research domains. Our first research domain is Augmented Reality. We designed and realised a hardware and software platform where we can test our ideas on interaction and Augmented Reality. There are several issues on interaction between real and virtual elements of a mixed environment. Both real and virtual humans have some limitations concerning interaction. A possible solution is developed by mapping characteristics of real elements into virtual environment.

Our second domain is NCVEs. We investigated several methods to develop hybrid networked environments, where real and virtual elements share the same mixed environment. In this paper we investigated interaction and participant representation issues in NCVEs. We used simple 3D objects with a live video stream texture mapped on it, as avatars.

In our case studies we focused on experimenting with video in NCVEs. Our NCVE platform VLNET provided us client/sever architecture for video distribution. For video sources more than five we experienced several difficulties concerning server load and network bandwidth. In future a proper video distribution like multicast will help to solve this problem. Another major issue with video over networked environments is expensive encoding methods. Affordable MPEG-2 encoders in near future will increase video stream quality (frame rate, image size and compression quality).

During our public demonstrations and experiments we figured out that public response to live video stream in a shared environment is generally positive. Seeing his/her own live image embedded into a virtual environment increases realism of the virtual environment. Additionally adding guided virtual humans and letting them interact with video participants creates the feeling of "being there".

As future work we plan to develop more computer vision based tools to acquire from real world. We will also focus on analyse and interpretation of this data flow. Correct mapping of real world into virtual world will enable virtual humans to interact with real environments autonomously.

Acknowledgement

The authors would like to thank Tolga Capin, who co-developed VLNET system used for tests, Patrick Keller who designed 3D models and Gael Sannier from MIRALab who worked on Madeira demo. This research was partly supported by ESPRIT project VISTA.

References

[BT97] Balcisoy S. and Thalmann D., "Interaction between Real and Virtual Humans in Augmented Reality", Proceedings of Computer Animation 97, Geneva, Switzerland, 1997
[CPNMTT97] Capin T.K., Panzic I.S., Noser H., Magnenat-Thalmann N., Thalmann D., "Virtual Human Representation and Communication in VLNET Networked Virtual Environments", IEEE Computer Graphics and Applications, Vol. 17 No. 2, March-April 1997.
[NT97] Noser H., Thalmann D., Sensor Based Synthetic Actors in a Tennis Game Simulation, Proc. Computer Graphics International '97, IEEE Computer Society Press, 1997, pp.189-198.

[BT96] Becheiraz P., Thalmann D., The Use of Nonverbal Communication Elements and Dynamic Interpersonal Relationship for Virtual Actors, Proc. Computer Animation '96, IEEE Computer Society Press, June 1996, pp.58-67.

[AK95] Ahlers K.H., Kramer A., Breen D.E., Chevalier P-Y., Crampton C., Rose E., Tuceryan M., Whitaker R.T., Greer D., "Distributed Augmented Reality for Collaborative Design Applications", EUROGRAPHICS 95, Maastricht, The Netherlands, 1995

An interactive face robot able to create virtual communication with human

Fumio Hara, Hiroshi Kobayashi and Fumiya Iida
Department of Mechanical Engineering
Science Univerisyt of Tokyo
1-3 Kagurazaka, Shinjuku-ku, Tokyo 162-8601, Japan
E-mail: hara@hafu0103.me.kagu.sut.ac.jp

We are studying the realization of natural human-like response of an animate 3-dimensional face robot in communicative interaction with human. The face robot can produce realistic human-like facial expressions and can recognize human facial expressions using facial image data obtained by a CCD camera mounted inside the left eyeball. We developed the real time machine recognition of facial expression by using a layered neural network and achieved the high correct recognition ratio of 85 % with respect to 6 typical facial expressions. And we also developed the new small size pneumatic actuator for display of dynamic facial expressions on the face robot and the same speed in dynamic facial expressions as in human was accomplished even in the swift expression of "surprise". For facial interactive communication between the face robot and human, we integrate these two technologies and the face robot can generate by itself the preferable facial expression to the human partner through the reinforcement learning. This implies a high technological potential for the animate face robot to undertake interactive communication with human when an artificial mind is self-organized through the interactive reinforcement learning.

KEYWORDS: Animate face robot, Virtual communication, Human robot communication, Facial expression, Recognition and production, Interactive learning

1. Introduction

Face-to-face communication between humans is considered as an ideal model in designing an agent such as intelligent software agent and/or intelligent human-cooperative robot that may create interactive communication with human, because the face-to-face communication is thought to play an essential role in our daily communication or in generation of the feeling of sharing something with our partners. The major feature of human face-to-face communication is the multiplicity of communication channels. A channel is a communication medium associated with a particular encoding method, for instance, an auditory channel for carrying voices such as speech, utterance, intonation and so on, and the visual channel for face actions including nodding motion of a head, facial expressions and so forth. Thus the face-to-face communication is a multi-modal communicative interaction between humans and has been a long-term, hard-work subject in socio-psychology as well as in cognitive psychology[1].

Concerning the face-to-face communication, Mehrabian[2] indicated that only 7[%] of message is due to linguistic language, 38[%] is due to paralanguage and 55[%] of it is transferred by facial expressions. This style of multimodal communication has attracted a keen interest among researchers involved in development of anthropomorphic human interfaces. However there is some discussions on the necessity of anthropomorphic interface for every intelligent software agent. It may strongly dependent on the task imposed on the agent. When we think of interactive communication between such software/hardware intelligent agent and human, an anthropomorphic agent may have a potential to create proactive interaction to human resulting in activating our brain ability for imagination, inspiration and creation of new things such as innovative ideas, artistic products, and/or helping us recover our brain activity. In face-to-face interactive communication, the facial expression is considered in psychology a major modality in transferring message between humans [2].We imagine that the anthropomorphic facial expression may, from the discussion above, be a potentially proactive modality in agent-to-human interactive communication. And thus we are interested in facial expression among many modalities such as hand/foot or limb/body motion, tactile action, prosodic voice and other body motion outputs.

When considered the facial expression for interactive communication medium between human and agent, there are at least two technological aspects; one is the recognition of facial expression, and the other is production of facial expression. For the first aspect, there have been quite a few research works. Moses et al [3] used the mouth valley contour which is a line between the upper and lower lips. They achieved the 100 % recognition rate for 5 different mouth shapes and could track the shape of the mouth at 50 Hz. Using Finite Element Method (FEM), Essa et al [4] modeled mechanics of facial tissue/skin and muscle (anatomicaly-based facial structure model). By using optical flow computation, they adjusted the anatomically based structure model onto the deformed face. According to the quantity of deformation of the model, they judged the facial expression in question and achieved the recognition rate of 98 % with respect to 4 facial expressions of 8 subjects. Yacoob et al [5] also used optical flow method for tracking the rectangular areas containing each of facial organs, i.e., eyebrows, eyes, nose, and mouth. Using the moving direction of each area, they obtained the recognitiion rate of 88 % with respect to 105 facial images of 6 typical facial expressions (surprise, fear, disgust, anger, happiness, and sadness) for 30 subjetcs. Black et al [6] did the tracking of each of the rectangular areas containing eyebrows, eyes, and mouth by using a kind of image brightness matching. They achieved the recognition rate of 90 % for 128 facial images of 6 typical facial expressions obtained from 40 subjects. We aslo developed a neural network recognition method by using the position data of 30 facial characteristic points (FCPs) that specify the shape change in eyebrows, eyes and mouth. We achieved the recognition rate of about 90 % for 6 typical facial expressions of 30 subjects [7]. Although these results have achieved a high recognition rate, they are not real time recognition of human dynamic facial expressions.

With regard to production of artificial facial expressions, there have been also quite a few research works [8, 7,10]. However they have been completely based on a computer graphic approach. We think that there is no necessity to confine the facial expression within 2 dimensional CRT display devices. Thus we have already developed a human-like, realistic face robot that can display various facial expressions [11].

This paper, in the first place, will summarize the achievement of real time machine recognition of dynamic facial expressions and then the real time production of facial expressions on the face robot. Thenafter we will integrate these two component technologies and explore the potential ability for the face robot to generate communicative interaction with human by demonstrating the learning ability of how to generate a preferavble facial expression to her human partner. Finally the works to be done in future will be briefly discussed. Note here that, in this paper, we are allowed to limit our present interest to the typical facial expressions such as surprise, fear, anger, happiness, disgust and sadness, which correspond to the emotions known in human cultures and are universally recognized [12].

2. Virtual communication

According to Nagao's definition of communication [13], human communication is a behavior to share something with other persons. He pointed out the difficulty in realizing a communication between a human and a machine (intelligent agent), and also indicated a suspicion to the necessity of human-machine communication. This is mostly due to the extreme difficulty in implementation of an "artificial mind" into a machine. However, as pointed out by Hara [10], a human would be able to feel as if he/she were mentally sharing something with a machine when the machine works at least along the following three functions [14]:

(1) Recognition of human partner's intention, feeling or state of mind,

(2) Decision of proper action, and

(3) Display it in appropriate form.

As we do not know whether or not the machine or intelligent agent really understands a human feeling and may have the "mentally-sharing feeling", we must say that there exists no real communication between a human and a machine. However, on the human side, he/she may have a high possibility to feel as if he/she feels satisfied with the message exchanged between him/her and the machine through anthropomorphic interface modalities such as 3dimensional facial expressions and voices. We thus point out that the "communication" between a human and a machine or intelligent agent / robot may be called "virtual communication" to clearly differentiate it from human-to-human communication.

In virtual communication, we deal with at least two types of information or message; one is factual information such as information composed of computer language and the other is psychological information such as human intention or feeling. In this paper we focus on the latter psychological information since we are interetsed in the aspect of communication between a human and a machine where a psychological message may play a major role to evoke feeling / affectiveness / emotion in the human partner.

3. Real time recognition of facial expression

The face robot is equipped with a CCD camera in the left eye and is able to collect facial image data. The data will be used for on-line recognition of human facial expressions. In this section we present a technology of real time recognition of dynamic facial expressions by using a layered neural network and show the recognition performance for 6 typical facial expressions such as surprise, fear, disgust, anger, happiness and sadness.

3.1 Data of facial image

We in the first place use a CCD camera(focus distance is 18[mm], resolution 256*240[pixel] and the brightness range from 0 to 256). The distance between the CCD camera and a subject is 1[m] for obtaining the face image taht covers the bottom of the jaw to the head. **Fig.1** shows the block diagram for obtaining face image data. A CCD camera is used in monochrome mode to take the brightness distribution data of human face. The numbers semi-circled in each block indicate a specific data processing (see Ref.[15]). We obtain brightness distributions along the vertical line segment crossing the iris shown in **Fig.2** from 10 subjects and the "base distribution of brightness (base data)" is acquired by calculating their average (see **Fig.3**).

By calculating a cross-correlation between the brightness distribution data and the "base data", we can extract the position of each iris of the eyes in terms of x-y coordinates in the face image. This is done by using a transputer system and 40[ms] are needed to extract the iris's position for one face image. The accuracy of the real time extraction of iris's position is evaluated for different modes of the subject's head motion. The results are shown in **Table 1** [15]. We find that the average difference between those obtained by our image processing system and by our naked eyes is about 3[mm]. Since this value is smaller than the radius of the iris, it is said that our image processing system realizes a high speed (about 40[ms]) and high accuracy automatic extraction of the center position of the irises.

By using the center position of the right and left irises, we determine each area including eyebrows, eyes and mouth respectively. And, we select the x-y coordinates for each of these areas empirically. Using the brightness distribution along vertical lines passing the facial organs such as eye, eyebrow and mouth, we build up the facial information for the recognition of facial expressions. Because the border lines of facial organs against face skin usually exists in horizontal direction and the change in facial expression appears in up or down movement of the border lines. In this study, we thus use the brightness distributions of the vertical lines crossing over the facial characteristic points (FCPs) [2], since the FCPs locate on these border lines. Then we select the 13 vertical lines crossing the FCPs shown in **Fig.4**.

In order to compensate the difference in the size of each subject's face, we normalize the face image so that the distance X , shown in **Fig.4** , between right and left irises becomes 20[pixel] by using affine transformation. From the X value and the center positions of both irises, we determine empirically the length of the vertical lines as to certainly include the eyebrows, eyes and mouth regardless of the test subjects. As the number of vertical lines is 13, the brightness distribution data then become 234[pixel](18*13). For emphasizing the characteristics of each facial expression, we need a special consideration to the modification of the brightness distributions [15].

3.2 Neural network training

We use the layered neural network(NN) composed of sigmoid-type units and shown in **Fig. 5** for the recognition of facial expressions. The unit number of the input layer is 234 corresponding to the number of facial information, the hidden layer unit number is 50 and the unit number of the output layer is 6 corresponding to that of 6 basic facial expressions.

We use the back propagation algorithm for NN training. As we already had the video tape recorded the facial expressions of 30 subjects, dynamically changing from "neutral" to each one of 6 basic facial expressions. We use them for the NN training and the recognition test. Since we will use the subjects, not used in the NN training, for the recognition test, the number of the subjects for the NN training is 15 at maximum, half of the total subjects. We select 15 subjects randomly for the NN training which is named as 15M.

As the brightness distribution data are ranged from 0 to 255, we normalize the range into

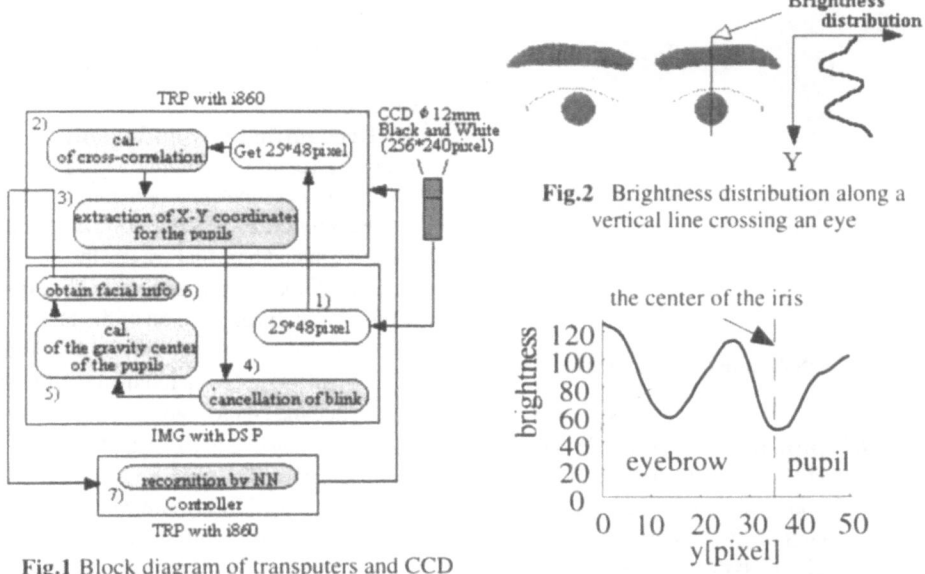

Fig.2 Brightness distribution along a vertical line crossing an eye

Fig.1 Block diagram of transputers and CCD camera to obtain face image data

Fig. 3 "basic" brightness distribution as the average over 10 subjects

Table 1 Measurement error in iris positioning (unit: mm)

subject (iris diameter)	right-left rotation	up-down rotation	right-left inclination	parallel disp.
A (9mm)	2.529	2.911	3.050	2.692
B (8.5mm)	2.714	1.907	1.682	1.861
C (7.5mm)	2.847	1.705	2.701	2.684

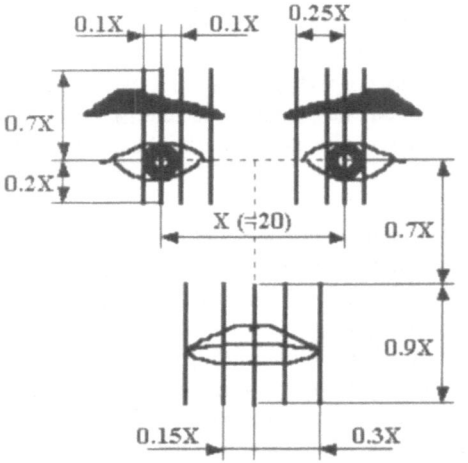

Fig. 4 13 vertical lines for obtaing facial information, X = 20 pixels

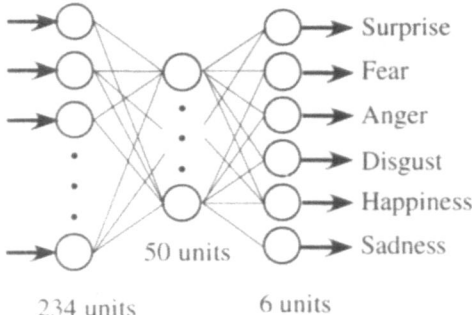

Fig. 5 Structure of neural network used

Table 2 Recognition results, training facial information: 15M

Facial expression	Recognized result					
	Sur.	Fear	Dis.	Ang.	Hap.	Sad.
Sur.	90	10	0	0	0	0
Fear	10	90	0	0	0	0
Dis.	0	0	60	40	0	0
Ang.	0	10	10	80	0	0
Hap.	0	0	0	0	100	0
Sad.	0	10	0	0	0	90

average : 85.0%

[0, 1] and use it as facial information which will be input into the NN.. As the teaching signal, we assign the value of 1 to the output layer unit corresponding to the same facial expression as that of the training information. The value of 0 was asigned to the other output layer units. We terminate the training process when the error between the output of the NN and the teaching signal becomes smaller than 0.01.

3.3 Recognition test and results

All processes from inputting a facial image data into our computer recognition system to the recognition by NN are done automatically. It is noted here that we use the off-line trained NN for the recognition test. The time needed from the acquisition of the facial information to the recognition is less than 15[ms]. All processes including the iris positioning and the NN recognition is performed within 55[ms]. However the image-processing time is not constant due to the size of face. Then the interval for taking the face image is set to 2/30[s] (66.7[ms]).

Though we obtained the recognition result at every 66.7 [ms] for dynamically changing facial expression, it was hard to tell the facial expression in the middle of its change from "neutral" to each of 6 typical facial expressions. Thus we employed the NN recognition result at the final time-step in the change of facial expression. **Table 2** shows the distribution of correct recognition ratio, misrecognition ratio, and the average of correct recognition ratio for 6 basic facial expressions, where the result was obtained from 15 subjects. From this table, we find that if we use the NN training information 15M, the average of correct recognition ratio reaches 85[%]. Bassill[16] reported that the average of correct recognition ratio for 6 basic facial expressions obtained by the trained persons was about 87[%]. This indicates that the NN has almost the similar ability of facial expression recognition as that of human subjects (see Ref.[15])

4. Facial expression by face robot

This section describes briefly the design and construction of 3-dimensional, human-like face robot and presents the performance in expressing 6 typical facial messages such as surprise, fear, disgust, anger, happiness, and sadness.

4.1 Design and construction of face robot

In the field of psychology, the movement of facial muscles is divided into 44 basic components called Action Units(AUs)[12]. Referring to the Action Units approach, we design the face mechanism to realize the indispensable AUs for expressing various facial expressions. **Table 3** shows the 14 AUs required to express the 6 typical facial expressions[12]. For these 14 AUs shown in **Table 3**, we select empirically the 18 points on the face skin shown in **Fig. 6**. We call these points as "control point". Each of the 14 AUs is found to be realized by the particular combination of control points as shown in **Table 4**. To move the control points appropriately in each facial expression, we employ small-size flexible microactuators (FMAs) [17] which are driven by air pressure. As FMAs for the control points 14-18 shown in **Fig. 6** must be installed in a jaw part, the size of the face robot jaw is 1.2 times as large as a human jaw and consequently the face robot is 20% larger than a human face.

The other structural characteristics of the face robot are as follows: eyeball has 2 degrees of freedom for its rotation in the same manner as in human eyeball. Inside the left eyeball we equip a CCD camera. The movement of the whole body of the face robot has 3 degrees of freedom as in turning, nodding and inclining motions. The face frame for disposing 18 FMA actuators is made of aluminium. The skull is made of plastics and installed onto the face frame as shown in **Photo.1**. The face is also installed with a pair of dentures for teeth and silicone rubber for skin. The thin wire connects the FMA actuators and the control points located on the back surface of the silicone face skin. This wire connection is made in one-to-one correspondence

Table 3 Required AUs for 6 typical facial expressions

AU No.	Appearance Changes.
1	Inner Brow Raiser
2	Outer Brow Raiser
4	Brow Lowerer
5	Upper Lid Raiser
6	Cheek Riser & Lid Compresso
7	Lid Tightener
9	Nose Wrinkler
10	Upper Lid Raiser
12	Lip Corner Puller
15	Lip Corner Depressor
17	Chin Raiser
20	Lip Stretcher
25	Lips Part
26	Jaw Drop

Table 4 Correspondence of AUs to control points

AU No.	Control Point	
	Right	Left
1	2	3
2	1	4
4	5, 6	7, 8
5	9	10
6	11	12
7	9	10
9	13	
10	13	
12	11	12
15	16	17
17	18	
20	14	15
25	18	
26	18 & Motor	

188

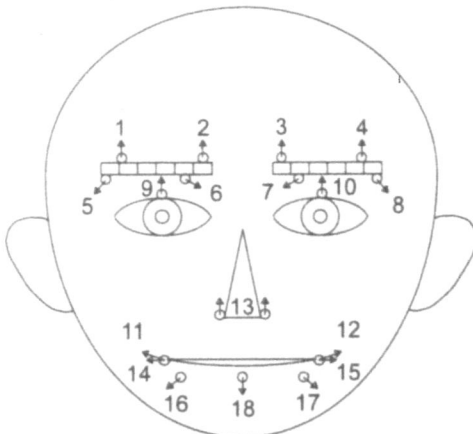

Fig. 6 Location of 18 control points

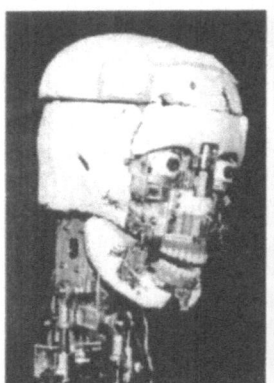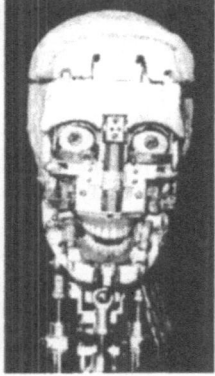

Photo. 1 Skull frame of the face robot

Table 5 6 typical facial expressions organized by AUs

Expression	Action Units (AUs)
Surprise	1+2+5+26
Fear	1+2+4+5+7+20+25,26
Disgust	4+9+17
Anger	4+5+7+10+25,26
Happiness	6+12(+26)
Sadness	1+4+15

between the actuator and control point. We put on the natural hair wig on the face robot head and make up it to look as natural as possible.

4.2 Experiments of facial expression display

We determine the combination of AUs[12] necessary to produce each of the 6 typical facial expressions on the face robot. The result is shown in **Table 5**. We then empirically determine the required movement in each of the AUs for each facial expression. Note that **Table 6** shows the 24 AUs to be realized on the face robot by combining the control points selected in this paper. This implies that the face robot has a large potential to make various kinds of facial expressions. According to the required movement of the AUs for expressing each of the 6 facial expressions, the control points are forced to move by the FMAs. Then the face robot expresses the 6 facial expressions. **Photo.2** shows the neutral face and the 6 facial expressions on the face robot.

We undertake the recognition test by showing each of the photos shown in Photo.2 to 30 subjects and ask these subjects to judge the facial expression they look at into 7 categories ("neutral", "surprise", "fear", "disgust", "anger", "happiness" and "sadness"). The results are shown in **Table 7**. **Table 7** shows that, although the facial expression "fear" tends to be recognized as "surprise", the average correct recognition ratio over the 6 facial expressions is about 83.3[%]. This ratio is almost equivalent to the ratio(87[%]) attained by trained students for recognizing facial expressions expressed by actors[16]. We believe the facial expression "fear" might be missrecognized due to a immature tuning of all AUs required for this expression since the "fear" involves 8 AUs. However we think this is not an essential problem and will be improved by a finer tuning of those AUs.

4.3 Faster response micro-actuator

We found that the FMA dynamic capacity was not enough to dynamically express each of 6 basic facial expressions at the same speed as in human facial expressions. The facial expressions "surprise", "fear" and "anger" required the time five times as much as in human facial expres-

Table 6 Implemented AUs in the face robot

AU No.	Appearance Changes	AU No.	Appearance Changes
1	Inner Brow Raiser	15	Lip Corner Depressor
2	Outer Brow Raiser	16	Lower Lip Depressor
4	Brow Lowerer	17	Chin Raiser
5	Upper Lid Raiser	20	Lip Stretcher
6	Cheek Raiser	25	Lips Part
	& Lid Compressor	26	Jaw Drop
7	Lid Tightener	27	Mouth Strech
9	Nose Wrinkler	41	Lip Drop
10	Upper Lid Raiser	42	Slit-Optional
11	Nasolabial Furrow	43	Eyes Close-Optional
	Deepener	44	Squint
12	Lip Corner Puller	45	Blink-Optional
14	Dimpler	46	Wink-Optional

Surprise   Fear   Disgust

Neutral

Anger   Happiness   Sadness

Photo. 2 Neutral and 6 typical facial expressions (FMA actuators used)

sions (2.2[s], 2.0[s], 1.9[s]), and those "disgust" and "happiness" needed the time about 4 times(3.0[s], 2.1[s]), and "sadness" needed the time about twice times(3.0[s]). The FMA had no measurement device of its elongation which made it impossible to mimic the dynamic movement of the facial characteristic points(FCPs).

In order to improve the above-mentioned two drawbacks of FMA, we developed the following new actuator. **Fig.7** shows the structural configuration of the new actuator "ACDIS(ACtuator for the face robot including DIsplacement Sensor)" developed.The ACDIS is equipped with a double action piston to make the actuator response to be fast. The ACDIS is driven by air pressure. A LED and a photo-transistor are equipped inside the ACDIS as shown in **Fig.7**. We control the piston displacement of ACDIS for tracking the FCP displacement obtained from the dynamic human facial expresisons. By using this control method, it is possible to carry out not only dynamic facial expressions on the face robot in the same manner as human facial expres-

190

Table 7 Recognition results of
6 facial expressions made by face robot

Facial expression	Recognized result					
	Sur.	Fear	Dis.	Ang.	Hap.	Sad.
Sur.	**97**	3	0	0	0	0
Fear	27	**53**	10	3	0	7
Dis.	0	0	**77**	20	0	3
Ang.	3	3	10	**84**	0	0
Hap.	0	0	3	3	**94**	0
Sad.	0	0	3	0	0	**97**

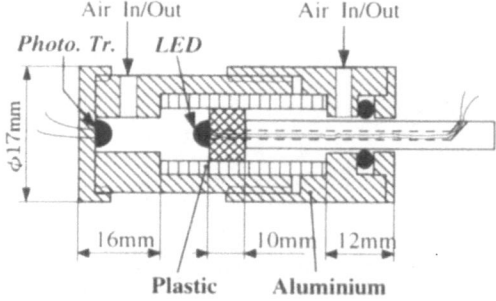

Fig. 7 ACDIS structure

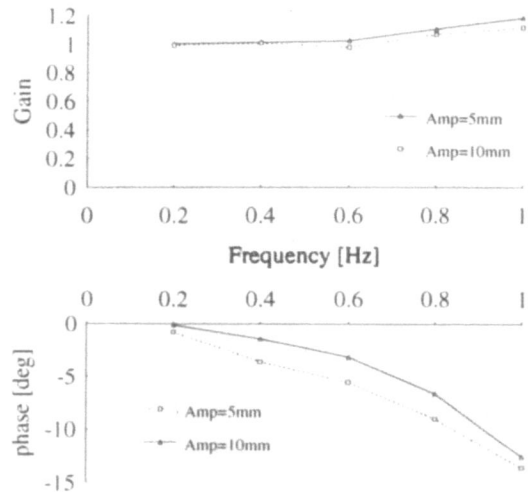

Fig. 8 Bode diagram of ACDIS

sions but also the arbitrarily speedy displacement of FCPs.

The dynamic characteristic of ACDIS control was examined in terms of the frequency response of the ACDIS to which a square of silicone rubber used as the face skin of the face robot attached. **Fig.8** shows the Bode diagram of ACDIS for the case of 10[mm]/5[mm] stroke which is corrrespondent to FCP no.2 movement in the vertical direction. This diagram shows almost constant gain and a slight phase delay over the frequency range needed for our face robot [18].

5. Face robot interaction with human

Since the face robot has not yet been implemented with eye-tracking function which is needed to see always her human partner's face, the human partner or subject is placed to sit directly at face-to-face position with about 1 m distance. Thus the face robot is able to obtain the face image of her partner in terms of the brightness distribution along the 13 vertical lines defined in Section 3. The lighting was carefully adjusted to obtain a proper human face image through a CCD camera installed in the left eyeball of the face robot.

5.1 Direct reflex of facial expression

All the neccesary initialization for the transputer system as well as for the computer to control 18 ACDIS actuators was done before the facial interaction experiment. When the subject started to make one of 6 basic facial expressions, simultaneously the face robot started to obtain the subject's face image. By using the brightness distribution, the face robot in the first place determined the location of two irises and then obtained again the brightness distribution along the 13 vertical lines.

After normilizing the brightness distribution data, they were input to the trained neural network (NN) for recognizing the facial expression. The time needed for this one facial recognition was almost 66.7[ms]. The face robot did output the result of recognition of the facial expression and stored the result.The recognition of facial expression was successively done. If the face robot obtained the same recognition result three times, then the face robot decided the subject' s facial expression as that obtained. Then the recognition result was transfered to the computer by RS-232C and the target displacement of each ACDIS actuator needed for the facial expression was given. Then the face robot started to drive the neccessary ACDIS actuators toward the target displacements in a fashion of displacement feedback control. Thus the face robot simply reacted to the facial expression displayed by the subject. If the robot would make a misrecognition, then the robot's facial expression would be different from that shown by the subject.

Photo. 3 shows two examples ((a) and (b)) of facial expression produced by the face robot when the face robot recognized the facial expression which is shown in the right hand side in the photos. The (a) facial expression displayed by the face robot was "sad" face which is apparently different from that of the subject. The (b) facial expression on the face robot is "angry" face which is a direct reflex to that shown by the subject even if the subject's mouth was not open [19].

5.2 Learning of preferable facial expression

At step i, the human partner or subject sitting in front of the face robot evaluates the facial expression. That facial expression was made by setting the displacement of each ACDIS actuator (action $a(i)$) needed for the specified facial expression. The evaluation was made as "very good (+1)", "good (0.5) ", "fair (0)", "not good (-0.5)", and "bad (-1)". The subject input his/her above numerical evaluation (reward $r(i)$) into the Q-learning algorithm [20] implemented in the face robot computer. Then the computer calculates the value function $Q(a(i))$ using the reward $r(i)$

$$Q(a(i)) = 0.5 \times Q(a(i-1)) + 0.5 \times r(i) \ \text{------------------------------------} \ (1)$$

and the probability defined by Boltsmann distribution

$$P(a(i)) = Exp\{Q(a(i)/T)\}/\Sigma Exp\{Q(a(j)/T)\} \ \text{--------------------------} \ (2)$$

where

$$T = 0.1 - 0.05 \times \{r(i-4) + r(i-3) + r(i-2) + r(i-1) + r(i)\} \ \text{-----------} \ (3)$$

 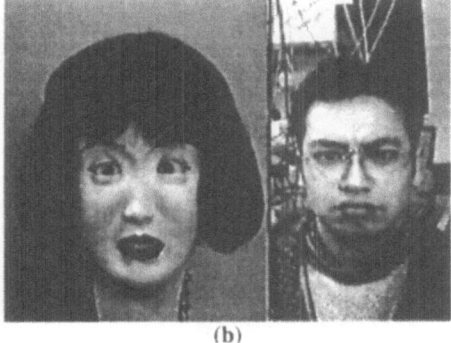

(a)   (b)

Photo. 3 Direct reflex of facial expression to the human facial expressions

Then one action a is selected out of the action set A according to the Roulette rule [21] based on the probability given in the above equation. The face robot takes the selected action a or changes the ACDIS displacements to the new ones resulting in production of another facial expression. Again at step i + 1, the human partner evaluates the facial expression in terms of the numerical values ranged between (+1, +0.5, 0, -0.5, -1). The same experimental procedure as above is repeated until the human partner will be satisfied with the quality of the specified facial expression, in other words, the facial expression produced at present step is preferable to the human partner.

The interactive learning experiment was carried out for "happy" facial expresion. In the experiment, ACDIS actuators positioned at the control points 2, 3, 11, and 12 were used and other ACDISs were set at the displacements corresponding to "neutral face". Each of 4 ACDIS actuators took the designed maximum or mimimum displacement at each time step i. This experiment was done for 5 subjects (college students) separately and we examined how the generated "happy" facial expression looks and how the learning process was proceeded.

Photo. 4 shows the "happy" facial expression produced at one of the initial period of the learning process and the one at the final learning period. The face robot can produce a really happy facial expression with a partial opening of her mouth showing her white teeth. **Fig. 9** shows the timewise change in the average value of the numerical evaluations given by 5 subjects, at which the reward value (+1, +0.5, 0, -0.5 and -1) were replaced by 4, 3, 2, 1, and 0, respectively. The human evaluation became better with increase in the number of the interactive learning steps. It is worthy to note here that the face robot did not use the ability to recognize her partner's

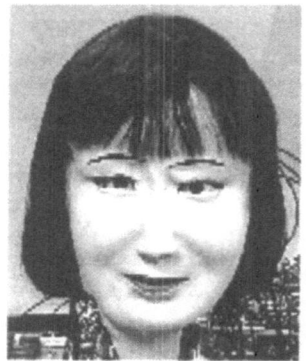 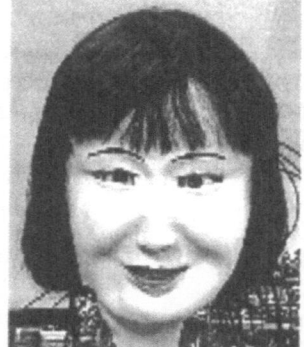

Photo. 4 "Happy" facial expressions in the interactive learning process

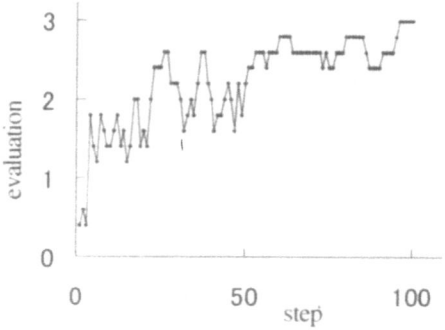

Fig. 9 Evaluation of "happy" facial expression with learning steps

facial expression or she was blind in the experiment. This was due to the reason that the learning algorithm used is based on the supervised learning, i.e., the reward is given by the human subjects.

From these two experimental results, we may conclude that the face robot that is implemented with a supervised learning algorithm will be able to generate the facial expression preferable to her human partner. These figures also suggest us the potentiality that, if the face robot is implemented with a learning algorithm and an evaluation mechanism to the human partner's facial reaction, it may also generate the facial expressions personalized to her human partner.

6. Concluding remarks

As explained in sections 3 and 4, the animate face robot developed is equipped with the function of real time recognition of human facial expressions and also with the function of real time production of 3 dimensional dynamic facial expressions. The former is surely correspondent to sensory function and the latter to motor function in the realm of human-to- face robot communication. The animate face robot implemented with these sensory and motor functions may have a potential to be used to develop an "artificial mind" through the interactive learning between the face robot and a human partner. In the interactive learning, the facial information corresponding to the movement of facial organs will be directly connected to the ACDIS actuators with some interconnection and weighting factors. Through facial interaction with human partner, the interconnection and weightings will be adjusted by the learning algorithm together with evaluation mechanism. From this point of view, we demonstrated an example of generation of "happy" facial expression through the supervised interactive learning. This implies that the face robot may generate her "personality" through the interactive learning with her human partner. Thus we may not need to implement any model of "artificial mind" into the face robot. However we need a thourough discussion about the evaluation mechanim for bettering the interactive communication between the face robot and humans. This may be crucial for seeking a solution to the challenging question always given to the face robot, i.e., what kind of "artificial mind" shoud be implemented ?

As pointed before it is surely better to additionally employ the other communication modalities such as voices. We are specially interested in prosody information processing in speech recognition and synthesis. As a new direction of our research, the integration of facial expression recognition with prosodical speech recognition is the most urgent and exciting one to improve the communicability.

The use of 3-dimensional, human-like face robot seems to be a breakthrough compared to the conventional 2-dimensional CRT display devices. This paper showed a promising potential of face robot as a more realistic, natural communicative agent. However it should be noted that several premature factors of the face robot fail to demonstrate its full potential advantages in the realization of human-robot communication. The face robot currently lacks Action Units corresponding to squeezing lips, breathing, and tongue motion. These are essential to make a synchronization of mouth movement with synthesizing prosodic speech. Another one of the future works on our animate face robot is, thus, pointed out as follows: Synchronization of mouth movement with synthesizing prosodic speech.

Then we can finally point out several potential applications of the animate face robot. The first application is considered a 3 dimensional physical agent with an ability of facial expression for interactive entertainment. Second application may be a new artistic interactive media like an interactive sculpture that may express various facial expressions when an audience comes to close to the sculpture face robot. The third one may be a new type of puppet show or robot-augmented opera where robots and human actors/actresses play opera together. Other applications may be rehabilitation of handicapped persons who have some difficulty in expressing their facial expressions or training of attractive facial expressions.

Acknowledgments

This research work was partially supported by the Research for the Future, JSPS, through 1996 to 2000. The authors thank to those involved and also to the students, Department of Mechanical Engineering, Science University of Tokyo, who assisted the experiments.

References

[1]   V. Bruce, " Recognising Faces (translated into Japanese)", *Science Pub. Co., 1990.*

[2]   A. Mehrabian, "Communication without Words", *Psychology Today, Vol.12, No.2, 1968*

[3]   Y. Moses et al," Determining Facial Expressions in Real Time", *Proc.of International Conf. on Computer Vision, 1995, pp.296 - 301*

[4]   I. A. Essa and A. Pentland, " Facial Expression Recognition using a Dynamic Model and Motion Energy", *Proc. of International Conf. on Computer Vision, 1995, pp.*

[5]   Y. Yacoob and L. Davis, " Computing Spatio-Temporal Representation of Human faces", *IEEE Trans. On Pattern Analysis and Machine Intelligence, 18 (6), 1994, pp. 636 -642*

[6]   M. J. Black and Y. Yacoob, " Tracking and Recognizing Rigid and Non-rigid Facial Motions using Local Parametric Models of Image Motion", *Proc.of International Conf. on Computer Vision, 1995, pp.374 - 381*

[7]   H. Kobayashi and F. Hara, " The Recognition of Basic Facia Expressions by Neural Network ", *Proc. of Joint International Conf. on Neural Network, 1991, pp.460 - 466*

[8]   A. Takeuchi and K. Nagao, " Communicative Facial Display as a New Conversational Modality", *Proc. ACM/IFIP INTERCHI, 1993, pp. 187 - 193*

[9]   S. Seto, Y. Nagata, Y. Yamashita and Y. Takebayashi, " Multimodal Response of a Real Time Speech Dialogue System", *Proc. 8th Human Interface Symposium, 1992, pp. 693 - 698 (in Japanese)*

[10] F. Hara, " A New Paradigm for Robot and Human Communication", *JSME Proc. Robotics and mechatronics, No. 940-21, 1994, pp. 1 - 9 (in Japanese)*

[11] H. kobayashi, F. Hara, G. Uchida and M. Ohno, " Study of face Robot for Active Human Interface", *Journal of the Robotic Society of Japan, 12 - 1, 1994, pp. 155 - 163 (in Japanese)*

[12] P. Ekman and W.V. Friesen, " Facial Action Coding System", *Consulting Psychologists Press, Palo Salto, CA. 1977*

[13] M. Nagao, " Some Problem in Communication between Human and Machine", *J. Artificial Intelligence, 8 -6, 1993, pp. 705 - 708*

[14] M.A. Arbib, "Neural Networks and Brain (translated into Japanese)", *Science Pub. Co., 1992,pp. 1 - 507.*

[15] H. Kobayashi, A. Tange, and F. Hara," Real Time Recognition of 6 Basic Facial Expressions", *Proc. IEEE International Workshop on Robot and Human Communication, 1995, pp. 179 - 186*

[16] J.N. Bassilli, "Emotion Recognition; The Role of Facial Movement and the Relative Importance of Upper and Lower Areas of Face", *Personality and Social Psychology, 37 - 11, 1979, pp. 2049 - 2058*

[17] Y. Suzumori, "Flexible Microactuator (in Japanese)", *Trans. of JSME(C), 55 - 518, 1989, pp. 2547 - 2552*

[18] H. Kobayashi and F.Hara, "Real Time Dynamic Control of 6 Basic Facial Expressions on Face Robot", *Journal of Robotic Society of Japan, 14-5. 1996, pp.677 - 685*

[19] H. Kobayashi and F. Hara, " Facial interaction between Animated 3d face Robot and human Beings", *Proc. IEEE Internationa Conf. on Systems, Man and Cybernetics, 1997, pp. 3732 - 3737*

[20] R. S. Sutton and A. G. Bato, "Reinforcement Learning", *MIT Press, 1998, p.322*

[21] D. B. Fogel, " Evolutionary Computation" , *IEEE Press, 1995*

A Flexible Prototyping Tool for 3D Real-Time User-Interaction

Roland Blach, Jürgen Landauer, Angela Rösch, Andreas Simon

Competence-Centre Virtual Reality
Fraunhofer Institute for Industrial Engineering (IAO)
Nobelstr. 12, D-70569 Stuttgart, Germany
phone: +49-711-970-2153, fax: +49-711-970-2213
Roland.Blach@iao.fhg.de
http://vr.iao.fhg.de

Abstract

High interactivity in real-time environments requires new system design concepts for virtual reality environments. We will define our understanding of a modern system and describe the prototypical system *Lightning*, which addresses some of these new features.

Keywords: Virtual reality, Virtual environments, Virtual reality development system, Immersive environments, Interactive real-time systems

1.0 Introduction

Virtual Reality (VR) in our understanding, is an interface technology which allows direct multimodal interaction with dynamic and responsive computer generated or so-called virtual environments. Responsive virtual environments should operate in real-time, that is, the response time and update rate of the system is high enough that it generates an experience of continuity. Continuity is a major precondition for the impression of an imperceptible boundary between user and virtual environment, the so-called interface. This is related to the idea of immersion or sense of presence, which is in our opinion a product of the used techniques and the content. Immersive interfaces seem to enable a different experience compared to classical interfaces. We consider this property to be one of the major differences between VR-systems and other 3d-systems such as CAD systems.

We see the main purposeof VR-technology in the enhancement of human computer interaction. Especially in problem domains of high complexity the use of immersive virtual environments enables more direct perception and manipulation. Obvious examples are complex evaluation or planning tasks like architecture or design, medical training, fluid dynamics in engineering, assembly planning, etc..

196

2.0 Basic Considerations

The user interface of a virtual reality system (VR-system) can be considered as a closed loop system where the user is an integral part of the system ('human in the loop'). The generalization of the user concept to other external systems including also more users seems obvious and useful.

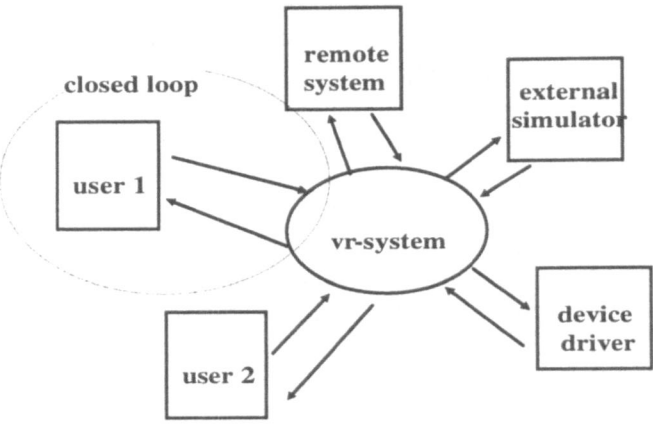

Fig. 1. General VR-System Structure

A VR-system can be divided in internal and external subsystems. As external we consider all subsystems where only the interface is known but there is no complete control in the sense of parameterization or restructuring during run-time. Obvious examples are human users, external simulation programs, hardware devices, etc.

The internal simulation system contains adequate abstractions of entities and their communication system to define the application and input/output modules. Basically it samples the outside world via sensors or other communication mechanisms. A new internal state will be computed according the inbuilt dynamics, behavior or interaction rules. The display modules sample the internal state of the simulation and generate the adequate output.

We see some similarities between complex artificial machines/organisms like robots and VR-systems. A minor difference is actually the embedding factor of reality and virtuality. In classical virtual reality systems the user is surrounded by computer generated environments. The VR-system has to capture 'only' the user, but has to generate the impression of a complete and convincing environment. A robot f.e. has to capture its physical environment and to compute 'only' the adequate output for its effectors. A major difference is the existence of a goal of the system. A virtual reality system has no defined end state or goal, it is a kind of open system. Some researcher have defined performance goals like frame rate and used control theory methodologies [13] to obtain these goals. Basic approaches are realized in visual rendering as for example frame-rate based level of detail (LOD) switching to achieve a constant frame rate, which is only a small part of the overall performance. Another approach are prediction schemes for motion tracking [14] where for example Kalman filtering was proposed.

This more general understanding of a virtual reality system leads us to the assumption that some of the problems might have been solved already in other research areas as for example in robotics, control and system theory or artificial life. Especially strategies to overcome the lack of information in case of sensors are needed. General synchronization schemes might be derived with these strategies. One of the challenges for system design is a flexible and extensible methodology of achieving consistency between known and unknown input and output modules and the internal simulation. We have concentrated in our concepts basically on space and time consistency which leads to the problems of synchronization and exact overlay of physical and virtual space. General consistency should consider basically all state information, as for example colour space matching is an important issue for augmented reality.

A virtual reality system distributes output, for example visual rendering and input tasks for example collecting position tracking data to independent process to be able to control request times. The application consists often of an event propagation module and sometimes if higher computing load is expected, independent simulation processes, for example a dynamic simulation of moving objects. But even today many systems do have an inflexible structure concerning the distribution of the application load in regard to heavy interactive user involvement. Main focus was the real-time capability of the display output, or mostly the visual rendering, although some researchers are concentrating also on other features like 3D acoustics [1] or force-feedback output [2][7]. Input processes run usually as an external process, as fast as the hardware device is able to deliver the data. In our understanding it is not just necessary to collect input-data in real-time, it has to be evaluated in real-time. Output should sample the internal real-time simulation at a physiological suitable and necessary rate. That implies a shift to a real-time input loop compared to today's systems where the focus is more on real-time output. Two main points have to be addressed:

- Real-time capability of the system behavior, that is evaluation and event propagation of the input data completely independent from output.

- Internal storage of sampled input data to produce continuous output at a later time.

This real-time capability is particularly interesting in case of dynamic behavior of objects in combination with user interaction.

In the following we will describe how our prototype *Lightning* addresses these considerations.

3.0 *Lightning*

The *Lightning* virtual reality system was first presented in 1996 [6] as a rapid prototyping tool for VR applications, particularly in the architectural and presentation domain. Since then it has evolved to a mature tool for interactive engineering environments, where prototyping of 3D user interfaces becomes an important issue.

3.1 Software architecture overview

The design of the system is inspired by a common event propagating paradigm similar to for instance VRML 2.0 [11] or Open Inventor [12], as it can be seen in the following section. Fig. 2. gives an overview of its system architecture.

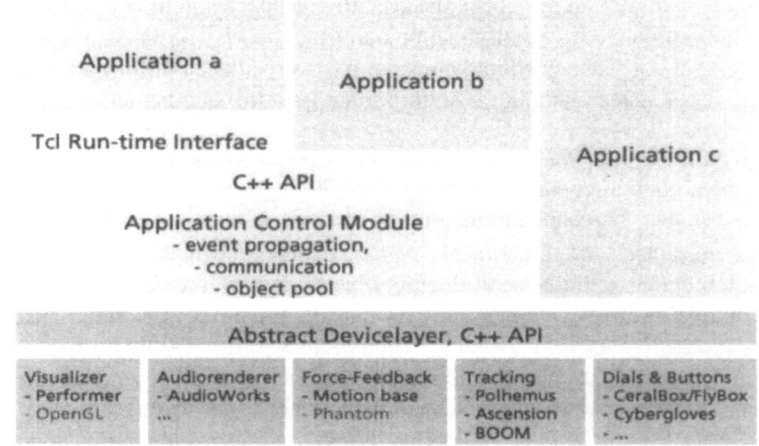

Fig. 2. *Lightning* overview

Its core component is a database called object pool. Application developers define the environment merely by creating or deleting objects within this database. The interactivity and the behavior can be introduced with function objects and communication channels, so-called routes. These communication channels define application specific event propagation and therefore the interactivity.

A basic object type is provided with several properties:

- Unified Interface slots so-called fields provide a standardized interface for the event propagation module.

- A uniform update function, which changes the internal state according to the data at the input fields and the internal state of the object.

- Execution of this update function, only if the input data has changed or the object has been handed to a specialized administration module, which always calls the update function. This is a generalized implementation of the so called sensor type in VRML2.0 [11].

Objects have a certain internal linkage, which connects them to the *Abstract Device Layer*. System or application developers can extend the system simply by providing a new object with the described field interface.

Generic render devices exist for visual and audio renderer. The specific implementation will be filled in via inheritance, which in case of the visual renderer provides the actual implementation is based on the IRIS Performer [10] graphical render library. The specific Performer renderer links the visual scene graph to *Lightning* objects and reports changes of the geometry of a visual object to the underlying library and, as a result, to the graphics device hardware.

3.2 Event propagation

Objects within the pool and their links form a directed graph (link graph) which is evaluated at each simulation step. Starting with output from sensor objects, information is propagated along links. The behavior description code of a behavior object node is re-executed as soon as all nodes prior to this node (along the path of links) produced new output or at least had a chance to do so. Finally, if all graphs are evaluated, the procedure repeats. Output is defined by objects like for example cameras, which are part of the object pool, but are sampled asynchronously by the various renderer.

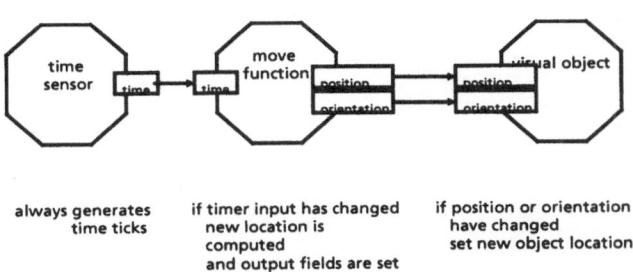

always generates	if timer input has changed	if position or orientation
time ticks	new location is	have changed
	computed	set new object location
	and output fields are set	

Fig. 3. Example of event propagation

3.3 Multilanguage/multiparadigm programming

Lightning does not rely on a specific language but supports a heterogeneous, mixed-language approach. That is, behavior objects written in, for instance, C++ can be freely replaced by objects written in an interpreted language and vice versa, even at runtime. So far, we have used the Tcl programming language [8] as it is easy to integrate into other systems and as a free software package many resources and extensions. With its self evaluating property, the "eval" command it also has an expressive power similar to the "lambda" of Lisp or other AI languages. This enables a compact description of high-level behavior.

3.4 Multiprocessing

Multiprocessing is provided on the device level. All devices, which have significant differences in the update-rate are scheduled in another process. This holds basically for all input devices. Conceptually all render modules have their own processes. The IRIS Performer render library provides its own extended multiprocess scheme. The *Application Control Module* can distribute independent subgraphs to different processes. Often a link graph can be divided into two or more subgraphs, which are not connected through links.

3.5 Superposition of virtual space and user space

One basic approach to designing a projection model is to achieve an exact match of virtual and physical space. That is, the apparent size of an object should be independent of the projection system. If this is the case, the handle of a teapot would have exactly the same size if seen on a CRT screen as if seen on a wall projection. Consequently, the user can interact naturally with the teapot without the need for scaling the geometry model. In *Lightning* the projection system is specified simply by providing a geometric model (with exact physical dimensions) of the projection environment. With this data, the projection is automatically configured by the system.

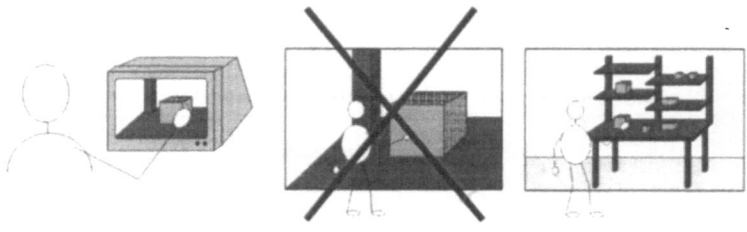

Fig. 4. Projection system independence of object size

Location measurement calibrations are actually also an important factor for exact spatial matching. In *Lightning* this feature is provided on device module level.

3.6 Synchronicity

Todays virtual reality environments often consist of various modules, each operating with different update rates. That is, they have different virtual time bases with different granularity. It is necessary to synchronize these modules to obtain consistent or causal system behavior. The internal use of virtual time by different parts of the system is completely transparent. An obvious case is the synchronization of rendering: The sound of a ping pong ball should be delivered by the acoustic renderer exactly in that moment when the user perceives the visual sensation of the ball colliding with the paddle. The *Lightning* system is designed to use a mechanism to transform discrete states into a continuous representation that is capable of serving an object state at a definite virtual time either via interpolation or extrapolation. This mechanism links different simulation modules to allow translation of different virtual time bases. The internal structure of the interpolation/extrapolation is considered as a basic system service and therefore it remains hidden for the application developer.

3.7 Extensibility

An important key feature of *Lightning* is its extensibility. All application objects are accessible via the Tcl interface. Behavior scripts can be developed to define the functionality of applications. New applications can be built completely on this layer.

On the core system layer we use a combination of object oriented techniques and operating system features for decoupling the modules. Application objects inherit the interface and communication properties from a base class. The communication process operates only on base class features. The configuration and initialization communication is strictly string based to enable run time coupling.

All *Lightning* system libraries are so-called shared objects, which are linked at runtime. This feature is used primarily for ease of maintenance. Application objects are by default shared objects and can be accessed immediately by the Tcl interface without coding or recompiling. This is a major advantage for the extensibility of the system. Application objects can easily be developed; only common system interfaces have to be included. The extension on C++ level is also independent of static linking with the system.

4.0 Related Work

This section reviews related work on VR system architecture. There have been a lot of proposals for augmenting visual output in VR with other media, especially for spatial audio output. But, often caused by hardware performance limitations, very few of them provide a common framework which uniformly integrates all media currently available. In VPL's Body Electric [2], users specify relations between virtual world entities and I/O devices in a dataflow diagram editor. This dataflow approach can also be found in a variety of similar systems such as SGI's Open Inventor[TM] [12]and VRML 2.0 [11]. A pure dataflow approach, however, came out to insufficiently support program modularity. Hence, VRML allows for defining complex object behavior within so-called script nodes, often written in the Java programming language. As mentioned earlier, the VRML model is very similar to our behavioral semantics system, particularly the object pool. But the specification of VRML is not without ambiguity, so behavior tends to depend on the actual implementation. Aimed mostly at internet applications, existing VRML browser, by contrast, do not provide ways for flexibly accessing modern output systems such as force feedback or wall projection with tracked shutter glasses. Many commercially available products such as Sense 8's WorldToolKit (WTK) or Division's dVS system provide good support for most visual and acoustic output configurations, but do not include force output. They usually provide programming interfaces for C++ and often specifically designed interpreted languages. Other researchers provide additional languages such as Python [9] OML [5], or, for high-level interaction, Scheme [3]. Aimed at a broad range of application domains, *Lightning* could not rely on a single language but had to provide means to support many existing paradigms. The Alice system [9] also automatically separates simulation and rendering into different processes. *Lightning* has adopted this approach, but provides a finer granularity as both simulation and rendering processes are automatically divided into subprocesses if more processors are available. The Avocado system of GMD [3] follows an approach similar to our system. It is based on a concept called 'Performer with fields' but is closer dedicated to the IRIS performer graphics library as *Lightning*.

5.0 Conclusion and future work

In this paper we have shown how recent requirements affect the architecture of VR systems. They need to take into account various i/o media and to provide ways for defining interactions and behavior and synchronize all these modules. The VR system *Lightning* has been implemented with these design issues in mind. It integrates audio and video output and is open for other media. Its multi-language behavior specification allows for more flexible and faster behavior prototyping. *Lightning* has shown its usefulness at various occasions in real-world applications ranging from engineering to entertainment.

Having implemented some of the design considerations the next step is to evaluate the performance. Next steps include research of the physiological and cognitive aspects of the perception of time, to be able to adapt system behavior better to the user. Furthermore the system should behave dynamically such that objects have weight and elasticity because it seems to be considerable useful to help user to interact more intuitively.

6.0 References

[1] Astheimer, P., Dai, F., Göbel, M., Kruse, R., Müller, S., Realism in Virtual Reality, Artificial Life and Virtual Reality, ed. by N. Magenat-Thalman and D. Thalman, 1994.

[2] Adachi, Y., Kumano, T., Ogino, K., Intermediate Representation for Stiff Virtual Ob-jects, Proc. IEEE VRAIS, Research Triangle Park, N. Carolina 1995.

[3] Hasenbrink F., Avocado system, Unpublished White Paper, GMD Department Visualisation and Media Systems Design, (Bonn St. Augustin 1997), (see http://viswiz.gmd.de/?hase/Avocado.html)

[4] Blanchard, C., Burgess, S., Harvill, Y., Lanier, J., Lasko, A., Obermann, M., Teitel, M., Reality built for two: A virtual reality tool, Proc. 1990, Symp. on Interactive 3D Graphics, Snow Bird, (Utah 1990).

[5] Green, M., and Halliday, S., A Geometric Modeling and Animation System for Vitual Reality, Communications of the ACM, Vol. 39, No. 5, (May 1996).

[6] Landauer J., Blach R., Bues M., Rösch A., Simon A.: Towards Next Generation Virtual Reality Systems, Proc. IEEE Conf. Mulitmedia Computing & System, (Ottawa 1997)

[7] Mark, W. R., Randolph, S. C., Finch, M., Van Verth, J. M., and Taylor, R. M., Adding Force Feedback to Graphics Systems: Issues and Solutions, Proc. ACM SIGGRAPH 96, (New Orleans 1996).

[8] Ousterhout, J., Tcl and the Tk Toolkit (Addison-Wesley, Reading, Massachusetts 1993).

[9] Pausch, R et al., A Brief Architectural Overview of Alice, a Rapid Prototyping System for Virtual Reality, IEEE Computer Graphics and Applications, (May 1995).

[10] Rohlfs, J., Helman, J., IRIS Performer: A High Performance Multiprocessing Toolkit for Real-Time 3D Graphics, Proc. ACM SIGGRAPH, (Orlando 1994).

[11] The Virtual Reality Modeling Language (VRML) Specification Version 2.0, ISO/IEC CD 14772, (see http://vrml.sgi.com/moving-worlds/spec/ index.html)

[12] The Open Inventor C++ Reference Manual, (Addison-Wesley, Reading MA 1995)

[13] Schraft et al.: A Fuzzy Controlled Rendering System for Virtual Reality Systems Optimized by Genetic Algorithms, Proc. 2nd Eurographics Workshop on Virtual Environments, (Springer, Wien, 1995)

[14] Azuma R, Bishop G.: A Frequency-Domain Analysis of Head-Motion Prediction, Proc. ACM SIGGRAPH 95, (Los Angeles 1995).

Reactive Virtual Environment System:
LivingWorlds multi-user world

Ryo Yoshida * and Carmine F. Greco

*Tokyo Research Laboratory, IBM Japan Ltd., Software Solutions, IBM Corp.

Abstract

We describe a VRML browser-and-server system that we developed to support the LivingWorlds specification for multi-user environments. Since the browser supports VRML version 2.0 with quality-of-service (QoS) control, the LivingWorlds module was implemented by using the VRML 2.0 Java application interfaces. We discuss the concept of designing systems with QoS control, and the problems encountered and solutions reached in actually implementing a LivingWorlds client-server system.

1   Introduction

Several VRML browsers have been developed over the past year, during the formative period of the VRML 2.0 specification [6]. One is a plug-in type of HTML browser, another is a helper application of the first, and a third is a non-VRML browser that can load and render VRML contents. VRML models have been created for various areas such as entertainment, manufacturing, and telecommunication, and thus the interests of people involved in VRML are moving in various directions, one of which is multi-user shared-state environments. Several research groups have created experimental distributed VR systems for multiple users. Their current goal is to support large numbers of participants simultaneously connected to a network. In a multi-user environment, a user can join a discussion in a virtual meeting room or go shopping in a virtual mall via an "avatar," which is the user's agent in that virtual world.

Several working groups (WGs) for VRML have been formed to discuss various themes in line with the interests of participants. Groups working actively on multi-user environments include the the Humanoid Animation WG, the GeoVRML WG, the Database WG, and the LivingWorlds WG. We are involved mainly with the LivingWorlds WG, in which the most important activity is lower-level (system-level) technical discussion of topics, including file syntax specification [3] based on the concept of the shared-state space and object model. Our project started before standardization of the VRML 2.0 specification got under way. The system we designed, called Reactive Virtual Environments

---

*1623-14   Shimotsuruma,   Yamato-shi,   Kanagawa   242-8502,   Japan, e-mail:yoshidar@trl.ibm.co.jp

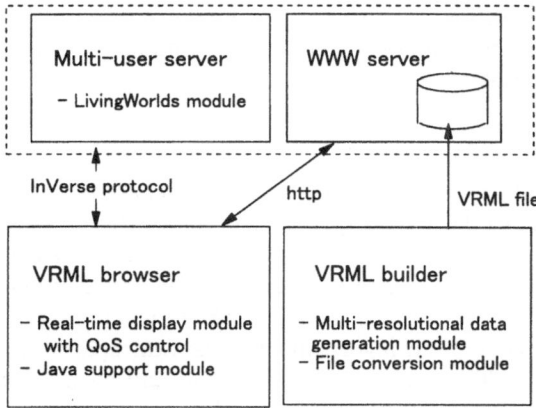

Fig. 1. RVE system overview

(RVE), consists of a VRML browser and two additional modules, a Living-Worlds multi-user server and a VRML file builder. Figure 1 shows an overview of the RVE system.

In this paper, we restrict our discussion to multi-user systems (browser and server). In section 2, we give an overview of system architectures and related work. In section 3, we introduce our VRML browser and server, and describe our implementation, which conforms to the LivingWorlds specification. We also introduce two examples of applications using our system. Section 4 discusses the direction of our activity, and Section 5 is a summary of the paper.

2 Multi-user systems

2.1 System architectures

In general, there are three architectures for building systems to realize a shared-state virtual world. The first is a client-server model. This model makes it conceptually simple to build a shared-state world, and is therefore used as a basis for multi-user systems. In this model, there is always only one reference world. The server maintains master versions of all of the objects in the world, and the client basically copies the master from the server when it initially loads the world. The second architecture is a peer-to-peer model in which all the clients maintain the same world among themselves, instead of copying the master from the server. The reference world is maintained by each of the clients. The third architecture is a hybrid of the above two models, using both the server-client model and the peer-to-peer model. The systems in this category have a wide variety of implementations; for example, the client may have a replica of the world and maintain it for reference, although the server also has the master world. Each model has strong and weak points. We use the client-server model for our RVE system, since it generally minimizes the required network bandwidth and computational power.

2.2 Related Work

There has been considerable research on multi-user shared-state environments. Sony's Community Place [1] is one system that supports the construction of a multi-user environment, using a client-server model. When the user changes the state of an avatar on a certain client, information on the avatar's position and orientation is sent to the server, and the server then dispatches that information to the chosen clients, using their algorithms to select the spatial areas of interest where the client exists. The protocol linking server and clients is a proprietary Virtual Society Client Protocol. To build a VRML shared-state scene, the user has to write it with Sony's proprietary defined nodes, and therefore the scene builder has to rewrite it when porting it to another system.

Another example of a multi-user system is SPLINE, designed by Mitsubishi Electric America [7], which is positioned as a platform for shared-state environments. A world named "Open Community" was built by using SPLINE. The Open Community specification includes an API, which is available with the SPLINE module and has comprehensive interfaces between the network layer and the world model layer. The scene generated by the system seems to be a multi-user shared-state world, but not a VRML world. If an implementor wants to develop a new browser or a new server using the Open Community API, he/she might need to use SPLINE's modules, since in practice it is not an open specification.

3 RVE architecture

The RVE system follows a client-server model. We developed the browser partly in C/C++, to display the scene-graphs, and partly in Java, to support the VRML Java platform scripting API for Script nodes and to communicate with the server. The server was developed only in Java.

Our project has two principal objectives: (1) to develop a VRML browser that can process interactions with users without serious delay and can also display large amounts of data in applications such as CAD geometry, and (2) to develop a client-server system that can share the state of a world simultaneously visible to many users across a network. Recently, multi-user environments, including systems conforming to the LivingWorlds specification, have been built with low-cost home computers, whereas in the past, distributed VR systems usually included many very high-performance and expensive computers. It is thus now possible to form a multi-user environment by using computers and connections with a wider variety of performance levels, such as low-cost PCs without any graphics accelerator boards connected to a network by modems, and high-performance graphics workstations connected via LANs. To realize a situation in which every user can see the same world almost simultaneously in

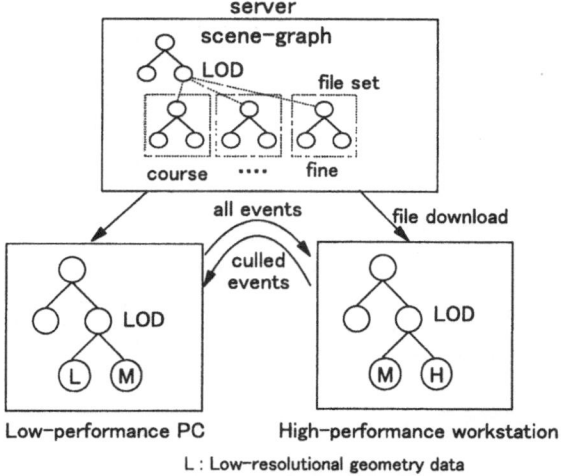

L : Low-resolutional geometry data
M : Mid-resolutional geometry data
H : High-resolutional geometry data

Fig. 2. QoS-able system

such a heterogeneous environment, the client needs to coordinate its own load to be able to reflect the results of user interactions by updating the display screen of a world at an appropriate frame rate. Otherwise, a user on a low-performance client PC will always have a delayed view of events and will miss some occurrences in the world, since they will be reflected to the client's display screen with a serious delay. To solve this problem, we applied the quality-of-service (QoS) control technology, whose concept is shown in Figure 2, to the VRML browser. The basic concepts of the technology are as follows:

- According to the performance of the machine, an appropriate level of detail is selected and the display frame rate for updating the scene is coordinated to reflect changes in the scene promptly without causing the frame rate to fall during display.

- For low-bandwidth networks, redundant event information transmitted from the server to clients is eliminated, to reduce the network traffic.

For example, in the case of a low-performance PC connected to a network by a modem, a smaller level-of-details (LOD) set of VRML data, that is, the coarser three levels of the five levels of LOD data set, is selected and sent to the client when it initially loads a world. At the time, the browser itself notifies the server of the performance level for the data set selection. Once the browser starts rendering a scene, in response to the user's dragging a mouse, a series of events can be partially culled. Thanks to this technology, even a low-performance PC user can join a multi-user (i.e. heterogeneous performance) environment without viewing of a scene being delayed.

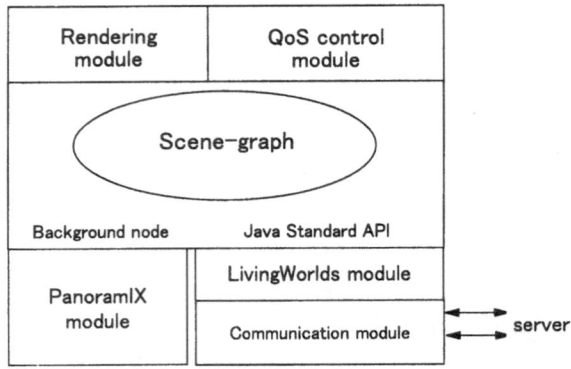

Fig. 3. RVE client

3.1 RVE browser

The RVE browser supports the VRML 2.0 specification; that is, it can load a scene-graph containing the VRML standard nodes, prototyping, and ROUTE. As the API of the Script node, the browser provides the Java in Script Nodes Authoring Interface (JSAI) implemented by Java version 1.1, but does not support any External Authoring Interface (EAI). By loading the initial VRML world, our browser works as a helper application of an HTML browser.

When the user does not enter a world that includes a shared-state space, the browser functions simply as a stand-alone VRML browser. Figure 3 shows the client architecture. In particular, the PanoramIX module enables the user to see VRML objects in front of a background panoramic image generated by the PanoramIX technology [2], if the input file contains a Background node with the PanoramIX control file name. The Rendering module calls the Direct3D API. The QoS control module estimates the load of the next frame by comparing the actual time from start to end of the display routine with the time expected in the previous frame. This QoS control module works for runtime; however, to select the appropriate LOD set of VRML data for the machine performance at the initial loading of the world, the QoSInfo node and QoSSwitch node defined by prototyping appear in the main VRML file. An example is shown in List 1.

In the current implementation, once the user enters the shared-state space, the browser contacts the server via a proprietary protocol (the InVerse protocol) that works on the IP network. The LivingWorlds module runs between the communication layer and the VRML Java platform scripting API layer.

3.2 RVE server

The RVE server supports functions specified in the LivingWorlds of August 1997. The function for communication between clients and server is provided

```
EXTERNPROTO QoSInfo {                EXTERNPROTO QoSSwitch {
    field    MFint32 range    []         eventIn    SFInt32 level
    field    MFFloat frameRate []        exposedField MFString url        []
    eventOut SFInt32 level               exposedField MFNode   children   []
} "urn: ....."                           field        SFVec3f bboxCenter 0 0 0
                                         field        SFVec3f bboxSize    -1 -1 -1
                                     } "urn: ....."

   ex. DEF QoS QoSInfo {
          range     [500, 2500, 10000]   # polygons per frame
          frameRate [5, 10]              } # frames per second
       DEF LodSelector QoSSwitch {
       url ["lowRes.wrl","midRes.wrl", "highRes.wrl"] }
       ROUTE QoS.level TO LodSelector.level
```

List 1. Prototypes for QoS control nodes.

by the module named "InVerse." Its communication infrastructure has two components: one controls the sender and receiver of the shared object's information, which changes every moment, while the other controls the registration and management of the clients connected to the server. The LivingWorlds module functions as a shared-state object information holder on the communication infrastructure, as shown in Figure 4. A QoS control module and Object drag & drop module on the server side will be added in the next version. The server maintains the information about the positions and orientations, as well as the specified field values of shared objects, which are routed to the LivingWorlds AssociativeStringArray. When the user enters the shared-stated world or moves around in the world, the browser sends the position and orientation information to the server, and the server then distributes the information to all or some of the clients. Since the system uses the concept of a proximity group of avatars, the information is sent to the chosen clients on which the user's avatars are mutually located in neighboring in the world. The server can currently maintain a single shared-state scene; however, if the user wants to create two independent worlds, he/she needs to run two servers to maintain these respective worlds.

In the client-server system we designed, while the server maintains one complete and independent scene including one zone, a client can connect to multiple servers. Therefore, when the client loads several independent scenes from the respective servers, it displays them as a world.

3.3 LivingWorlds module

All the nodes defined according to the LivingWorlds specification are written in PROTO/EXTERNPROTO with several VRML standard nodes, including the Script node working with a Java program. Each Java file is required to be compiled into a class file that includes invocations of the Java interfaces (JSAI). Here, we note that nodes related to the "lock" have not been implemented, because to implement its function we may need to define what should be protected, whom we have to protect it from, and how we should protect it. It may

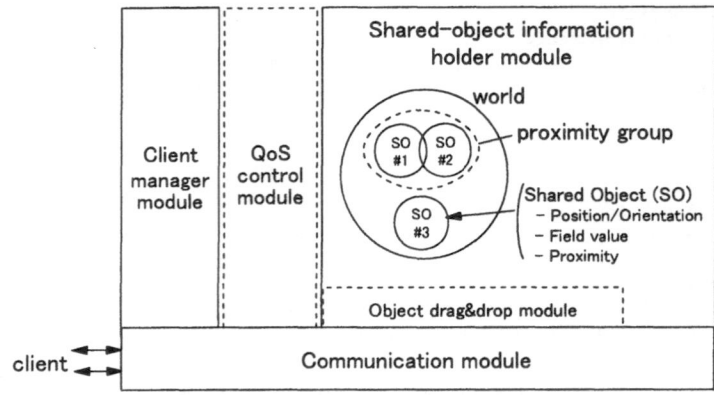

Fig. 4. RVE server

be a better approach for the run-time performance to implement the Living-Worlds node as a native node such as a VRML standard node rather than as a prototyped one in PROTO/EXTERNPROTO, although a VRML file including those native nodes does not have compatibility on the VRML 2.0 browsers generally used. On our browser, the QoS control module is also useful for solving this performance-related problem; that is, it distributes CPU power not only for scene rendering, but also for execution of the Java program that implements the LivingWorlds functions.

In accordance with the LivingWorlds concept, IBMZone and IBMSharedObject were implemented for MuTech technology, in addition to Zone, PrivateZone, SharedObject, PrivateSharedObject, Selector, SelectorItem, all converters, and AssociativeStringArray. The details of these functions are stated in the Living-Worlds specification. For us, there were two issues involved in implementing LivingWorlds modules by using the RVE client-server system: one was proto-typing with the Script node, and the other was processing events between nodes. Moreover, there was one important issue involved in authoring a world.

The prototyping problem is caused by the syntax of VRML, in which the exposedField declaration is not allowed for the Script node. In prototyping the various LivingWorlds nodes, we solved the problem by applying PROTO, which has no prototype definition. Among the LivingWorlds nodes, those to which it was applied were those whose PROTOs have an exposedField VRML field-type, such as SharedObject, PrivateSharedObject, or Selector. For instance, the prototyping of Selector, shown in the right side of List 2, has a selectorItems field, and therefore this field was divided into two fields, a selectorItems field and a set_selectorItems eventIn field, for the Script node. Another problem related to the prototyping is at the initialization when the browser loads the

```
#VRML V2.0 utf8                      #VRML V2.0 utf8
EXTERNPROTO Zone [                   PROTO Selector [
  field     SFNode private            exposedField MFNode selectorItems []
  .....                                eventIn      SFBool enabled
] "Zone.wrl"                          field        SFBool isTearOff FALSE
EXTERNPROTO PrivateZone [             eventIn      MFNode addItems
  field        SFNode zone            eventIn      MFNode removeItems
  field        SFNode muTech        ] {
  exposedField MFNode children         DEF G Group { }
  .....                                PROTO ExposedFields [
] "PrivateZone.wrl"                    exposedField MFNode selectorItems []
EXTERNPROTO IBMZone [                 ] { }
  field SFString nameServer           DEF EF ExposedFields {
  field SFNode   zone                   selectorItems IS selectorItems }
  field SFNode   privateZone          Script {
  .....                                  field SFBool isTearOff IS isTearOff
] "IBMZone.wrl"                          eventIn MFNode set_selectorItems
DEF Z Zone {                                               IS set_selectorItems
  private DEF PZ PrivateZone {          eventIn SFBool enabled IS enabled
    muTech DEF MZ IBMZone {             eventIn MFNode addItems IS addItems
      nameServer "lw.ibm.com"           eventIn MFNode removeItems
      zone USE Z                                          IS removeItems
      privateZone USE PZ }            field     SFNode exposedfields USE EF
    zone USE Z                        field     SFNode group USE G
    children [ ..... ] }                ...... }
}                                    }
```

List 2. VRML file with LivingWorlds nodes and PROTO of Selector

prototype. The VRML 2.0 specification did not mention that VRML event processing occurred during the loading of several prototyped nodes. As a result, a different world may appear, event though the same VRML file is loaded, if the user uses the browser designed by a different developer, because one browser can process all events occurring throughout the loading of the files, but the other can only process the events received after initialization of the prototyped node. Hence, to support the LivingWorlds module, the RVE browser enables all events received while the browser loads each prototype to be processed regardless of the order of the prototype initialization.

The second issue concerns the VRML event flow. The problem is caused by the event cascade processing when two events have the same time-stamp. For instance, suppose that an event is transmitted between PrivateSharedObject and SmoothMover (Figure 5). The event sent to PrivateSharedObject from the network is forwarded to SmoothMover, which then returns the value to PrivateSharedObject. The value is calculated on the basis of the value input to SmoothMover. Here, to be exact, the ROUTE of the event is not the loop defined in the VRML specification; however, the PrivateSharedObject node has to be evaluated twice to end the entire processing of an event cascade routed to the node, even though every event has the same time-stamp. To solve this problem, in our browser, while events with the same time-stamp are mainly evaluated at the same time, they are evaluated one by one if the VRML file

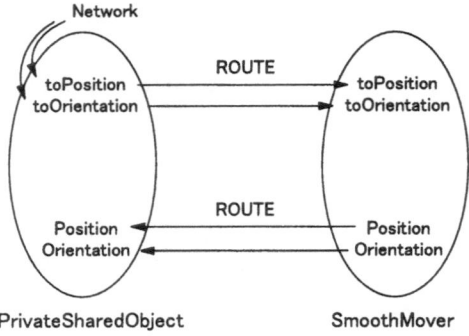

Fig. 5. Event loop between two nodes

```
EXTERNPROTO SFNodeToASA [                    EXTERNPROTO ASAToSFNode [
    exposedField SFNode shared    NULL           eventIn      MFString input
    field        SFString tag     ""             field        SFString tag     ""
    field        SFString access ""              field        SFString access ""
    eventOut     MFString output                 exposedField SFNode shared    NULL
] "urn: ..."                                 ] "urn: ..."
```

List 3. Proposed prototype for sharing

includes a loop that needs to be evaluated twice [5].

The last issue is related to AssociativeStringArray. In the current specification, it is generally difficult for us to set two values to the same AssociativeStringArray simultaneously, since this causes the fan-in problem. Without
a solution, a user is not allowed to create a scene in which the shoulder joint
and elbow joint of an avatar are simultaneously bent at arbitrary angles. We
proposed prototypes of SFNodeToASA and ASAToSFNode with an owner field
named "access" for access control. With this syntax, a node described as a value
of the SFNode "shared" field is considered as a shared node; that is, all the field
values of this node are conceptually the same for all the clients referring to the
scene. These prototyped nodes are used in the same way as the other converters
described in the LivingWorlds documentation. This description does not cause
the fan-in problem, since the field value of this prototyped node is not likely to
be frequently changed.

3.4 Application examples

We are investigating applications in the manufacturing and distribution industries, while of course applications in the entertainment areas such as chat spaces
are still important for multi-user environments. We created two application ex-

amples using the RVE system: a virtual used-car shop, and an on-line hotel reservation desk. In the virtual used-car salesroom demonstration, a user can visit the salesroom and view several displayed usedcars as an avatar, and start negotiations with the merchant's avatar through text chat. We also provided a function that allows the merchant to show a price board for the car preferred by the user; however, there was scope for improvement of the browser's performance in this connection, to allow the users to enjoy stress-free operation.

In the case of the hotel reservation desk content, the system allows the operator in charge of room reservation and the customer to share a 3D window in VRML and a 2D window in HTML on the Netscape Web browser. For this demonstration, the system needs to run with the WebShare program [4]. When filling out an on-line reservation form in the shared window of the Web browser, the user can receive instructions by following the mouse cursor controlled by the operator. For example, which is the text box where he/she should type in his/her credit card number? Which is the button that he/she can use to choose the type of room? The operator can input text on behalf of the customer, simultaneously talking via Internet phone. This function for sharing 2D Web pages is offered by WebShare. When negotiating the arrangement of tables and chairs in the reserved room through the shared VRML window, the user can be shown the VRML model room controlled by the operator; for example, where are these tables located? The RVE panorama viewing function using PanoramIX also enables the user to look around the room while turning through 360 degrees. This 3D sharing function is offered by the RVE system. In the shared windows, updates related to both 2D and 3D contents modified by the operator are reflected in the customer's window in realtime.

4 Future Direction

As explained in tne previous section, we are investigating applications in the manufacturing and distribution industries. For this purpose, the items we are currently working on are: (a) a model for processing events across the network for multi-user environments, (b) function extensions including file syntax and implementation for multiple zones and multiple servers, (c) integration of the 3D-space-sharing program with the 2D-page-sharing program, and (d) performance improvements for the browser and server.

The first item is related to both the system architecture and the Living-Worlds architecture. To reduce the network traffic, it is possible to notify other clients only of the target events that originally caused event cascades, while ignoring the other events transmitted in ROUTE. The former are generated at VRML sensor nodes and script nodes. As it is, the MUTechSharedObject requires events to be transmitted by ROUTE according to the LivingWorlds architecture, and we are therefore working to incorporate the algorithm effectively into our system.

As regards the second item, function extensions we are adding several functions to make it possible to: 1. Restrict accesses for changing the values of fields. This makes it possible to divide users into groups with different access

```
EXTERNPROTO ConnectedPoint [
    field SFString url         ""
    field SFString rootName    ""
    field SFString nodeName     ""
    field SFString worldId      ""
    field SFVec3f connectPoint 0 0 0  ]
```

List 4. Prototype for connecting scenes

authorities, so that group "A", for example, can change any fields of any nodes, while group "B" can change the fields of only some nodes. 2. Transfer multi-resolutional data for LOD from the original server to the destination one. This makes it possible to transfer objects from one zone to another.

As explained in the previous section, the client displays several scenes downloaded from each server as a world. Each scene received from the servers generates a complete scene itself, so if the author designs the scenes well, they can be connected to give the appearance of a single world, such as a shopping mall with many shops. If the author has access control to change a field's value, he/she can build a world in which the shop owner can move an article for sale to another place, but a buyer in the shop cannot take it away. If the article is moved from one zone to another, the LOD data set of the article must be copied to the server maintaining another scene. This is because, when the article is introduced into the scene, it needs to be displayed on the screen of every user looking at the same scene in a heterogeneous environment. As a prototyped node for connecting scenes, we are considering a prototyped node shown in List 4. If this type of node exists as a leaf node in two independent scene graphs, the browser interprets the node as one instance jointly owned by two graphs, that is, as one merged scene graph composed of two scene graphs. In this representation, the strict relation between two spaces is not defined, but the representation would be useful as a hyperlink in HTML, for example. The remaining definitions could be left to the world author.

The third item is related to the business application that we have already prototyped as an example. The system, which completely integrates a 3D-space-sharing program such as the RVE system with a 2D-page-sharing program such as WebShare, allows users to consult merchants about on-line shopping. When a customer wants to buy furniture or electric appliance, he/she first looks for it in a catalog on a Web page. If the user cannot find the desired item, he/she contacts a consultant who has information about all of the items and can show several alternative items to the customer through the 3D shared window of the Web browser. Using the VRML model of the item with movable or combinable parts, the consultant shows how to operate each feature or how to put together several parts as a real-time collaboration. After the consultation, the customer may take the chance to try again by himself/herself. Once the customer has decided on an item, he/she can be instructed how to fill out the purchase form through the 2D shared window. As explained above, a VRML/HTML shared-state system may be a good front-end for an electronic payment system.

As regards the last point, we need to improve the performance to display very large amounts of data, such as complex CAD geometries or bone structures captured from CT scans, with user interaction. In addition, we need to port the functions of the AssociativeStringArray node and convertor nodes such as SFFloatToASA to those of the new NetworkState nodes described in the latest LivingWorlds (Core LivingWorlds) specification.

5 Conclusion

We have described the browser and server of the RVE system with the Living-Worlds implementation. The design of our system architecture is based on the concept of quality-of-service control in VR multi-user network environments. Problems in implementing the browser following the LivingWorlds specification have also been described. We have completed the development of the first stage of the RVE system, which consists in implementing the LivingWorlds client-server, and are now working on the next stage, which consists in adding functions for QoS control, access control, and object drag-and-drop function using multi-servers. Multi-user environments will give all VRML users and all Internet users a chance to communicate expressively through an intuitive user-interface. We hope that such environments will accelerate the evolution of VRML.

Acknowledgments

The authors would like to thank all the reviewers of this paper. We are grateful to Tatsuo Miyazawa, Masaaki Taniguchi, Takaaki Murao, and Fumio Ando for useful discussions and comments. Many thanks also to the the RVE development team for their invaluable contributions. The project was funded by the Ministry of International Trade and Industry of Japan in 1996, 1997, and 1998.

References

[1] R. Lea et al., "Community Place: Architecture and Performance," *Proc. Second Symposium on the Virtual Readlity Modeling Language*, pp. 41-50, 1997.

[2] J. Lipscomb et al., "PanoramIX", *http://www.software.ibm.com/net.media/panoramix/index.html*, 1998.

[3] Mitra et al., "Living Worlds," *http://www.livingworlds.com/draft_2/index.htm*, 1997.

[4] T. Sakairi et al., "Collaboration Framework: A Toolkit for Sharing Existing Single-User Applications without Modification," to appear in *Proc. Third Asia-Pacific Computer and Human Interaction*, July 1998.

[5] M. Taniguchi, "Event Processing for Complicated Routes In VRML2.0," *Proc. Third Symposium on the Virtual Reality Modeling Language*, pp. 83-88, 1998.

[6] VRML Consortium Inc., "The Virtual Reality Modeling Language ISO/IEC 14772-1:1997," *http://www.vrml.org/Specifications/VRML97/*, 1997.

[7] R. Waters et al., "Scalable Platform for Large Interactive Networked Environments (SPLINE)", *http://www.merl.com/projects/spline/index.html*, 1996.

Strolling Through Cyberspace With Your Hands In Your Pockets: Head Directed Navigation In Virtual Environments

Anton Fuhrmann, Dieter Schmalstieg, Michael Gervautz
Vienna University of Technology

email: fuhrmann@cg.tuwien.ac.at
http://www.cg.tuwien.ac.at/research/vr/hdn/

Abstract: Head-Directed Navigation is a simple and efficient method for navigating large virtual spaces. For walkthrough applications such as architectural visualization or games, the user is often required to cover simulated distances. In doing so, inexperienced users often have a hard time learning complicated navigation patters with 3-D mice or similar input devices. In large virtual worlds, this frequently leads to disorientation. With head directed navigation, the user navigates the virtual environment only by orienting his or her head. An orientation tracker mounted on the head-mounted display worn by the user is used to derive the navigation commands. Besides the approach's simplicity, the user's hands are left free for other tasks.

1. Introduction

Navigating through virtual environments can no longer be considered a task reserved for the expert. 3D-worlds and architectural walkthrough applications [Mine95a] for the common user require new, intuitive interface techniques. We present a simple navigational metaphor for immersive walkthrough applications called *head-directed navigation*. This method requires only the tracker attached to a head-mounted display (HMD). It is extremely easy to learn and doesn't require additional input devices, thereby leaving the users hands free for other tasks. In the following we discuss the properties of established navigation methods together with related work. We then give an overview of our approach together with details on implementation, evaluation and results.

2. Related work

The choice of the navigation method to be employed for a virtual reality (VR) application is constrained by both the need of the application and by the physical setup. The latter can broadly be categorized into desktop VR (screen and mouse only), fishtank VR (desktop VR with shutter glasses) and fully immersive setups (using head-mounted displays). While desktop systems usually have to employ navigation methods using simple devices such as mice or joysticks (e. g., [Strommen94]), immersive setups can make use of the larger number of degrees of freedom (DOF) provided by tracking systems [Meyer92], which have led to a variety of proposed navigation methods.

We discuss this related work with respect to their applicability for walkthrough applications. We therefore limit ourselves to methods that couple the user's view to the camera used to render the scene, and that are suited to general exploratory behavior (as opposed to object or goal driven movement such described in [Mackinlay90]).

Mine [Mine95b] identifies the following techniques for specification of direction in immersive virtual environments:

- Physical walking: While being most natural, the range of current tracking systems [Ward92] prevents the use for walkthrough applications. We also do not further consider "exotic" devices such as treadmills or stationary bicycles [Waters97].
- Gaze-directed: moving in the direction the user looks at. The head-directed navigation method proposed in this paper falls into this general category.
- Pointing: moving in the direction the user points the hand or prop (e. g. wand)
- Cross-Hair: moving in the direction from head to hand
- Physical controls: The use of physical controls (such as a steering wheel) and corresponding "vehicle" metaphors is often difficult in immersive settings, as the user cannot see the devices
- Virtual controls: These are often difficult to operate for their lack of haptic feedback.

Other forms of navigation involve obtain a global view of the virtual environment, such as "world-in-hand" metaphor of [Ware90] or "world-in-miniature" [Stoakley95]. However, these approaches are not strictly methods for walkthrough applications.

An approach related to ours was presented in [Hix95]: Pre-Screen projection allows the user to control the viewpoint in a fishtank VR setup by moving her head relative to the screen. However, their approach is limited to panning and zooming operations with a stationary viewpoint and cannot easily be extended to a fully immersive walkthrough application.

3. Quality factors for walkthrough navigation

Bowman et al. [Bowman97] state that navigation methods should be evaluated according to specific quality factors rather than to their suitability for particular applications, as the requirements of applications may be very different. These quality factors can then be used to determine the right navigation method for an application.

In the following, we discuss the most relevant quality factors for walkthrough applications. The intended application scenario is that of a walkthrough application with general exploratory character (e. g., for architectural visualization) used by people without computer experience and without training in an ad-hoc fashion. Such situations regularly occur when using VR for demonstrations to customers.

Many different criteria for efficient navigation have been proposed [Bowman97]. We consider the following to be of importance for walkthrough applications:

1. **Easy to learn and easy to use**: A complicated navigation metaphor would be counterproductive in most cases: An architect who wants to show a new building to a client in a VE cannot expect the client to learn complicated commands and interaction with new devices, a police officer would like to concentrate on the mission goals and not on how to walk around the next corner.

2. **Minimum of additional devices**: The use of additional input devices for movement is not desirable. A soldier in a simulation should be able to hold his rifle in his hands and not some kind of navigation device like a joystick or 3D-mouse. When using fishtank VEs, the user is in a standard desktop environment, where the use of special input devices is acceptable, but when in a fully immersive environment requiring an additional device for movement distracts the user from the tasks at hand. Besides, if larger audiences are targeted, technical and financial constraints make the use of additional devices increasingly difficult.

3. **Avoid fatigue of the user**: Devices like a 3D mouse or a glove, used for pointing, strain the user into adopting unnatural positions caused by the necessity of lifting the device up into the field of view and lead to unnecessary gesticulation.

4. **Spatial awareness**: Exactly the ease with which one can change viewpoint and direction in a VE is one of the pitfalls of many navigation metaphors: turning around on the press of a button or the twist of a dial doesn't correspond to any movement of the user in reality. The result can be loss of orientation similar to turning around blindfolded. Any instantaneous translational movements, like "teleporting" to a new location, equally disrupt the coherence of the mental map.

5. **Avoid translational limits**: Immersive VEs which simulate a person moving by foot in a contained space allow an easily comprehended one-to-one mapping (the user simply walks around in the simulated space), but place a physical limit on the distances the user can cover. An acceptable metaphor should extend this range without preventing the user from making small adjustments of viewpoint by changing position in reality.

6. **Make use of the floor constraint when appropriate**: When moving around in reality, one naturally accepts that ones feet always touch the floor, while in VEs, users are often allowed to fly. This additional degree of freedom however doesn't help the user; on the contrary it requires the user to make additional height adjustments. For walkthrough environments, reducing the freedom of movement from 3 to 2 dimensions improves the ease of navigation.

In the following paragraphs we will show how our approach covers all these criteria.

4. Head Directed Navigation

Imagine a little kid playing "airplane": It holds out its arms and tilts its whole upper body according to the direction in which the "plane" should move. It behaves like an airplane, rolling and yawing according to the laws of aerodynamics even without any knowledge of these laws (Figure 1). This observation inspired our approach of *head directed navigation*.

Figure 1: A little kid playing airplane naturally employs our approach

Of course this kind of interaction is not directly applicable in our case, since it involves directing the forward motion by foot ("running around the playground"), but if we sacrifice one degree of freedom - in our case the ability to move up and down, we are able to map head rotations to the movements of the whole user. Since our movements are already constrained to the plane of the floor ($\Rightarrow$ requirement 6, above), we can use the up- and downward sweeping motion of the head to control our speed. Moving forward is accomplished by nodding in the right direction. We gain the direction of motion from the horizontal component of the head direction - yaw - and the speed from the angle between the head direction and the horizontal plane (pitch).

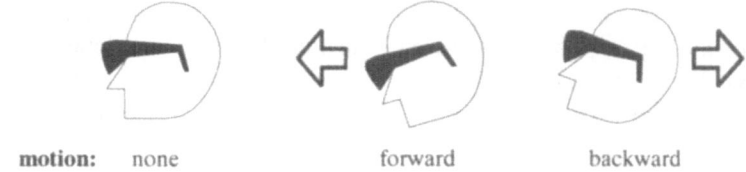

| **motion:** | none | forward | backward |

Figure 2: Association of pitch to translational motion

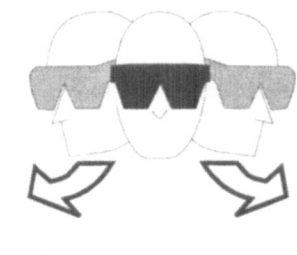

| **motion:** | right | left |

Figure 3: Steering is done by head rotation

In a head-tracked setup, navigating can now be achieved by head rotation alone. Note that a 6DOF tracker is not even fully utilized, as only the three rotational measurements are needed.

This yields essentially the kind of behavior we aimed for in our "kid-playing-airplane" metaphor: The user moves forward by simply inclining her head while gazing at the target, stopping is done by leveling out the direction of view and moving backwards by leaning back (Figure 2). Steering is done by turning the head in the desired direction (Figure 3).

4.1 Discussion

Head-directed navigation can be seen as the equivalent to the navigation method used for desktop 3D browsers or computer games that have only a joystick or even cursor keys at their disposal. In these desktop applications, a horizontal axis controls the heading, while a vertical axis controls the movement.

No additional input devices are required besides the head tracker. This reduces the required hardware for the installation, which saves cost and also allows a larger number of simultaneous users if the number of tracking sensors is the limiting resource. It also simplifies briefing and dress-up if a larger group of users and short turnaround times are desired (e. g., trade shows or theme parks).

As navigation is controlled by head movements alone, the hand are left free for other tasks. If no additional devices are used, the arms can be placed in a comfortable position for complete avoidance of fatigue, a problem known to occur when using wands or 3D mice. Alternatively, a hand-held 3D input device can be completely dedicated to object manipulation.

Often an immersive application hosts a number of first-time users together with a guide or tutor, who is supposed to have more control over the environment than the users. Head-directed navigation allows the construction of an asymmetric application where the guide carried a wand or other 3D input device to control the application, while the other users are only equipped with a head-tracker for individual control of viewpoint, but not more.

Head-directed navigation does not fully utilize a tracker, as only the rotational DOF are used for input. The remaining positional DOF can be used to walk small distances by foot when examining a room or object. In this way, a combination of unconstrained movement and direct physical walking can be achieved.

The main restriction of head-directed navigation lies in the requirement that the environment must have a ground floor constraint. However, a significant number of applications is compatible with such a requirement.

Problems arise when the user inadvertently moves while trying to look around. This happens for example when the user doesn't look absolutely horizontal. We solved this by using a linear mapping from pitch to speed with a small zone – about 10° – of zero speed around the horizontal direction to tolerate slight head movements while standing still. Alternatively, if a higher top speed is desired to cover large distance, a pitch threshold can be defined beyond which a non-linear mapping from pitch to speed, as proposed in [Song93].

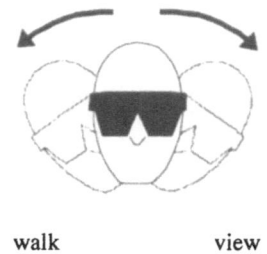

mode: walk   view

Figure 4: Mode switch

Scrutinizing a nearby object from top to bottom also cannot be accomplished without moving back- and forward. This is solved by defining a view mode with a stationary viewpoint and a walk mode where head-directed navigation is active. Switching between walk and view mode can either be done by an additional device (e. g., a button), if available, or by using the remaining DOF of the head tracker. The solution we developed works by tilting ones head to one side (Figure 4). This allows the user to switch modes while still keeping her hands free and utilizes a seldom used head position.

4.2 Example usage

Let us give some examples of navigational tasks which can easily be accomplished with our method:

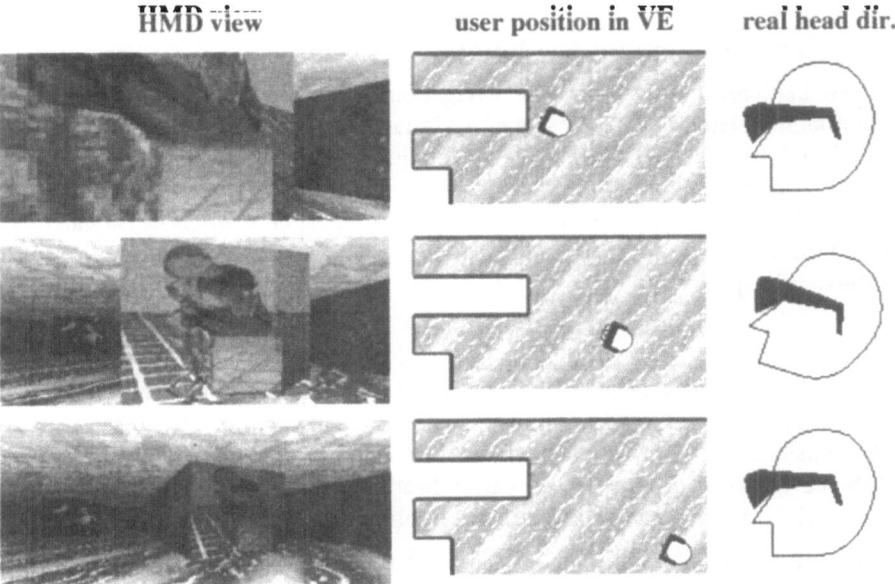

Figure 5: Moving away from an object is done by leaning back

Moving away from an object to gain an overview: The user leans her head back, until a sufficient distance has been reached (Figure 5).

HMD view

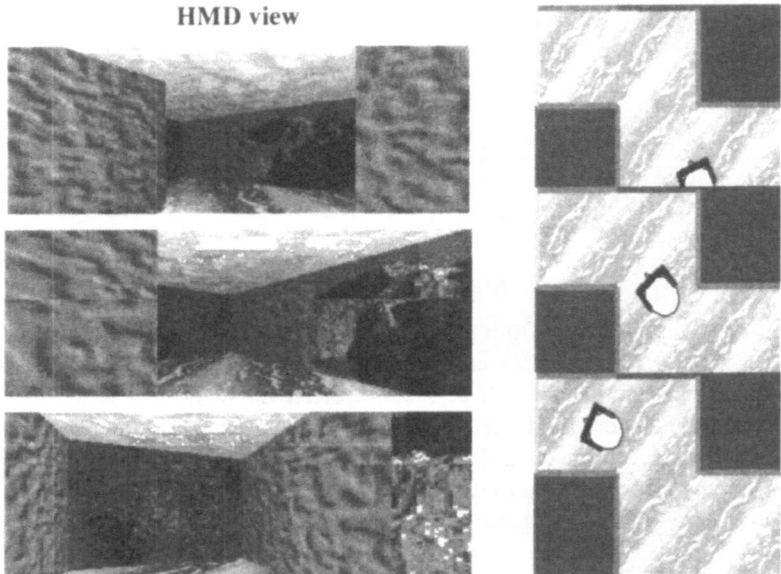

Figure 6: Walking around a corner is done by gradually inclining ones head

Walking around a corner: The user looks slightly down and parallel to the wall until reaching the corner, then turns by looking around the corner (Figure 6).

5. Implementation and Evaluation

We first implemented head-directed navigation as motion metaphor in a PC-based walkthrough system which represented a virtual gallery. HMD and tracking devices were virtual-io i-glasses, an inexpensive solution capable of displaying stereoscopic graphics. The integrated tracker uses gravity and a compass to track three rotational degrees of freedom and is orders of magnitude cheaper than professional 6DOF magnetic tracker systems. The implementation was a straightforward application of the above principles.

5.1 Setup

Our setup consisted of a PC with attached HMD. The graphics output was additionally routed to a large monitor which allowed bystanders and experimenter to see the same as the immersed user. This enabled potential users to get a preview of the environment and the navigational method by comparing head movements of the immersed user to the view of the VE and generally shortened briefing of new users.

Our demonstration environment consisted of a labyrinth containing a gallery of images depicting work done at our department. To enliven the environment we implemented sliding doors which react to proximity and one exit which stops the program when reached by a user. The task of finding the exit provided an additional goal to the otherwise pure exploratory character of the environment. We used a straightforward implementation of head-directed navigation without mode switches. By using the DOF normally used for mode switching to implement movement to the left and right (strafing), viewing of the gallery while moving sideways was made possible.

5.2 User responses

Since the advisor had to introduce every user to the virtual environment and the navigation within, we were able to obtain an informal sample of user responses. Unfortunately, the situation at the fair precluded a comparison with other navigational methods. Thus we are not able to draw a direct comparison, but the user responses were throughout positive.

After the initial orientation period, many first-time users were fascinated by the possibility of moving around in a virtual environment and soon concentrated on experimenting with doors and different points of view while apparently not focusing on navigation itself. With a few exceptions, most users also liked the hands-free approach. When we interviewed users on their experiences in the virtual environment, they often used phrases like "when I was walking through the door on the right", which indicated to us that users accepted navigation without thinking about it.

The most severe complaints we recorded did not concern the navigation, but the small field of view of the HMDs, which we compensated by using a fisheye view into the environment.

5.3 Observations

Because of its simplicity, our approach proved extremely easy to learn. Most users quickly overcame initial steering problems, which mostly consisted of mastering control of the head to velocity mapping. These initial problems can be compared to the adaptation process one goes through when using a new mouse with unfamiliar resolution. After about a minute, most users grew accustomed to velocity control and were able to easily navigate the environment. Since the orientation of the user in reality and virtuality is the same, disorientation due to lack of bearing almost never occurred.

Head-directed navigation requires a minimum of activity in head movements. Therefore, we did not observe the almost paralyzed posture typical for first time HMD users who are not aware that they can move around or too frightened to do so. The method of moving along the gallery by sliding sideways had to be suggested to most users, but was then readily adopted.

As our navigational method constrains the user to movement on a ground floor, it requires control of only two independent dimensions, which is a minimum for navigation in a realistic environment. Therefor users were not bothered with unnecessary freedom of control which can quickly lead to disorientation in "flythrough" navigational situations, as we have observed from other applications. The use of an additional monitor not only enabled the advisor to help the user adjusting to the VE but also reduced initial reservations of novice users regarding the HMD.

6. Conclusion and future work

From our experience we have learned that head-directed navigation is a simple and intuitive way of navigation. While is limited to walkthrough applications that work with a ground floor constraint, the method in its simplicity is particularly useful for novice users and when virtually no training time is available. The lack of need for additional devices apart from the head tracker is helpful when cost is a factor or when multiple simultaneous users must be supported with limited hardware resources.

Future work is planned to develop head-directed navigation as an aid for the disabled.

For further information, see http://www.cg.tuwien.ac.at/research/vr/hdn/

7. Acknowledgments

This work has been supported by the *Austrian Science Foundation (FWF* project number P-12074-MAT) and the city of Vienna (*Hochschuljubiläumsfonds der Stadt Wien*).

8. References

[Bowman97] D. Bowman, D. Koller, L. Hodges: Travel in Immersive Virtual Environments: An Evaluation of Viewpoint Motion Control Techniques. Proceedings of VRAIS'97, pp. 45-52 (1997)

[Hix95] D. Hix., J. Templeman., R. Jacob: Pre-Screen Projection: From Concept to Testing of a New Interaction Technique. Proceedings of ACM CHI'95 Conference, Denver (1995)

[Mackinlay] J. Mackinlay, S. Card, G. Robertson: Rapid controlled movement through a virtual 3D workspace. In Proc. SIGGRAPH'90, pp. 171-176 (1990)

[Meyer92] K. Meyer, H. Applewhite, F. Biocca: A Survey of Position Trackers. Presence, Vol. 1, No. 2, pp. 173-200 (1992)

[Mine95a] Mine M., Weber H.: Large Models for Virtual Environments: A Review of Work by the Architectural Walkthrough Project at UNC. Presence, Vol. 5, No. 1, pp. 136-145 (1995)

[Mine95b] M. Mine: Virtual Environment Interaction Techniques. SIGGRAPH'95 Course, No. 8 (1995)

[Song93] D. Song and M. Norman: Nonlinear Interactive Motion Control Techniques for Virtual Space Navigation. In Proceedings of IEEE Virtual Reality Annual International Symposium, pages 111-117 (1993)

[Stoakley95] R. Stoakley, M.J. Conway, and R. Pausch: Virtual Reality on a WIM: Interactive Worlds in Miniature. In Proceedings of ACM CHI'95, Denver CO, pages 265-272 (1995)

[Strommen94] E. Strommen: Children's Use of Mouse-Based Interfaces to Control Virtual Travel. Proceedings of CHI (Boston MA), pp. 405-410 (1994)

[Ward92] M. Ward, R. Azuma, R. Bennett, S.Gottschalk, H. Fuchs: A Demonstrated Optical Tracker With Scalable Work Area for Head Mounted Display Systems. SIGGRAPH Symposium on Interactive 3D Graphics, pp. 43-52 (1992)

[Ware90] C. Ware and S. Osbourne: Exploration and Virtual Camera Control in Virtual Three Dimensional Environments. Proceedings of SIGGRAPH Symposium on Interactive 3D Graphics 1990, pages 175-183 (1990)

[Waters97] R. Waters, D. Anderson, J. Barrus, D. Brogan, M. Casey, S. McKeown, T. Nitta, I. Sterns, and W. Yerazunis: Diamond Park and Spline: Social Virtual Reality with 3D Animation, Spoken Interaction and Runtime Extendability. Presence, 6(4):461-481 (1997)

Automatic Facial Expression Composition
from Base Faces

Moonho Park*⁺   Heedong Ko*   Hyeran Byun⁺
lausdeo@chopin.kist.re.kr   ko@kistmail.kist.re.kr   hrbyun@aipiri.yonsei.ac.kr

Imaging Media Research Center

Korea Institute of Science and Technology*

39-1, Hawalkok-Dong, Sungbuk-Ku, Seoul, 136-791, Korea

TEL: +82-2-958-5646 / FAX: +82-2-958-5769

Department of Computer Science

Yonsei University⁺

134, Shinchon-Dong, Seodaemoon-Ku, Seoul, 120-749, Korea
TEL: +82-2-361-2719 / FAX: +82-2-365-2579

Abstract. This paper describes a method to create a facial expression of a virtual character inhabiting in the virtual environment. The proposed method is to search for facial expression from a facial image and to map the expression to a virtual character. In general, it is a time-consuming and laborious job to create a facial expression manually. In order to extract components of facial expression from facial images automatically, Genetic Algorithms and Simulated Annealing are used. With the proposed method a realistic facial expression of the virtual character can be created more easily and efficiently.

1 Introduction

In virtual environments, it is important to increase the quality of social interaction for the sake of enhancing the sense of reality. The realistic modeling and animation of a virtual character may enhance the sense of reality. In general, as human mainly exposes his internal state on the face, facial expression plays an important role in the communication of emotion and in the regulation of social interactions. When we want to know what someone is thinking, how they are feeling, the first place we frequently look is their faces. In the case of virtual environments, a virtual character's facial expression also plays an important role to increase the reality and presence. In multi-participant distributed virtual environments, facial expression of virtual human representing each participant is an important factor to perceive and to feel the other participants.

There has been a great advance in the development of the realistic facial expression modeling and animation technology in the last few years[1][2][3]. So, a variety of algorithms and technologies have been developed. As a result, it is possible to create very realistic and intimate facial expressions.

Recently, some virtual characters such as Jack[4], Kyoko Date[5] in Japan, Adam[6], Lusia[7] and Cyda[8] in Korea have been created from all over the world academically and commercially. The movements by the virtual character is often animated by a motion capturing device that detects the movements of each joint by an acting person. Thereby, the animator is smoothing the captured movements before storing into the database of primitive movements that are later retrieved to compose the desired movements.

When creating an animation of a facial expression, the animator still resorts to manual modeling by viewing the video clip of a live character making the facial expression over and over again. This is a time-consuming and laborious job especially when we have to create the facial expression of a person whose face is familiar to us and have us believe the animation is from that person.

An animator can model the desired facial expression more easily and efficiently if he can retrieve a large number of facial expressions already prepared in the database as a basis to compose the right facial expression that is input by capturing an image of a person making a face. Here, we propose a method for 3D modeling of a facial expression from an image by composing the base facial expression models in the database. We are constructing facial expression database for creating facial expression of virtual character such as Adam, Korean virtual character, and developing automatic method for constructing facial expression database as a Multimedia Contents Project in Korea. The proposed method in this paper will be used for the project.

2 Motivation: From Image To Model

Facial expression is very important to represent the intention and mood of a character. So far, the mouth movement with speech and the gesture is mainly used. Generally speaking, facial expression is created using one of the following methods: key-framing, shape blending or motion captures of a character performance[9].

In the case of shape blending, the blending ratio among several facial expressions has been determined manually. To determine the right blending ratio, we have to choose a particular blending ratio to apply the result. Unless the resultant expression is close to the desired face, another blending ratio is chosen and tested. The manual generation and test cycle is repeated until a desired facial expression is obtained. This process is very time-consuming and almost impossible to extract the precise blending ratio.

So, we propose a method to search for the blending ratio among several facial expressions to fit the arbitrary facial images automatically. By the proposed method, the components of facial expression are extracted from arbitrary facial images automatically, and the extracted components are mapped to characters. That is, a facial expression of virtual character can easily be created from human facial images captured by camera to facial models.

Using the proposed method, we can construct a variety of facial expression database efficiently and automatically. Moreover, the searched facial expression is included to new facial expression component, and can be used to create a facial expression. So we can incrementally construct base faces used for creating facial expression of virtual character.

3 The Facial Expression Explorer

The facial expression can be analyzed and described as a blending ratio of several base faces and it is possible to set up several base sets of faces for the analysis. The base set may be different according to the objective and viewpoint of the facial analysis. An analytic method is determined according to a base set prepared for the facial analysis. The information obtained by a base set can be applied to other objects. By applying the same analysis methodology, it is possible to transform the base set to another base set.

In this paper, the proposed system, Facial Expression Explorer sets up 6 typical facial expressions and a normal facial expression as a basis for the facial analysis. The Facial Expression Explorer searches for a blending ratio among the 6 typical facial expressions and a normal expression needed to create character's facial expression from a facial image.

The extracted facial information can be applied to a corresponding character, so it is possible to create very realistic and natural facial expression as well as expect to lighten the difficulty of job. Fig. 1 shows the procedure of the Facial Expression Explorer.

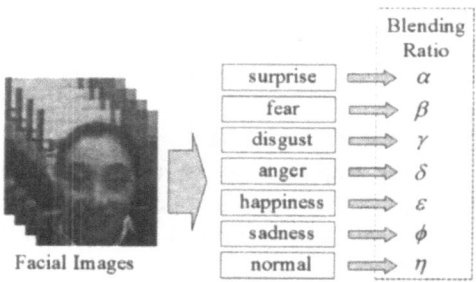

Fig. 1. The procedure of Facial Expression Explorer.

3.1 Creation of 6 Typical Facial Expressions

FACS(Facial Action Coding System) was suggested in order to describe a human facial expression. According to the FACS, there are 44 primitive muscular movements in a human face called action unit, and a facial expression can be synthesized by the combination of action units[10]. Consequently, one can create all facial expressions using the combination of necessary action units according to the information of a facial expression. A facial expression can be expressed as a set of 3D vertices as follows.

$$f_{exp} = \begin{bmatrix} x_1 \ y_1 \ z_1 \\ \cdots \\ x_i \ y_i \ z_i \\ \cdots \\ x_N \ y_N \ z_N \end{bmatrix} \qquad (1)$$

where x_i, y_i, z_i are x, y, z values of an ith vertex, and N is total vertex number of a face model.

As a human facial expression has various forms and shapes expressing human emotion, there is no fixed rule to describe a facial expression of a human emotion. Nevertheless, there are 6 typical facial expressions, which are clearly classified as universals, that is, surprise, fear, anger, disgust, happiness and sadness. These 6 typical facial expressions and normal expression, that is $f_{surprise}$, f_{fear}, f_{anger}, $f_{disgust}$, $f_{happiness}$, $f_{sadness}$, f_{normal} can be described as follows.

$$F_n = \begin{bmatrix} x'_1 & y'_1 & z'_1 \\ \cdots \\ x'_i & y'_i & z'_i \\ \cdots \\ x'_N & y'_N & z'_N \end{bmatrix} \tag{2}$$

$$\Delta f_e = \begin{bmatrix} \Delta x_1 & \Delta y_1 & \Delta z_1 \\ \cdots \\ \Delta x_i & \Delta y_i & \Delta z_i \\ \cdots \\ \Delta x_N & \Delta y_N & \Delta z_N \end{bmatrix} = \begin{bmatrix} x_1 - x'_1 & y_1 - y'_1 & z_1 - z'_1 \\ \cdots \\ x_i - x'_i & y_i - y'_i & z_i - z'_i \\ \cdots \\ x_N - x'_N & y_N - y'_N & z_N - z'_N \end{bmatrix} \tag{3}$$

$$f_{surprise} = \Delta f_s + F_n \tag{4}$$

$$f_{fear} = \Delta f_f + F_n \tag{5}$$

$$f_{disgust} = \Delta f_d + F_n \tag{6}$$

$$f_{anger} = \Delta f_a + F_n \tag{7}$$

$$f_{happiness} = \Delta f_h + F_n \tag{8}$$

$$f_{sadness} = \Delta f_{sa} + F_n \tag{9}$$

$$f_{normal} = \Delta f_n + F_n \tag{10}$$

where F_n of Eq. 2 is normal expression, Δf_e is a facial expression displacement from normal expression, Δf_s, Δf_f, Δf_d, Δf_a, Δf_h, Δf_{sa} and Δf_n are the facial expression displacements of surprise, fear, disgust, anger, happiness, sadness and normal, respectively from normal expression.

In order to apply a facial expression using a combination of action units, a 3D model of a human face is produced from a facial image captured by CCD camera. The 3D model of a human face is fit to the facial image by giving 39 feature points manually.

3.2 Exploring Blended Facial Expression by GAs

The Facial Expression Explorer applies GAs(Genetic Algorithms) to find the right combination of the blending ratio from a desired facial expression. GA is based on the genetic processes of biological organisms[11][12]. In GA, the major parts of the modeling problem are the chromosome representation and the evaluation function which assigns a figure of merit to each coded solution. During the evolution, parents must be selected for reproduction, and recombined to generate the offspring.

Arbitrary facial expression can be described in terms of blending ratio like Eq. 11.

$$f_{exp} = \begin{bmatrix} \Delta f_s & \Delta f_f & \Delta f_d & \Delta f_a & \Delta f_h & \Delta f_{sa} & \Delta f_n \end{bmatrix} \begin{bmatrix} \alpha \\ \beta \\ \gamma \\ \delta \\ \varepsilon \\ \phi \\ \eta \end{bmatrix} + F_n \qquad (11)$$

where $\alpha, \beta, \gamma, \delta, \varepsilon, \phi$ and η are the blending ratios among the 6 facial expressions and a normal expression. In this case the blending ratio ranges from 0 to 1 and is normalized to prevent abnormal facial shapes deviated from natural human facial expressions. This also helps to prevent the generation of illegal chromosomes. So, a modeling of a chromosome is given in Fig 2.

0.14	0.25	0.21	0.18	0.03	0.17	0.02
α	β	γ	δ	ε	ϕ	η

Fig. 2. A modeling of a chromosome.

According to the information of a chromosome the content for the facial expressions is determined. That is, a chromosome determines a facial expression, the facial expression is applied to the expressionless facial mesh data, so the coordinate values of the mesh model are changed. The differences between the changed coordinate values and the target values can be used by an evaluation function of GA. For the implementation of Facial Expression Explorer, the evaluation function is as follows.

$$\begin{bmatrix} \delta x_1 & \delta y_1 & \delta z_1 \\ \cdots \\ \delta x_i & \delta y_i & \delta z_i \\ \cdots \\ \delta x_N & \delta y_N & \delta z_N \end{bmatrix} = \begin{bmatrix} x_{t1} & y_{t1} & z_{t1} \\ \cdots \\ x_{ti} & y_{ti} & z_{ti} \\ \cdots \\ x_{tN} & y_{tN} & z_{tN} \end{bmatrix} - \begin{bmatrix} x_{e1} & y_{e1} & z_{e1} \\ \cdots \\ x_{ei} & y_{ei} & z_{ei} \\ \cdots \\ x_{eN} & y_{eN} & z_{eN} \end{bmatrix} \qquad (12)$$

$$f_{eval} = \sum_{i=1}^{N} |\delta x_i| + |\delta y_i| + |\delta z_i| \qquad (13)$$

where $\delta x_i, \delta y_i, \delta z_i$ are 3D difference values between target facial expression vertices and compared vertices, x_{ti}, y_{ti}, z_{ti} are target vertex values, and x_{ei}, y_{ei}, z_{ei} are compared vertex values.

Through evolution of chromosome populations, one can efficiently get the necessary blending ratio among the facial expressions.

In the process of the evolution, there may be a variety of chromosomes with high fitness or low fitness. But, through the many generations, the evaluation value of the better chromosome gets to approach global optimum value.

3.3 Another Method: Simulated Annealing

Simulated Annealing(SA) can also be used to find right combination of the blending ratio from facial expressions. SA is a stochastic computational technique derived from statistical mechanics for finding near globally-minimum-cost solutions to large optimization problems[13][14].

SA has a direct analogy with thermodynamics, specifically with the way that liquids freeze and crystallize, or metals cool and anneal. At high temperatures, the molecules of a liquid move freely with respect to one another. If the liquid is cooled slowly, thermal mobility is restricted. The atoms are often able to line themselves up and form a pure crystal that is completely regular. This crystal is the state of minimum energy for the system, which would correspond to the optimal solution in a mathematical optimization problem. However, if a liquid metal is cooled quickly i.e. quenched, it does not reach a minimum energy state but a somewhat higher energy state corresponding, in the mathematical sense, to a sub-optimal solution found by iterative improvement or hill-climbing.

The simulated annealing procedure uses the Metropolis Algorithm[15][16] but varies the temperature parameter from a high value (system at "melting point" i.e. accept most new configurations) to a low value (system at "freezing point" i.e. accept no new configurations). The full SA procedure for minimization is then as follows.

```
Initialize T
Generate random configuration Xold
WHILE T > Tmin DO
        FOR i = 1 to Nc DO
                Generate new configuration, Xnew
                Calculate new energy, Enew
                Calculate ΔE=Enew-Eold
                IF ΔE < 0 or random < e^{-ΔE/T} THEN
                        Xold ← Xnew
                        Eold ← Enew
                END IF
        END FOR
        Reduce T
END WHILE
```

where X is parameterized state vector that represents a problem, the configuration of parameter is like Eq. 14.

$$X = (\alpha, \beta, \gamma, \delta, \varepsilon, \phi, \eta) \qquad (14)$$

where each element of X is blending ratio of base faces and normal face. The cost function $E(X)$ (analog of energy) used to calculate energy E is the same as Eq. 13, Nc is the number of random changes in configuration at each temperature T and is chosen so that the configuration has reached a minimum energy state for the current temperature. The variable *random* is a randomly generated number in the range [0,1].

4 Experimental Result

The arbitrary facial expressions of a character are analyzed and synthesized with the base faces of a character and the extracted blending ratios. The base faces are selected for facial analysis and synthesis, and we get to know the base faces are not necessary to be orthogonal by the experiment. The combination of weighted base faces is sufficient for facial analysis and synthesis of virtual characters.

To get a good solution by GA, the harmony of the convergence and the diversity is necessary. In the implementation of GA, a selection schedule is the mixture of methods using both roulette wheel and expectation value of each individual, the adaptive rate of crossover and mutation is used. So in the beginning of evolution, the rate of crossover, 0.7 and the rate of mutation, 0.01 are applied, according to the progress of evolution the rate of crossover is decreased, on the other hand the rate of mutation is increased to expedite the convergence. For the implementation of SA, Nc is 200, the temperature is decreased by a factor of 0.1.

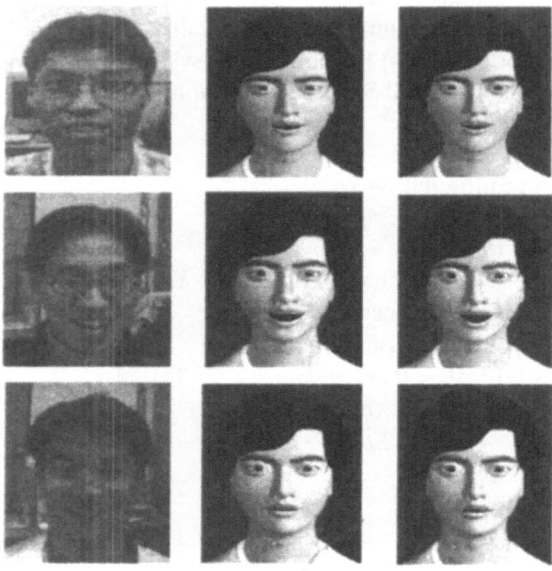

(a)facial image   (b)GA method   (c)SA method

Fig. 4. The resultant facial expressions of Korean cyber character, Adam from the corresponding facial images.

Using the facial information extracted by the Facial Expression Explorer, the following facial expressions of a Korean cyber character, Adam(middle & right) are obtained according to the corresponding real facial images(left) of three persons like Fig. 4. Middle facial expressions is created by GA, right facial expressions is created by SA. As one can see in Fig. 4, GA method and SA method produce comparable results in our applications.

The machine used for graphics, 3D modeling, GA and SA is SGI Indigo2 without any special hardware. We also used Open Inventor, X-Window(Motif-API) and SGI Video Camera for the implementation of the experiment.

5 Conclusion and Future Work

The facial expression is the reflection of one's emotion and thought. Therefore, by trying to find out its components, we have proposed a method for facial expression generation and constructed a basis for the facial analysis. The proposed system extracts the facial expression information from a facial image automatically. So, the extracted facial information can be used for generating facial expression of virtual character and the analysis of human emotion.

Using the facial expression generating method proposed in this paper, we can create realistic facial expression of a virtual character inhabiting in the virtual environments more easily and efficiently. Therefore it'll be helpful to construct very intimate virtual environments, and we may give and receive our feeling by virtual character's facial expression in the virtual environments like the way we do in the real environments.

We plan to use the proposed method to build a large store of facial expression database so that an animator can create facial expression of a virtual character easily. Furthermore, we continue to extend the system capabilities: including full body-motion capturing system, facial expression movements from video images, and their synchronization.

6 Acknowledgement

The authors would like to greatly appreciate the kind help of Adamsoft Co., Ltd. for creating the resultant photographs of Korean cyber character, Adam, and comments from Dr. Jeffrey T. Deutsch of Deutsch Research Inc.

References

[1] Y. Lee, D. Terzopoulos and K. Waters, Realistic Modeling for Facial Animation, SIGGRAPH 95 Proceedings, pp. 55-62, 1995.
[2] P. Litwinowicz and L. Williams, Animating Images with Drawings, SIGGRAPH 94 Proceedings, pp. 409-412, 1994.
[3] S. Glenn, VActor Animation Creation System, Computer Graphics Visual Proceedings, pp. 223, 1993.
[4] http://www.transom.com.
[5] http://www.dhw.co.jp/horipro/talent/DK96/index_e.html.
[6] http://www.adamsoft.com.
[7] http://www.lusia.com.
[8] http://www.cyda.co.kr.
[9] B. Robertson, Read My Lips, Computer Graphics World, Vol. 20, No. 8, pp. 26-36, 1997.

234

[10] P. Ekman and W. V. Friesen, *Facial Action Coding System*, Consulting Psychologists Press Inc., 1978.

[11] D. E. Goldberg, *Genetic Algorithms in search, optimization & Machine Learning*, Addison-Wesley, 1989.

[12] H. Ko, J. H. Kim and J. H. Kim, Searching for Facial Expression by Genetic Algorithm, Proc. of 2nd Eurographics Workshop on Virtual Environments, Monte Carlo, Monaco, Jan 1995.

[13] http://www.cm.cf.ac.uk/User/S.U.Thiel/ra/subsection3_7_3.html.

[14] W. H. Press, S. A. Teukolsky, W. T. Vetterling and B. P. Flannery, *Numerical Recipes in C*, 2nd Edition, Cambridge, 1992.

[15] N. Metropolis, A. Rosenbluth, M. Rosenbluth, A. Teller, and E. Teller, Equation of state calculations by fast computing machines, Journal of Chemical Physics, Vol. 21, pp. 1087-1092, 1953.

[16] S. Kirkpatrick, C. D. Gelatt, and M. D. Vecchi, Optimization by Simulated Annealing, Science, Vol. 220, No. 4598, pp. 671-680, May 1983.

Symbolic representations of exclude and include for audio sources and sinks:
Figurative suggestions of
`mute`/`solo` & `cue` and
`deafen`/`confide` & `harken`

Michael Cohen and Jens Herder
Spatial Media Group
University of Aizu
Fukushima-ken 965-8580
Japan
voice: [+81](242)37-2537; fax: [+81](242)37-2549
e·mail: {mcohen,herder}@u-aizu.ac.jp
www: http://www.u-aizu.ac.jp/~{mcohen,herder}

Abstract

Shared virtual environments require generalized control of user-dependent media streams. Traditional audio mixing idioms for enabling and disabling various sources employ `mute` and `solo` functions, which, along with `cue`, selectively disable or focus on respective channels. Exocentric interfaces which explicitly model not only spatial audio sources, but also location, orientation, directivity, and multiplicity of sinks, motivate the generalization of `mute`/`solo` & `cue` to exclude and include, manifested for sinks as `deafen`/`confide` & `harken`, a narrowing of stimuli by explicitly blocking out and/or concentrating on selected entities. This paper introduces figurative representations of these functions, virtual hands to be clasped over avatars' ears and mouths, with orientation suggesting the nature of the blocking. Applications include groupware for collaboration and teaching, teleconferencing and chat spaces, and authoring and manipulation of distributed virtual environments.

Keywords: CSCW (computer-supported collaborative work), groupware, narrowcasting functions, articulated mixing console

1 Introduction

1.1 Virtual Mixing

Non-immersive perspectives in virtual environments enable fluid paradigms of perception, especially in the context of frames-of-reference for conferencing and musical audition [Coh95] [Coh98]. Traditional mixing idioms for enabling and disabling various sources employ $\boxed{\text{mute}}$ and $\boxed{\text{solo}}$ functions, which, along with $\boxed{\text{cue}}$, selectively disable or focus on respective channels. Exocentric interfaces which explicitly model not only spatial audio sources, but also location, orientation, directivity, and multiplicity of sinks, described by Table 1, motivate the generalization of $\boxed{\text{mute}}$/$\boxed{\text{solo}}$ & $\boxed{\text{cue}}$ commands to exclude and include, manifested for sinks as $\boxed{\text{deafen}}$/$\boxed{\text{confide}}$ & $\boxed{\text{harken}}$, a narrowing of stimuli by explicitly blocking out and/or concentrating on selected entities [Coh97] [CK98]. ($\boxed{\text{harken}}$ is used to describe focusing on one's own sink.)

	Role	
	Source	Sink
Function	radiation	reception
Level	amplification	sensitivity
Direction	output	input
Instance	speaker (human or loud-)	listener (human or dummy-head)
Organ	mouth	ear

Table 1: $^{s}\text{OU}^{rce}_{Tput}$ and $^{s}\text{IN}^{k}_{put}$

1.2 Exclude and Include Audio Functions

A source can be disabled with $\boxed{\text{mute}}$; its complement $\boxed{\text{solo}}$ disables all non-$\boxed{\text{solo}}$ed sources. The semantics of $\boxed{\text{mute}}$ and $\boxed{\text{solo}}$ can be described in predicate calculus notation:

$$\text{active}(\text{source}_x) = \neg\text{mute}(\text{source}_x) \wedge (\exists y\ \text{solo}(\text{source}_y) \Rightarrow \text{solo}(\text{source}_x)) \quad (1a)$$

As sinks are duals of sources, the semantics of $\boxed{\text{deafen}}$ and $\boxed{\text{confide}}$ (& $\boxed{\text{harken}}$) are analogous:

$$\text{active}(\text{sink}_x) = \neg\text{deafen}(\text{sink}_x) \wedge (\exists y\ \text{confide}(\text{sink}_y) \Rightarrow \text{confide}(\text{sink}_x)) \quad (1b)$$

These two predicates can be described by a generalized representation, using "exclude" to stand for $\boxed{\text{mute}}$ and $\boxed{\text{deafen}}$ and "include" to stand for $\boxed{\text{solo}}$ and $\boxed{\text{confide}}$ (& $\boxed{\text{harken}}$):

$$\text{active}(x) = \neg\text{exclude}(x) \wedge (\exists y\ \text{include}(y) \Rightarrow \text{include}(x)) \quad (2)$$

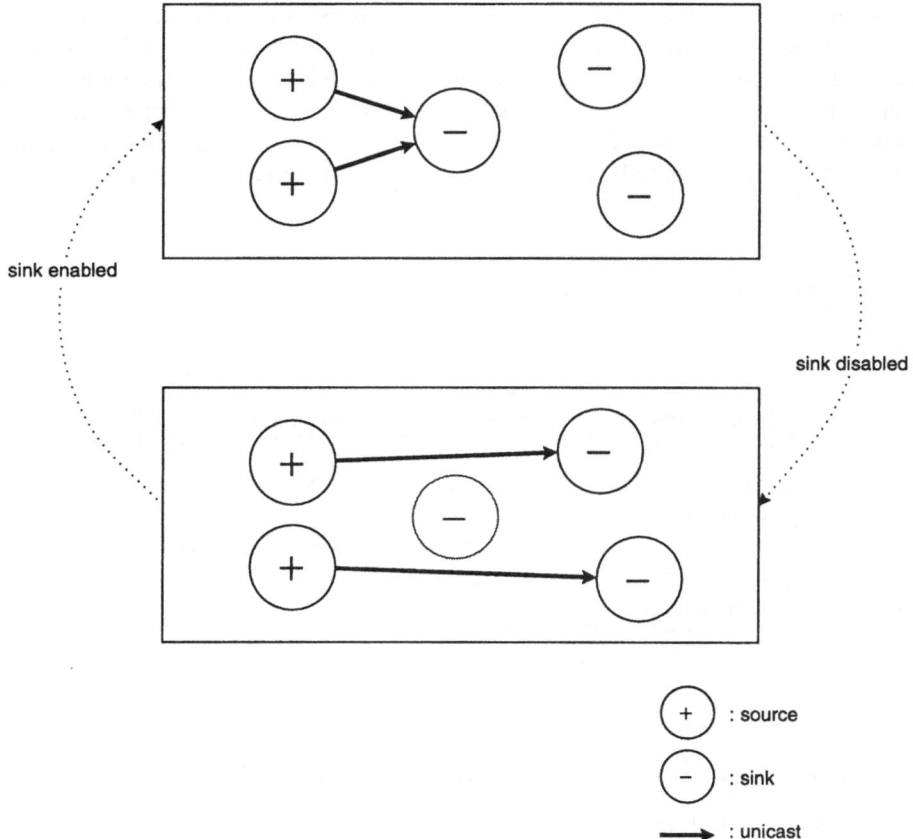

Figure 1: Unicast Source → Sink Transmissions: orphaned sources adopted by sinks

Such functions can be applied not only to other users' sinks for privacy, but also to one's own sinks for selective presence [HC96]. Multiple sinks are useful in both groupware, where a common environment implies social inhibitions to rearranging shared sources like musical voices or conferees, and individual sessions in which spatial arrangement of sources, like the configuration of a concert orchestra, has mnemonic value. As shown by Figure 1, an "autofocus" mode can be used to adjust source→sink mappings, depending on sink activation.

2 Figurative Avatars

User (human pilot)	Delegate (representative, projected presence)
human body	avatar
carbon community	electronic community
RL (real life)	virtual life
	synthespian (**synthe**tic **thespian**)
meatspace	digital puppet
human actor	vactor (virtual **actor**)

Table 2: User and Delegate

2.1 Representation of Exclude Audio Functions

A human user can be represented in virtual space by one or more avatars, as suggested by Table 2. A figurative avatar in virtual space is naturally humanoid, including especially a head, since it not only embodies a center of consciousness, but also important communication organs: ears, mouth, and eyes. Exclude and include source and sink operations can be visually represented by iconic attributes which can distinguish between operations reflexive, invoked by a user associated with a respective icon, and transitive, invoked by another user in the shared environment. Distributed users might typically share spatial aspects of a groupware environment, with attributes like `mute` dness or `deafen` dness determined and displayed on a per-user basis.

For example, as shown in Table 3, a source representing a human teleconferee denotes `mute` edness with an iconic hand clasped over its mouth, oriented differently (thumb up or down) depending on whether the source was `mute` d by its owner (or one of its owners) or another, unassociated user. (In the former case, all the users in the space would observe the `mute`, but in the latter, only users disabling the remote source would typically see the `mute`.) An audio muffler could be wrapped around an iconic head to denote its deafness, but to distinguish between self-imposed deafness, invoked by a user whose attention is directed elsewhere, and distally imposed, invoked by a user desiring privacy, hands clasped over the ears should be oriented differently depending on the agent of deafness. As such attributes are orthogonal, simultaneously applied filters could be represented by interpenetrated virtual models.

	action	
	deafen (muffle)	mute (muzzle)
object	sink	source

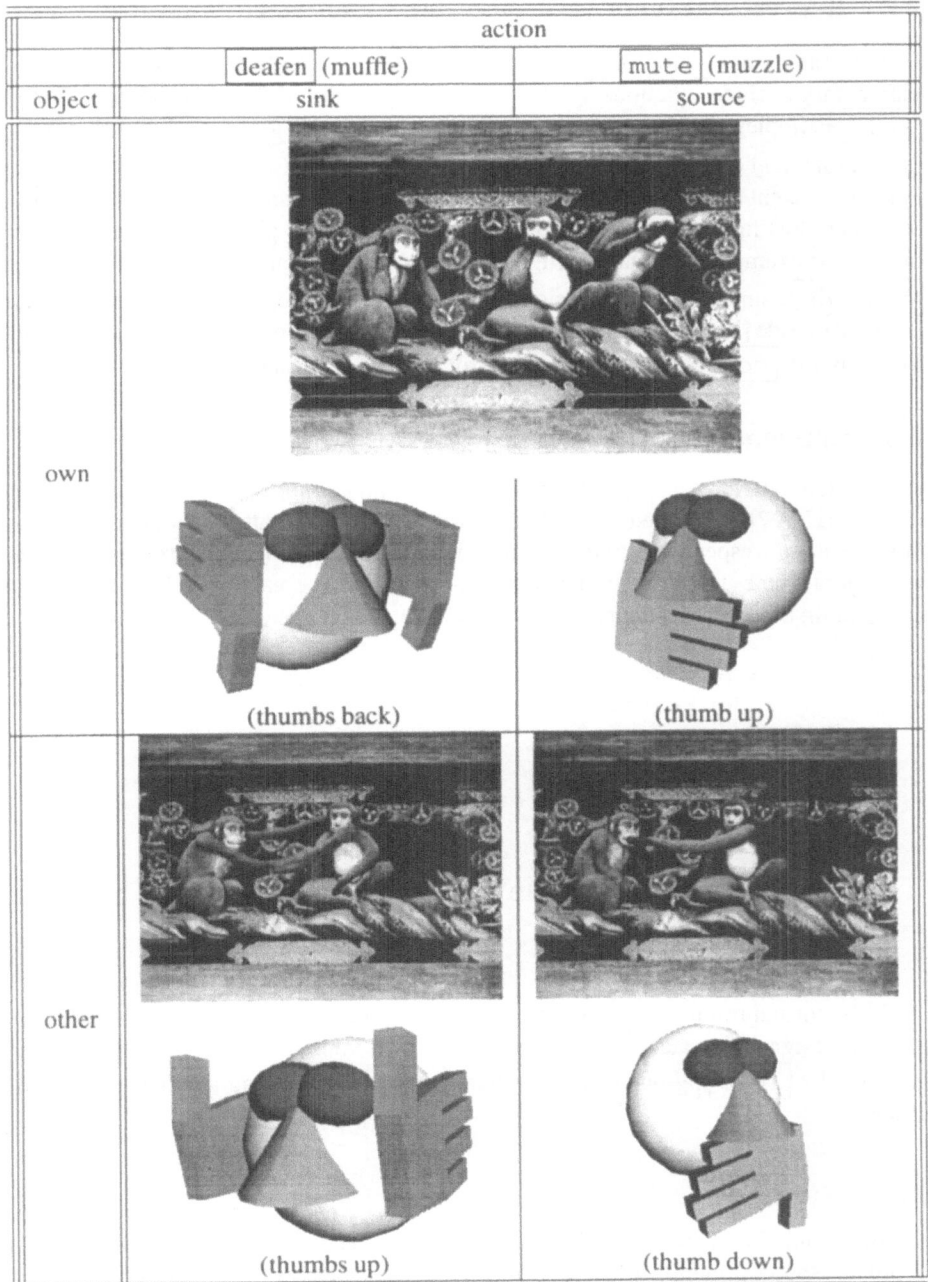

own	
(thumbs back)	(thumb up)
other	
(thumbs up)	(thumb down)

Table 3: Deafening and Muting One's Own and Others' Avatars

2.2 Representation of Include Audio Functions

Include functions (`solo` and `confide`) manifest visually as the respective complementary exclude functions applied to the complement of the appropriate selection. `solo` is implemented as a straight-forward extension of `mute`, effectively muting the complement of the `solo`ed selection, as `confide` (& `harken`) `deafen`s the complement of the selection. These pairs of fields are maintained separately, however, anticipating a visual idiom that distinguishes the explicit and implicit operations. For example, a visual spotlight could be used to denote `solo`ed sources or `confide`d sinks. Future extensions will distinguish these attributes aurally as well; a whisper mode [Mar97] suggesting confidences is a transparent affordance appropriate for explicitly `confide`d sinks, but not for un`deafen`ed ones!

2.3 Implementation

Our implementation uses Open Inventor [Wer94] and a sound spatialization framework [HC97] [Her97] developed at the University of Aizu. The attributes are maintained in the avatars' respective VRML or Open Inventor nodes as lists of users[1] setting the boolean attributes, along with a "represents" field, whose value is a list of the users designating the avatar as theirs, as shown below:

```
DEF AvatarA Avatar {
   geometry Separator {...}
   source SoundSource {...}
   sink SoundSink {...}
   represents [useridA, useridB]
   mute [useridA, useridB, ...]
   solo [useridA, useridC, ...]
   deafen [useridB, useridD, ...]
   confide [useridB, ...]
}
```

If the virtual room is a chat space, in which each user's voice is projected from all of their designated avatars, one can hear their own voice remotely (as with a studio monitor) by `solo`ing one of their avatars and `confide`-ing another in the same space.

2.4 Groupware

Actions along the main diagonal of Tables 3 and 4, i.e., applied to one's own sinks or to others' sources, manifest locally (in the respective user's spatialization process and soundscape), while actions along the secondary diagonal, i.e., applied to others' sinks or to one's own sources, manifest remotely (in other users' spatialization processes and

---

[1] Human users are tagged by <userid, qualified host name> pairs. In fact, the mapping between users and such tags is many↔many, and such an assumption can be subverted by a user choosing to have multiple ids and/or multiple login hosts, or to share their accounts with someone else.

avatar	own	other
mode	reflexive	transitive
sink	deafen	deafen
	harken	confide
source	mute	mute
	solo	solo

Table 4: Reflexive and Transitive Audio Exclude and Include Operations

soundscapes). Such medial attributes do not propagate to distal users' soundscapes; a normal user can `mute` a personally undesired source, but can't prevent its disturbing others.

2.5 Applications

These features are demonstrated with a prototype of a helical keyboard [HC96], a virtual environment to experience music attributes which are normally not directly portrayed, featuring separate sinks, selectively disablable, to normalize the octave. Besides musical audition, such conventions will also have immediate application to teleconferences and voice chat spaces.

Another, as yet unimplemented application, is a language lab in which students practice conversation in several talk scenarios. The groups are monitored by the teacher, who virtually moves from one group to another, actively or passively joining the conversation. This participation can be perceivable (visible/audible) to the students depending on the teacher's choice. In such an example not all users (i.e., the students) have supervisory control.

Acknowledgments

Hiroki Sato prepared the monkey illustrations. Kimitaka Ishikawa made the hand model.

References

[CK98] Michael Cohen and Nobuo Koizumi, *Virtual gain for audio windows*, Presence: Teleoperators and Virtual Environments **7** (1998), no. 1, 53–66, ISSN 1054-7460.

[Coh93] Michael Cohen, *Throwing, pitching, and catching sound: Audio windowing models and modes*, IJMMS: the Journal of Person-Computer Interaction **39** (1993), no. 2, 269–304, ISSN 0020-7373.

242

[Coh95] Michael Cohen, *Besides immersion: Overlaid points of view and frames of reference; using audio windows to analyze audio scenes*, Proc. ICAT/VRST: Int. Conf. Artificial Reality and Tele-Existence/Conf. on Virtual Reality Software and Technology (Makuhari, Chiba, Japan) (Susumu Tachi, ed.), November 1995, pp. 29–38.

[Coh97] Michael Cohen, *Exclude and include for audio sources and sinks: Analogs of mute/solo & cue are deafen/confide & harken*, Proc. ICAD: Int. Conf. Auditory Display (Palo Alto, CA), November 1997, pp. 19–28.

[Coh98] Michael Cohen, *Quantity of presence: Beyond person, number, and pronouns*, Cyberworlds (Tosiyasu L. Kunii and A. Luciani, eds.), Springer-Verlag, 1998, ISBN 4-431-70207-5, pp. 267–286.

[HC96] Jens Herder and Michael Cohen, *Project report: Design of a helical keyboard*, Proc. ICAD: Int. Conf. Auditory Display (Palo Alto, CA), November 1996, `www.santafe.edu/~icad/ICAD96/proc96/herder.htm`, pp. 139–142.

[HC97] Jens Herder and Michael Cohen, *Sound Spatialization Resource Management in Virtual Reality Environments*, ASVA'97 — Int. Symposium on Simulation, Visualization and Auralization for Acoustic Research and Education, April 1997, Tokyo, Japan, pp. 407–414.

[Her97] Jens Herder, *Tools and Widgets for Spatial Sound Authoring*, Compugraphics '97, Sixth International Conference on Computational Graphics and Visualization Techniques: Graphics in the Internet Age (Vilamoura, Portugal) (Harold P. Santo, ed.), GRASP, December 1997, ISBN 972-8342-02-0, pp. 87–95.

[Mar97] William L. Martens, *Acoustics and perception of sound sources at close range*, 1997, In preparation (`http://www.u-aizu.ac.jp/~wlm/whisper`).

[Wer94] Josie Wernecke, *The Inventor Mentor*, Addison-Wesley, 1994, ISBN 0-201-62495-8.

„The Virtual Endeavour"- a VR-Gallery Application for Remote Multimedia Data Access

Christoph Brandt, Klaus Meyer
Heinz Nixdorf Institut, University of Paderborn, Germany
James Johnson, John Benfield
The Natural History Museum, London, United Kingdom

Abstract

As part of the european ACTS research project SICMA (Scaleable Interactive Continous Media Server - Design and Application) the Heinz Nixdorf Institute together with several european partners has developed a Virtual Gallery application based on Captain Cook's ship Endeavour. The virtual environment is populated with 3D objects, each providing access to underlying digital media data. The data is retrieved from the SICMA server over high bandwidth networks.

1 Introduction

The rapid development in computer technology, the explosion of interest in the internet and interactive media by diverse organisations is a clear sign of the potential for distributing information via new media to audiences. Networked multimedia technology is undoubtedly the fastest growing medium for outreach currently available, part of its success being due to the innovative way in which information can be presented to a large number of people. Many museums, galleries and similar institutions have now started to digitally record their accessions and to get prepared for their future in the information society. Naturally this has lead to discussions on how the digital information derived from or related to the collections may be made accessible to the public.

Fig. 1. „The Virtual Endeavour" real time environment.

Among the potential advantages of an effective digital medium the more important ones might be

- providing access to representations of objects otherwise physically remote from their potential audiences

- bringing together representations of objects which are physically held remotely from one another, in separate museums for example improving access to objects by using representations where the conservation requirements of the original artefact limit their display

- providing access to objects which no longer physically exist

- putting objects in context with an exhibition space which can not be build by a museum

- taking interpretative gallery design to a remote audience as a vehicle for education and enjoyment

Among emerging media technologies Virtual Reality is one of the most promising technologies which could lead to new ways how museums interpretate and present their material to the public. The conceptualisation of a 'virtual gallery application' is therefore based on a 3D environment populated with representations of artefacts with supporting interpretative materials. These are stored in high resolution data format on a scalable media server remotely accessible over high bandwidth networks.

2 General approach

The Natural History Museum holds a significant collection of artefacts that are derived from the first voyage of Captain Cook. This historic voyage culminated in the detailed charting of New Zealand and the East Coast of Australia in 1771. The voyage also had a particular significance, as it was the first to carry on board a group of professional scientists who made detailed astronomical and biological observations supported by detailed collecting and recording. After considering alternative options the concept of creating a digital replica of Cook's ship Endeavour and populating this with digital objects derived from the museums and other collections was adopted as the 'virtual gallery' application.

Fig. 2. View into a cabin of the virtual gallery.

Fig. 3. Users get prompted background information.

Fig. 4. A videostream is downloaded from the server.

The exhibition therefore takes place in a realtime rendered 3D model of the Endeavour (figure 1). The application enables users to explore a continuous, seamless, virtual exhibition defined on the first level by a virtual environment (the ship) inhabited by 2D and 3D rendered objects (figure 2). The visitors can treat these objects as interfaces to reveal further levels of multimedia data (figure 3 to 4). These include interactive programmes, video clips, animated renderings, digitised 2D and 3D scans of original artefacts ranging from navigation equipment, charts, and specimens collected on the voyage, to the mundane stores of a sailing ship of the period. The objects are supported with interpretative information (figure 5 and 6).

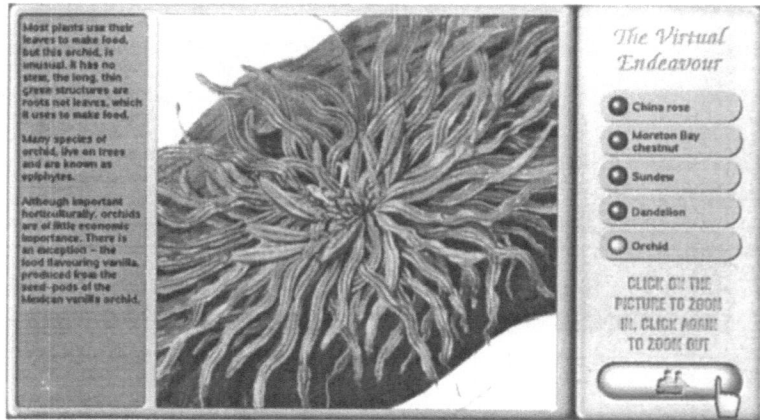

Fig. 5. 2D image interface.

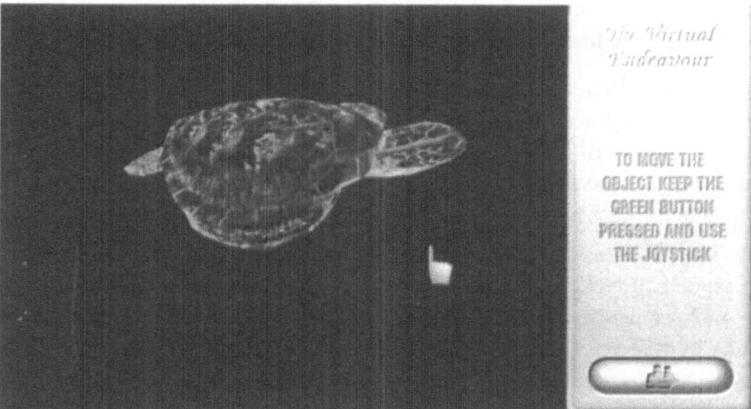

Fig. 6. 3D object interface.

In this concept the virtual environment becomes an access mode to the underlying layers of multimedia, a 3D browser for any kind of digital data. The amount of information a 'virtual gallery application' could hold is limitless, as the application is scaleable. In principle 'virtual museums' can be extended limitless in breadth they occupy in the virtual environment and in depth in the underlying levels of information accessed from the „virtual objects". These issues of breadth and depth of interpretation can of course be targeted to meet the needs of different types of audience.

3 System design and implementation

3.1 Geometric Modeling

The digital replica of the ship is based on the best available detailed historical data. The vessel itself and the interior of the cabins were created according to original drawings and plans [MAR95]. All geometric modeling was done with 3-D modelling tools. The geometry data was then converted to a realtime data format using several converting steps. Realism of the models was enhanced by applying realistic materials and texture maps onto the surfaces of the models. To achieve the maximum visual quality for the targeted system environment the complete 3D dataset was processed with a radiosity illumniation tool developed at the University of Paderborn [LS97]. Furthermore, a lot of effort was put into optimizing the 3D dataset for use in a real-time environment. The whole geometric dataset consists of 350K polygons and 10 MByte textures.

3.2 Real-Time Environment

The simulation model is executed through the real-time environment. The most important requirement of the system is to deliver real-time frame rates (more than 20 frames/sec) on the target platform. This is crucial to maintain the illusion of an interactive virtual world. The hardware resources needed to process the complete „Endeavour" dataset in real-time unfortunately is a magnitude greater than what the SGI Octane MXI graphics hardware is able to process at the desired framerate.

In recent years the increase in complexity of virtual environments has outpaced the improvements of graphics hardware. Thus there is an ongoing research in reducing the geometric complexity of a given scene for real-time rendering. Among others the most important strategies are level-of-detail hierarchies [FS93] visibility culling [ARB90], [Tel92], occlusion culling [CT97] and image based rendering utilizing texture maps [SLS+96]. The „Endeavour" virtual environment takes advantage of several of these advanced rendering techniques. The implementation was based on the IRIS Performer real-time API for rendering [RH94]. The number of polygons to be drawn in every frame could be reduced to less than 15,000/frame, which allows a smooth walkthrough on an Octane MXI system.

3.3 Multimedia data

The application is designed to serve as a 3D information browser connected to a scaleable parallel media server via a variety of networks. The basic service of the server is to deliver media streams, containing video, audio, images or general data over a network infrastructure. The client systems retrieve all the background multimedia data for the application from the server across a ATM network. Video information is stored in MPEG-2 Transport Stream format, audio information as MPEG audio layer 2 streams on the server. All other data is stored in common used formats, for example pictures have been stored as RGB files. The multimedia database contains 11 MPEG-2 videoclips (3-5 min), 30 images, three 3D-scans, 12 audioclips and supporting text material. More information about the SICMA Multimedia Server can be found in [BKL+98] and [BLR97].

4 System demonstration

During the trial conducted at The Natural History Museum in London the application was displayed on SGI Octane MXI systems in a public gallery. Two duplicate presentation theatres gave visitors access to the 'Virtual Endeavour' application where it was projected onto large, 1.7m x 3m screens (figure 7).

Fig. 7. Physical gallery setup in the Natural History Museum

A navigation console was installed in front of each projection. At any given time, navigation through the virtual environment was controlled by one user in each theatre. Up to ten other people were able to view the projected graphics. This provided the opportunity for a semi-immersive environment where group participation was possible.

The option of using fully immersive head mounted displays was rejected on two counts. Immersive headset technology is unreliable and not durable enough for general gallery use without significant supervision. It is also not available at high enough resolution at reasonable cost. Secondly, from a human interaction point of view, head mounted displays exclude interaction between visitors, an essential component of normal gallery experience.

Parallel to this trial a demonstration of the application was displayed in a similar arrangement in the Gallo Romains Museum at Tongeren in Belgium.

5 Critical assessment of the project

The SICMA project, application development and culmination of the first trial has provided exciting and interesting insights to the areas of exploration described above:

What has been most impressive was the visitor reaction to the „Virtual Endeavour" application. On the basis of audience responses there is a clear potential audience of people who would be interested in access to interactive, interpreted content of the type in the demonstrator. The potential is enormous for the medium generally and for potential content provision from Museums, Galleries and Heritage (MGH's) within the cultural sector. An indication of the visitor interest is particularly evident through the holding power of the demonstrator application where attention spans of 20mins were typical against an average holding power of museum gallery exhibits generally in the order of 20 seconds with 3 minutes normally being considered ambitious. That visitors would spend such a proportion of their prime visit time exploring the virtual museum demonstrator in direct competition with the opportunity to explore the physical museum was an unexpected result.

Much of the success with users reported here is, we believe, due to the intuitive, interactive, exploratory nature of the physical controls and graphical interface. From the visitor analysis [BBJ+97] these have significantly contributed to dispelling the 'technology phobia' across the age and sex demographics of the sampled audience previously reported in studies of computer based communication systems.

It is important to report here that the success of the application as a 3D virtual interface to an underlying rich, interpreted multimedia data base has been noted by key industrial players. In particular Silicon Graphics Computer Systems Ltd. not only provided support for the first trial, they have since given significant attention to the applications intentions and success and are responding to it in their 'Heritage Sector Strategy'. This is largely due to the fact that the SICMA application has paved a way for a reconsideration of the potential of VR applications. Previously the emphasis in the industry has been on very high-end, high-resolution graphic reconstructions such as the virtual Coliseum by Infobyte, these are essentially devoid of context and content interpretation. The problem with this approach being the identification of application use and target audiences within the MGH sector. The SICMA application marks a significant shift for several reasons:

- the development of high-end VR products has been treated as too financially and technologically limiting in the near term for most MGH's, particularly as the exploitation routes are unclear.

- the use of high-end digital representations and in particular 3D representations of objects was perceived by the MGH partners as too financially and technologically limited in the near term to play a significant role in museological archive and recording systems where 2D images and „QuicktimeVR" solutions are simpler options for implementation.

- our preferred re-focussing instead towards the outreach potential of VR, within a multimedia application with rich content, distributed via networks and set-top boxes to wide audiences, appears to have been clearly vindicated by the visitor evaluation.

The main limiting factor identified by the MGH's involved in the project for the future exploitation of the approach is of course the current state of the art:

- Few MGH organisations could afford the risk at this stage of creating applications of this sort from their own resources and could only work in commercial collaborations that are still poorly defined.

- The network infrastructure for this type of application is still too immature to reach a wide public audience, although this is rapidly changing it is still a disincentive for the sorts of collaborations referred to above.

Certainly suitable set-top boxes that are both reliable and affordable and capable of allowing wide distribution of applications in the mould of the SICMA prototype are still to be developed. Given the generation time of technological advances to come to the market it does seem likely that the next generation of high-end PCs will begin to provide this functionality at an acceptable price, so this limitation may be overcome within the next 2-3 years.

Without easy and accessible generic application software tools the time and skills involved in developing applications similar to the SICMA prototype are still largely prohibitive. This is one of the major limitations on the economic viability of projects containing rich, interpreted multi-media data and where there is significant opportunity for software developers to shift the balance.

Once the physical access developments and the software tools have significantly improved we are confident, on the basis of research within the limitations of the first trial, that there would be a public demand for interactive, cultural/educational applications similar to the type developed and trialed here.

6 References

[ARB90] Airey, J. M.; Rohlf, J. H.; Brooks, F. P.: Towards Image Realism with Interactive Update Rates in Complex Virtual Building Environments, In Computer Graphics, Volume 24, Number 2, March 1990

[BBJ+97] Benfield J.; Bloomfield B.; Johnson J.; White, I.: Evaluation report of the first trial, SICMA project deliverable D7, Bussels, 1997.

[BJM97] Brandt, C.; Johnson J.; Meyer K.: SICMA - A Networked VR Application, The Fourth International Conference on Hypermedia and Interactivity in Museums, Paris 1-5th September 1997.

[BKL+98] Brandt, C.; Kyriakaki, G. ; Lamotte, W.; Lüling, R.; Maragoudakis, Y.; Mavraganis, Y.; Meyer, K.; Pappas, N.: The SICMA Multimedia Server and Virtual Museum Application, Proceedings of European Conference on Multimedia Services Applications and Techniques, ECMAST'98, Berlin, 1998.

[BLO97] Bloomfield, R.: Remote Access to Museums Exhibits, The 6th International Forum on Leisure and Entertainment Attractions, Straßbourg 24th-26th June 1997.

[BLR97] Berenbrink, P.; Lüling R.; Rottmann V.: A Simple Distributed Scheduling Policy for Parallel Interactive Continuous Media Servers, Workshop on Parallel Computing and Multimedia, 11th International Parallel Processing Symposium, Geneve1997.

[CT97] Coorg, S.; Teller, S.: Real-Time Occlusion Culling for Models with Large Occluders, Proceedings ACM Symposium on Interactive 3-D Graphics, 1997

[FS93] Funkhouser, T. A.; Sequin, C. H.: Adaptive Display Algorithm for Interactive Frame Rates During Visualization of Complex Virtual Environments, Proceedings of SIGGRAPH '93, in ACM Computer Graphics, 1993

[LS97] Lange, B.; Schmidt, O.: Virtuelle Wände - Parallele Bildgenerierung basierend auf der physikalischen Simulation, Proceedings, BMBF Statustagung, 1997.

[MAR95] Marquardt, K.-H.: Captain Cook's „Endeavour", Anatomy of the Ship Series, Conway Maritime Press, 1995.

[RH94] Rohlf, J.; Helman, J.: IRIS Performer: A High Performance Multiprocessing Toolkit for Real-Time 3-D Graphics, Proceedings of SIGGRAPH '94, in ACM Computer Graphics, 1994

[SLS⁺96] Shade, J.; Lishinski, D.; Salesin, D. H.; DeRose, T.; Snyder, J.: Hierarchical Image Caching for Accelerated Walkthroughs of Complex Environments, Proceedings of SIGGRAPH '96, in ACM Computer Graphics, 1996

[TEL92] Teller, S. J.: Visibility Computations in Densley Occluded Polyhedral Environments, Ph.D. thesis, Computer Sience Division (EFCS), University of California, Berkeley, 1992

[ZMH⁺97] Zhang, H.; Manocha, D.; Hudso, T.; Hoff, K. E.: Visibility Culling using Hierachical Occlusion Maps, Proceedings of SIGGRAPH '97, in ACM Computer Graphics, 1997

Automotive Panel: Using VR in the Automotive Business

Ulrich Lang

Panel Participation
Panel Chair:
Dr. Ulrich Lang, HLRS Visualisation Department, Universität Stuttgart

Panellists:
Thomas Reuding, BMW AG, CAD Projects R&D
Dr. Walter Gillner, Daimler Benz AG, VR Competence Centre
Christoph Gümbel, Porsche AG, Manager Vehicle Development Computation
Kai Schrader. Volkswagen AG, VRLab

Opening Questions
During the opening of the panel discussion some general elements of the current situation of Virtual Reality were presented by the panel chair to initiate the theme. These elements were:

- Media hype   vs.   Disappointing state of usage
- Marketing usage   vs.   Engineering usage
- Heterogeneous techniques vs.   Integration in work processes
- Under development   vs.   Turnkey systems
- Long introduction times vs.   Quick usage
- Own development   vs.   Off the shelf aquisition

Positional Statement of Panellists
The panellists and their automotive companies are all involved in virtual reality oriented activities, but the approach varies greatly. The positional statements of the panellists were (in alphabetical order of companies):

BMW AG:
The pressure for companies in the automotive industry to remain competitive has led to the adoption of concurrent engineering. The largest percentage of design and manufacturing costs for a new product are pre-determined in the concept definition stage of a project, yet this phase is characterised by the need to evaluate complex engineering scenarios under conditions in which the relevant information is either only partially available or the correctness of underlying assumptions regarding the viability of certain technical solutions is not yet proven.

Therefore decisions made during this early stage should be supported by all means, especially those of information technology. CAD and CAE systems are widely used and the rise in model complexity, data quantity, computing performance and accuracy makes performance predictions and functional evaluations possible long before the results of real prototype tests are available.

So, on one hand we increasingly find ourselves lacking the tools, methods and metaphors to deal with the amount of information that is being generated, on the other hand physical prototypes still play an important role due to their spatial presence. The advent of immersive virtual environments means that the user of digital information has also finally arrived in 3D space. The basic philosophy behind the use of VR technology is to provide a communications platform for supporting multidisciplinary concurrent engineering.

Apart from the need for technical maturity for many of today VE components, a profitable implementation of the technology also very much depends on our understanding of human factors involved as well as the social implications on the workforce.

Daimler Benz AG:

The global competition between manufacturers of high-quality technical products leads inevitably to increased requirements in terms of product quality, the flexibility to react quickly to changing market demands, and the efficiency of the production process.

In this context, the complete description of new developments in digital product data bases, and in particular the introduction of Virtual Reality techniques, are becoming a key technology, which industrial enterprises have to master to remain competitive.

Due to the increasing performance of computer hardware and the general application of CAD methods, the way is open now for interactively controllable real-time visualisation. Interactive Virtual Reality applications not only allow improvements in the product development process. With this technology, an entirely new quality can be achieved in the design, construction and ergonomic assessment of new products.

The general introduction of Virtual Reality applications in industry has been impeded so far by the insufficient standardisation of interfaces in particular of peripheral devices and tracking systems, by the lack of acceptable haptic feedback mechanisms and by high investment costs. Now we are on the verge to overcome these problems.

Porsche AG:

To bring new products like cars successfully to market, short design and development cycles are decisive advantages. In order to reach this goal, complex computer simulations (virtual prototyping) are done. This leads to more complex computations on increasing amounts of data. The analysis of the vast amount of resulting data requires new kinds of visualisation tools.

In the area of crashworthiness simulation and CFD usual post processing tools are not sufficient anymore to provide for high quality analysis of computer simulation results. A big improvement can be achieved by using virtual reality methods. Virtual reality performs real time animations and allows the user to interact with the visualised data.

Volkswagen AG:

The motivation to work with VR technology is to reduce the huge costs and long times from a styling idea to the production start of a new car. Important production decisions have to be taken for design, marketing and manufacturing planning, before a first prototype is manufactured. Virtual prototypes can help in solving problems at an early stage of development, can improve communication and shorten iteration cycles in the design.

Since founding the Volkswagen Virtual Reality Lab in 1994 as a research facility, some of the initial research topics have already been established in the development process. A few of the applications that have been realised are:

- Visualisation of CAD data for surface inspection
- "Virtual Car Clinic": The presentation of a complete car for marketing research purposes.
- "Virtual Showroom": Presentation of models and manipulation of materials (colours and textiles) in an immersive environment.
- "RAMSIS-VR" - Coupling of the ergonomic dummy "RAMSIS" with VR
- FEMwalk - A dynamic postprocessor for the evaluation of results from FEM calculations.

Discussion

In the presentations and discussions it became quickly clear, that the given title "Using VR in the Automotive Business" was reaching too far. The usage of virtual reality has not reached a level of maturity, that allows to introduce it as turn key solutions into the work processes of automotive companies.

While bigger companies appear as early adopters of such techniques, smaller companies are evaluating the usefulness of virtual reality techniques in very focused projects in co-operation with external experts.

The broadest approach has been chosen by Daimler Benz AG, which established a Virtual Reality Competence Centre as a central reference point for all VR activities within the Daimler Benz AG. Volkswagen AG also established a central Virtual Reality Lab, which focuses on the evaluation of VR usage in certain application contexts. BMW AG follows the conceptual approach of multidisciplinary concurrent engineering to determine, where VR techniques can provide the biggest benefit. Porsche was engaged in selective projects where external specialists provided a VR solution to certain presentation requirements.

On the technology side, it can be said that Virtual Reality has in some areas matured from a "tool of weird scientists" to a "state of the art" tool. In some areas there is still a lot of research to be done before applications will be useable. Due to missing force feedback devices, accurate and wireless tracking devices or speech recognition systems the whole user interaction is still not as intuitive as it should be.

There were also large differences on the perception, what and how much VR can contribute in different application areas. While Porsche stated, that VR as a tool does not improve the result of a computer simulation, Daimler Benz and BMW see the possibility to discover the unexpected in complex simulation results.

While all companies showed a rather conservative and cautious approach to introduce VR usage in different application fields, they are all firmly dedicated to continue on the established paths and increase the involvement in this field.

Panel: Virtual Reality in the telecommunications industry - current state and future

Organizer:

Jürgen Landauer, Fraunhofer IAO, Germany, *Juergen.Landauer@iao.fhg.de*

Participants:

Yoichi Kato, NTT Human Interface Laboratories, Japan, yoichi@nttlabs.com
Ola Ødegård, Telenor, Norway, ola.odegard@kjeller.fou.telenor.no
Paul Rea, British Telecom, UK, paul.rea@bt-sys.bt.co.uk

Panel abstract

Distributed virtual worlds, projects linking broadcast media such as TV with virtual worlds, and virtual chat spaces show that virtual reality technologies enable telecommunications industries to provide new content for their networks.

Panelists's statements:

1. Yoichi Kato, NTT Multimedia Communications Laboratories Inc.

InterSpace: A Shared 3D Communication Environment (http://www.intsp.com)

Evolution of Communication Media

The development of communication media in the modern age can be considered as creations of virtual spaces. For example, people on the phone can be thought of not in the real space where they actually exist but in a virtual space where only the two people share and only the voice can propagate.

In this context, to introduce a shared virtual 3D space, like InterSpace, is a quite natural movement of communication medium enhancement. It is because one of the streams of medium evolution is to simulate the real space as far as possible in order to move people's activities in the real space to in virtual ones.

InterSpace

The objective of NTT's InterSpace is to provide a system to support diversified interactions and communications among people and/or with the environment.

Introducing a concept of avatars in shared 3D virtual spaces combined with multi-user communication and multimedia technologies, InterSpace provides the most integrated communication environment currently available. In addition, InterSpace is a total solution including streaming audio/video, HTML page rendering, various user management functions, user directory/data base, resource (content files) management/auto download and update, scripting platform of 3D object behaviors and an authoring tool. The distributed server architecture provides a high scalability and robustness.

Its application includes electric commerce, distance learning, telecommuting, online gaming, any sort of online community (e.g., an online community for a hobby) and so on.

Community in Virtual Spaces

We have been operating experimental InterSpace sites for a year. So far the community is well maintained. However, inappropriate behaviors are seen occasionally. InterSpace has added a function to filter "unwelcome" user in the browser recently but we don't think this is a final answer.

As a communication medium becomes more like a public space, social aspect of the medium should be considered more seriously.

2. Paul Rea, BT Labs, British Telecom

Introduction

In 1968, Ivan Sutherland developed what is accepted to be the world's first Virtual Reality (VR) system. Sutherland's system used a head-mounted display to immerse users in the same space as objects rendered in wire-frame. In the thirty years since Sutherland's groundbreaking work, efforts to deploy VR have been hampered by high development and deployment costs, and inadequate system performance. However, over recent years, the emergence of the World Wide Web and associated technologies - in particular VRML and Java - coupled with faster hardware has meant that developers can finally start to focus on delivering systems where VR is a significant component in the user interface.

VR activities at BT Labs – An overview

At BT Labs we believe the growth in VR applications over the next ten years will be in the area of community-based networked virtual environments, which we term Shared Spaces. Given this we have been engaged in experiments to try to understand the dynamics of virtual communities and the role companies like BT will have in supporting these communities beyond simply provisioning technical building blocks. In our model, the future of communications is about more than the evolution of the telephone, and the research we are undertaking is exploring issues of technology, interface and applications in delivering this new medium.

Inhabited Television

Over the last 18 months much of our work has involved developing a concept we refer to as Inhabited TV. The advent of digital broadcasting when combined with the convergence of the Internet and broadcast television will lead to new and exciting opportunities for creating and delivering engaging interactive services using VR. To date, we have explored the concept through the development and delivery of two major experiments: 'The Mirror' and 'Heaven & Hell – Live'.

'The Mirror', created through a collaboration involving BT, the BBC, Sony and Illuminations, an independent television production company, was an experimental social environment run in association with the BBC's information technology television programme 'The Net'. 'The Mirror' focused on how a virtual environment might be used to support communication and interaction in an online community formed around a television series. The worlds comprising 'The Mirror' were opened to the public on January 13th, 1997 and closed seven weeks later. During this experiment a number of special events were staged, including debates, a virtual art exhibition; a game show; and a virtual marriage. The importance of the special events should not be underestimated as they provided a focus, particularly during the early days, for the community to gather and interact in the world.

'Heaven & Hell – live' was conceived as an experiment to take the Inhabited TV concept to the next stage beyond The Mirror. Our intention was to develop a much tighter coupling between the users in the world and television broadcast. Indeed, the shared space and the events within it formed the major part of a live, one-hour broadcast shown on UK national television. The broadcast component of 'Heaven & Hell – live' was commissioned by Channel 4 as part of late-night series of programming entitled 'Renegade TV'. Celebrating the subversive, the marginal and the underground, 'Renegade TV' consisted of three blocks of programming shown over a three-week period in August 1997. On the day of the broadcast, over 175 people logged in to the space with the population peaking at 142 during the actual broadcast.

The Inhabited TV experiments referred to previously used PC and IP over dialup PSTN connections. Our work is now starting to explore the issues that arise from porting these applications to a set top box environment. From a more content oriented perspective, we are involved with eRENA, a European Union funded project running over three years, which is exploring new forms of cultural experience spanning arts, performance and entertainment. Inhabited TV is one of the application domains targeted by the eRENA consortium.

Business conferencing

Over the last decade more people have started to work within teams that are separated both geographically and temporally. Traditional Groupware and conferencing solutions have solved, for the large part, the problems of exchanging information amongst team members. However, these systems have been less successful in supporting the patterns of social interaction that typically emerge within collocated teams. A project called The Forum is studying how Shared Spaces can be used to support these patterns of formal and informal group interaction – typically, a formal interaction might equate to a meeting structured through an agreed agenda, while an informal interaction might embrace chance encounters. This work has also extended to exploring the issues that arise from integrating VR with more traditional interfaces.

Education

BT offers a range of services aimed specifically at the needs of UK education sector. Through services like Campus, many schools are being connected to the Internet and it is becoming an important tool for both teachers and pupils. We believe that services that deploy Shared Space interfaces will, quite literally, add a new dimension to the learning experience. We believe education to be one of the richest domains to understand some of the opportunities of the technology. To date, we have introduced Sony's Community Place browser and server software, and a world construction package into a number of local schools in the Ipswich area. Initial feedback has been quite positive with pupils actively creating and sharing virtual environments based upon subject matter from their studies. In the future, this area of our work is likely to increase in importance with the prospect of creating global learning environments.

Immersive environments

The work described so far has been targeted at conventional display platforms. In addition to this work, we have an ongoing activity studying the use of immersive environments, like the Vision Dome, for applications requiring large, high resolution displays and high quality rendering. One of the recent highlights from this activity was a demonstration of a network training simulation for the defence industry. During this task three sites; BT Labs, Silicon Graphics, and Matra BAe, were connected via an ISDN point to point network running the Distributed Interactive Simulation (DIS) protocol. The real novelty derived from the fact that the three sites used heterogeneous display systems, namely BT's Vision Dome, Silicon Graphics' Reality Centre and Matra BAe's synthetic environment facility, to provide mixed VR and video conferencing. With the numbers of installations set to increase, we are likely to see increasing opportunities for networking these systems to create testbed for exploring new forms of collaborative working.

Technologies – barriers and opportunities

Standards

BT is not interested in developing our own Shared Space client/server solutions. Rather we seek to predict service opportunities built from available and complementary technologies. This means we are particularly supportive of efforts to develop usable and useful standards. Until quite recently there were very few standards in the VR field, which made it difficult to contemplate deploying services. The picture has now changed with the emergence of VRML and, to a lesser extent, Java 3D. Although VRML has not been greeted with acclaim by all developers, its existence has drawn attention to the potential of VR. Java 3D is still in its infancy, however, it does present an important milestone for developers in the way that it uncouples the scenegraph describing the world from the display and interaction devices. Separating these issues will result in a much simplified development process, which will reduce development costs.

Client platforms

One of the biggest problems faced by VR developers is how do they create applications which meet the often inflated user expectations on platforms that are not always suited to the task. This problem is exacerbated by the legacy of outdated and underspecified machines used by the majority of potential users. In some domains, the greatest barrier to overcome in deploying VR application may not be user attitudes, as one might expect, but rather the hardware and software systems being used. Consider the business conferencing example discussed previously. Although it may deliver undoubted benefits, it may be difficult to deploy because many corporate PC's are not capable of running the application. In addition to performance, applications targeted at certain devices are either not available or do not support the rendering and communications subsystems required. Inhabited TV, targeted as it is at a set top box, is unlikely to be supported by first generation devices because their performance will be poor since the rendering pipe would have to be implemented in software.

Access network

The two large-scale Inhabited TV experiments discussed previously required participants to have access to at dialup-network connection running at 28.8Kbps; the type of connection typically used by home users in the UK to access the Internet. The advent of new access technologies based upon Digital Subscriber Line (xDSL)[1] and fibre access systems (FTTx)[2] will mean that the network will be less of a bottleneck for delivering content and applications, and will enable media streaming within Shared

---

[1] xDSL is the commonly use collective abbreviation used to describe the various Digital Subscriber Line technologies. Examples of such systems include Asymmetric DSL (ADSL), Symmetric DSL (SDSL), and Very high bit rate (VDSL).

[2] FTTx usually refers to either Fibre To The Curb (FTTC) or Fibre To The Home (FTTH).

Spaces. To reap the full rewards of increasing bandwidth, lower latency and reduced jitter will demand suitable increases in the client performance.

Challenges facing the VR community

There are many challenges, these represent some of the more important issues:

- Further work is required on quantifying the value and applicability of using VR interfaces for solving particular classes of problem.
- More intuitive forms of navigation and interaction are required particularly in the desktop domain.
- Workable standards, as stated previously, are important to our work.

The work discussed in this paper demonstrates our belief that VR will form an important component in the information systems of the future. Over the next few years we expect to start to see a number of these applications moving from the research domain into commercial applications where they will offer early adopters a competitive advantage.

Virtual Reality and the Link between Design and Engineering Analysis

Thomas Reuding [+], Martin Schulz [++]

[+] BMW AG, Entwicklung Karosserie, D-80788 München, Germany
thomas.reuding@bmw.de
[++] University of Erlangen, Computer Graphics Group (IMMD IX)
Am Weichselgarten 9, D-91058 Erlangen, Germany
schulz@informatik.uni-erlangen.de

1. Introduction

The pressure for companies in the automotive industry to remain competitive has led to the adoption of concurrent engineering to reduce the lead time for new products. Concurrent engineering is a systematic approach to the integrated concurrent design of products and related processes. When using concurrent engineering, specialist knowledge and expertise from downstream tasks of a design and engineering process are introduced during the early phases of product development. Since the largest percentage of design and manufacturing costs are allocated during the concept definition stage of a project, decisions made during this early stage should be supported by all means, including those of information technology. Since CAD and CAE systems are widely used in the automotive design and development process, large amounts of 3-dimensional digital product data are available. Nevertheless, physical prototypes still play an important role, their benefits compared to digital models arising mainly from their spatial presence.

The advent of immersive virtual environments means that the user of digital information has also finally arrived in 3D space.

The basic philosophy behind the use of virtual reality technology is to provide a communications platform for supporting multidisciplinary concurrent engineering. This should encourage the consideration of as many product development issues as possible during the crucial concept development phase. Such considerations should result in fewer unexpected problems during subsequent development stages and consequently fewer design iterations, reduced development time and costs, and better product quality.

This paper describes the implementation of a virtual environment for supporting different design and engineering applications significant for the concept stage of the automotive development process. The potential that virtual reality technology might offer are discussed and examples are given.

2. Virtual Reality for Automotive Engineering Design Evaluation

Virtual Reality can be used in several ways in the design and engineering process: to assess the overall impact of the design, to conduct visual quality inspections, carry out ergonomics studies and make the results of engineering simulations from fields such as structural mechanics, aerodynamics, acoustics and climatization more transparent and communicateable. Some of these aspects will be discussed in the following.

Design Impact

Immersive, stereoscopic viewing as a fundamental part of VR technology is very effective in determining the first reaction to a design concept. By sitting inside a virtual interior, the user can experience the spatial aspects of the geometry and check for accessibility or occlusion of instruments. Visual problems caused by the A-pillars or the lower and upper windscreen edge can be examined for instance, as well as the position and the layout of control panels (Fig. 1).

Fig. 1. Visibility of instruments

Other studies can be conducted to determine the effect of occupant height variation as well as the interdependence between the perception of interior spatiousness and the variation of exterior design elements. This is achieved by allowing the virtual A-pillars to vary in angle, thereby changing the relative position of the roof frame (Fig. 2).

264

Fig. 2. Perception of interior roominess

Visual quality inspection extends to digital subassemblies of body-in-white parts which can be checked for collision and clearances as well as water drainage and accessability of anti corrosion coatings.

Engineering Analysis

Numerical analyses play a key role in car body engineering, enabling performance predictions and functional evaluations long before results of real prototype tests are available, and extending to a variety of applications such as structural mechanics, aerodynamics, acoustics and climatization, to name just a few.

In each of these fields, the task at hand is twofold: first to predict the physical behaviour of a complex technical system both as a whole or as individual components; second to use the analysis results to effectively introduce the necessary engineering changes to compensate for detected design shortcommings.

However, with the rise in model complexity, data quantity, computing performance and accuracy, we increasingly find ourselfs lacking the tools, methods and metaphors to deal with the information that is being generated. This is supported by the observation that currently about 30 percent of the efforts involved in a typical simulation go into the preprocessing phase and about 10 is taken up by the actual computation, while approximately 60 percent goes into the analysis and communication of the results.

Clearly there is a strong incentive to reduce the last percentage through the use of a virtual environment that provides insightful, intuitive visualization and allows effective communication between engineers.

We have developed a virtual environment which is written in C++ and has been implemented on Silicon Graphics workstations (Octane and Onyx). It is devided into a high-end VR part and a VRML based part for Internet/Intranet access and it supports a variety of interface hardware and interactive functions. Currently available are a Fakespace BOOM, stereoscopic large screen projection was well as conventional workstation display. In addition the user can choose between a CyberGlove, a 3D mouse or a conventional 2D mouse and a keyboard for input (Fig. 3). This flexibility supports different usage scenarios - from two or three engineers discussing details to design-build teams of ten people engaged in a project meeting. A simple menu is used to control the visualization. Since not every application needs the full depth of immersion, VRML files can be created and used for documentation and web-based communication.

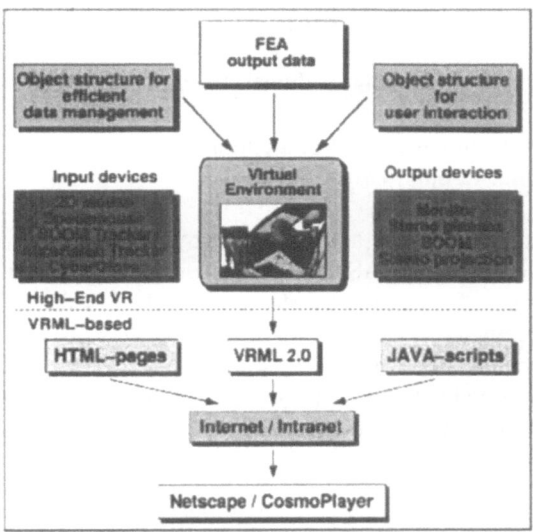

Fig. 3. System design

The study of realistically simulated scenarios in structural and fluid mechanics involves very large transient data sets, therefore the visualization will, in general, be in motion. Because moving objects can be difficult to analyse, users must have the opportunity to lock on what they want to see. We provide the ability to attach oneself to arbitrary objects in the scene, thereby observing only relative motion. This can provide the user with, for instance, the crash-test dummy´s perspective of driving the vehicle. In addition, individual objects can be selected and freely moved during the animation. Furthermore scalar values calculated at runtime are displayed either as color maps on the selected geometry or as a function of time and location drawn on a virtual sketch pad appearing in the users peripheral field of view (Fig. 4).

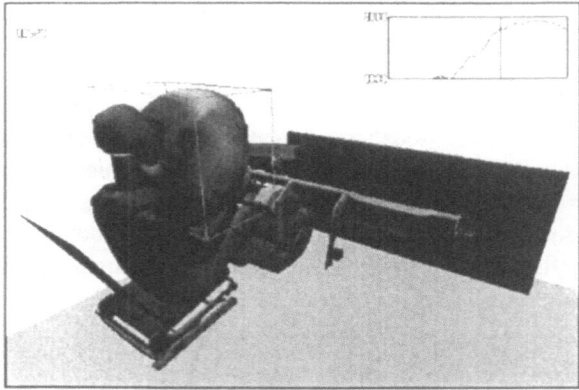

Fig. 4. Virtual sketch pad

Another interactive feature is the use of a cutting plane. It can also be moved freely in virtual space and slice through virtual objects.

The crash-test simulation results are calculated by the non-linear, transient, dynamic finite element solver PAM-CRASH in sixty discrete time steps. A single data set consists of a geometry for every time step and a set of scalar values for each finite element of that geometry. Typically we have to deal with approximately 400.000 finite elements per time step. Geometry data and physical properties data like stress, strain, acceleration or velocity are displayed to illustrate the performance of the whole vehicle or any subset of components (Fig. 5).

Fig. 5. Frontal offset crash

Vibrational analysis is computed as a linear modal eigenvalue simulation of the car body structure. As opposed to the crash-test simulation there is only one complete geometry description which contains the nodes and the element connectivities. Over the course of the animation the vehicle vibrates with a user-defined amplification factor and the engineer can analyse the simulation more clearly than by interpreting a set of displacement vectors in 3D space (Fig. 6)

Fig. 6. Amplified door vibration

The noise level,(or preferably the absence thereof) in the passenger compartment is a feature of relatively high customer value because it is easily noticeable. This noise occurs when the volume of air that occupies the passenger compartment is subjected to a change in pressure caused by the exitation of resonating components such as the floor panel or the fore and aft firewalls. In the virtual environment the volume of air consists of about 20.000 voxels and we display the scalar value of air pressure as a function of time and location by means of time dependent iso-surfaces (Fig. 7). The source of the noise and the noise level can be localized and the propagation of the wavefront through the passenger compartment visualized.

Fig. 7. Noise level wavefront

3. Conclusions

Currently, VR technology for industrial applications that fall outside the multi-media industry still has many deficiencies: The tradeoffs between scene complexity, image quality, frame rate and interactivity are very high. Many display devices are either bulky and cumbersome or lack a sufficient image resolution and field of view, or all of the above. Tracking systems to record a 3D position in space have high latency, an overly short range and are by far too imprecise in a real working environment. The absence of haptic and force feedback when manipulating virtual objects necessitates further research regarding a combination of automatic constraint recognition and allowable motion techniques to support the accurate positioning of virtual objects using 3D input devices such as data gloves. Data preparation and data exchange are still issues which are unsatisfactorily resolved regardless of STEP, IGES and other standardization efforts.

The vision of prototyping in virtual environments would be to merge VR and CAD/CAE tools which would allow us to design in a virtual environment. The designer could shape a new concept and pass it on to engineering analysis. Then, not only crash simulation, structural dynamics, acoustics or climatization data can be viewed, but the product developers can "experience" a design concept, walk into the simulation space of the engineering data and examine details or properties sometimes not accessable in the real world.

Finally, virtual reality is an interdisciplinary science: human factors, psychology, physics and computer science - they all have something to contribute to the development of VR applications. Therefore, the future of industrial VR will depend on how well these groups get along and develop applications and user interfaces. Also, the development of new hardware peripherals, software and the ability to adopt VR technology in commercially interesting applications will greatly influence the impact of VR on industrial product development processes.

4. Acknowledgements

Many of the ideas in this paper were generated by discussions with Sven Kuschfeld and Michael Holzner of BMW as well as Thomas Ertl of the University of Erlangen. Conceptual inspiration came from the work of Steve Bryson et al. on the *Virtual Windtunnel* project at NASA Ames. We would like to thank Edith Zimmermann and Manfred Weiler of the University of Erlangen for their contribution to software development and finally, we are grateful for the continuing support by the University of Erlangen, BMW, ESI Group Paris and Sense8 Europe.

5. References

Beier, K.-P., Virtual Reality in Automotive Design and Manufacturing, The University of Michigan, Virtual Reality Laboratory, Dept. of Naval Architecture and Marine Engineering, April 1994.

Bryson, S., Levit, C., The Virtual Windtunnel: An Environment for the Exploration of Three-Dimensional Unsteady Flows, NASA Ames Research Center, Technical Report RNR-92-013, Oct. 1991.

Bryson, S., Approaches to the Successful Design and Implementation of VR Applications, SIGGRAPH 95.

Dai, F., et al., Virtual Prototyping Examples for Automotive Industries, Virtual Reality World '96, Stuttgart, Germany.

Kuschfeldt, S., Holzner, M., Sommer, O., Ertl, Th., Efficient Visualization of Crash-Worthiness Simulations, IEEE Computer Graphics and Applications, 1998.

Kuschfeldt, S., Schulz, M., Reuding, Th., Ertl, Th., Holzner, M., Visualizations of Crashworthiness Simulations using Virtual Reality Techniques, Proc. International Conference on High Performance Computing in Automotive Design, Engineering and Manufacturing, Paris, 1996.

Schulz, M., Einsatz von Virtual Reality Techniken zur Darstellung von Ergebnissen der Karosserieberechnung, Proc. VisEng '97, Rechenzentrum Universität Stuttgart, Germany, 1997.

Schulz, M., Reuding, Th., Ertl, Th., Crashing in Cyberspace - Evaluating Structural Behaviour of Car Bodies in a Virtual Environment, Proc. IEEE Virtual Reality Annual International Symposium (VRAIS '98), Atlanta, 1998.

Schulz, M., Zimmermann, E., Reuding, Th., Ertl, Th., From High-End VR to PC-based VRML Viewing: Supporting the Car Body Development Process by Adapted Virtual Environments, Proc. CGIM'98, IASTED, Halifax, Canada, 1998.

Yeh, T., P., Vance, J., M., Combining Sensitivity Methods, Finite Element Analysis and Free-Form Deformation to Facilitate Structural Shape Design in a Virtual Environment, Proc. 23rd ASME Design Automation Conference, Sacramento, CA. 1997.

Editors' Note: see Appendix, p. 333 f. for colored figures of this paper

Virtual Environment for Education and Training in Safety Engineering and Maintenance

Dipl.-Ing. Thomas Flaig

Demonstration Centre for Virtual Reality,
Fraunhofer-Institute for Manufacturing Engineering and Automation, IPA
Nobelstraße 12, D-70569 Stuttgart
flaig.t@ipa.fhg.de

Abstract. Education and training depends on perception of, information about and self-driven examination of unknown environments. The paper describes a virtual environment for education and training in safety engineering and maintenance. The characteristics of the environment is a combination of 3D-visualization, real-time simulation and multimedia representation of information. The user will interact in a realistic environment of manufacturing engineering facilities with dynamic behavior, real-time interactivity and free control of information support. First experiences will be presented form different projects.

1 Introduction

International competition is characterized by the reduce of the innovation time. Therefore the success of new products strongly depends on the necessary time for their development and the nearness to market. Virtual Reality, as a new 3D human-computer interface accelerate significantly the processes of creating and handling 3D date, in 3D space for design and validation proposes. Virtual Reality, providing advanced human-computer-interfaces can make a valuable contribution to improve simulation and control tools. The operator, using a dataglove and a head-mounted stereo display could act in a virtual world and is no longer a passive observer [1]. Characteristic in Virtual Reality is the interaction and the perception in a virtual environment. This is only possible by real-time simulation and rendering. This led to high performance computer technology with nowadays high prices.

The use of Virtual Reality in the rapid development of products and industrial production environments is nowadays a great challenge. Engineers and customers have the possibility to test virtual products for fulfilling their needs. The results of those tests depend on the accuracy of the behavior of the virtual prototypes [2]. Especially environments which depends on human performance need virtual environments for validation. High degree of presence in combination with real physical behavior of the simulation is necessary for usable validation results. For example safety systems are very complex systems and the development a difficult task for design engineers [3]. A lot of rules and laws have to be disregarded for the design. Mechanical and electrical know-how is necessary for the technical design, ergonomic and psychological know-how for the logical design, depending on human factors.

2 State of the Art

Simulation of industrial environments is well known since the upcoming of computers. The ongoing in the computer graphic technology shows new 3D oriented tools for simulation of industrial processes for planning and optimization. Well known are IGRIP from Deneb Robotics [4] and ROBCAD from Technomatix [5]. Both tools came up at the end of the 80´s and use high-end computer graphics systems. They have been designed for robot simulation and off-line programming of robot working cells and are mostly used in automotive industry. The tools have been designed originally not for real-time graphic simulation in immersive environments known as virtual environments. Recent developments show a new orientation of both tools to virtual environment with real-time graphic and advanced interaction devices. At the leading edge of these developments is CLARUS [6] in Sweden. The use of common 3D simulation systems for safety design is not usual. Normally safety design will be done parallel to the design of the robot work cells. Only validation of the technical design is possible in common simulation systems. Validation of the logical design is possible only partly because of the lack of immersion. First steps towards immersive environments for safety design have been done at VTT Manufacturing Technology [7]. Experiments had shown, that the use of 3D simulation systems will decrease the design faults significantly.

Safety design is a human oriented task for designers. Workers have to control and handle the technical environment. The demands are to fulfill ergonomics and psychological requirements. Nowadays all 3D simulation systems include human models for ergonomic studies. But real-time control of these virtual humans is not possible because of the used graphical system. Therefore ergonomic validation and also training is static and not dynamic, with less effective results. Safety engineering is a very complex task for the designers because of the different requirements. Beside technical aspects also human factors have to be fulfilled. Examples show that the use of 3D simulation systems and immersive environments will offer opportunities. Problems to be solved are the design of virtual environments for design, validation and training tasks, real-time oriented human model and validation of the target control code.

The quality of a product is increasingly judged not only on the basis of its performance, but also in terms of the after-sales services such as maintenance. Indeed, the maintenance costs of a product can be a sizeable portion of the total lifetime costs and, therefore, a key competitive factor. While suppliers currently often make a handsome income from charging maintenance costs, increasing global competition may well force them to actively seek to reduce the costs for the client. Because of the importance of maintenance, it has been identified as a key application area of new information technology in production [8].

From the supplier side there is a major dilemma in providing maintenance assistance:

- As products become more complex with an increasing number of subsystems, have more customer specific features and shortening lifecycles, the costs of providing comprehensive and up-to-date maintenance documents can become prohibitive.
- On the other hand, to reduce the costs of having to provide support on site, it is preferable for the customer to carry out as much servicing as possible himself on the basis of the documentation provided.

3   Method

As described in the state of the art, no common 3D simulation system fulfill all requirements for training and education in safety engineering and maintenance. The use of Virtual Reality needs developments we will focus now.

3.1   Virtual Environment

The paper describes a virtual environment for education and training in safety engineering and maintenance. The characteristics of the environment is a combination of 3D-visualization, real-time simulation, interaction and multimedia representation of information (Fig. 1.).

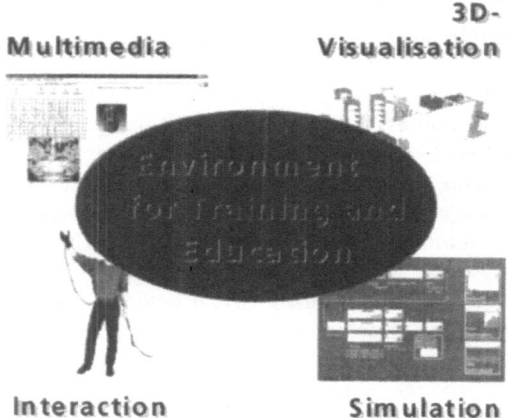

Fig. 1. Virtual Environment for Training and Education

3D-visualization allows the user to percept an environment as realistic as possible, so that you have a close correlation to a real environment. The characteristics are:
- Realistic spacious representation of objects,
- Navigation and interaction in real-time,
- Intuitive perception.

The realism of an environment depends not only on visualization but also on a realistic object behavior. To realize this you need real-time simulation:
− Simulation of object characteristics and behavior.

To behave in an virtual environment as you will do in a real you need realistic interaction:
− Intuitive interaction with objects,
− 3D-navigation.

The described characteristics are the same you would use in an industrial Virtual Reality application. For training and education you need further information about objects. The best way to present these information to the user is the use of multimedia:
− Use of text, pictures, sounds, video clips,
− Increasing perception of information by multimodal presentation.

3.2   Immersion versus Performance

A great advantage of Virtual Environments are the ability to give immersion to the user. Especially in training and education it is very important to immerse. Learning depends on trying and gaining insights from failures. Therefore, the higher the level of immersion the better is the performance for learning.

But the advantage of a virtual environment for solving a problem is not constant. It depends on the needs of the work process (necessary interactions) and the degrees-of-freedom (DOF) of the interaction devices in VE (possible interactions). The method to configure interaction devices in a VE is based on a classification from Ware-MacKenzie [9]. Interaction devices will be classified in DOFs and goes on in five steps:

1. Classification and valence of necessary interactions for the control and observe of the VR system based on DOFs.
2. Classification and valence of necessary interactions for the application in the VE based on DOFs.
3. Classification and valence of the interaction devices based on DOFs.
4. Valence of the combination of interaction devices with input[output functions.
5. Choice of interaction devices by the use of the valences and comparison.

The method shows a systematic way to choose interaction devices depending on the exercises to have be solved in the VE. Dead locks in the method will be solved by mapping the task to another channel of human perception [10].

3.3   Simulation of the Control Environment

Validation of the electrical aspects includes the test off the functionality of the control code for the safety functions. Most simulation systems have not the possibility to use the target code (PLC code) for simulation. They use a higher simulation language different to PLC code and are therefore not able to give a final guarantee for correct functionality. Only the use of the target code gives a final guarantee.

The PLC level is the lowest logical level in a technical system and is bit-oriented for the control of technical components. The control components receive signals from sensors to get a display of the technical process and transmit signals to actors for interacting with the process. The program running a PLC is assembler oriented and programmed in statement lists, ladder diagram or function block diagram. The logical behavior of those systems depends strongly on the programming style and the three-dimensional arrangements of sensors. Therefore a simulation of the real behavior of the PLC is necessary for decent results.

The realization in the simulation system is based on the structure of the PLC system S5 from SIEMENS. This system has a characteristic register and memory structure which is widely used and the basis for the IEC standard 1131-3 for PLC programming languages. In the simulation system each component has its own PLC program, the same structure as in the real environment. The very close link to the real environment allows the use of existing PLC programs in the simulation or the use of programs from the simulation in a real environment. Therefore all described programming languages are available in the simulation system [11].

The PLC program module in the simulation is an executable C-code converted from the PLC language by a compiler. The communication with the simulation, sensors and actors is done by shared memory areas corresponding to real environments [12].

4 Implementation

4.1 Environment for Safety Engineering

The test environment for the virtual prototyping of safety systems consists of a robot working cell with two drilling machines and separate working stations.

The robot takes work pieces form a storage carrier, put it into the drilling machine and does this steps then for the second drilling machine. After this steps he takes the piece out of the first drilling machine, put it to the working station and set it in a second storage carrier. This steps will be repeated for the second drilling machine. A worker has to interfere with the system by the programming or reprogramming of the robot system, by exchanging the storage systems and by the repair of failure functions of the robot system, the drilling machines and the working stations. Fig. 2 shows the geometrical model of the robot working cell with the safety system components. Safety in technical systems depends not only on the design and functionality of the components but also on the educational know-how of the workers. The better the education the lower is the failure rate. Nowadays education of the workers is done theoretical or by training in the real environment. The costs of the training limits the possibilities and therefore the success.

The use of a virtual prototype in an immersive environment allows the unlimited training of workers. The computer controlled environment gives the possibility to run training programs with exercises and lessons. This test can be analyzed for ranking the educational know-how of a worker. The immersive VE guarantees concentration of the test persons and therefore the base for successful training.

To support the learning process an interactive information system has been included based on a HTML environment. The user can browse in an online data base with relevant information about safety guidelines, functionality of components and the work environment (Fig. 3.).

Fig. 2. Environment for Safety Engineering

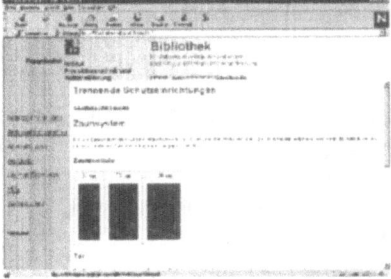

Fig. 3. Tool in the safety engineering environment for information and introduction

4.2 Environment for Maintenance

The test environment for education and training of maintenance workers is based on a logistic center of a shoe manufacturer [13]. Shoe boxes come from the production line are put on carriers, called tablar, by workers. The filled tablars run on conveyer belts to the storage area. The storage warehouse consists of ten automatic storage devices for loading and unloading tablars. If a customer order comes into the system tablars are unloaded from the warehouse and brought to special commission areas, where shoe boxes are be collected. On twenty commission belts the customer orders are collected for further manual handling. The industrial project was done for the product presentation of spacious logistic environments on an exhibition. The graphic model consists of nearly 700.000 textured polygons. The simulation environment consists of about 150 technical components with 450 sensors and 350 information links between the components. Up to 1000 objects are manipulated by full operating rate of the simulation. The simulation cycle time is about 40 ms and accuracy is about 80 ms, which is useable for logistic environment simulation. The frame rate of the system is 20 frames per second rendered on a SGI INFINITY.

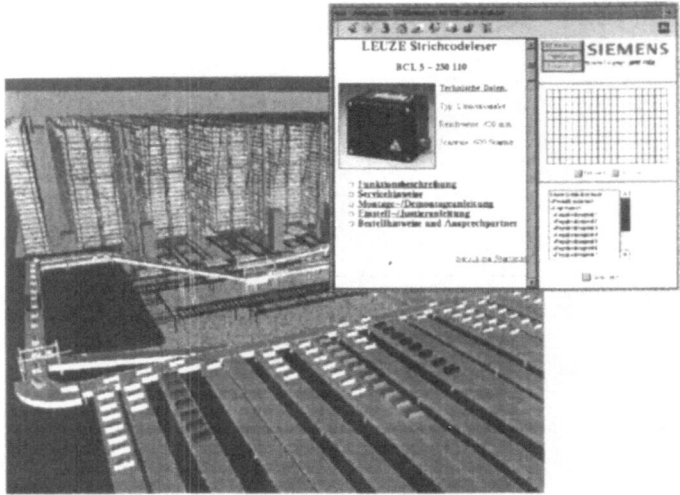

Fig. 4. Environment for Maintenance

The environment itself consists of a Virtual Reality simulation running on an high-end graphics computer and a hardware independent HTML information window.

The characteristics of the Virtual Reality simulation are:
- Navigation of the user in an immersive environment,
- Interaction with graphical objects,
- Use of textures,
- Use of kinematics,
- Collision detection,
- Real-time dynamic simulation,
- High-end computer hardware.

The HTML information window is connected to the VR Simulation by a JAVA server. So the information window can be started on hardware independent computer system connected via LAN.

The characteristics of the HTML information window are:
- Multi-frame window with text, pictures and video clips,
- Sensitive text frames,

- JAVA applets for object identification,
- JAVA applets for output of parameters,
- Hardware-independence.

To fulfill maintenance work tasks in virtual environments the worker needs tools for navigation in the available information in the HTML window. These tools are for: search & identification, information & introduction and observation & control (Fig. 5.).

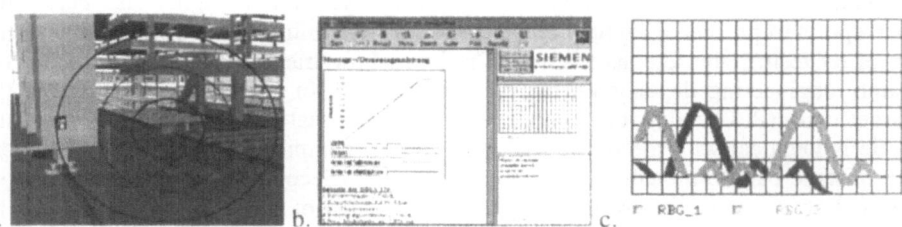

Fig. 5. Tools in the maintenance environment for: a. search and identification; b. information and introduction; c. observation and control

Search & Identification
- Choosing components in 3D environment or from an index
- Marking components with color and wave

Maintenance workers have often the problem of identification of facility components. There are two solutions for that problem in the virtual environment. First the worker chooses a component from an index in the HTML window. The chosen component will appear then in a red color and a blue wave will run continuously to its position. The same happens if the user picks a virtual object for identification.

Information & Introduction
- Direct linking of information to components
- Handbook for assembly and service
- Multimedia display

If a component is identified the worker will have fully access to all available information like hand books for assembly or service tasks. All information will be displayed in multimedia technique for gaining best information transfer to the workers.

Observation & Control
- Online output of dynamic process parameters
- Online Manipulation of process parameters

By the direct connection with the simulation the worker is able to observe control all parameters like sensor signals or velocity and acceleration of movable facility components. So the worker can test which system reaction will happen by a given parameter set. Learning by doing, the best method for training and education.

5   Results

The use of VR technology in training and education has been put into action in a test environment at the Fraunhofer IPA. Therefore a VE has been designed for the specific requirements of safety engineering and maintenance.

Safety depends on the education of the workers. The immersive environment with real dynamic behavior is well adapted to training requirements. It is cheaper using a virtual prototype of a robot working cell for training than a real environment or do training theoretical. The results show that the success is higher the better the perception of presence. Another advantage is the possibility to control the educational level by testing the lessons learned. The know-how transfer in an environment for safety engineering depends on the realistic behavior of the system. The use of the target code (PLC code) for simulation shows two great advantages. First, the used code is identical with the target code and no post-compiling is necessary. Therefore no mistake can be included after validation in VE. Second the critical combination, know-how of the worker versus complex functionality of the technical system, can be tested.

Training and education in a virtual environment shows great advantages in know-how transfer to the workers. All tasks can be done on graphics computers. The following advantages derive from the use of Virtual Reality:
− Fasten up the learning process by use of multi media,
− Increasing the quality of the learning process by the use of more scenarios,
− Increasing the working performance in real environment,
− Increasing transparency of processes,
− Increasing the safety of working processes in real environments,
− reduction the necessary time for learning and training.

These are intermediate results from user observations and interviews at our institute. The tests will go on to get more measurable results with selected test persons. The goal is to value learning performance depending on different levels of immersion in virtual environments. Further test will be done by Siemens in Munich for the benefit of the maintenance environment.

6   Conclusion

The VEs have been tested in a test environment. Virtual Reality technology can make significant contributions in training and education for complex industrial facilities. Especially the use for better understanding of safety and maintenance aspects have shown great advantage. The easy to use graphical environment has the potential to play with the displayed problem case and to increase human performance and work quality by lower risks for the workers´s health.

7 References

1. Flaig, T.: „Echtzeitorientierte interaktive Simulation mit VR4RobotS am Beispiel eines Industrieprojektes", Tagungsunterlagen des 2. VR-Forum ´94, Anwendungen und Trends, Februar 1994, Stuttgart, Deutschland.
2. Flaig, T; Thrainsson, M.: „Virtual Prototyping - New Information Techniques in Product Design". In: Rolf D. Schraft (Hrsg.); M. Munir Ahmad (Hrsg.);William G. Sullivan (Hrsg.); Fraunhofer-Institut für Produktionstechnik und Auto-matisierung (IPA); CIM System Research Center; Department of Industrial and System Engineering: 5th Inter-national Conference on Flexible Automation and Intelligent Manufacturing, FAIM ´95. Begell House Inc., 1995. S. 338-348.
3. Flaig, T.; Grefen, K.: „Auslegung sicherheitstechnischer Einrichtungen mit Virtueller Realität". In: Fachtagung SA, Simulation und Animation für Planung, Bildung und Präsentaion; 29. Februar - 01. März 1996, Magdeburg, Deutschland.
4. N., N.: „IGRIP", „QUEST", „Virtual NC", Technical Product Description, Deneb Robotics Inc., 1994, Michigan, USA.
5. N., N.: „Information über ROBCAD", Technische Produktinformation, Tecnomatix Automatisierungssysteme GmbH, Offenbach, Deutschland.
6. N., N.: „Prosolvia opens new worlds", Technical Product Description, Prosolvia: Clarus AB, Calstedt Research & Technology AB, Pronima AB, 1996, Göteborg, Sweden.
7. Kuivanan, R.: „Methodology for simultaneous robot system safety design", VTT Manufacturing Technology, Technical Research Centre of Finland, ESPOO 1995.
8. Flaig, T; Wapler, M.: The Hyper Enterprise. In: Roller, Dieter (Hrsg.): Simulation, Diagnosis and Virtual Reality Applications in the Automotive Industry: Dedicated Conference on ...., Proceedings, Florenze, Italy, 3rd-6th June 1996. Croydon, England: Automotive Automation, 1996.
9. Herndon, K. P.; van Dam, A.; Gleicher, M.: „The Challenges of 3D Interaction; A CHI´94 Workshop". In: SIGCHI Bulletin Literatur zur Kollisionserkennung (1994) Vol. 26, No. 4, pp 36-43.
10. Flaig, T.: "Work Task Analysis and Selection of Interaction Devices in Virtual Environments". In: Proceedings of the 1st International Conference on Virtual Worlds, Paris, France, 1st- 3rd June 1998, accepted.
11. N.N.: „SIMATIC S5", Technical Product Description, Siemens AG, Industrial Automation Systems, Nuremberg, Germany.
12. Neuber, D.: „Spezifikation und Implementierung von Datenstrukturen zur echtzeitorientierten Simulation von Speicherprogrammierbaren Steuerungen", Diplomarbeit am Fraunhofer IPA, Februar 1995, Stuttgart, Deutschland.
13. Flaig, T.; Grefen, K.; Neuber, D.: „Interactive Graphical Planning and Design of Spacious Logistic Environment". In: Bergamasco (ed.): FIVE ´96, Framework for Immersive Virtual Environments: Proceedings of the Conference of the FIVE Working Group; 19-20 December 1996. Pisa: PERCRO, Scuola Superiore S. Anna, 1996, pp 10-17.

Window into Virtuality -
A Sales-Support-System based on ideas and technology components out of the Virtual Reality area

Christoph Stratmann, strat@artcom.de
ART+COM GmbH, Berlin, Germany, http://www.artcom.de/

1. Background

In product marketing and sales virtual reality applications are relatively common. This report exemplifies the development of an application by the example of the ART+COM project „Virtuelles Fahrzeug" comissioned by Mercedes-Benz. The shown prototype of an electronic sales system resulted from the first phase of development.

This case study shows, that in the field of virtual reality, application development rarely is only a matter of technological development. Especially in the common case of a rather vague project specification, the development of a VR application will become a synergetic process combining conceptual work, technology and software development, design competence and content production.

2. Objective

The objective was to implement virtual reality concepts and technologies in order to create an application supporting the sales process at the sites of the sales partners. The device should accompany the sales representative during the sales talk and support the customers individual configuration of his or her ideal vehicle. This requires a system able to present all possible variants of the vehicle.

The device should mediate an experience, but the form of presentation should at the same time differ substantially from conventional VR-Installations in the field of product marketing. The implementation of VR may constitute an outstanding experience for the user, but at the same time the VR-technology is supposed to stand back in order to leave center stage to the product automobile.

3. Concept

The fundamental concept is to substitute the real vehicle in favour of a virtual one at its traditional places of presentation: the podium and showroom. Essentially the car is represented on a 1:1 scale. The user may walk through and view the virtual car with the help of a flat screen (LCD) attached to a swivel arm. The representation is updated in real time relative to the position and point of view of the user.

4. Computer Human Interface

Utilising a LCD with integrated touch screen that can be freely moved in 3D-Space, the user may experience the car through a window to the virtual world. The display is framed and mounted to a swivel arm.

5. Interactive concept

The screen permits the examination of the vehicle including all its features and, by way of its touch sensitivity, allows for the car to be invidually re-configured. If the user selects a piece of equipment he is presented with all available options from which he may choose the most pleasing to his individual taste. In this manner all of the available vehicle options are available to be chosen from, from color, engine, wheel rims, seats down to style of gear shift knob.

Virtual Reality Applications
for
Spacecraft Operations

Roland Luettgens
European Space Agency
Robert Bosch Str. 5, 64293 Darmstadt, Germany, Tel: (49) 6151 90 2797,
e-mail: rluettge@esoc.esa.de

Introduction

The Virtual Reality (VR) technology appears to offer promising potential to spacecraft operations. Typical applications that can be considered include the support of ground personnel in the control of spacecraft, the validation of procedures, the assessment of planning products and timelines, as well as the "look and feel" of operations such as tele-operations, for unmanned satellite missions and servicing missions, but also for manned missions.

Present operations environments are constrained by a flat data-driven "world" with individual abstract data representations and models tailored to each team member in the operations team.

The VR environment enables the entire ground operations team to be placed in a synthetic environment with a multi-dimensional logical representation of the on-board system, allowing each member the control of the assigned subsystems and payloads whilst at the same time allowing all members full insight in the overall operations progress and tasks performed by other members.

Today's communication technologies further enhance the VR capabilities, supporting remote cooperative operations. Applying this communications technology together with the VR technology enables individual ground operators to work in the same environment whilst located at different geographical places. Adding additional multimedia capabilities, such as 3-dimensional audio may further enhance the team's perception of the operations at hand, through acoustic orientation in the VR environment. Systems such as this one could also be applied to other areas with similar operational environments, thus offering a potential for knowledge transfer to other space and ground applications.

The VR technology appears to be well suited for applications in the area of preparation for and execution of spacecraft control tasks. Already pursued fields of VR include tele-manipulation, -robotics, and tele-presence.

Creating a virtual environment for a ground operations team may well constitute a major step forward from today's systems which are limited to a flat data-driven "world" with individually tailored, abstract data representations and models.

Overview

The European Space Agency together with Industry is in the process of developing and evaluating a VR system in support of spacecraft operations. This VR system represents the spacecraft subsystems as logical components together with a semi-realistic representation of the spacecraft itself. The functionality of these subsystems, e.g. onboard computers, thermal control systems, power distribution systems etc. are represented by a 3-dimensional model located close to the model of the spacecraft. Interaction with these models and monitoring of the overall system behavior gives an instant system level overview of the state of the spacecraft together with spatial information identifying the subsystem locations. This representation allows easy orientation within the VR environment without loosing the relation to the spacecraft physical systems.

The Columbus Orbital Facility (COF) was taken as the reference mission for the implementation of the subsystems. The COF is the European Pressurized Laboratory for Microgravity Missions in the Material, Fluid Physics and compatible Life Science and Technology Disciplines, launched and serviced by the Shuttle, permanently attached to the International Space Station (ISS). Its subsystems provide the necessary infrastructure, in terms of electrical Energy, Environmental Control and Data Management, to support those Missions.

Architecture

The VR System Architecture is based on the main components of the COF physical structure including the locations of the subsystems components, as well as the architecture of its subsystems. An exploded view of the COF gives a brief overview of the system and equipment locations together with the physical structure.

The main usage of the physical architecture used for the VR System is to correctly represent and the identify the location of the subsystems.
In order to derive the VR System Architecture, the basic hierarchical model of the COF and its subsystems was used together with the subsystem enditems to be taken into account. Those enditems are, in principle, functional groups, such as the power distribution units and their corresponding possible physical and logical measurements, which define the states of the subsystems, e.g. Voltages, Switch on-off states.

The breakdown of the COF System together with the breakdown of its subsystems into logical components is the basis to derive the VR System graphical structure. The physical and logical structure is mapped onto a graphical structure, which represents the spacecraft as a virtual system with some degree of abstraction, combining a physical and logical view of the COF.

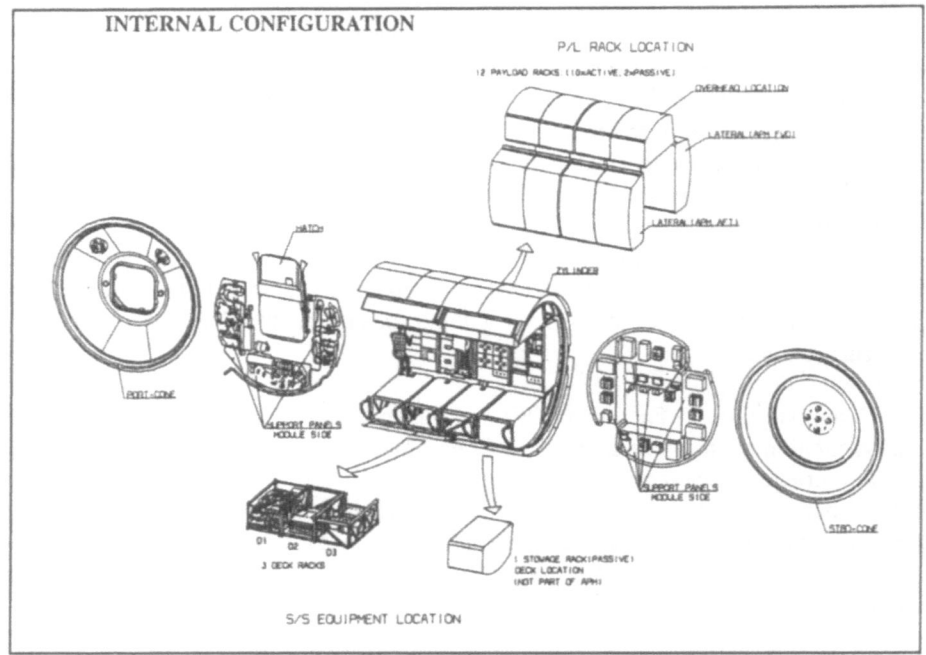

Fig. 1. Internal Configuration

One of the main goals to achieve was a representation of the COF in a way, such that it reflects the logical structure of its subsystem, rather than a physical representation. The physical representation is used to identify the location of subsystems and to provide the mechanism to interact with the model in a VR environment.

The logical structure was derived from the main classes of COF subsystems together with their physical location within the COF structure, as indicated in Figure 1. Five main COF subsystems are identified related to data management, thermal control, power distribution and payloads. Each class has associated states and measurements that can be taken from a set of sensors or parameters, which define the overall status of the class. The classes are further categorized in functional groups, each of which represents a major function of this class, such as the power distribution or the heater control. Each of those functional groups together with its individual enditems are reflected in the VR System and provide the instantaneous view of the state as an abstract component of the VR System.

The system level overview is shown in Figure 2. It indicates that a physical model of the COF is used as a reference to identify its subsystems, which are represented then as classes and functional groups to interact with.

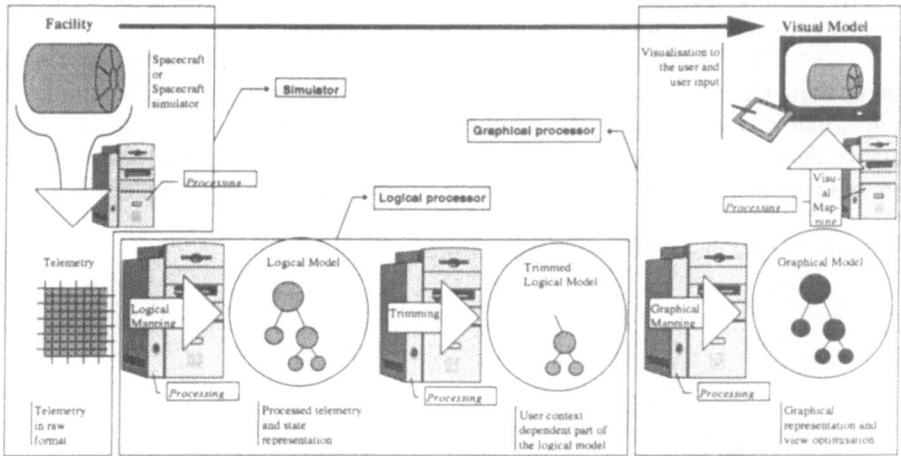

Fig. 2. System Overview

Implementation

The implementation of the graphical part of the VR System requires to keep a constant overview of the COF subsystems as a whole. At the same time it shall be possible to focus on a particular subsystem that requires attention and therefore needs to be monitored in detail. This has led to the concept of unfolding the graphical representation of the spacecraft and being able to set the focus on a particular subsystem.

Figure 4. shows the unfolded graphical structure as represented in the VR System. It is possible to use the nominal 3-D interaction capabilities to navigate around the model. The interaction with the model itself allows to locate a subsytem, to select and focus on a subsystem and interact with the subsystem itself.

A single view as shown in Figure 4. provides a system level overview, as a combination of traditional 2-D areas, showing in a semitransparent way the detailed parameters or measurements of a subsystem enditem. The 3-D model can be unfolded and its components can be placed anywhere in the environment, such that a complete disassembling of its components is possible. In case subsystems, located in different areas of the model, are interconnected, e.g. electrical wires, thermal connections etc., these interconnections will be kept such, that the relationships between those parts are still visible. These interconnections are functional or logical connections rather than physical connections, to provide the necessary abstraction from the physical model of the system.

Predefined arrangements of the model can be used and recalled at any time. Functional group components or enditem symbols are animated showing the dynamics or operation of those. Functional groups consists of various subsystem components so that a functional group or class as a whole, visualizes its behavior through animated enditems. Detailed representation of the data related to the functional group is shown as 2-D semitransparent windows.

Each enditem allows interaction, such as sending commands to the system, through a popup window next to it with all possible commands listed. A further capability is to visualize through avatars which classes or functional groups are set on focus by other users of the system. This allows for multiuser interaction with the VR System.

Examples of those enditems are shown in Figure 3.

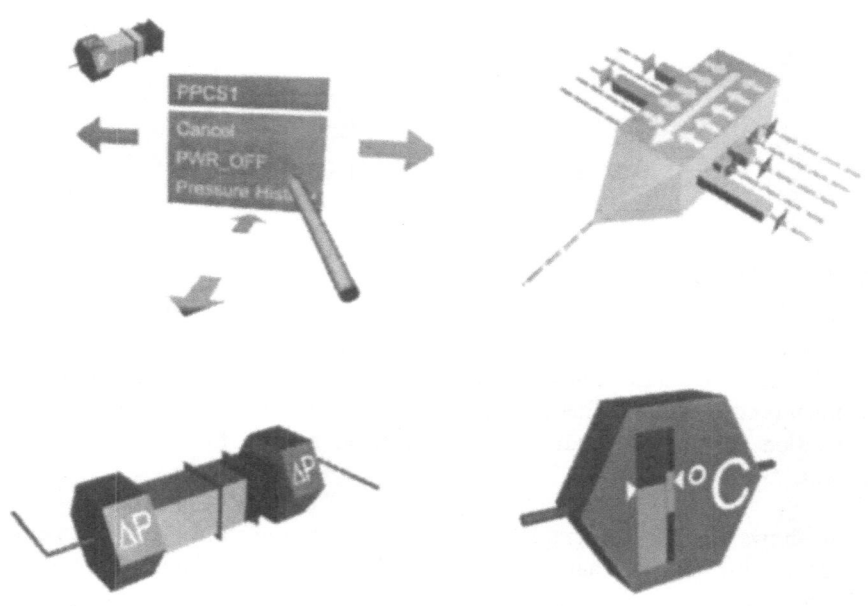

Fig. 3. Symbols

The implementation of the VR System will allow to work with a large amount of parameters in a wide logical context. Through the utilization of abstraction represented in a virtual reality environment, the behavior of nearly all complex physical systems can be represented very efficiently. Attention can be given by setting the focus on a particular functional group and monitoring the detailed underlying behavior and data.
It further provides a powerful and easy filtering of information, providing a fast, clear and overall view of the system.

It provides fast and intuitive navigation within the VR environment, keeping the relationship to the physical model.

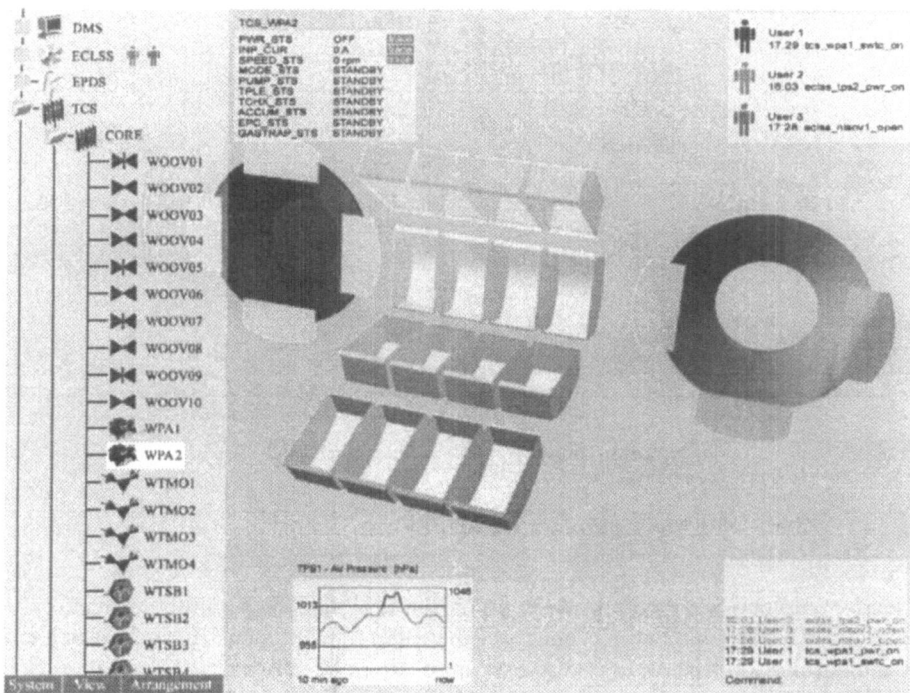

Fig. 4. Unfolded View

Conclusion

The features described in this paper represent the current state of the development. A prototype of the VR System will be available early 1999. The work conducted so far has shown, that the VR technology provides a step forward utilizing modern technologies in support of spacecraft operations. It provides the right level of abstraction necessary to get a fast system level overview of a complex system, such as the European COF. It allows easy and intuitive navigation within the VR environment as well as interaction with the VR environment without loosing the context to the overall system state.

Industrial Application Potential of Virtual Reality

An Empirical Study of Demands, Barriers, and Drivers

Thomas Lechler

Alexandre Saad

1 Virtual Reality between Forecast and Reality

Nearly everyone is pulled into the spell of Virtual Reality upon initial contact. VR is already a fixed ingredient in products of the entertainment industry, and has achieved meaningful market shares in a very short time.

In the VR industry we are still dealing with a threshold technology. According to various market researchers, this is due to change dramatically over the next few years. Some successful pilot applications in the aviation and automobile industries indicate the considerable potential of the VR technology. The application of VR curtails development time, since the time-consuming process of building prototypes is partly omitted, and rapid iteration in the development process is made possible.[1] Communication between user and developer in the evolution of complex products is substantially facilitated through application and evaluation in virtuality. The application of virtual models of products is seen as a common basis of co-operation as it supports interdisciplinary and decentralized teamwork. Faster recognition and resolution of diverse problems are the result.

Market forecasts are also apparently based on this potentially high usage. Unanimously, all market researchers proceed from an enormous market growth for VR

---

[1] cf. Bickel (1996) S.2, Miller (1996) pp.15, Schmid (1996 a,c),

technologies in the next few years. This reflects the high expectation of the future use of VR technologies.

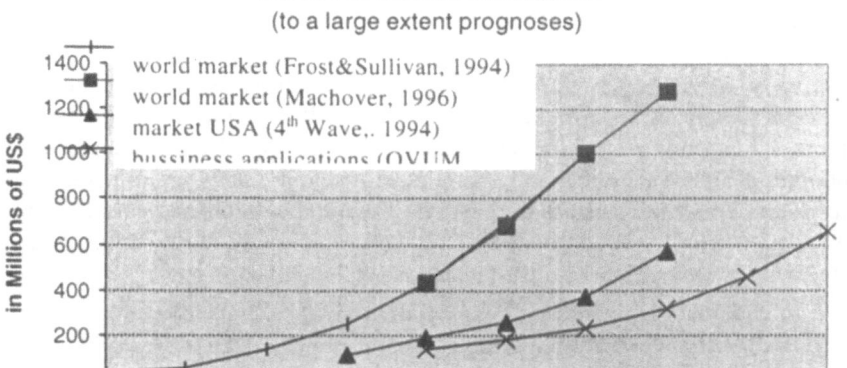

Growth of Various VR Markets
(to a large extent prognoses)

Fig. 1: Market growth of VR: Worldmarket - Market USA - Business Applications

Source: Frost & Sullivan, 4th Wave in: Bauer (1996) pp.182 ff.; OVUM in Leston et al. (1996) pp.154ff. Machover (1996) pp.32

Are these expectations realistic or do they result from the initial euphoria of an innovative technology? The high growth prognoses are based particularly on the expansion of Virtual Reality in the industry. In the entertainment industry, only small growth rates are expected, and their relative proportion of the world market volume have sunken to 27%. If one regards the prognoses more carefully, then one can say that the growth curves shift continuously to the right according to the date of the respective study. This development may have several causes.

Up to now, no clear structure is apparent in the VR market. Rather, the VR market is still shaped by a multiplicity of small enterprises, which „briefly emerge, then sink out of sight."[2]

The measurement or estimation of the size of the market is hindered by the fact that VR is a very new market, in which still no clear, predominant sector has developed.[3] The further dependency of VR to related technologies brings about various descriptions of the size of the market. If, for example, complete flight simulator systems are to be

---

[2] Bauer (1996) pp.215, pp.176 f.

[3] cf. IMO (Hrsg.) (1995) pp.14

regarded as VR systems, the unit price being 25 million US$ and a sales volume of 10 units per year, the market would double in size according to some estimates.[4]

Additionally it is to be considered that in particular large VR projects in the industry can be subject to the secrecy, so that these projects are not contained in current turnover figures.[5]

In summary, it should be noted that in industrial applications delays occur, and „... *scepticism is needed when looking at estimates of VR market size.*"[6] So far there is still a lack in reports over actual operational integration of VR technologies from the standpoint of the user[7]. Apparently the unique potential of VR is not yet apparent to many users: To which purpose the resulting "pictures" should serve, is evident only to the least of companies. Does this mean that in the future the broad application of VR technology will remain solely limited to the entertainment sector?

2   Study Objectives

The development and proliferation of VR is influenced by the cooperation between researcher, manufacturer, the service bureau, and the final user. In this process, these roles are linked together according to different objectives and achievements. VR researchers look at an abstract level for fundamental solutions and develop standards to create a framework for possible applications. Manufacturers of VR tools take these solutions and offer concrete applications to a group of users as large as possible. Above all, they are interested in what demands are placed on their products by the clients and to which degree they can link it to a market potential. Co-operation between manufacturers and their customers is reciprocal. The client incites the manufacturer with new requests and questions, thereby evaluating the use of the given VR products. Should fundamental problems occur in solving the user request, then the manufacturer initiates projects in research. Rarely does the final user come into contact with research. This case occurs with very complex, research based applications, for example in the military sector of the aviation industry or in the automobile industry.

Meanwhile, numerous VR tools and environments used in creating virtual products and worlds are on the market. A projection requires a suitable selection of tools and often additional developments, in order to satisfy concrete demands placed by the user. This customizing, depending on the size of the market, is adopted by a specialized service bureau. Usually it is a reseller, who is intimate with the concrete

---

[4] ibd. pp.14

[5] cf. Wilson pp.15

[6] IMO (Hrsg.) (1995) pp.14

[7] cf. Wilson et al. (1996) pp.13 ff.

problems of the customer and, using their application know-how, creates the corresponding solutions. Even service bureaus place demands on the tools.

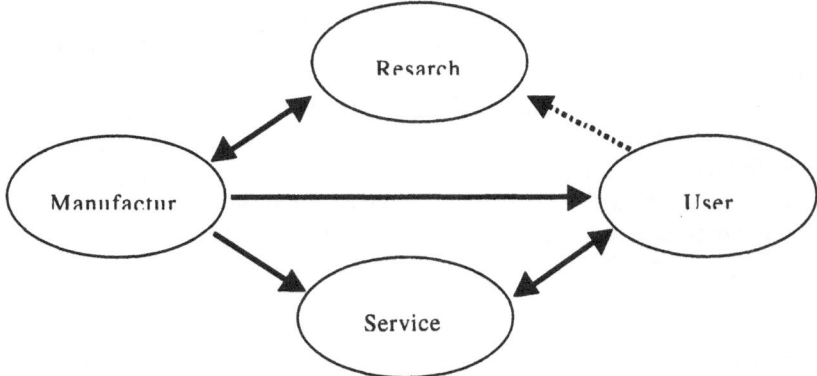

Fig. 2: Roles and Relational Structure of VR Development and Application

Thereby, the perception of problem-solving and concrete demands of the users become central issues in the industrial use of VR. This is the starting point of our investigation: based on the perspective of a potential client-profile we will establish the demands of the VR technology.

Due to the described deficits in application areas, the conditions for an VR application from the viewpoint of 111 potential or current users. The following questions are to be discussed:

- *What are the barriers to using VR?*

- *In which area of business does the user see applying VR?*

- *What sort of demands would a potential industrial user place on the use of VR?*

- *Which driver could promote a break-through of an industrial VR application?*

The central term of this study is defined as ‚VR technology' or also ‚VR application'. Following BAUER, Virtual Reality is defined as a technology which offers interaction in real time with three-dimensional, computer animated models, and "by technique of immersion" gives the user the impression, that he finds himself within the the computer generated, artificial environment.[8] In this sense, Virtual Reality actually stands for the technology and does not define the artificial environment that is created by VR. Rather, there are possible concrete applications or products, with which these applications can be created.

---

[8] cf. Bauer (1996) pp.16, Bishop et al. (1992) pp.156

3   Data Collection Design and Database

To establish goals of the study, it is necessary to determine the potential VR market from the viewpoint of the potential and already practicing user. The estimates of a large number of mechanical and electrical engineering firms in reference to VR technology were recorded using a questionnaire. On the basis of a 5 point scale, the companies answered 48 items. 206 firms in both industries were randomly selected in November 1996 and contacted by telephone[9]. The topic of the survey encountered a large interest, reflected in the fact that only three companies immediately declined participation. From 203 initial firms, altogether 111 responded, which represents a return ratio of approximately 55%.

The distribution of the size of the respondents corresponds to that of a medium-sized firm in the electrical and mechanical engineering industry. Over half of the companies (61%) employ fewer than 500 employees. Almost a third (31%) were medium sized companies with 500 to 2000 employees, and only 8% of the answering companies concerned large-scale enterprises with more than 2000 employees.

4   Barriers of Industrial VR-Application

The application of VR technologies occurs in the most diverse industries, yet remains limited to few applications[10]. In their world-wide study in 1993, Helsel & Doherty could identify only 805 projects with a VR component.

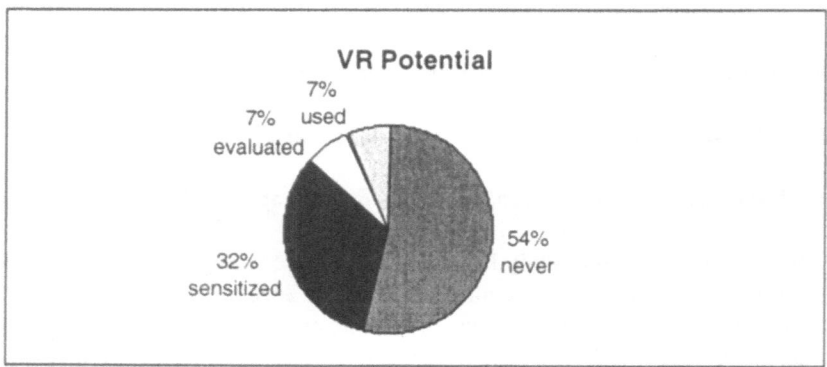

Fig. 3: Employment of VR-Technologies in the Survey

---

[9] Boris Reis and Bernhard Kusch did the data collection as part of their master thesis.

[10] Helsel & Doherty (1993) in: Burdea et al. (1994) pp.258

The low degree of application and recognition of VR technology are confirmed by the survey data. Only 7% of the firms use VR technologies, whereas 54% have never used VR, and 32% claim to be sensitized to the new technology.

Corresponding to the small degree of application and recognition of VR, is the sense of urgency associated with the use of VR. About 42% of the firms wish employ VR in two years at the earliest, or not at all. Nevertheless, 46% of the firms can imagine using VR applications within the next year.

Direct or indirect association with a minimal scope of application and recognition produce further barriers.

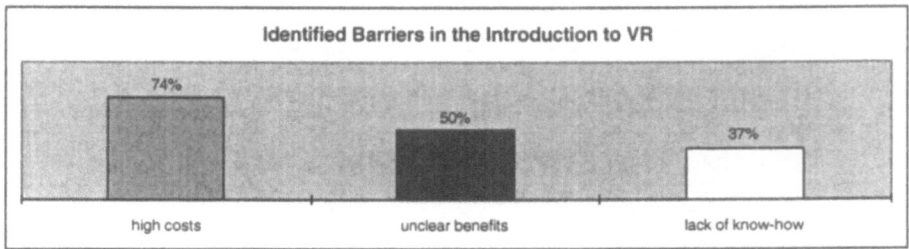

Fig. 4: Barriers in the Introduction to VR from the Point of View of an Enterprise

The two most frequently mentioned factors are 'high costs' and 'unclear benefits'. They point to the cost/use relation assumed by the users as the main barrier of a VR application.[11] Along with the small range of application and the minor relevance of VR comes the 'lack of know-how barrier' assumed by many users (34%). Missing VR experiences augments the assumed cost/use relation, which again closes the cycle.

5   Demands of the User on VR

One of the most important determinants for investments in a new technology is its expected use. The higher the companies perceive the benefits of VR, the higher the probability of its application. Due to the lack of proliferation and few available applications the entire spectrum of use is clear neither to the manufacturers, service providers, nor to the group of users.

So far the application of VR has above all been technologically motivated (technology push). In order to achieve as large a group of users as possible, the next development

---

[11] cf. Bullinger et al. (1994a) pp.15, o.V. (1996a) pp.55; this result is confirmed by other studies. cf. Wilson et al. (1996) S.37, Machover (1996) pp.34

must more strongly stem from the market (market demand). Available market studies and aforementioned barriers do not indicate which demands or expectations users place against VR technologies. The current study would like to close the gap and present both the expectation of the user and technical demands of VR applications.

5.1 Expectations of Users towards VR

Due to the diversity of VR applications, the expectations of the potential users must be surveyed in detail. The estimation of the application potentials can be discussed systematically on the basis of a value chain according to the operational business functions of construction, sales, and service.

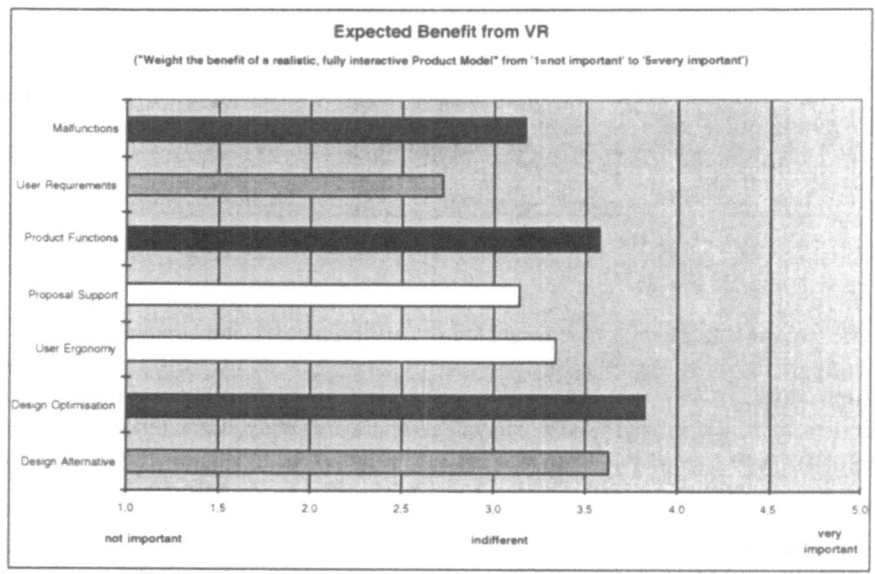

Fig. 5: Averages of Individual Potential Uses

In the area labeled Product Design ('Design Optimization' and the generation of 'Design Alternatives') the surveyed firms estimated the benefits for the use of VR technologies to be the highest.

They see the smallest use of VR in the determination of customer requirements. 'Rapid Prototyping' has obviously not been brought in connection with VR yet. Nevertheless, the highest estimate was in the use of VR in the design process, in the visualization of malfunctionings and product functions.

It can be summarized that at the moment firms see no particularly high benefits in operational business functions. None of the calculated average values exceeds the value of 3.5 on the response scale. The relatively undifferentiated responses correspond to the aforementioned lack of application knowledge.

5.2   Technical Demands of the User towards VR

The application of the VR technologies depends not only on potential use, but also on technical features of VR products. A current dilemma of many firms is the integration of various software systems. The ability of integration particularly applies to VR, since it can only enhance rather than replace other software applications[12]. All surveyed enterprises used CAD systems in construction. This means that 2D or 3D data from existing CAD systems must also be suitable for VR modelling, [13] because:

> *„Potential industrial users ... do not want to waste the investment*
> *they feel they have already made in CAD and other data files. "[14]*

The current situation of VR is comparable with the diffusion process of CAD technologies, which became generally accepted with the availability of low-priced standard workstations.[15] Therefore, the second technical demand on VR applications is that they run on standard computers. Which technical demands the surveyed companies have will be shown by the following analyses (cf. Fig. 6).

According to their technical standard, the most important factor for the firms is to run VR applications on 'standard computers', as well as the 'data import or export with CAD systems'. The high meaning of these two features is connected to the small application experience of the firms surveyed. It can be observed that those features are judged as particularly important, which indicates close linkages to the background experience of the firm. This partly explains the high meaning of the ability to simulate.

Audio support is least valued, although the proximity to reality of VR models is regarded as particularly important. It is also interesting to note that the internet capability hardly plays a role, although it is an important function for a teleservice-based VR solution.

---

[12] cf. Wilson et al. (1996) pp.93 f., D'Cruz et al. (1996) pp.8

[13] cf. Bickel (1996) pp.5 f., Kress (1995) pp.326 ff., Riedel (1996) S.24, Wilson et al. (1995) pp.308

[14] Wilson et al. (1996) pp.94

[15] cf. Vince (1995) pp.3

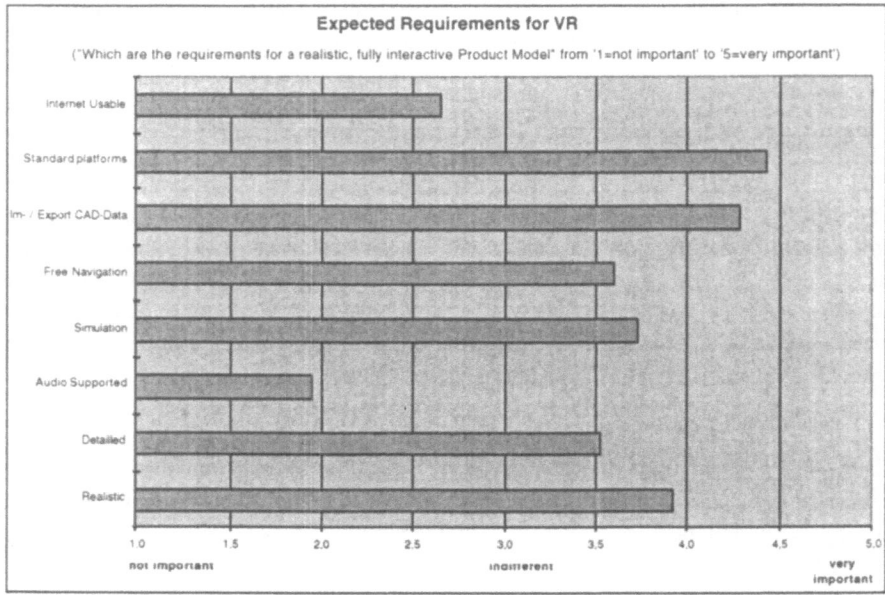

Fig. 6: Requirements of VR Technologies

6   Drivers of Industrial VR Applications

The discussion of barriers, perceivable benefits, and demands lead to incentives in broad range of industrial VR application. In view of the high rating of the executability of VR software on standard computers, it can be regarded as being indispensable to the dissemination of VR applications. In reference to technical platforms the operating system also plays an important role. Windows NT platforms are frequently found beside Unix platforms, even in medium-size companies. Rapid industrial diffusion is conceivable only if VR applications can be used on standard personal computers.

A further critical point results from the cost to use relationship, whereby the high costs are estimated as being a substantial barrier. On the other hand, the benefits of VR has not yet been realized. One must create pilot applications with referential effects. Funding from the European Union was made available in ESPRIT II,III, and IV. The 5th program will include the promotion of the development and application of VR based intuitive user interfaces and applications.

Competition between users is also seen as a driver. If a direct competitor is known to use a VR application, then their direct competitors will seriously consider appropriate application possibilities.

A driver in the diffusion of VR appears to be the effort, which a potential user is ready to take, the various partners and the competition. The development of these three drivers are to be explicitly analysed on the basis of the survey results.

6.1 Effort

High costs were already identifies as being a substantial barrier to the industrial usage of VR. But how much efforts are users willing to invest? Instead of asking for the direct costs, companies were asked what sort of effort and manpower they were willing to invest.

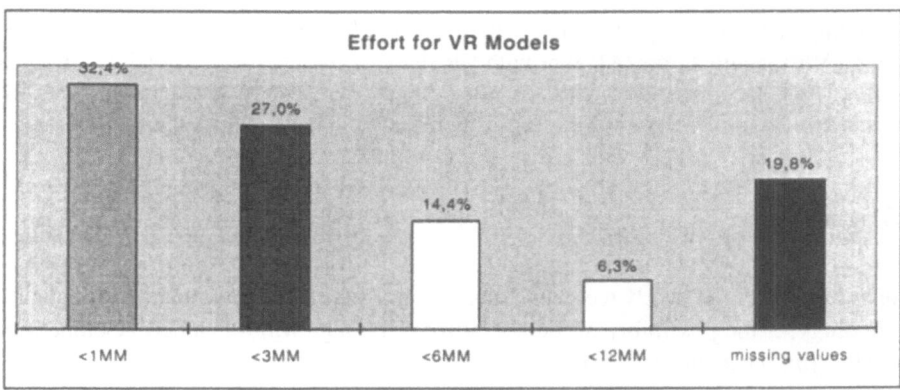

Fig. 7: Willingness to put Effort into VR Applications

The responses were unique. Approximately as 60% of the firms are ready to invest at the most 3 person months into the creation of a VR model. Inexperience and unrealistic or wishful thinking guided many potential users. On the other hand, it becomes clear once again that every possibility for the reduction of costs needs to be investigated, in order to achieve a faster diffusion of VR.

6.2 Consultants

An important factor in the application and publication of VR are the various consultants. Which importance the user attaches to the given consultants is shown in the following analysis:

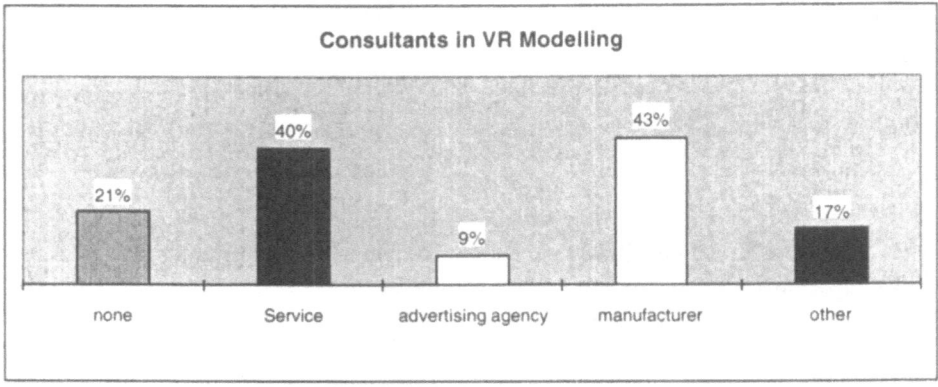

Fig. 8: Consultants in VR Modelling

The companies clearly prefer the creation of an VR application the co-operation of either a VR manufacturers (43%) or with VR service provider (40%). Much less was the willingness for co-operation with advertising agencies (9%). It has become clear that the surveyed companies of VR apply particularly to the technical areas of application.

6.3 Competition

Companies will more likely feel compelled to, or at least agree to evaluate an innovative technology, if the possibility of a competitive advantage will be gained. Competition thereby stimulates the sensitivity of a user for a new technology.

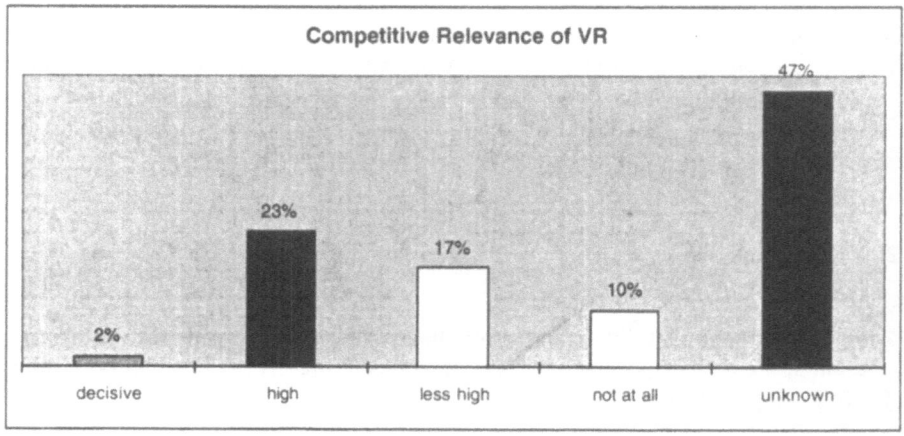

Fig. 9: Awareness of a Competive Advantage through VR

A substantial reason for the limited degree of current use of VR is that about 47% of the surveyed companies can not predict the possible competitive advantage attained through the use of VR. According to 23% of the companies which perceive a high competitive importance in applying VR technologies, the first steps for a successful VR adoption were done. Two companies even regard the use of VR as being crucial to competition.

Additionally, the influence of the competition on the use of VR is strengthened by the possibility that a competitor implements VR technologies successfully. Two of the four companies which use VR stated, that competitors already apply VR with perceptible competitive advantages. However, altogether 82% of the companies indicate they are not aware of the usage of VR by a competitor. The fact that in the meantime, all large automobile manufacturers use VR, reinforces the meaning of competitive pressure in the transfer of a new technology.[16]

7   Summary and Outlook

As demonstrated by the answers of 111 companies of the mechanical and electronical industries, the application of VR in Germany is characterized by many unknown factors. Especially the expected ‚high cost‘ and ‚unclear benefits‘ of VR applications impede the diffusion of VR technologies. This general result has been confirmed by answers with respect to the potential application of VR in specific operational business functions: none of the calculated averages were graded as being very important.

The results also show that the early forecasts of the market potential of VR were to optimistic. Whether or not the use of VR remains limited only to the entertainment sector, depends on various factors. The demands to be met are clear. Applications must take ‚existing CAD investments‘ into consideration, and be able to run on standard computers; meaning to avoid high costs. Astoundingly, according to the answers, the potential use of VR in the internet does not play an important role.

The main drivers for a rapid diffusion of VR are inexpensive, industrial reference applications created in cooperation with VR manufacturers or service providers. Although in many cases the competitive advantage cannot (yet) be estimated, the application of VR by a competitor creates a sensitivity for this technology and promotes its broad industrial adoption.

---

[16] cf. Dai et al. (1996) pp.3 ff, Harms (1996) S.32, Kress (1995) pp.334 f., Leston et al. (1996) pp.327 ff. ,
    Miller (1996) pp.15, Schmid (1996b) S.20

8   References

Bauer C. (1996): "Nutzenorientierter Einsatz von Virtual Reality im Unternehmen: Anwendungen - Wirtschaftlichkeit - Anbieter ", München: Computerwoche-Verlag.

Bickel D. (1996): "Anwendungen von Virtual-Reality-Werkzeugen in der Fertigungsindustrie", Virtual Reality World '96, Stuttgart, Feb. 1996.

Bishop G. und Fuchs H. (1992): "Research Directions in Virtual Environments", in: Computer Graphics, Vol. 26, Nr. 3, S.153-177.

Bullinger H.-J. und Bauer W. (1994a): "Strategische Dimensionen der Virtual Reality (1)", in: Office Management, Nr.3, S.14-18.

Burdea G. und Coiffet P. (1994): "Virtual Reality Technology", New York: John Wiley & Sons.

D'Cruz M., Eastgate R., Wilson J. (1996): "Towards a Structured Methodology for the Industrial Application of Virtual Reality ", Virtual Reality World '96, Stuttgart, Feb. 1996.

Dai F., Felger W., Frühauf T., Göbel M., Reiners D., Zachmann G. (1996): "Virtual Prototyping Examples for Automotive Industries ", Virtual Reality World '96, Stuttgart, Feb. 1996.

Encarnacao J., Göbel M., Rosenblum L. (1994): "European Activities in Virtual Reality", in: IEEE Computer Graphics and Applications, Bd. 14, Nr.1, S. 64-74.

Göbel M. (1996): "Industrial Applications of VEs", in: IEEE Computer Graphics and Applications, Bd. 16, Nr.1, S.10-13.

Harms U. (1996): "Daimler-Benz konstruiert in Zukunft ihre flotten "Sterne" im Cyperspace ", in: Computer Zeitung, Nr.49, S.32.

Helsel S., Doherty DeNoble S. (1993): "Virtual Reality Market Place 1993: Insights from the Meckler Database", in: Proceedings of Virtual Reality '92, S.209-211, San José CA..

IMO (Hrsg.) – Information Market Observatory (1995): "Virtual Reality – The Technology and its Applications", http://guagua.echo.lu/impact/imo/9503fnl.html, 13.10.1996.

Kress H. (1995): "Integration Aspects within a Virtual Prototyping Environment", FAIM '95, Flexible Automation and Intelligent Manufacturing Conference,

Stuttgart, Jun. 1995, S.326-337.

Leston J., Ring K., Kyral E. (1996): "Virtual Reality - Business Applications, Markets and Opportunities", London: Ovum Ltd. .

Machover C. (1996): "What Virtual Reality Needs", in: Information Display, Nr. 6, S.32-35.

Miller F. (1996): "Durch Simulation und Virtual Reality sparen die Unternehmen Zeit und Geld", in: Computer Zeitung, Nr.4, S.15.

Riedel O. (1996): "Virtual Reality in der Praxis", in: Computer Zeitung, Nr.47, S.24.

Schmid M. (1996a): "Wie Unternehmen "so tun als ob" - und dabei auch noch richtig Geld sparen", in: Computer Zeitung, Nr.23, S.20.

Schmid M. (1996b): "Virtual Reality spart bei der Automatisierung Geld", in: Computer Zeitung, Nr.28, S.20.

Schmid, M. (1996c): "Digitale Luftschlösser sparen Entwicklungszeit und Planungskosten", in: Industrie-Anzeiger, Nr.11, S.54-57.

Vince J. (1995): "Virtual Reality Systems", Wokingham, England: ACM Press Books.

Wilson J., Brown D., Cobb S., D'Cruz M., Eastgate R. (1995): "Manufacturing Operations in Virtual Environments (MOVE)", in: Presence: Teleoperators and Virtual Environments, Vol. 4, Nr. 3, S.306-317.

Wilson J., Cobb S., D'Cruz M., Eastgate R. (1996): "Virtual Reality for Industrial Application: Oppportunities and Limitations ", Nottingham: Nottingham University Press.

Layout Planning of Manufacturing Systems with VR-based Construction Sets

Jürgen Gausemeier, Michael Grafe, Raphael Wortmann
Heinz Nixdorf Institut
Fürstenallee 11
33102 Paderborn, Germany
grafe@hni.uni-paderborn.de
wortmann@hni.uni-paderborn.de

Abstract - **The technology of virtual reality (VR), as a new user interface for 3D computer aided design (CAD), introduces a completely new perspective for the design of technical manfacturing systems. As with well-known construction sets, such as LEGO or Fisher-technic, the planning engineer models a virtual manufacturing system in virtual reality. Materials are chosen from virtual construction sets and are positioned in a virtual manu-facturing hall. The user works with typical VR in- and output instruments such as a head mount display (HMD), stereoscopic (3D) glasses and 'pinch gloves'. This article describes the conception of a virtual construction set and the realisation of its prototype, using as an example the rail transport system, MONTRAC, as manufactured by the company MON-TECH AG, Switzerland. The description of the development of this construction set is supplemented by an illustration of the hardware and software components used.**

1. Introduction

The planning and realisation of flexible manufacturing systems in industrial compa-nies necessitates a large investment of time and money. The pressure due to time and cost is intensified as a result of ever shortening product lifetimes and also the product modifications often undertaken during production. As a consequence of these pressu-res, many industrial companies now use software tools in their manufacturing planning process. These tools contribute to shortening and improving the quality of the planning process. 3D-CAD software systems are increasingly being used in the planning of manufacturing systems, particularly in the micro or 'fine-layout' planning stages [1],[2]. They enable the planning engineer to fit machines and apparatus into the future manufacturing hall via the use of a 3D model. Here they can be positioned without danger of collision. In addition to this, more advanced systems allow computer visua-lisation of the manufacturing process. Hence, control programs for installed machines, transport and handling apparatus may be developed 'offline' [3],[4].

Despite the great utility of today's 3D CAD systems, they have one major disadvan-tage. These systems are complex to use and necessitate a long tutoring and learning period for effective use. As an example, a graphic interactive user interface is shown in fig.1. Virtual reality (VR) suggests a new solution to this problem. It relies on a new generation of 'man-machine' interfaces. With the help of innovative input and output apparatus, these interfaces enable the user to immerse himself in a computer generated 3-dimensional environment. The user can navigate through and interact with this com-puter generated environment and can manipulate his surroundings within it. The intro-duction of VR as a new user interface for 3D-CAD systems enables a completely new approach to the development of manufacturing systems. In analogy with well known technical modelling systems such as LEGO or Fishertechnic, the planning engineer models a virtual manufacturing system in virtual reality. In doing this he uses the same simple intuitive methods and modelling techniques as would normally be employed in a true modelling process.

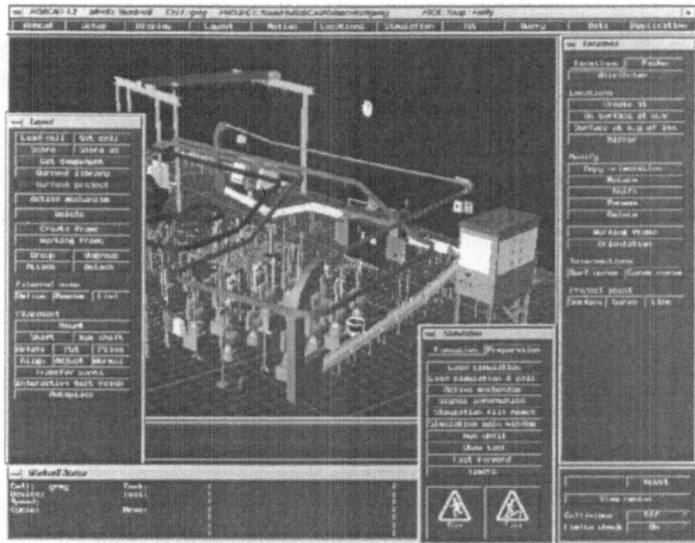

Fig. 1. User interface of a 3D-CAP-system (ROBCAD, Tecnomatix)

As with real construction sets, the planning engineer grasps the 3D model of the manufacturing and transport system from the virtual construction kit. Building blocks from the virtual tool-box are used to construct the entire system. This method of progress corresponds directly to the modular construction of many manufacturing and transport systems and accelerates the activity of the planning engineer significantly.

2. Conception of a Virtual Construction Set for a Rail Transport System

The method of designing technical systems using virtual construction sets was applied to the development of a modular monorail transport system and from this a prototype was produced. Essential components of the virtual construction set include 3D models of the fundamental construction elements, i.e. building blocks. These are created using a conventional 3D CAD system or other 3D modelling tools. In addition to modelling the structure of the system, its behaviour and that of its components must be also modelled accurately.

2.1 Construction functions

A 'real' construction of a monorail transport system depends on joints made simply with adhesives and screws etc.. This type of joint necessitates a high degree of precision in positioning which must be available to the user of the VR system.

Construction of building blocks. The building blocks of the track system can be represented by fundamental solids. A track is described by a cuboid, a bend through an extruded arc of a circle, a shuttle by several cuboids etc. These fundamental solids are in turn described by surfaces. The surfaces of the various building blocks are joined to one another during the construction of such a track system. Vector pairs, (j,k, j',k'), with a specific direction are positioned on top of one another at right angles on the surface of the building elements (here blocks A and B, see fig.2).

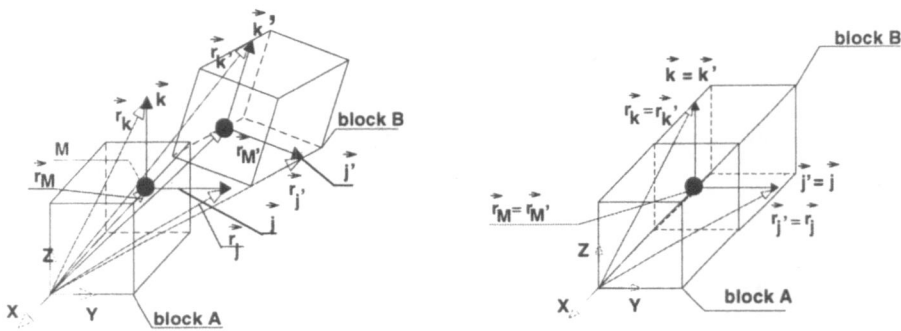

Fig. 2. Snap function: construction elements A and B are free to move

Fig. 3. B completely snapped to A

The points from which these vectors originate, have, as a further means of identification, an attribute such as a name or colour. This attribute ensures that an assembly function is only available to bricks where this is desired. If the attributes agree, the assembly function ('snap-together') will be allowed. If the attributes do not agree, the bricks will not snap to one another. The position of these points (i.e. the origins of the vector pairs) can also be described by a vector (rM, rM'). Suppose a brick (e.g. brick B) is moved towards another brick (e.g. brick A) already positioned in space. In the case of the brick separation becoming less than a particular tolerance value, brick B snaps to the points on the surface of A that are described by the vectors rM and rM' (rM=rM'). This happens as long as the identifying attributes of the points agree with one another. In the case of further movement of B about the point M, the two vectors j',k' will approach the direction of the respective equivalent vectors, j,k. If in the course of this reorientation a particular tolerance value exceeds the difference in direction of the vectors, then the coordinates of the respective vectors are fitted to the coordinates of the target vector. Hence, B snaps successively to brick A, as seen in fig. 3.

In order to avoid that bricks being grouped together prematurely (i.e. when grouping is not desired), a tolerance value must be defined. This value determines at what distance the vector coordinates of the brick being positioned will be set the same as (overwritten by) the coordinates of the target brick. Snap-range S_R is introduced as an expression for this tolerance. In the choice of this snap-range, the size of the brick to be positioned must be taken into account. Large bricks necessitate a larger snap-range than smaller bricks to enable a sensible grouping function. Since in this environment the geometry is described by its surfaces, snap-range may be defined by the equation (1):

$$S_R = \frac{1}{10} \sqrt{\frac{A_1 + A_2 + \ldots + A_n}{n}} \tag{1}$$

The expression under the root sign gives an arithmetic description of all surfaces $A_1, \ldots A_n$ of the brick with n=number of surfaces. Through the root a ´characteristic size' is defined and the snap-range S_R is output as 10% of this. In order to avoid the correction of an error that has become too large, it should also be possible for the snap-range to be manually corrected (input).

Construction of the track system. In order to be able to build the track system the building blocks of the MONTRAC system must be defined and assigned vectors and attributes as described above. To guarantee a simple illustration, colour was chosen as an attribute. In place of colour other different properties could be chosen, as long as each attribute is used for only one snap-function. The various coloured markings split the blocks into groups. Each colour represents one attribute. Bricks that find themselves in a common '(attribute)-group' can be joined to one another by certain surfaces.

Straight track sections. When generating a construction function, building block surfaces and their associated vectors and attributes must be taken into account. Straight track sections are taken as an example of how this is done. In addition it is described, how the length of the track sections is defined. Simple tracks (straight) have four points where they may be joined with other blocks. A joint (red -E-) is an attachment to other track elements. In fig. 4. only the vector pair on the front side of the block is illustrated. A vector pair, which points in the same direction, is also found on the back surface. The direction of the vectors is meaningful since on one side of the track the necessary current for the shuttle is carried, and on the other side attaching of information elements ('nodes') is supported. To preserve this flow of current a track may only snap to another track in a particular direction. On the underside (in blue -B-), the block may attach itself to the foundations. The yellow vectors (-D-) enable positioning of shuttles on the tracks. The shuttles may only snap to the tracks in one direction, since they are supplied with power on one side and with information on the other side. The correspondingly defined vectors take care of this.

The vectors associated with information elements (info-nodes) are shown in black.(-A-) It should be noted that here three vectors are considered. This due to the fact that such a node must be able to operate in the plane of the tracks (i.e. direction of travel) as well as the perpendicular direction in order to be able to pass relevant information (halve speed, stop etc.) to the shuttle. Of these black vector pairs only one is shown.

There should be at least 3 per track, one in the middle and both others at either end of the track. Hence - through the track and 'stop' nodes - a stopping point can be defined.

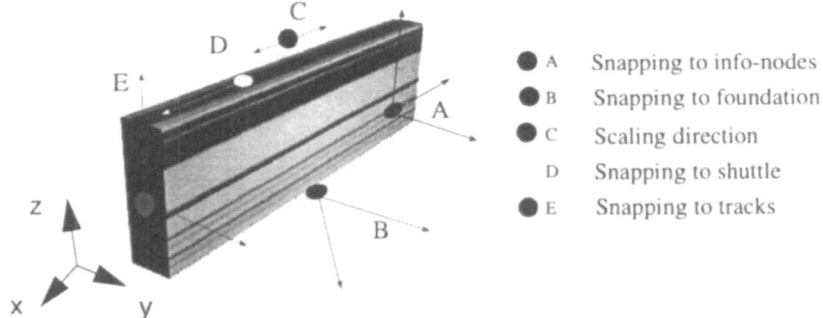

Fig. 4. Track construction element (straight section)

In reality tracks are cut to a preferred length. This length function can be realised in virtual reality in the following way. The track element is stretched or compressed in length (see brown arrow -C-, fig. 4). This scaling function can be defined by assigning degrees of freedom (DOF) and corresponding constraints. A scaling DOF ensures that the tracks can be stretched and compressed in the length direction. It should be noted that the tracks when being scaled in the length direction are not also proportionally scaled in the other directions. This avoidance of simultaneous scaling of all track dimensions can be realised by assigning constraints. Thus tracks may stretched in length while all other directions where scaling is possible remain the same. These constraints naturally do not affect the translation and rotation operations that are also needed for positioning blocks. The modelling of the other building blocks proceeds analogously.

Choice of building blocks. The construction set should allow specific model frameworks, i.e. digital mock-ups to be tested, and modified if necessary. Hence the possibility of ungrouping grouped objects from one another must exist. A building block e.g. a track, which has been built into a track system can be detached from the track system (from the framework) through identification by hand by grasping or touching the block using an input object such as a pinch glove or space mouse. The block can be displaced by a specified distance (L) in height (z-direction) by pressing a specific button (in case of a space mouse) or through a particular finger combination (pinchgloves). In the case of further displacement, the detached object should not immediately snap back to its old position. Therefore L must be greater than the snap-range. L is defined as $1{,}2S_R$. After the block has been detached from the track system it can naturally be moved to another point or deleted.

2.2 Animations

In a 'real world' manufacturing plant the following construction elements would be required for the operation of a transport system: shuttles, switching points, crossings and elevation sections. In a real factory the shuttle moves along the tracks from starting station through intermediate stations to its destination. In the course of this moveable track elements (such as switching points and elevation sections) are moved so that the shuttle reaches the desired point. In VR these movements can be orchestrated such that blocks that are to move follow a path predefined by the programmer. This may be implemented as follows. Points in virtual space are defined and the desired route between two of these points (A and B) is calculated. The time which may elapse between moving the block from A to B must be specified. From the time and distance the corresponding speed may be calculated. Since the track system illustrated here must be constructed from a large number of moving parts, the software itself must generate the animation.

Movement of shuttles. Each shuttle has its own personal animation data, or special section of animation data assigned to it (the assignment may be made for example by object name). If a shuttle now traverse a track, then that track writes data from track beginning to end into the shuttle animation data. This means that when a shuttle passes over e.g. a straight track section, the data of the start and end points of the track will be written into the animation data of the shuttle. This track data is well defined since the track elements are described by vectors during construction. Now suppose that, on approaching the end of the straight track section, the shuttle must now travel round a corner. The shuttle is handed over, so to say, from the straight track to the bend. The straight section communicates with the bend, telling it what the object is (object name). The data of the shuttle is passed form the straight track-block to the corner-block. The bend then writes its animation data into the animation data of that shuttle.

Movement of track elements. Track elements have a pre-defined method of motion. Elevation sections translate in a particular direction and crossings and points rotate about a particular axis. In addition, the positions that these three elements may take are predefined. As a result of this predefined motion and position, animation data can be created automatically in a similar manner to the shuttles.

2.3 Information and energy flux

To drive the system and generate a flow of information a 'piloting philosophy', whose complexity should not be under estimated, is necessary. To explain such a system in this work would exceed the scope of this article. Therefore, as an example of such a piloting philosophy, we refer to the work of Förste [5], 'Conception and prototypical realisation of a decentralised material flow pilot system based on local operating networks (LON)'.

The electrical power supply for the shuttles is provided through the tracks. On one side they accommodate the power requirements of the shuttle, keeping them continually supplied with power. For the purposes of a simulation, as described above, this means that we may assume that there is always enough electrical energy available to run the shuttles. The motion of active track elements (points or elevation sections) functions in reality electro-pneumatically. For the purposes of the simulation described it may be assumed that nothing prevents these elements from functioning correctly.Realisation of a Prototype

For the prototypical realisation of a virtual construction set, the MONTRAC monorail transport system, with self-drive carriages (shuttles) was taken as an example [6]. This is a modular system whose standardised base components must allow varied factory configurations to enable connection of work-areas, machinery and commissioning stations etc An exemplary transport system ist shown in fig. 5.

Fig. 5. The MONTRAC monorail transport system

3.1 Hard- and software environment

Hardware. The virtual environment with the virtual construction set is generated and controlled by a four processor graphics workstation (SGI Onyx). The workstation is equipped with two separate graphics subsystems to generate stereoscopic images. The system is installed in the „Software Theater", a cinema-like auditorium equipped with 30 seats and a large-scale stereoscopic projection screen (see fig.7). This facility, located in the Heinz Nixdorf MuseumsForum next to our institute, was designed by our group for the presentation of CYBERBIKES and other virtual reality applications[8][9][10].

Software. The prototype was realised using 'SmartScene' software (Multigen Inc., USA). SmartScene enables the user to work interactively in a virtual environment [7]. Thanks to natural hand-eye co-ordination the user can assemble building blocks in a 3D space. The system allows development of virtual construction sets with self-defined 3-dimensional building blocks.

The necessary basis functions, such as the storage of solution elements or the aving of modelled transport systems are enabled with SmartScene via virtual menus. Furthermore the system supports the installation of various VR peripherals such as a data helmet, pinch gloves and a tracking system.

These essential components of the graphical user interface of the interactive Smart-Scene environment are shown in fig. 6. On the right hand side one sees two scenes in which blocks from the virtual construction set have already been assembled. 'Snap cursors' (in red) and pointers (shown in yellow) allow the user to grasp blocks and use the menu window (tool box and model set) on the left of the picture. The snap cursors and pointers are the equivalent, in the VR environment, of hands. It is possible to grasp, move and position objects with them. Furthermore, fundamental commands such as saving the last modified model, saving the whole scene, deletion of blocks etc. can also be carried out using these cursors.

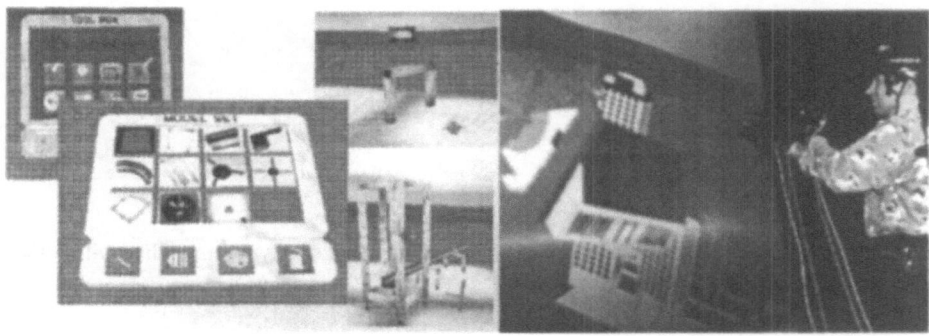

Fig. 6. SmartScene - User interface of the virtual construction kit   **Fig. 7.** The Software Theatre at the Heinz Nixdorf MuseumsForum

To use SmartScene hardware components are also necessary. These include a head mount display (HMD) or a similar component, e.g. stereo glasses to interact (fully) in the environment. A tracking system detects the motion of the virtual reality visitor. Grasping of objects and the movement of the user through the scene to various points is made possible through the tracking system and the opening and closing of contact with the gloves (pinch gloves)

3.2 Working with the virtual construction set

Having started the SmartScene program, the user (equipped with HMD, pinch gloves and tracking system) finds himself in a scene such as that in fig. 8. Through the hardware components, blocks from the construction set (see fig. 6) can be brought into the VR scene and assembled with help of the construction functions. If the pieces to be assembled are brought close enough to one another, they snap together. Pinch gloves serve as input apparatus for the assembler. With the help of these pinch gloves and the tracking system, the snap cursor illustrated in the pictures can be moved. The hands of the assembler are symbolised by the yellow crosses.

Fig. 8. Assembly of construction elements using the Snapp-cursor

Fig. 9. Virtual reality assembly line with MON-
TRAC system

The red snap-cursors aid the design process as follows. If the user moves his hand (the cross) with the snap cursor near a block the snap-cursor snaps to the block and shows the user that this block is 'touchable'. A corresponding finger combination (through the pinch gloves) brings the block to the hand of the assembler (the block snaps with the help of the snap cursor to the cross). The block can now be repositioned, deleted or scaled etc. Hence the user is now in a position to build a track system 'with his own hands'. Blocks of the track system can now be built into an installation. This can then be used for further application within SmartScene or be saved after assembly. In this case SmartScene saves the scene as an 'open-flight' model. This may then be inserted into a VR scene and can be displayed as seen in fig. 9 by a 3D-realtime rende- ring system like dVS from DIVISION Ltd., UK [11].Here one can see a MONTRAC system that supplied the assembly line in a virtual bicycle factory with parts. As men- tioned at the start of this article, a simulation/animation of such a system using the methods described has not yet been carried out. The corresponding animation of the shuttles has in this case been carried out using Key Frame Animation.

3. Summary and Outlook

The Prototypes described have shown that the use of VR based construction sets in the technical planning and projection process is beneficial. In several trials the invol- ved planning engineers needed only a short time of 30-60 minutes understanding the functions of the VR-based user interface.The efficiency of the systems mainly depends on the number and quality of construction elements available in the virtual construction set. These results could be transformed for the planning of similar technical systems (e.g. further development systems or entire machines and factories). Furthermore, the VR-based virtual construcion set can be used as a planning aid in other areas besides manufacturing. Examples include the furniture, kitchen and building industries. Construction sets which contain kitchen units, house elements, interior design objects etc. could be developed.

Next steps in the further development of the system is the functional integration of LON-based piloting system. It will allow an easy and interactive apporach to the off-line programming of the shuttles within the virtual environment.

4. References

[1] Aggteleky, Béla: *Fabrikplanung, Werksentwicklung und Betriebsrationalisierung*, Band 2: Betriebsanalyse und Feasibility-Studie; Carl Hanser Verlag, München, 1982

[2] Deutschländer, Arthur: *Integrierte rechnergestützte Montageplanung*; Carl Hanser Verlag, München, 1989

[3] Wiendahl, H.-P. / Enghardt, W.: Rechnerunterstützte Grobplanung von Fabrikanlagen unter Einbezug praxisgerechter Randbedingungen; in *wt-Werkstattstechnik*, 1986, 76, S. 741-744

[4] Jäger, Andreas: *Systematische Planung komplexer Produktionssysteme*; Springer-Verlag, Berlin, 1991

[5] Förste, Stefan: *Konzeption und prototypische Umsetzung einer dezentralen Materialflußsystemsteuerung auf der Basis von Local Operating Networks (LON)*; Heinz Nixdorf Institut, Paderborn, 1996

[6] MONTECH: *MONTRAC Produktprospekt*; MONTECH AG, Derendingen (CH), 1996

[7] MultiGen: *SmartScene Version 1.1 Release Notes*, MultiGen Inc., San Jose (USA), 1997

[8] Gausemeier, J.; von Bohuszewicz, O.; Gehnen, G., Grafe, M.: Cyberbikes: An Immersive Virtual Environment controlled by real CIM-Applications. *Proceedings of the FIVE 1996 Conference*, Pisa, December 1996

[9] Ebbesmeyer, P.: *Dynamische Texturwände - Ein Verfahren zur echtzeitorientierten Bildgenerierung für Virtuelle Umgebungen technischer Objekte*, Dissertation, Heinz Nixdorf Institut, Universität-GH Paderborn, 1997

[10] Gausemeier, J.; Brandt, Ch.; Grafe, M.: *Nutzenpotentiale von Virtual Reality in Industrieunternehmen*. In: Dangelmaier, W.; Gausemeier, J. (Hrsg.): Fortgeschrittene Informationstechnologie in der Produktentwicklung und Fertigung. 2. Internationales Heinz Nixdorf Symposium für industrielle Informationstechnik, Paderborn, 20./21. November 1996, HNI-Verlagsschriftenreihe, Band 19, Paderborn, 1996

[11] *Division Limited: dvs User Guide; Division Ltd., Bristol (UK), 1996*

Creating VR-based setups for the study of human motor behaviour

T. Kuhlen, R. Steffan, M. Schmitt, and C. Dohle

Abstract

The present paper demonstrates that study of human motion behaviour can be usefully assisted by Virtual Reality (VR) techniques, building up motion tasks in which subjects interact with virtual instead of real objects. A tool is introduced by which an experimenter can easily build up VR-based reach to grasp experiments. Virtual objects are presented to the test subjects by means of a viewer centered projection onto a high resolution graphics monitor. Experiments for the visual perception of viewer centered visualized objects show that inaccuracies, resulting from the curved surface of the screen. and discrepancies between convergence and accomodation, can be neglected when the negative parallax is not too large. Using the developed tool, the results of a first experiment related to the study of human motion behaviour are presented, which show that VR-based experiments can indeed lead to concrete hypotheses about human movement organization: the results suggest that not only the transport and the grasp component are represented by two separate visuomotor channels in the human brain, but that also the grasp component itself is divided into two separate programs, one for the acceleration phase and the other for the deceleration phase of a reach to grasp movement.

1 Introduction

In the last years, the development of advanced measurement technology, being able to register even complex movements in three dimensions, has lead to an increasing number of human motion studies. The goal of most studies is to identify kinematic characteristics of human motor behaviour and, further on, to get new ideas and hypotheses about the organization of voluntary movements. All in all, neurologists and physiologists want to find an answer to the question how the human brain completes the task of planning and executing movements (Flash, 1990).

In motion studies, reach to grasp experiments play an important role. Although reaching and grasping is a complex movement several joints are involved in, it is highly automated. Furthermore, it requires the interaction with the environment, i.e., with the object to be grasped. In order to perform such a movement successfully, two tasks have to be completed: the hand must be transported towards the object (transport component), and the fingers must be adapted to the object's size and shape (grasp component). The question comes up whether these two components are represented in the brain by two separate motor programs, and if so, in which way these programs are coordinated (Paulignan and Jeannerod, 1996).

To create experimental setups for grasping studies, Virtual Reality technology can provide a powerful means. Here, subjects interact with virtual, computergraphic objects instead of real objects. The use of such VR-based setups is motivated by the exact control of computer-generated, programmable environments. Stimuli such as shape, characteristics and behaviour of objects can be varied and presented separately.

For the first time, the use of virtual target objects makes it possible to examine motor behaviour in reach to grasp experiments when haptic feedback is lacking. In addition, perturbation studies can be carried out, in which one or more object characteristics are modified unexpectedly while the subject is grasping. Such experiments, which up to now can only be insufficiently generated by physical setups (Kuhlen et al., 1996a), promise new insights into the coordination of transport and grasp component.

For this reason, a VR-based tool has been developed and will be introduced in the next sections, which allows an experimenter to interactively and easily create flexible experimental setups for perturbation studies. Section one will explain what visualization technology has been used for the presentation of virtual scenarios to the subjects. It will be shown that visual perception of real and virtual objects are nearly identical. Section two will demonstrate the graphical user interface for the experimenter, while section three will describe the principle setup for all VR-based experiments. Finally, section five shows the results of a first experiment, which compares the motor behaviour while grasping real and virtual objects, respectively.

2 Visualization technology for VR-based motion studies

When developing virtual scenarios suitable to replace real scenarios in neuropsychological experiments, special care must be taken to the visualization of the objects the test persons have to interact with. The visual presentation of a virtual object must not influence the subjects' motor behaviour. This can only be guaranteed if visual perception of real objects and virtual objects are identical. In particular, for reach to grasp studies the following requirements exist:

- Subjects must keep visual contact to their own, real hand.

- A target object must be visualized three-dimensionally in free space, otherwise it cannot be grasped.

- Since the subjects' heads are usually not fixed during a grasping experiment, a target object has to be perceived as stationary in 3-D space, independent from a subject's viewpoint.

As a consequence of the first requirement, an immersive visualization technology using a head-mounted display cannot be applied here, since a subject's hand would have to be visualized by a computergraphic counterpart. Instead, a visualization technology called 'viewer centered projection' or 'Virtual Holography' is preferable (Kuhlen et al., 1996b). This technology, well known from virtual environments based on CAVEs and Virtual Workbenches (Krueger and Froehlich, 1994), combines stereo shutter glasses and head tracking, and meets all three requirements mentioned above.

By means of a viewer centered projection, all physiological and psychological cues for a spatial visual perception can be realized with one exception: subjects have to focus their eyes onto the screen surface, even when a virtual object is positioned, e.g., in front of the screen. A mismatch between accomodation and convergence arises, which may influence the visual perception of virtual object and in consequence the subjects' motion behaviour.

Furthermore, technical limitations such as the sample rate of the head tracking system, a curved surface of the projection plane when using a graphics monitor, or ghosting, an effect caused by the inertia of the phosphor layer of a CRT, may disturb the visual perception.

These restrictions make it necessary to carry out preliminary experiments about the perception of virtual objects. In these experiments, which are described in detail in Kuhlen (1998), subjects have to determine the corner positions of virtual cubes, visualized on a graphics monitor by the method of viewer centered projection. The distances of the cubes from the screen surface have been varied. The results of this study, partially shown in figure 1, can be summarized as follows:

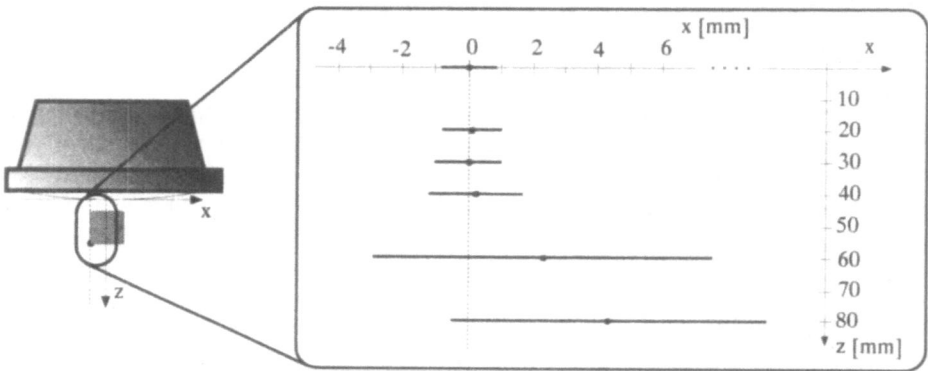

Figure 1: View from above onto the monitor: discrepancy (mean value and standard deviation) between the perceived x-position and the required x-position for several distances z between object and screen. Changing mean values for the perceived object position can be explained by the curved surface of the screen, whereas increasing standard deviations with larger distance between object and screen are caused by the growing mismatch between accomodation and convergence.

As expected, a larger distance of the virtual object from the projection plane leads to an increasing inter- and intra-individual variablility in visual perception, reflecting the conflict between accomodation and convergence. The results show however, that for a distance of no more than 4 cm from the projection plane, the perception errors are not greater than 1.5 mm, which can be regarded as acceptable for the execution of reach to grasp experiments.

The results have also shown that few subjects have difficulties to perceive stereo-scopically visualized objects in three dimensions. As a consequence, all subjects have to be tested with regard to this capability before participating in a VR-based reach to grasp study.

Finally, the experiments demonstrated that it is not sufficient to apply a single interocular distance for all subjects. Taking into account the interocular distances of individual subjects in the algorithm of viewer centered projection significantly enhances the accuracy of of visual perception.

3   Interface to the experimenter

Typically, an experimenter coming from the clinical field does not have any programming knowledge. For this reason, a graphical user interfaces is implemented in the tool, by which a researcher can easily build up reach to grasp experiments with or without perturbation. Figure 2 shows one of several dialogues available to the user. A perturbation can affect the shape, size, postition, orientation or colour of one or more virtual objects. For a moving object, any velocity can be

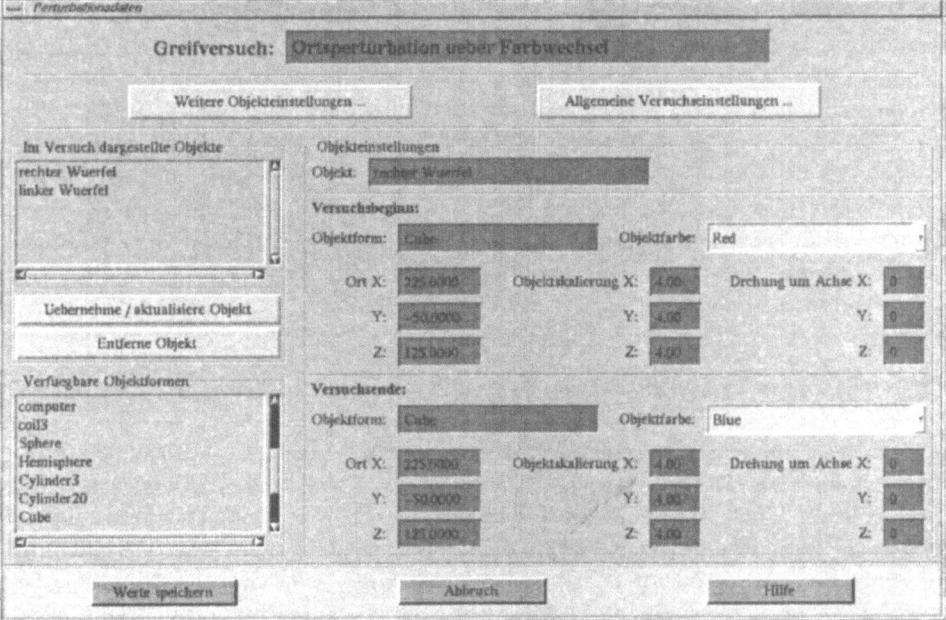

Figure 2: Part of the graphical user interface to create VR-based perturbation experiments

selected. Furthermore, an experimenter can define several external signals on which a perturbation starts.

Usually, perturbation studies are realized as a series of experiments, in which single perturbations occur randomly in order to avoid an anticipation by the subject. The user interface takes care that the frequency of perturbation in such a series and the accompanying random protocol can be controlled by the experimenter.

Due to the limited performance of any simulation computer, there always exists a time delay between the initiation of a perturbation and its visualization. The experimenter must take this effect into account while interpreting subjects' reaction times. Therefore, the tool is implemented in a way that it guarantees a constant response time for an experimental setup. The response time is displayed to the experimenter.

4   Principle experimental setup

Figure 3 shows the principle experimental setup proposed for all VR-based reach to grasp studies. Since grasping experiments do not require a large interaction volume, virtual target objects can be visualized using a standard graphics monitor. Head tracking, necessary for a viewer centered projection, is completed by an electromagnetic tracking system.

In order to register a subject's hand and arm movements, an optoelectronic motion recording system is applied. Small infrared led markers are attached to the skin, of which the three-dimensionsional positions are calculated from the frames of two optoelectronic cameras. In reach to grasp experiments, optoelectronic motion tracking is preferable to instrumented gloves, since the fingertip positions are of high importance for later motion analysis. By optoelectronic methods, these positions can be measured directly by placing markers at the fingertips.

At the begin of an experiment, subjects have to put the hand on a pressure sensitive plate, which does not only signal the begin of a movement, but can also serve as a signal for the start of a perturbation.

5   Experiment: Grasping real and virtual objects

While the influence of variation of object size and position on movement kinematics has been studied extensively, few is known about the influence of haptic information. The experiment presented here, uses the developed tool to compare subjects' motion behaviour when reaching and grasping a real and a virtual cube of 4x4x4 cm, respectively (see fig. 4, "real grasping" and "virtual grasping"). By such an experiment, the role of haptic feedback in the neural organization of human movements can be examined for the first time, since this feedback is lacking when touching a virtual object.

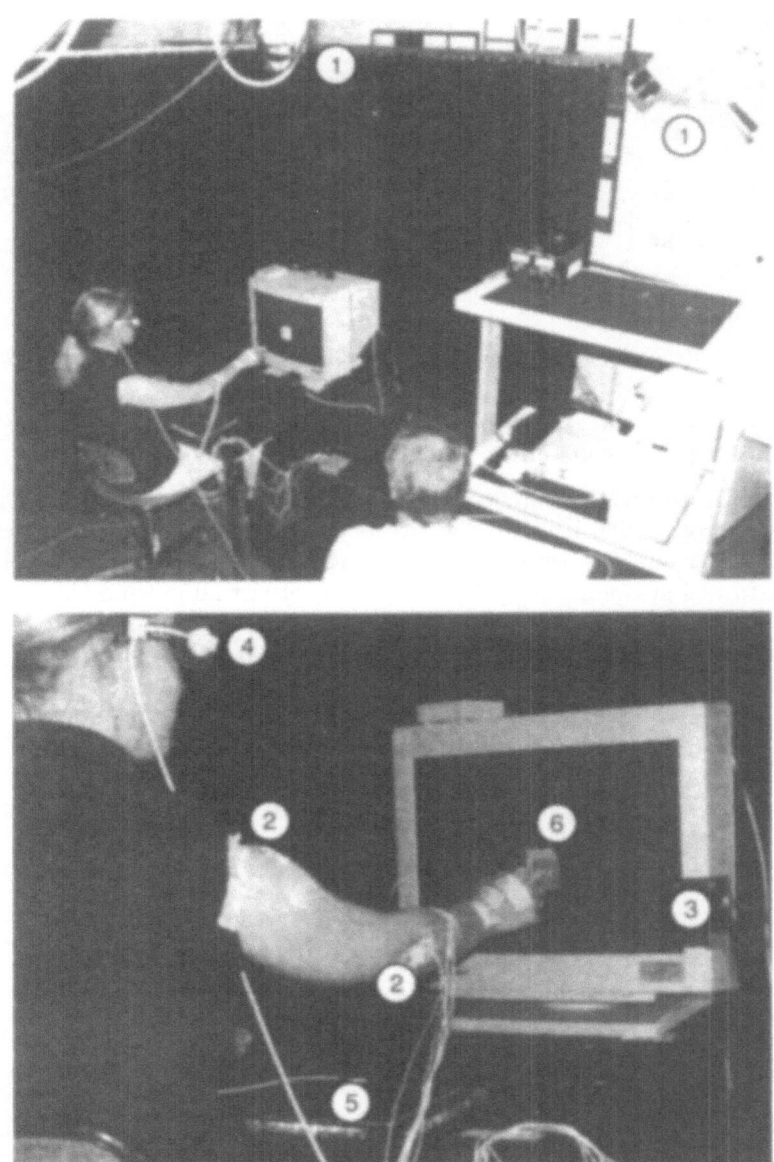

Figure 3: Experimental setup for VR-based reach to grasp studies 1: Infrared cameras, 2: Infrared-leds, 3: Emitter of the tracking system, 4: Shutter glasses with receiver of the tracking system, 5: Pressure sensitive plate, 6: Virtual target object

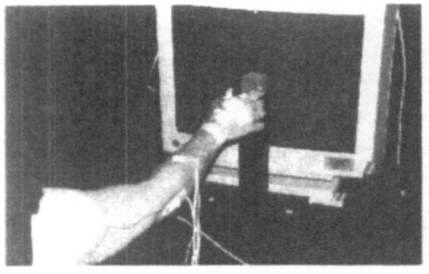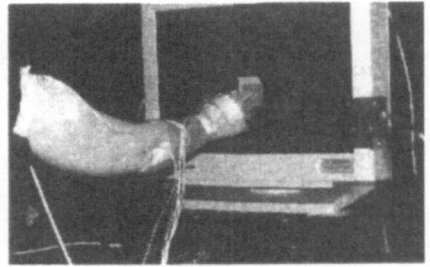

Figure 4: Reaching and Grasping a real cube and a virtual cube, respectively

The whole experiment is described in detail in Kuhlen (1998). This paper will concentrate on the results of the study.

Grasp component. Researchers characterize the grasp component by means of the aperture profile, i.e., the distance between thumb and index finger over time. A cluster analysis using Self-Organizing Feature Maps has shown that, in contrast to real grasping, the grasp component of virtual grasping is characterized by a heterogeneous behaviour. Looking closer at the behaviour of single subjects, two different strategies can be distinguished (see fig. 5).

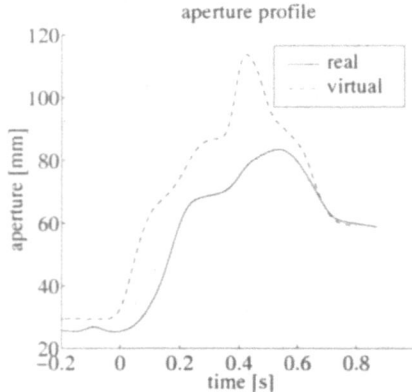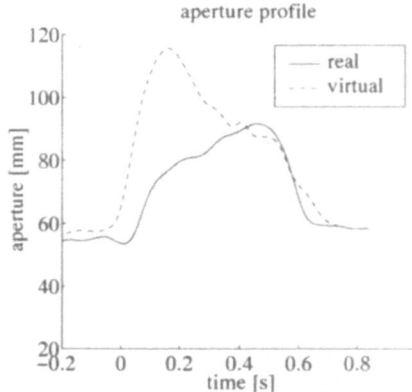

Figure 5: Strategies 1 (left) and 2 (right) for the grasp component of virtual grasping in comparison to real grasping

Strategy 1: The aperture profile of subjects following strategy 1 is is determined by a correction of the finger opening that starts at the beginning of the deceleration phase, about 15 cm away from the virtual object. This correction leads to a larger aperture maximum in comparison to real grasping. The aperture velocity profile typically shows two maxima. The amount and time of the first one corresponds to the maximum observed in real grasping (at about 15 percent of movement time). Consequently, the real and virtual grasp components of these subjects show no differences in the aperture opening phase. The second, larger and therefore absolute maximum appears in the deceleration phase (at about 40 percent of movement time).

Strategy 2: The grasp component of subjects following strategy 2 typically shows a very early and fast opening of the fingers. As a result, the kinematic parameters show an earlier time of maximum aperture and a larger maximum aperture velocity to a slightly earlier time. Here, closing of the fingers takes 70 percent of movement time (only 40 percent in real grasping for all subjects and in virtual grasping for subjects with strategy 1) and is already initiated at 30 cm from the object. In contrast to strategy 1 being, among others, characterized by a larger aperture maximum, subjects who follow strategy 2 do not show a uniform reaction with regard to the amount of maximum aperture.

During repetitions in virtual grasping, no subject showed a learning effect or a switch from one strategy to the other.

Transport component. The transport component of a reach to grasp movement is usually characterized by the velocity profile of the wrist. As in real grasping, the transport component in virtual grasping is determined by an asymmetric velocity profile with a single maximum. Movement times are nearly identical. the deceleration phase takes about 2/3 of this time. Small but significant differences arise from smaller velocity and deceleration maxima in virtual grasping. No significant difference between grasping strategies can be established.

Discussion. The lack of haptic feedback has a unique influence on the transport component, but can lead to two different strategies for the grasp component. This result proposes that transport and grasp component are programmed separately by the human brain. In this regard, the experiment supports M. Jeannerod's hypothesis of two different visuomotor channels for the transport and the grasp component (Jeannerod, 1981). In addition, the results support the hypothesis established by R. Marteniuk et al. (1990) of a functional, task specific rather than invariant, temporal coupling between the components. They found that increasing requirements lead, among others, to an earlier finger opening. These findings are supported here: Grasping a virtual object is obviously more difficult than grasping a real one, resulting partially in an earlier maximum aperture (strategy 2), or being compensated for by means of a larger aperture in the deceleration phase (strategy 1), a reaction that can also be observed in fast reach to grasp movements (Wing et al., 1986).

As reaction on the presentation of a virtual instead of a real object, the aperture profile either changes in the deceleration phase, or vice versa, i.e., it starts in a normal way and continues with a change in the deceleration phase. This finding supports the hypothesis recently proposed by Kudoh et al. (1998) that not only reach and grasp component but also the grasp component itself can be subdivided into two separate programs, responsible for the acceleration phase and the deceleration phase, respectively. The lack of haptic feedback then leads, specific for single subjects, to a variation of one of the two programs.

6 Summary and future work

A tool has been introduced which uses Virtual Reality technology to create experimental setups for the study of reach to grasp movements. Here, virtual target objects are presented to the subjects by means of a viewer centered projection, a visualization technology for which it could be shown that it is suitable for a realization of motion studies. An experiment comparing motion behaviour when reaching and grasping a real and virtual cube has been carried out, of which the results have shown that a VR-based study can lead to concrete hypotheses about how movements are organized in the human brain.

Current work is about VR-based perturbation studies. Using the graphical user interface of the developed tool, an experimenter can build up such experiments without any programming knowledge. A first perturbation study is being carried out now which refers to a sudden change of object position.

References

Flash, T. (1990). *The Organization of Human Arm Trajectory Control*. In *Multiple Muscle Systems: Biomechanics and Movement Organization*, chap. 17. Springer-Verlag, New York.

Jeannerod, M. (1981). *Intersegmental Coordination During Reaching at Natural Visual Objects*. In *Attention and Performance*, chap. 9. Erlbaum, New York.

Krüger, W. and Fröhlich, B. (1994). Responsive Workbench. Towards a user-centered, application-driven multimedia human-computer interface. In *IPA/IAO-Forum Virtual Reality - Anwendungen und Trends*. Springer-Verlag.

Kudoh, N., Hattori, M., Numata, N., and Maruyama, K. (1997). An analysis of spatiotemporal variability during prehension movements: effects of object size and distance. *Experimental Brain Research*, 117:457–464.

Kuhlen, T. (1998). *Entwurf und Validierung eines klinischen Diagnose-Assistenten zur Klassifikation des Greifverhaltens nach realen und virtuellen Objekten*. PhD thesis, Lehrstuhl für Technische Informatik der RWTH Aachen.

Kuhlen, T., Dohle, C., Walter, P., Schmitt, M., Hefter, H., Kraiss, K.-F., and Freund, H.-J. (1996a). Impact - a VR-based system for diagnosis and therapy of sensorimotor disturbances. In *Virtual Reality World '96*, Stuttgart. Computerwoche Verlag, München.

Kuhlen, T., Kraiss, K.-F., Szymanski, A., Dohle, C., Hefter, H., and Freund, H.-J. (1996b). *Virtual Holography in diagnosis and therapy of sensorimotor disturbances*. In *Technology and Informatics 29*, chap. 22. IOS Press, Amsterdam.

Marteniuk, R., Leavitt, J., MacKenzie, C., and Athenes, S. (1990). Functional relationships between grasp and transport components in a prehension task. *Human Movement Science*, 9:149–176.

Paulignan, Y. and Jeannerod, M. (1996). *Prehension Movements – The Visuomotor Channels Hypothesis Revisited*, chap. 13, pages 265–282. Academic Press.

Wing, A., Turton, A., and Fraser, C. (1986). Grasp size and accuracy of approach in reaching. *Journal of Motor Behavior*, 18(3):245–260.

Applying the Third Dimension to E-Commerce

J. Dauner, M. Wittkowski, A. Müller
Fraunhofer IAO
http://vr.iao.fhg.de

Introduction

The Internet technology offers a high potential to market and sell products world-wide. Internet based Electronic Commerce systems have improved quickly. Distributing products like CDs, books or tickets has already been established and most likely other products and branches will be put on the E-Commerce channel as well. Selling products over the Web works well as long as the objects are easy to describe and to present. But how are manufacturers of modular products supposed to utilize Electronic Commerce systems, as long as their product ranges demand a high grade of personal consulting?

This paper offers a solution combining interactive 3D visualization with personal communication to improve the quality of electronic commerce and thus broaden the range for new product categories ready for E-commerce.

Related Work

Already for some years now immersive Virtual Reality has been applied for product presentation as sales support system. Matsushita uses VR for product presentation in its Virtual Kitchen project [1], a retail application set up in Japan to help people choose appliances and furnishings for the rather small kitchen apartment spaces in Tokyo. Users bring their architectural plans to the Matsushita store, and a virtual copy of their home kitchen is programmed into the computer system. Buyers can then mix and match appliances, cabinets, colors, and sizes to see what their complete kitchen will look like - without ever installing a single item in the actual location.

Reaching the limits of Electronic Commerce

For many companies selling products over the Web means a revolution of their traditional sales channels because it enables to shorten the sales chain and to be able to do without intermediates like dealers. But despite of increased margins and proximity to customers, renouncing to sales assistants also means to do without personal and individual consulting. This might still work with products like books, software, tickets and similar products, but a limit is reached soon if more attributes of the objects are important for the buyer:

- Visual appearance in terms of design, shape or color
- Visual appearance in combination with other objects or appearances
- High amount of attribute variability (i.e. color, textures, model)

- Complex information on product specific information (i.e. ergonomic usage) or technical clues

A large range of products is based on modular composition: Basic elements can be combined according to customer's demands. Though this trend leads to customized and individual system solutions, it also provoques problems with the mediation of all configuration possibilities. Too big is the amount of miscellaneous object attributes, additionally these vary due to production conditions. Using conventional product presentation media such as catalogues the customer or distribution partner is confronted with numerous tables of colors, shapes and patterns as well as the corresponding order strings. This complicates an easy, clear and error-free configuration.

For instance, the lamp manufacturer Steng offers about a dozen lamps with different shapes. For each of them a dozen colors and/or surface patterns are available. Even their printed catalog does not provide an image of all these combinations. Instead, little color samples are provided and the real appearance of the product is left to the customer's imagination. Most manufacturers already have to cope with non-electronic commerce due to their highly configurable product range and because of an intensive communication effort to dealers and customers. Employing conventional E-Commerce systems, these manufacturers will not be able to offer the sales support, which is necessary.

Objectives of 3D E-Commerce Systems

This envisioned combination of various multimedia technologies allows the development of a configuration system which can be used by customers, sales persons or distribution partners.
Combining the visualization power of Virtual Reality and the communication potential of the Internet, a new dimension of sales support will be reached. With a spatial visualization of the product users can select any combination of variants and see the result of their selection in real-time.

Interactive, spatial product configuration and planning

Based on Web 3D technologies like VRML (Virtual Reality Modeling Language) objects can be viewed within a Webbrowser as 3D models. Furthermore, object attributes such as color, position etc. are variable - with a mouse click the spatial visualization is updated in real-time.
Especially for interior design planning, the combination of products within an environment (i.e. a room) is a good example for 3D E-Commerce systems: The user can walk through a room and view a layout from all perspectives. Ground plans, drawn on digital graph paper, can be risen into the third dimension and can be used further on for the planning process. Configuration limits, material consumption, current price and similar information are considered and displayed in the system. After having finished the layout, the user can place an online order.

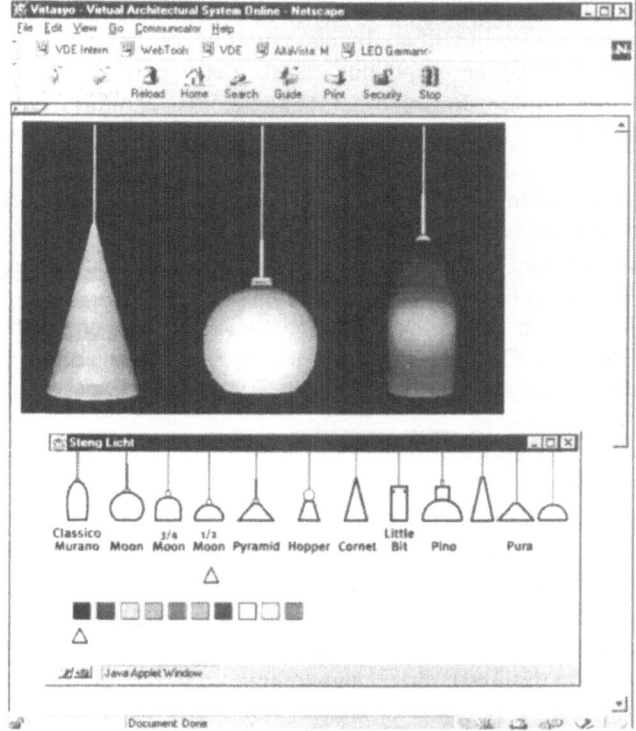

Figure 1: Product Configurator of Steng lights

Communication, Conferencing, Call Center

A lot of products (especially those of the building and furnishing branch) have a strong need of individual consulting. In order to satisfy this demand, we envision 3D E-Commerce systems to be enhanced by two major features:

1. Distributed multiple participant sessions

Layout planning sessions can be performed by a large number of participants, who access the system via the Web, independent of their actual position. The planning process can be conducted collaboratively, attribute changes (i.e. the color of an office desk) are distributed to the other participants and visualized immediately on their local simulations. This kind of conferencing is similar to conventional multi-user VR systems (like Blaxxun's community Player and Server system [2] or the High-End system GreenSpace [3]. But in order to save bandwidth and to keep the software module no avatars will be displayed.

2. Parallel Communication

The level of communication will be divided into three succeeding steps depending on the improvement of Internet bandwidth: first voice communication via a parallel telephone line; second, transferring to Internet telephony and third, adding Web based video conferencing.

Adding these features to the Web based 3D planning systems shifts these tools to a new application dimension: applying work group conferencing. For example an architect living in Milan, a building owner in Frankfurt and a consultant in Hamburg can work together to optimize and discuss a room layout.

Connecting this system to a call center, companies are able to perform consulting, service and Electronic Commerce entirely media based. Sales and service activities can thereby be extended globally.

Case studies: Virtual Design Exhibition, Virtasyo

The objective of the collaborative project Virtual Design Exhibition, that was established by the Fraunhofer IAO and seven well-known interior design companies in 1997, was to explore the combination of Virtual Reality and the Internet for interactive product presentation. On the one hand 3D models of furnishing have been shown in attractively designed, virtual showrooms, on the other hand a system to plan rooms was developed.

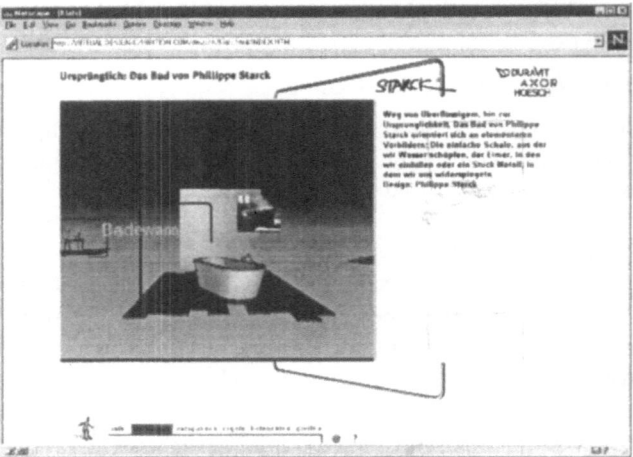

Figure 2: Showroom of the Virtual Design Exhibition

The concept of interactive showrooms (Figure 2) was to replace a static flat catalog picture showing a product in a suitable environment by a lively interactive world, where the visitor can walk around and get more information about the selected object with a mouse click. In collaboration with the Milanese Design and Architecture bureau Studio De Lucchi a new kind of architecture was designed for these showrooms: Floating showareas and panels with a collage of 3D models and 2D information and images.

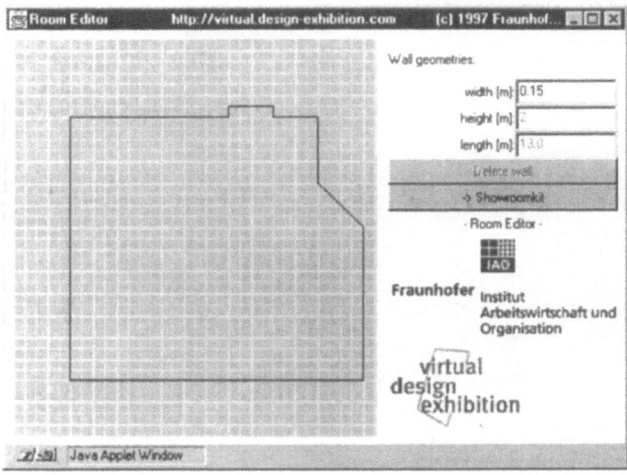

Figure 3: The room editor of the Showroomkit

The second part of the project, a layout deciding tool for interior design called Showroomkit, is used for interactively furnishing a room. This tool is based on Java and VRML. In this application users such as salespersons or their customers first create a 2D floor plan of a room (figure 3). Then they choose products such as furniture or accessories from the Virtual Design Exhibition database. When a product is selected, a request to the JDBC server is generated and the VRML geometry of a default variant of the product, a list of possible variants, and associated product information such as pricing or ordering is downloaded (figure 4). The product is placed at a default position in the world. Users can now move the product within the currently selected viewing plane by using the mouse. Changes of variants are stored in a dynamic list, which can be further processed for online ordering.

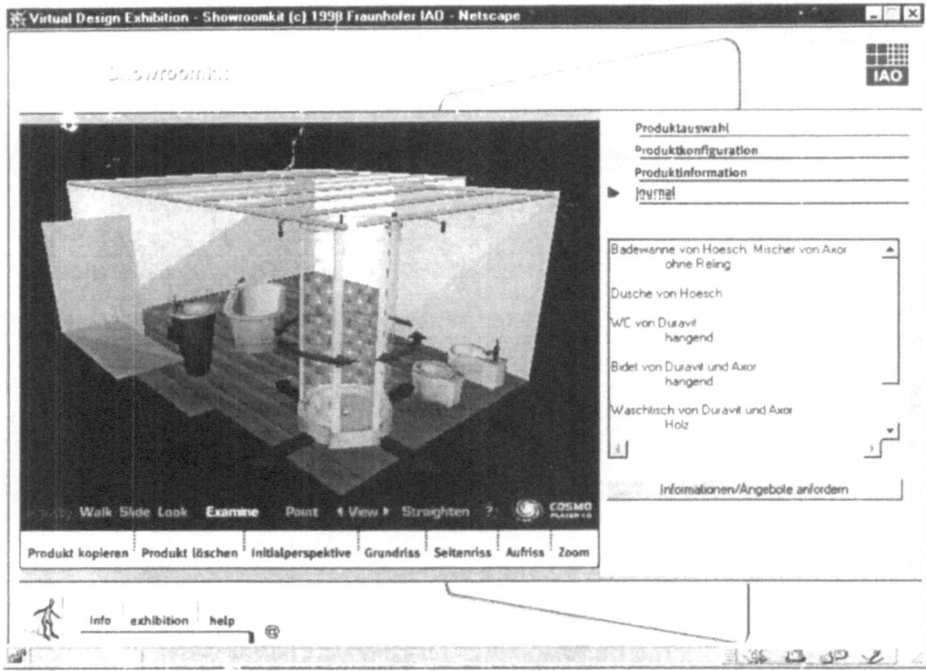

Figure 4: the Showroomkit 7 Virtasyo prototype

The Showroomkit forms the base for a new concept which is currently developed in collaboration with BauNetz, a leading German information platform for architecture and construction: Virtasyo, (Virtual Architecture System Online). It comprises a set of modules and systems enabling online configuration and planning of products of the building and furnishing industry. Additionally, the above mentioned concept of conference communication is being implemented . Virtasyo offers the manufacturers the possibility to make their products available in a digitized, three-dimensional way. The user can retrieve details of the product online at his workplace and make it part of his planning process.

Conclusions

In this paper we discussed how the combination of 3D visualization and Internet technology can be used for Electronic Commerce. Problems of presentation limits and the lack of personal consulting can be solved by using interactive 3D product configuration enhanced by conference systems with voice and video communication. The projects Virtual Design Exhibition and Virtasyo have implemented initial stages of this concept. Nevertheless, the pace of 3D enhanced E-Commerce systems depends on the employed Web 3D technologies in terms of stability, performance, functionality and availability as well as on the bandwidth of the Web.

Acknowledgements

We would like to thank BauNetz for their support. Special thanks to Oliver Riedel and Wilhelm Bauer for their support. Also thanks to our students Jens Böhmler, Mark Kaufmann, Alexander Barth, Kai Todenhöfer, Elmar Loth.

References

[1]   K. Sawada. Tokyo Showroom, Proceedings VR commercial impact Congress, Graz, 1998

[2]   R. Rockwell. Getting Together in Cyberspace, Proc ACM VRML95, Monterey, 1995.

[3]   .J. Mandeville, J.; Furness, T.; Kawahata,, M Dauner, J.: GreenSpace. Creating a Distributed Virtual Environment for Global Applications. In Proceedings of IEEE Networked Virtual Reality Workshop (1995)

[6]   J. Dauner. 3D Product Presentation Online: The Virtual Design Exhibition. Proc ACM VRML98, Monterey, 1998.

Appendix: Colour Images

Lutz and Ziegler

Fig. 1. Partly colored greyscale image
(Courtesy of Wismut GmbH)

Fig. 2. Color image
(Courtesy of Wismut GmbH)

Fig. 3. Dump Beerwalde (current state)
(Courtesy of Wismut GmbH)

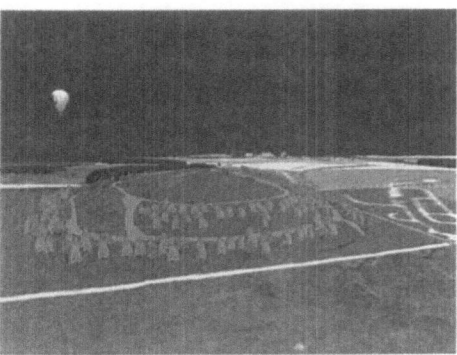

Fig. 4. Dump Beerwalde (planned state)
(Courtesy of Wismut GmbH)

Fig. 5. Spa garden, actual state
(Courtesy of Wismut GmbH)

Fig. 6. Spa garden, planned state
(Courtesy of Wismut GmbH)

Fig. 7. Current state (Courtesy of Wismut GmbH)   **Fig. 8.** In construction (Courtesy of Wismut GmbH)

Fig. 9. Planned state (Courtesy of Wismut GmbH)

Fig. 10. Actual landscape
(Courtesy of Wismut GmbH)

Fig. 11. Planned landscape
(Courtesy of Wismut GmbH)

Reuding and Schulz

Fig. 1. Visibility of instruments

Fig. 2. Perception of interior roominess

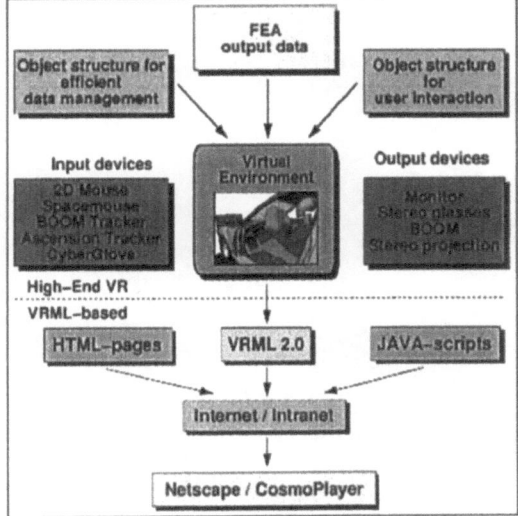

Fig. 3. System design

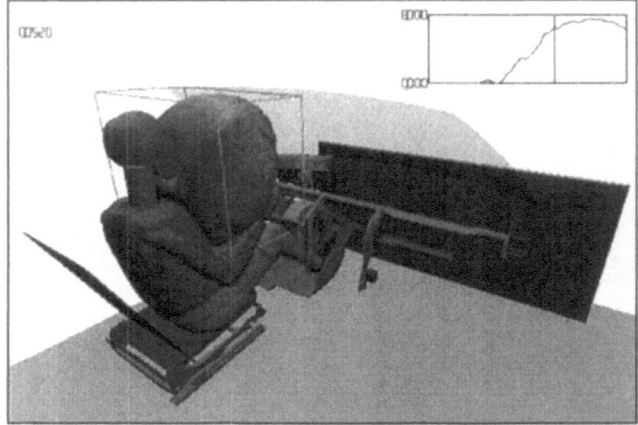

Fig. 4. Virtual sketch pad

Fig. 5. Frontal offset crash

Fig. 6. Amplified door vibration

Fig. 7. Noise level wavefront

SpringerEurographics

Dirk Bartz (ed.)

Visualization in Scientific Computing '98

Proceedings of the Eurographics Workshop
in Blaubeuren, Germany, April 20–22, 1998

1998. 82 partly coloured figures. VII, 151 pages..
Soft cover DM 85,–, öS 595,–
ISBN 3-211-83209-2

In twelve selected papers common problems in scientific visualization are discussed: adaptive and multi-resolution methods, feature extraction, flow visualization, and visualization quality.

Four papers focus on aspects of mesh reduction, mesh compression, and increasing the quality of the resulting mesh. Two extentions on particle tracing are presented as well as a paper on the simulation of material transport. Two papers are on feature extraction in dynamics systems and on the accuracy of algorithmic extracted features. Three papers focus on stereoscopic volume rendering, on the visualization of atomic collision cascades and of quality of visualization systems in general.

SpringerWienNewYork

Sachsenplatz 4-6, P O Box 89, A-1201 Wien, Fax +43-1-330 24 26
e-mail. order@springer at, Internet http //www.springer at
New York, NY 10010, 175 Fifth Avenue • D-14197 Berlin, Heidelberger Platz 3
Tokyo 113, 3-13, Hongo 3-chome, Bunkyo-ku

SpringerEurographics

George Drettakis, Nelson Max (eds.)

Rendering Techniques '98

Proceedings of the Eurographics Workshop
in Vienna, Austria, June 29–July 1, 1998

1998. 231 partly coloured figures. XI, 339 pages.
Soft cover DM 118,–, öS 826,–
ISBN 3-211-83213-0

Some of the best current research on realistic rendering is included in this volume. It emphasizes the current "hot topics" in this field: image based rendering, and efficient local and global-illumination calculations. In the first of these areas, there are several contributions on real-world model acquisition and display, on using image-based techniques for illumination and on efficient ways to parameterize and compress images or light fields, as well as on clever uses of texture and compositing hardware to achieve image warping and 3D surface textures. In global and local illumination, there are contributions on extending the techniques beyond diffuse reflections, to include specular and more general angle dependent reflection functions, on efficiently representing and approximating these reflection functions, on representing light sources and on approximating visibility and shadows. Finally, there are two contributions on how to use knowledge about human perception to concentrate the work of accurate rendering only where it will be noticed, and a survey of computer graphics techniques used in the production of a feature length computer-animated film with full 3D characters.

 SpringerWienNewYork

Sachsenplatz 4-6, P.O Box 89, A-1201 Wien, Fax +43-1-330 24 26
e-mail. order@springer.at, Internet http://www.springer.at
New York, NY 10010, 175 Fifth Avenue • D-14197 Berlin, Heidelberger Platz 3
Tokyo 113, 3-13, Hongo 3-chome, Bunkyo-ku

SpringerEurographics

Panos Markopoulos,
Peter Johnson (eds.)

Design, Specification and Verification
of Interactive Systems '98

Proceedings of the Eurographics Workshop
in Abingdon, U.K., June 3–5, 1998

1998. 119 figures. IX, 325 pages.
Soft cover DM 118,–, öS 826,–
ISBN 3-211-83212-2

Does modelling, formal or otherwise, have a role to play in
designing interactive systems? A proliferation of interactive
devices and technologies are used in an ever increasing
diversity of contexts and combinations in professional
and every-day life. This development poses a significant
challenge to modelling approaches used for the design of
interactive systems.

The papers in this volume discuss a range of modelling
approaches, the representations they use, the strengths and
weaknesses of their associated specification and analysis
techniques and their role in supporting the design of interactive systems.

SpringerWienNewYork

Sachsenplatz 4-6, PO Box 89, A-1201 Wien, Fax +43-1-330 24 26
e-mail order@springer.at, Internet http://www.springer.at
New York, NY 10010, 175 Fifth Avenue • D-14197 Berlin, Heidelberger Platz 3
Tokyo 113, 3-13, Hongo 3-chome, Bunkyo-ku

SpringerEurographics

Michael Douglas Harrison, Juan Carlos Torres (eds.)

Design, Specification and Verification of Interactive Systems '97

Proceedings of the Eurographics Workshop in Granada, Spain, June 4–6, 1997

1997. 129 figures. VIII, 320 pages.

Soft cover DM 118,–, öS 826,–

ISBN 3-211-83055-3

Wilfrid Lefer, Michel Grave (eds.)

Visualization in Scientific Computing '97

Proceedings of the Eurographics Workshop
in Boulogne-sur-Mer, France, April 28–30, 1997

1997. 92 partly coloured figures. VII, 187 pages.

Soft cover DM 85,–, öS 595,–

ISBN 3-211-83049-9

Daniel Thalmann, Michiel van de Panne (eds.)

Computer Animation and Simulation '97

Proceedings of the Eurographics Workshop
in Budapest, Hungary, September 2–3, 1997

1997. 121 partly coloured figures. VIII, 203 pages.

Soft cover DM 89,–, öS 625,–

ISBN 3-211-83048-0

Julie Dorsey, Philipp Slusallek (eds.)

Rendering Techniques '97

Proceedings of the Eurographics Workshop
in St. Etienne, France, June 16–18, 1997

1997. 172 partly coloured figures. IX, 342 pages.

Soft cover DM 118,–, öS 826,–

ISBN 3-211-83001-4

SpringerWienNewYork

Sachsenplatz 4-6, PO Box 89, A-1201 Wien, Fax +43-1-330 24 26
e-mail order@springer at, Internet: http //www.springer.at
New York, NY 10010, 175 Fifth Avenue • D-14197 Berlin, Heidelberger Platz 3
Tokyo 113, 3-13, Hongo 3-chome, Bunkyo-ku